John D. (John Denison) Baldwin

Pre-historic nations; or, Inquiries concerning some of the great peoples and civilizatins of antiquity, and their probable relation to a still older civilization of the Ethiopians or Cushites of Arabia

John D. (John Denison) Baldwin

Pre-historic nations; or, Inquiries concerning some of the great peoples and civilizatins of antiquity, and their probable relation to a still older civilization of the Ethiopians or Cushites of Arabia

ISBN/EAN: 9783741151620

Manufactured in Europe, USA, Canada, Australia, Japa

Cover: Foto ©ninafisch / pixelio.de

Manufactured and distributed by brebook publishing software (www.brebook.com)

John D. (John Denison) Baldwin

Pre-historic nations; or, Inquiries concerning some of the great peoples and civilizatins of antiquity, and their probable relation to a still older civilization of the Ethiopians or Cushites of Arabia

PRE-HISTORIC NATIONS;

OR, INQUIRIES

CONCERNING SOME OF THE GREAT PEOPLES AND
CIVILIZATIONS OF ANTIQUITY.

AND

THEIR PROBABLE RELATION TO A STILL OLDER
CIVILIZATION OF THE ETHIOPIANS OR
CUSHITES OF ARABIA.

By JOHN D. BALDWIN, A.M.

NEW YORK:
HARPER & BROTHERS, PUBLISHERS,
FRANKLIN SQUARE.
1869.

Entered, according to Act of Congress, in the year 1869, by
HARPER & BROTHERS,
In the Clerk's Office of the District Court of the United States for the Southern District of New York.

Copyright also secured in Great Britain, and entered at Stationer's Hall, London, and translation reserved.

THIS WORK IS RESPECTFULLY INSCRIBED

TO THE

AMERICAN ORIENTAL SOCIETY,

OF WHICH THE AUTHOR

HAS THE HONOR OF BEING A MEMBER.

Montesquieu says: "Il y a des choses que tout le monde dit, parce qu'elles ont été dites une fois." Many stupidities of history and dogmatic denials of the past have no other warrant. Instead of repeating anything "because it has been said once," it is better to accept the results of conscientious investigation.

CONTENTS.

	Page
I. INTRODUCTORY GENERALITIES	9
II. PRELIMINARY SUGGESTIONS RELATIVE TO THE CURRENT CHRONOLOGIES, THE RELATION OF HELLAS TO CIVILIZATION, AND THE MEANING OF PRE-HISTORIC TIMES	23
The current Chronologies	24
Hellas and Civilization	39
Pre-Historic Times	49
III. PRE-HISTORIC GREATNESS OF ARABIA	55
An early Civilization in Arabia	56
Arabia was the Ancient Ethiopia	57
Misapprehension concerning Arabia	67
The two Races in Arabia	73
Concerning the Old Race	78
Ancient Arabian Ruins and Inscriptions	80
The ancient Arabian Language	88
— Concerning the Origin of Alphabetic Writing	91
Ancient History of Arabia	95
Greek Notices of Arabia	99
Arabian Recollections of the Past	102
Fragments of Old Arabian History	108
The Cushite System of Political Organization	112
Cushite Science, Astronomical and Nautical	116
IV. THE PHŒNICIANS	129
Origin of the Phœnicians	130
The Immigration doubted	135
Renan's Theory	137
Their Cushite Religion and Architecture	141

Contents.

	Page
Antiquity of the Phœnicians	145
Periods of Phœnician History	147
The Building of Gades	150
Extent of Phœnician Influence	158
The Pelasgians	162
Minos and his Conquests	165
Phœnician Language and Literature	167

V. CUSHITE OR ARABIAN ORIGIN OF CHALDEA ... 173

Chaldean Civilization and Learning	174
History of Chaldea by Berosus	180
Chaldean Antiquities and Traditions	185
The Chaldean Ruins and Inscriptions	188
The Origin of Chaldea	192
The Cushite Language in Chaldea	194
Political Changes in Ancient Chaldea	196
The Year 2234 B.C.	199
Concerning an old Chaldean Temple	202
Assyria and the Semitic Race	204
A Theory concerning the Chaldeans	205
Concerning Chaldean Ancient History	206
Hypothetical Scheme of Chaldean History	209

VI. INDIA, SANSKRIT, AND ANTE-SANSKRIT ... 216

The Indo-Aryans preceded by the Cushites	218
The Rock-cut Temples of India	228
The Dravidian Race and their Language	238
Aryan History and Antiquity	243
The Veda and the Vedic Age	247
Religious History of Sanscrit India	253
Modern Brahmanism	258
Indian History and Chronology	260
The Ancient Malayan Empire	263

VII. EGYPT PREVIOUS TO MENES ... 267

Manetho's History of Egypt	269
Origin and Antiquity of Egypt	271
The old Sanskrit Books on Egypt	277

Contents.

	Page
Dionysus, called Osiris and Bacchus	288
Mythology and Mythological Personages	292
The Ages before Menes	296
Antiquity of Writing in Egypt	300
Attempts to measure Egyptian Antiquity	303

VIII. AFRICA AND THE ARABIAN CUSHITES ... 304

The Races in Africa	307
A brief Essay on Races	311
The Arabian Cushites in Africa	322
Traces of African Ancient History	326
Northern Africa in Pre-Historic Times	335
The Berbers, especially the Touaricks	338
Navigation round Africa	345

IX. WESTERN EUROPE IN PRE-HISTORIC TIMES ... 349

An ancient Civilization in Western Europe	353
The Age of Bronze in Western Europe	358
The Ancient Race in Western Europe	366
The Ancient History of Italy	371
Western Europe anciently called Africa	375
The old Sanskrit Books on Western Europe	378
The Ancient History of Ireland	381
The Keltic Language	389
Ancient Communication with America	392

PRE-HISTORIC NATIONS.

I.

INTRODUCTORY GENERALITIES.

THE origin of man, and the date of his first appearance on earth, have always been subjects of speculation. We see this in the cosmogonic myths and legends of antiquity, and in the dogmatic chronologies that have been allowed currency in modern times; but, so far as we know, it is only in very recent times that visionary speculation on these topics has given way to enlightened inquiry. The cyclical schemes of the ancient Eastern world, which computed by tens of thousands and hundreds of thousands the years of man's existence on earth previous to the regular beginnings of history, may be treated with small ceremony now; but they are quite as scientific as Archbishop Usher's scheme of chronology, for the men who invented them were skilful astronomers; and whoever undertakes to show that they are not quite as reasonable, may discover that something can be said on the other side of this question.

These cyclical estimates of the past may turn out to be as near the truth as Usher's system of chronology, but neither the one nor the other can now be accepted as an intelligent and truthful exposition of the antiquity of the human race. The whole tendency of scientific investigation and discovery, at the present time, is to class them together as alike unwarranted and worthless. We moderns have underrated the antiquity of man. This is shown more and more clearly in two departments of inquiry, where the greatest results are yet to be realized—geology and the science of language. Conscientious geologists are forced to say, "The date of man must be carried back farther than we had heretofore imagined;" and accomplished scholars and thinkers respond from the field of linguistic science, "Late discoveries are showing us that the antiquity of the human race upon earth must be much greater than has been generally supposed."

These two sciences bring important aid to the study of pre-historic times, by compelling us to throw off the trammels of false chronologies, and by showing us room in the past for those great pre-historic developments of civilization, and those long pre-historic ages of human activity and enterprise, which are indicated by the oldest monuments, records, and mythologies. It is impossible to study faithfully the ancient mythologies, or the results of exploration in the oldest ruins, or the fragmentary records in which the ancients speak of what to them was misty antiquity, without feeling that, to accept all they signify, we must enlarge the past far beyond the limits of any scheme of chronology known to modern times. If we lack strength and boldness to break down the barriers of unreason and pursue inquiry with unfaltering reverence for truth, we may find refuge in the oracular cave of historical skepticism, where little or nothing is seen beyond the first Greek Olympiad save barbarism, lying fables, and general chaos. But human intelligence cannot remain imprisoned there, especially in this age, when so much is constantly added to our knowledge of the past, and when increasing means for a careful and hopeful study of antiquity so stimulate inquiry as to make it irrepressible.

The oldest writings in existence are inscriptions found in the ancient ruins of Egypt and Southwestern Asia. The oldest books, leaving out those of China, are those preserved by the Indian and Iranian branches of the Aryan family—the Rig-Veda, a translated fragment of the Desatir, and portions of the works of Zoroaster; next to these come the Hebrew Scriptures; then follow the works of Homer, and some other books and fragments of books, in the Greek language, representing the culture of the Ionians of Asia Minor. These books show us the civilization of the communities in which they originated, but they do not tell us when or where civilization first appeared. The mythologies, the ruins, the discoveries of linguistic science, and the general voice of tradition, lead us to the conclusion that, so far as relates to the Cushite, Semite, and Aryan races, its first appearance was somewhere in the southwestern part of Asia; but we can not describe the agencies and methods of its first development, nor give the date of its origin.

We nowhere find a continued and permanent advancement of any nation or community of these races, but we see a constant progress of civilization from lower toward higher degrees, from the few to the many, and from limited and special toward many-sided and all-embracing development. Nations rise, flourish, and sink again to obscurity. The Egypt of to-day is not that Egypt which we see in the monuments of its Old Monarchy; Chaldea is not now the ancient Chaldea which we study in its ruins; to-day we inquire in vain on the coast of Asia Minor for that Ionian confederacy whose marvelous culture, passing over into the Hellenic peninsula, illumed Athens, and made that city the glory of Hellas. It is long since Carthage and Rome ceased to exist. But, while communities and nations have disappeared, this old civilization has remained; sometimes checked and lowered for a succession of ages, but always reappearing with new developments of its forces and new forms.

The Reverend Dr. Lang, in his "View of the Origin and Migrations of the Polynesian Nation," is led by the subject to make this observation: "In Tuscany and in Egypt, in India and in China, and, I will add, even in the South Sea Islands and in both Americas, we behold the evidences of a primitive civilization, which, in some instances, had run its course anterior to the age of Homer, but which, at all events, acknowledged no obligation to the wisdom or refinement of the Greeks." Few will question the fact he states, so far as relates to Italy and Asia, although not many who carefully study the past will describe all that civilization as "primitive." Dr. Lang himself is not quite satisfied with this description; for, in attempting to explain the origin of the ancient civilization which had nearly run its course in different countries previous to the time of Homer, he adopts the notion of Bailly and others, that it was originated by the antediluvians, and brought through the Deluge to their successors by the family of Noah. Without fully exploring it, he saw a fact that was much too large for his chronology—a fact for which there was not sufficient room in the past, as he measured it.

The great civilization, so apparent in various nations of antiquity that present themselves to view just beyond the borders of regular history, was not the work of a single people nor of a single period of national existence. Those nations were preceded by others no less great and important, although more hidden from observation by their greater distance from us in time. The civilization of the Phœnicians, Egyptians, and other nations of the East passed to the Greeks, the Romans, and the magnificent empire of the Caliphs, making some losses and receiving new developments. Without speaking of what we received from the Kelts, whose civilization was greater than history has admitted, the civilization of modern Europe has grown partly out of that of Greece and Rome, and also out of that of the Saracens to a much greater extent than is generally recognised. So has the mental and social cultivation, first seen in Western Asia, flowed on through the ages, from people to people, from the civilizers of Egypt, Chaldea, and India to Europe and America, never defeated entirely, and always surviving the "dark ages" that obscured it. We have the highest and widest development it has ever reached. To find its starting-point and write its early history, we must be able to explore the obscurest deeps of antiquity.

And yet what seems in these inquiries to be the obscurest antiquity becomes extremely modern when considered in connection with what geology says of the antiquity of man. Those familiar with the later discoveries of this science know how slowly, and against what persistency of incredulity and doubt, geologists themselves have been brought to admit the evidence which shows the existence of the human race in the latter part of the geological period which Lyell and others describe as Post-pliocene. This period, which next precedes the "Recent," or that in which we live, seems as modern as yesterday in relation to the countless geological ages that went before it; but some

tentative efforts at computation make us feel how far away
it is from yesterday. Sir Charles Lyell's lowest estimate
of the time required to form the present delta and alluvial
plain of the Mississippi is more than 100,000 years. It belongs almost wholly to the Recent period. The lower
portion of the peninsula of Florida has been created by a
constant growth of coral reefs toward the south, and this
growth is still in full activity. "The whole is of Post-tertiary origin," say Agassiz and Lyell, "the fossil zoophytes
and shells being all of the same species as those now inhabiting the neighboring sea;" that is to say, the commencement of the growth was later than the beginning of
the Post-pliocene formation, and probably not much older
than the beginning of the Recent period. Agassiz, having
ascertained as nearly as possible the average rate of this
coral growth, estimates that the gradual formation of the
southern half of Florida must have filled a period of not
less than 135,000 years.

It is no part of my purpose to discuss geological questions. The questions presented in this volume, and the
conclusions reached, do not in any way depend on geological estimates of past time. It may, however, be observed
that the discoveries of geology show plainly that the prehistoric ages in Western Europe were not wholly barbarous. They show us the remains of a very remote "Age of
Stone," in which there is no trace of civilization; but they
also bring to light manufactured articles, sepulchral customs, and old structures, the remains of other remote ages
when civilized peoples inhabited that part of Europe;
such are the monuments of the "Age of Polished Stone"
and the "Age of Bronze." Western Europe has its ancient ruins that invite careful study. Its antiquities of

this kind are not as grand as those at the East, although the old temple at Abury was not destitute of grandeur in the days of its glory. They have nothing to rival the amazing architecture or the multitudinous inscriptions found in the old ruins of Egypt and Chaldea, but they show us remains of civilized peoples of whom history gives no account.

We must turn to Asia to discover the earliest manifestations of civilized life, and ascertain how far they can be traced back into the past. Here we see two great developments of ancient civilization, entirely disconnected from each other, and, so far as we can see, nearly equal in age. The origin of each is hidden by the shadows of very remote antiquity. At the East is China, with literary records claiming to be more than nineteen centuries older than the Christian era, and with a culture in science, industry, literature, and the arts of civilized life scarcely inferior to that of the most enlightened nations that have appeared in history. Tried by the standards of modern Europe, it takes a very high place in the respect and admiration of those best acquainted with it. Professor Whitney, in his "Language and the Study of Language," says very justly, "No race, certainly, outside the Indo-European and Semitic families, and not many races of those families, can show a literature of equal value with the Chinese."

This Chinese culture is one of the most remarkable facts in the world's history. Instead of passing from nation to nation, and taking new forces and new forms in a grand progress round the globe, it has neither wandered far from home, nor shown any remarkable variety of development. It has remained chiefly in the country where it grew up, and in the hands of the people by whom it was originated

—dwelling apart from what we call history, as if China were a world by itself.

At the West arose another civilization, that seems to have originated somewhere near the waters of the Persian Gulf and Indian Ocean. Unlike the Chinese in character and history, it was enterprising; it went forth into the world; it established communication with all peoples within its reach; it colonized and occupied other lands; its influence became paramount "from the extremity of the East to the extremity of the West;" it changed its seat from nation to nation, ever developing, more and more, a wonderful power of life; it created India and Egypt; its light was kindled all around the Mediterranean; and, finally, by way of Western Europe, it travelled to America, where it seems likely to have its widest and richest development.

It is not in our power to explain with certainty those primitive groupings of mankind which determined the origin of diverse races, and created distinct families of language. The diverse races exist, although, at the present time, there are not anywhere on the face of the globe many communities where any original race is found entirely free from mixture with some other; and the separate families of language exist, so radically and absolutely unlike that we find it impossible to believe they all proceeded from a common source. The essential unity of mankind in all the peculiar characteristics of humanity is an incontestable fact which cannot be affected by any differences of race or language. Whatever theory denies this fact, or makes it uncertain, is false to human nature, as it appears and speaks for itself in every race and in every language. This is not questioned by those who attempt to solve the problem by adopting the hypothesis that the human race came into existence, originally, at different points on the earth, by simultaneous or successive creations, each primordial group being the source of a separate race and a separate family of languages.

Those primeval traditions of the Hebrews, which Moses deemed truthful and worthy of record in the sacred books of his nation, relate almost entirely to the Semitic, Cushite, and Aryan families, which, on any hypothesis, must have had a common origin. Their languages constitute three distinct families, for linguistic scholars are making the discovery that the Cushite tongues are a family by themselves, although they more closely resemble the Semitic language than that of the Aryan race. Neither of these families differs from the others as they all differ from the Chinese. Between these three races there is no physiological difference whatever; and their differences in other respects are not so great as to exclude entirely the possibility of their having issued from a common primordial source, and separated in the early infancy of their first dialects. They have played connected parts in the work of human development; and now the Aryan race, enriched with the acquisitions of their combined influence, seems destined to possess and rule the whole planet on which we live.

The Cushite race appeared first in the work of civilization. That this has not always been distinctly perceived is due chiefly to the fact that the first grand ages of th.. race are so distant from us in time, so far beyond the gr nations of antiquity commonly mentioned in our ancient histories, that their most indelible traces have long been too much obscured by the waste of time to be readily comprehended by superficial observation. In the earliest Hebrew traditions, older probably than Abraham, and immediately connected with a description of the "land of Eden," where "the Lord God planted a garden" for Adam, Cush (translated Ethiopia) is mentioned as a country or geographical division of the earth; the Hebrews saw nothing geographical more ancient than this land of Cush. In the tenth chapter of Genesis, the names recorded are professedly used, for the most part, as ethnical and geographical designations; but this ethnical geography of Genesis, which, excepting the interpolations, was probably more ancient than even the Hebrews themselves understood, must be referred to a period anterior to that great immigration of Cushites from Arabia into the valley of Mesopotamia, the primeval home of the Semites, which brought civilization and gave existence to the old cities of Chaldea.

It seems to me impossible for any free-minded scholar to study the traditions, mythologies, fragmentary records, mouldering monuments, and other remains of the pre-historic ages, and fail to see that the people described in the Hebrew Scriptures as Cushites were the original civilizers of Southwestern Asia; and that, in the deepest antiquity, their influence was established in nearly all the coast regions, from the extreme east to the extreme west of the Old World. This has been repeatedly pointed out with more or less clearness, and it is one of those incontestable facts that must be accepted. In nearly all the recorded investigations of scholars for the last two centuries, it has appeared among those half-seen facts which dogmatic criticism could treat as fancies without troubling itself to explain them. It could not be otherwise; for, to see and fully comprehend the significance of Cushite antiquity, we must have greater freedom in the matter of chronology, and a more accurate perception of the historic importance of Arabia, than have usually appeared in such investigations. Neither Usher's chronology, nor the little country known to the Greeks and Romans as Phœnicia, will suffice to explain that mighty and wide-spread influence of the Cushite race in human affairs, whose traces are still visible from Farther India to Norway.

Here, as well as everywhere else in the advancement of learning from the old to the new, from the explored to the unexplored, the investigator must settle his relations with the professional conservatism of what passes current as "orthodox" scholarship. This conservatism, like all other conservatisms, has its eminent oracles, whose influence is too frequently allowed to limit inquiry and shape its results. It is less malignant than some other conservatisms, but no less self-assured, and no less ready to chastise bold inquiry. In the history of mankind, it has been common to see wig mistaken for wisdom, while authority usurped the place of reason; but nothing else has the force of truth; it may wait for recognition, like Boucher de Perthes on the field of geological science, and, while waiting, be rudely treated as a visionary; yet it will surely sweep all obstructions out of its way, and constrain the oracles to pronounce in its favor.

The influence of what is accepted as "orthodox" learning sometimes deals very summarily with both the work and the reputation of venturesome innovators, who flout its oracles, question its wisdom, criticise its methods, and undertake to show that important additions can be made to its stock of knowledge. Controversies with such all-wise conservatism, however, are incident to all inquiry by which progress is maintained. Each profession instinctively disallows and resists any interference with its established creed, and becomes a castle where the old is vigorously defended against the new. So it is in theology, in law, in politics, in medicine, in science of every kind, and in every department of learning. We can not reasonably expect our archæological and historical studies to escape this influence; nor should we very much desire it. If conservatism needs movement, innovation needs to adjust its relations with whatever truth is already established. The innovator proceeds by means of the sharpest methods of criticism; therefore he can afford to endure criticism. Soon or late, whatever investigations sweep away venerable rubbish and open the way to progress in knowledge will enforce their claim to respectful consideration; and nowhere is this surer to be realized than among enlightened scholars, where no ardor of feeling can become fanaticism, nor any prejudice or pride of opinion be transformed into eureless bigotry.

One purpose of this volume is to point out what may be known of the ancient Cushite people, and of the great part they played in developing and spreading civilization. In doing this, it becomes necessary to criticise and discredit some influential theories, speculations, and methods of investigation, which I find to be obstructions in the path of inquiry; and also to show that Usher's chronology is a very false measure of the past, that the antiquity of the human race is much greater than he supposed, and that there can be no intelligent study of antiquity where his or any similar scheme of chronology, or any other dogmatic falsification of the past, is allowed to paralyze inquiry and dictate conclusions.

I do not write for learned archæologists. They have

written for me. It is possible, however, that those most deeply learned in archæology and the science of language may find in this volume suggestions worthy of their attention. Perhaps it will enable them to discover a more satisfactory solution of certain ethnical and linguistic problems with which they are familiar. It can hardly fail to do this if it shall succeed in convincing them that the original Ethiopia was not in Africa, and that the ancient home of the Cushites or Ethiopians, the starting-point of their great colonizing and civilizing movements, was Arabia. I do not write for historical skeptics. Their use of reason is so poor and their credulity so great, when they deal with antiquity, that no common influence is likely to break the spell that makes them incapable of looking wisely into the past, and studying pre-historic times with any hope of enlightenment. Their habit of accepting preposterous and monstrous absurdities, in order to deny the historical significance of myths and traditions, and discredit the discoveries of linguistic and archæological science, must be left to play out its comedy without interference.

Others, whose interest in these studies may be stimulated anew, or for the first time awakened, by reading this work, will perhaps desire to pursue the subject in a more minute and elaborate way. If so, they can find in the works of German, Danish, French, and English explorers and scholars abundant materials to aid investigation; and in the department of linguistic science, which in these inquiries is of the highest importance, there are very valuable works by several American scholars, such as Whitney, Marsh, and others. On looking over what I have written, I find that I have criticised many of the linguistic and archæological theories of that eminent and accomplished investigator, Ernest Renan, without properly expressing my sense of his great services in these departments of science. If his works relating to the subjects I discuss were not so rich and attractive, or if his style of writing were not so perspicuous and eloquent, it may be that I should have given him less attention.

II.

PRELIMINARY SUGGESTIONS CONCERNING THE CURRENT CHRONOLOGIES, THE RELATION OF HELLAS TO CIVILIZATION, AND THE MEANING OF PRE-HISTORIC TIMES.

HUMBOLDT says in his Cosmos, "What we usually term the beginning of history is only the period when the later generations awoke to self-consciousness." It requires an enlightened view of the past and considerable mental freedom to see and accept what this signifies; but the tendency of scientific studies at the present time is to make it clear and establish it as a commonly accepted truth. Our studies of Ancient History have been embarrassed by two strong but not very wise influences—a false chronology, and a false estimate of the Hellenic people in their relation to civilization. These influences have been supported until lately by the theological training and the scholarship of modern times, and they have mutually supported each other; for those who maintain that enlightened civilization began in Hellas very easily accept the rabbinical notion that man was created only about 4000 or 5000 years previous to the Christian Era, while those who uphold this unwarranted system of chronology very readily accept the belief that mankind did not get far away from barbarism previous to the literary and artistic development that brightened Athena. It is impossible to think correctly of the past, or to comprehend the testimony of its monuments, where these views are received as infallible oracles and allowed to regulate investigation; therefore it seems necessary to make them the subject of a few preliminary observations.

THE CURRENT CHRONOLOGIES.

Rollin, writing Ancient History, and giving his view of the time and greatness of Ninus and Semiramis, whom he described as the immediate successors of the first founder of the Assyrian empire, made this confession: "I must own that I am somewhat puzzled by a difficulty that may be raised against the extraordinary things related of Ninus and Semiramis, as they do not seem to agree with times so near the Deluge; I mean such immense armies, such a numerous cavalry, and such vast treasures of gold and silver, all of which seem to be of later date." According to Rollin's chronology, the Assyrian empire began its great career 2234 years before Christ, or about 115 years after the Deluge, and 235 years previous to the death of Noah. The Hebrew Scriptures inform us that "Noah lived after the flood three hundred and fifty years." Rollin never doubted this record, and did not revise his chronology. Therefore he must have believed (although he carefully avoided saying so) that Noah outlived the founders of that empire, and saw its progress and grandeur during more than two centuries. It is not surprising that he was puzzled by chronological difficulties. His system afforded no relief from them. It is true that in writing of Ninus and Semiramis he followed that ready fabler, the Carian physician Ctesias. The first princes of the celebrated Assyrian monarchy lived nearly a thousand years later. The great empire existing in that part of Asia at the date given by Rollin was Chaldean; but there is nothing in this to remove his perplexity, and later researches afford it no relief, for it is now certain that there were great monarchies in Asia much older than the year 2234 B.C.

Such embarrassments as that felt by Rollin multiply as we increase our knowledge of ancient times by a more careful study of the mythologies and traditions of the ancients, by investigating the monumental records of the older nations, by exploring the oldest ruins (the oldest now, because others that were much older have gone to dust), by comprehending the great revelations of linguistic science, and by searching intelligently the memorials of past time presented in the discoveries of geology. The absurd chronology by which they are created, not capable of serving as a guide, becomes an obstruction that must be removed. Could we have the literary records of all the pre-historic nations, or even the lost libraries of the Phœnicians, Chaldeans, and Egyptians, its most confident supporters would become ashamed to urge its claim to respect, and scholars everywhere would hasten to disown the absurdities it has introduced into Ancient History. As it is, enough is known, without calling in the testimony of geology, to show that the period between the creation of man and the birth of Christ is much longer than any of the current chronologies are able to measure.

I can not wonder at the amazement, trepidation, and even rage with which some of the dogmatic chronologists behold the revelations of geology. My purpose, however, does not require an appeal to what geology says of the antiquity of man. It is manifest, without such aid, that the time between the beginning of the human race and the Christian Era may have been, as Bunsen maintained in his work on Egypt, five times 4004 years, and even much lon-

B

ger than Bunsen supposed. The great past was certainly long enough for all that human existence and activity in pre-historic ages of which so many traces are found. There is nothing to require, indicate, or suggest that the current chronologies should be treated with the smallest degree of respect, while, on the other hand, there is much that demands for the pre-historic ages the longest measure intelligent inquiry has ever proposed.

The business of constructing systems of "biblical" chronology has furnished employment for a large amount of learned ingenuity which otherwise might have been led to write great folios on the word "Selah" in the Psalms, or to expound the natural history of ancient giants, or to interpret in a very marvelous way the prophetic mysteries of the Apocalypse. It has been chiefly the work of monks and rabbins, and its relation to historical science is very much like that of conjuring astrology to the science of astronomy. But it is not wholly useless. It has undoubtedly furnished many satisfactions to those whose calling did not afford a more profitable occupation for intellectual activity, or whose learning had not introduced them to a more enlightened study of antiquity. The authority of what is falsely called "biblical" chronology is no longer very potent. It can not maintain itself against that progress of science which constantly increases our knowledge of the past. It must soon disappear, and take its place in the rubbish of the ages with other legendary absurdities which in their time dishonored religion, oppressed the human intellect, and misled honest people by claiming immortal reverence.

Any system of chronology that places the creation of man only about 4000 or 5000 years previous to the birth of Christ is a mere invention, a scholastic fancy, an elaborate absurdity. There is nothing to warrant it, and not much to excuse it. Those who profess to find it in the Bible misuse and falsify that book. We may as well seek in the Bible for a perfected science of astronomy or chemistry. It is not there; and no such chronological scheme ever grew out of scientific inquiry. Moreover, there is a remarkable want of harmony among those who have constructed such schemes. The various systems of "biblical" chronology claiming attention are at variance among themselves. According to the Jewish rabbins, man was created 3701 years before Christ; the Greek and Armenian churches have been taught to say 5500 years; Eusebius said 5200; Panadoras, a learned Egyptian monk, having solved the problem with great care and exactness of demonstration, said 5493; we and the nations of Western Europe have followed Usher, a romancing archbishop of Armagh, who maintained, with great particularity of dogmatic demonstration, that the human race began to exist on earth precisely 4004 years before Christ; others have argued, with ingenuity quite as marvelous, to establish the validity of figures different from any of these.

In all these attempts to construct systems of "biblical" chronology, nothing is more apparent than utter lack of scientific method and purpose. The aim has been, not to discover facts, allow their influence, and accept the result, but to compel facts to harmonize with a preconceived theory and support given conclusions. A point has been assumed in the past beyond which the date of man's first appearance on earth must not be carried; and this assumption, not having the support of science, has feloniously sought that of revelation. Thus chronological dogmatism has perpetrated an atrocious outrage on the Bible by impiously claiming for itself the reverence due to religion. Even learned and religious men have sought to identify this false chronology with Christianity itself, and have pursued their investigations of antiquity with a purpose, deliberately expressed, to force every fact of science, and every date of ancient history, to agree with it. Maurice's "Indian Antiquities," and his "Ancient History of Hindustan," are valuable works. They were first published about eighty years ago, but no one can read them now without respect for the author's learning and ability; yet the style in which he upheld this dogmatism of the "biblical" chronologists is nowise likely to be imitated at the present time by any scholar having the same enthusiasm for archæological researches. In his preface to the "Antiquities" he wrote thus:

"The daring assertions of certain skeptical French philosophers with respect to the age of the world (whose arguments I have attempted to refute—arguments founded principally on the high assumptions of the Brahmins and other Eastern nations in point of chronology and astronomy), could their extravagant claims be substantiated, would have a direct tendency to overturn the Mosaic system, and with it Christianity." In his first volume of the "History," on page 276, he renewed the subject as follows: "I am not inclined violently to dispute any positions on this head (chronology) that do not tend to subvert the Mosaic chronology, and I am decidedly for allowing the Eastern historians, as a privilege, the utmost latitude of the Septuagint chronology. It is not for a century or two, more or less, that we wage the contest with infidelity, but we cannot allow of thousands and millions being thrown into the scale."

There was a time when it was deemed a sacred and incontestable proposition that Hebrew, given by miraculous inspiration, was the original language of mankind, and the primeval mother of all other languages. To assume, as a vital thing in religion, that linguistic inquiry must not be allowed to show any thing contrary to this proposition, would be just as rational as this violent assumption of Maurice in behalf of what he calls the "Mosaic" system of chronology; and yet with what lordly arrogance of authority his "Mosaic" system was set forth! It would condescendingly allow its own largest limits "as a privilege," but facts must take care to exist in submissive accordance with its permission, or they would be treated as infidel heresies, for inquiry can have no legitimate aim but to show its infallibility!

What crimes against Christianity have been committed by some of its zealous friends! and not the least of these crimes is that which makes it responsible for such follies as this. Nothing can be more unwarranted than to assume that any scheme of chronology is "Mosaic" or "biblical;" nor does it seem possible to do infidelity a greater service than to use Christianity as the antagonist of honest inquiry and intelligent progress in knowledge, or to talk as if she were not sufficiently great and comprehensive to wear her crown of glory in presence of any development of science or any progress of civilization. Modern astronomical discoveries were at first treated as grave heresies that should be suppressed by the Inquisition. Geology, the most reverent of sciences, has been treated as an infidel. It is not surprising that discoveries relating to pre-historic times, which set aside the current chronologies, have encountered similar criticism; but it would be very surprising if this unchristian dogmatism could maintain itself anywhere much longer. At any rate, truth is not discovered by such methods as that indicated by Maurice.

There are many considerations which should have checked the confidence with which dogmatic chronology has limited and falsified the past. The origin of nearly everything in our civilization is lost in the obscurity of ages that go back far beyond the oldest historic period. The arts of writing, building, spinning, weaving, mining, and working metals—in a word, nearly all the arts and appliances of civilized life, came to us from pre-historic times. They were brought to Europe chiefly by the people known in history as Phœnicians, or through their agency; but, as I have already stated, neither history nor tradition can tell us when or where they originated. Evidence of the riches and magnificence they had created in very remote ages abounds in the records, ruins, and other remains of antiquity, but neither Chaldea nor Egypt could give a clear account of their beginnings and early history. One thing, however, is certain: they indicate the existence, in pre-historic times beyond the reach of tradition, not only of civilized communities and nations, but also of long periods of civilized life; and they give special significance to such statements of the old writers as the following from Diodorus Siculus: "Asia was anciently governed by its own native kings, of whom there is no history extant, either as to any memorable actions they performed, or so much as their names." He says this at the beginning of his account of Ninus, and applies it to the ages preceding Nineveh and Babylon.

The great antiquity of some of the sciences is incontestable. If there were no monumental records of ancient Chaldea, Egypt, Arabia, and India, we should still have convincing evidence of their great attainments in that knowledge which was "the excellency of the Chaldees" and "the wisdom of the Egyptians;" Euclid, an Egyptian, would still be recognised as one of the foremost writers on geometry, and we should find it necessary to refer the origin of the science to an age more ancient than the oldest date of even Egyptian chronology. At the same time, it could be shown by authentic quotations from the literary remains of antiquity that some of the scholars of Ionia, which preceded Hellas in civilization, taught by the Phœnicians, Egyptians, and Chaldeans, had a knowledge of astronomy and of other sciences that was not retained by the scholars of Hellas, and seems to have disappeared from the Grecian world with the disciples of Pythagoras.

The most ancient peoples of antiquity, at the earliest periods in which we can see and study them, show us that civilization was older than their time. It is apparent in their architecture, in the varied possessions and manifestations of their civilized life, in their riches and magnificence, and in the splendor of their temples and royal palaces, that they had many of the arts and sciences, which we deem modern. Meanwhile, we can not easily deny their great attainments in astronomy, in presence of the general admission that the sphere filled with constellations, and the zodiac with its twelve signs, are at least as old as the Chaldeans. Humboldt, stating the result of inquiry on this point, says: "The division of the ecliptic into twelve parts originated with the ancient Chaldeans." They had the zodiac, and gave it to the Western countries. So much is easily seen. But the Chaldeans themselves may have received the zodiac from the more ancient civilizers of their country.

During the present century, much has been added to our knowledge of the past by exploration in the ruins of Egypt and Chaldea. The researches in Egypt have given us dates as authentic as the monuments themselves, which confound the current chronologies, and open the past to our view somewhat as the discoveries of Columbus opened the world to the geographers of modern Europe. It is now as certain as anything else in ancient history that Egypt existed as a civilized country not less than 5000 years earlier than the birth of Christ. The monumental and sepulchral records of that country, marvelously abundant, have substantially confirmed Manetho's history of Egypt. There was never any good reason for doubting the correctness of his dynastic list, as prepared by himself. He was an Egyptian of great learning and wisdom; he wrote with the libraries and monuments of Egypt before him; his dates are as authentic as those of any other historian; and the only objection to them, of any account, comes from the dogmatism of that false chronology which assumes with oracular confidence that the past has not room for such dates. We meet here, much less awful than formerly, the same blind arrogance of old prejudice that could see nothing but heresy in the astronomical discoveries of Galileo. But prejudice is not reason; false chronology is neither science nor religion; and the lesson of every age is, that sure defeat awaits those who forbid progress in knowledge, and employ against it the menaces of any tribunal of intolerance.

The magnificent discoveries in Egypt, by confirming Manetho's history, have seriously troubled this dogmatism. How can it allow that Menes, who first united all Egypt under one government, began his reign not less than 3893 years previous to the Christian Era? And where can it find respectable logic to discredit such dates against the evidence by which they are supported? It is amusing to observe the effect of these discoveries on certain eminent and admirable English scholars who have given much attention to studies of this kind, one of them being an accomplished Egyptologist. They cannot deny the facts, and have no inclination to deny them; but their Oxford and English Church associations seem to have interfered to prevent a frank acceptance of the incontestable antiquity of the Old Monarchy of Egypt. For a time they sought to reconcile it with the current chronology which orthodox churchmen hold in great reverence. When this became impossible, and compelled their acknowledgment of the impossibility, they adopted silence as the best policy under the circumstances, intimating that they could not solve this Egyptian problem in a satisfactory manner. Meaner men can sneer, deny violently, falsify the record, and, with godless infatuation, denounce the whole investigation as "business fit only for infidels." Christianity must be divine, for it is able to survive the championship of these meaner men.

It will not be questioned that blind reverence for this false method of chronology has been very powerful to discredit facts and dates against which there could be no valid argument, solely on the ground that they seemed disastrous to its authority. It has controlled the judgment of learned and conscientious men more than they could admit to themselves—more than will seem credible a few centuries hence, when its character will be explained chiefly by recollection of its absurdities. It comes into every archæological investigation, to mislead inquiry and hide the true explanation of every fact that implies great antiquity, too frequently sure of success because it has been incorporated with the investigator's thought and imagination from the moment when he began to think and acquire knowledge. Its influence grows weaker every day, and yet those who are sufficiently free in thought to disregard it entirely frequently find it moving them to utter apologies for doing so.

A free-minded and accomplished archæologist, speaking of the dates furnished by the chronology of Egypt (Revue des Deux Mondes, tome lvi., p. 666), says: "I know how appalling these figures are, and what grave apprehensions they awaken. I have shared these apprehensions; but what can we do against the concurring lists furnished by Manetho, Eratosthenes, the Turin papyrus, and the Egyptian tablets of Abydos, Thebes, and Sakkara?" This tone of apology may have some good use, perhaps, but does it express anything that can actually be found in his own conviction or feeling? Such dates can alarm nothing but false chronology, for which he cannot feel much concern. Instead of being hostile to any thing else in which a human interest is possible, they are friendly and full of satisfactions.

It seems astonishing that the authority of false chronology should ever have been sufficient to secure toleration for some of the absurdities it has originated. Take, for instance, its very surprising representations concerning the time of Zoroaster. It was necessary to recognise Zoroaster as a real personage, representing a great religious epoch of the Iranian people. It was seen that all accounts of him placed the time of his appearance far back in the past, the Greeks saying that he lived 5000 years before the Trojan War, and 6000 years before the death of Plato. But facts must not be stubborn, for here, as everywhere else, the current chronology, being supreme, must read the testimony and construe the facts in its own way; therefore it was assumed falsely that Zoroaster lived in the sixth century before Christ, during the reign of Darius Hystaspes, or during that of his father, who, as we know, was not a king, and never reigned at all. And this absurdity, already inexpressible, was heightened by a miraculous operation of "Mosaic" zeal, which transformed the great Iranian teacher into a Jew. The Rev. Drs. Hyde and Prideaux (the former in his "Veterum Persarum et Medorum Religionis Historia," and the latter in his "Connexions"), with solemn gravity befitting the wonderful announcement, represented Zoroaster as a native of Palestine, born of Jewish parents, who first appeared in Persia as a menial servant in the families of Ezra and Daniel.

Here was brilliancy almost equal to that of a Rev. Dr. Joshua Barnes, of the last century, who published an elaborate work to prove that Solomon wrote the Iliad.* It is not common to see Zoroaster transformed into a Jew, even by those who refuse to see that he lived many ages before Abraham. Even a hundred and seventy years ago, when Dr. Hyde wrote, not many "biblical" chronologists were "Mosaic" to this extent. Anquetil du Perron, and others who followed him, adhered to the incongruous chronological *dicta* already established, although larger information should have qualified them to apply the proper criticism and present a more intelligent view of Iranian antiquity.

---

* Scientific investigation is accustomed to the remarkable brilliancies of this kind of learned acumen. Dr. Hitchcock says in a work on Geology: "Felix Plater, professor of anatomy at Basle, referred the bones of an elephant found at Lucerne to a giant at least 19 feet high, and in England similar bones were regarded as those of the fallen angels!"

According to the Desatir, the Dabistan, and the old Iranian histories, there was a great king of that branch of the Aryan people known as Kai Khusro, who was a prophet and an ascetic. He had no children, and after "a glorious reign of sixty years" he abdicated in favor of a subordinate prince named Lohorasp, also an ascetic, who, after a long reign, resigned the throne to his son Gushtasp. It was during the reign of Gushtasp that Zoroaster appeared. Gushtasp was succeeded by Bahman, his grandson; Bahman by Darab, who was slain by rebels; and Darab by Sekander, who restored order and became famous in Iranian history. These were not kings of Persia; they reigned at Balkh, and lived many centuries before Persia became an independent kingdom. The Desatir calls their realm the kingdom of Hiras, and their people the Hirasis, names that seem to be modifications of the word Arya.

All this implied that the time of Zoroaster was far away in the past. The current chronologies were "frightened" at the mention of its possible distance from us. Such antiquity must be disallowed; therefore the kingdom of Hiras was transformed into the kingdom of Persia, Kai Khusro into Cyrus the Great, and Gushtasp into Darius Hystaspes or his father. And why was this done? The answer is, "Because this period is less subject to chronological difficulties than many others." This is the only reason that can be given for a stupidity that is wellnigh matchless. The chronological system used does not allow room in the past for the true period. The time of Darius Hystaspes or his father is the best it can afford, although the true period may have been several millenniums previous to that time. It was certainly many ages before either Media or Persia was heard of as a distinct nation. The kingdom of

Hiras belongs to remote ages previous to Babylon and Assyria, and, it may be, previous to Chaldea and Egypt, so far as relates to its origin and the first periods of its history.

The time has come when our current chronologies must more definitely adjust their relations with the history of China. This has already been attempted without satisfactory results, and there have been efforts to discredit the great antiquity implied by the civilization and literary records of that country. It is nowise likely that a more complete acquaintance with Chinese historical literature will make the task easier. It seems evident now that actual harmony between our chronology and Chinese antiquity is impossible. Heretofore we have seen China from a distance, heard reports of its civilization from mariners and merchants who have been permitted to visit some of its ports, from missionaries who have seen something of the interior, and from embassies that have seen its magnificent roads and its royal court; and Chinese books collected and brought to Europe have engaged the attention of scholars. But the commercial intercourse with Eastern Asia now opening across the Pacific begins a new era in the history of the world, and China, withdrawn from a seclusion no longer possible, will become as familiarly known to us as any other cultivated nation with which we have intercourse.

It is impossible to deny the vast antiquity of that country without using methods of criticism that would destroy the credibility of all history. Litse, an eminent Chinese historian, after describing the fabulous and mythical ages, comes to "the reigns of men" during long periods of time of which there is no chronology, although some knowledge of those old rulers is recorded. One of them, named Suishin, "took observations of the stars, and investigated the five elements." Next come the "Five Rulers," who are mythical representatives of historical epochs in "the period before Yao." They are named as follows: 1. Fu-hi, who cultivated astronomy, religion, and the art of writing, and whose dynasty consisted of fifteen kings: he represents a great epoch in Chinese history; 2. Shin-nung, who promoted agriculture and medical science, and had a line of successors. 3. Hoang-ti, a great sovereign, who put down a revolt, and in whose time the magnetic needle was discovered, the written character improved, and many appliances of civilized life carried to greater perfection; the 4th and 5th of these "Rulers," or heads of dynasties, were descendants of Hoang-ti. The "Five Rulers" were followed by the second period, called "the period of Yao and Shin." Next came the period of the "Imperial Dynasties," which began with the Emperor Yu, or Ta-yu, the great and good Yu. The great historical work of See-ma-thi-an, written about 2000 years ago, narrates events chronologically from the year 2637 B.C. to 122 B.C.

In the earliest times brought to view there appears a degree of civilization and culture which must have been the growth of many previous ages. One fact stated is important in its relation to "the period of the Five Rulers." It is said that the Chinese cycle of 60 years was established in the 61st year of Hoang-ti's reign. This being so, it follows, by mathematical demonstration, that Hoang-ti's reign began in the year 2698 B.C., for the 75th recurrence of this cycle was completed with the year 1863 A.D. The time of Fu-hi was probably 500 years earlier; and previous to him were the more ancient rulers, some of whom cultivated the science of astronomy. It seems impossible to avoid the conclusion that Chinese civilization is as old as Usher's date for the beginning of the human race, and, perhaps, much older.

I assume, in these inquiries, that the current "biblical" chronologies have no warrant from either science or the Bible, and that they must not be allowed to pass for more than they are worth.

HELLAS AND CIVILIZATION.

The false chronologies, and slowness to admit that prehistoric times were not necessarily barbarous, have troubled our histories of the people called Greeks. Heretofore the scholarship of modern Europe has too much fostered a belief that enlightened civilization, science, and art all began with the people of Hellas, and had their first great development at Athens. Hellenic egotism, inherited with Hellenic literature, has not served as the best qualification for writing or reading histories of the Greek race. What belongs to several families of this brilliant group of the great Aryan people has been given to one, and that the latest in development; and what they all received from the Phœnician or Cushite culture, which immediately preceded them in the same regions, has not been well considered. This influence has sometimes made it difficult to see that even Babylon, Egypt, Assyria, and Persia had any thing higher or more enlightened than a certain greatness of "barbaric pomp and splendor."

That interpretation of antiquity which begins its history of civilization with the Hellenes and the Romans, and excludes every thing not recognized and celebrated by their literary oracles, is not entitled to the highest degree of respect. Neither the Hellenes nor the Romans gave an intelligible account of the beginnings of their own history. Their literature betrays no clear consciousness of the brilliant civilizations that preceded them in Thrace, Asia Minor, and Etruria, and furnishes only confused and uncertain notices of the Phœnicians, Egyptians, and Persians previous to Alexander the Great. This is not altogether true of Herodotus, who was an Ionian; but it is true of what has heretofore passed current as most orthodox and authoritative in Greek literature, and has done most to regulate modern opinion.

In certain respects Mr. Grote's history of Greece is admirable, so far as it professes to be a history of the Hellenic peninsula; but his treatment of what is usually termed the "Legendary and Heroic Age of Greece" is chiefly remarkable as an elaborate display of unphilosophical skepticism. He begins the history with the year 776 B.C., and finds nothing but "interesting fictions" in the myths and legends representing the previous ages. The history of Hellas did not go back into the past many generations beyond that date. Hellas was scarcely as old as Homer, who was not a native of that country, and did not represent its culture. Grote's positive and not always ingenuous skepticism may be as reasonable as that theory of Greek antiquity which finds in the myths and legends nothing more than a "legendary and heroic age" of the Hellenes. It is false to the past, but not much more so than this theory itself.

The Greek race—settled around the Ægean Sea, in Asia Minor, Thrace, Macedonia, Thessaly, Epirus, and throughout the Grecian peninsula—consisted of a group of tribes or families as closely related in origin and language, probably, as the Scandinavian group in Northwestern Europe. They inherited the culture of their predecessors, the Phœnicians, or Cushites, and the Pelasgians, who, in more ancient times, established the oracle of Dodona, made Thrace eminent as a seat of civilization and science, established enlightened communities in Asia Minor, and carried their civilizing influence into the Grecian peninsula itself. The earliest and greatest known development of the Greek race was that which created the Ionian confederacy of Asia Minor; the latest was that of Hellas.

Very true it is that the Argonautic expedition, the legendary sieges of Thebes, the oracle of Dodona, the cities of Mycenæ and Tiryns, and such personages as Orpheus, Musæus, Olen, Linus, Cecrops, Cadmus, Pelops, and many others, have very little to do with the history of Hellas; but it is not true that they are *all* mere fictions or illusions. Criticism that destroys narrow and false interpretations of the legendary lore of the Greeks deserves respect, but it should not be content with skepticism, and assume too readily that "the curtain is the picture." It may be true, as Cousin says in his lectures on the History of Philosophy, that skepticism is the first appearance of common sense in our philosophizing; but it is not the only appearance of common sense on that field, for skepticism is neither the middle nor the end of true philosophy. Historical criticism should be able not only to destroy falsehood, but also to establish truth.

Mr. Grote might reasonably find in the Hellenic myths and legends nothing belonging to the history of Hellas; but, however brilliantly or weirdly arrayed by imagination, they are the children of Fact; they contain recollections, not of the first ages of Hellenic history, but of communities and nations more ancient. True interpreters of antiquity see this; it could not be seen by Mr. Grote, who adopted what he describes as "the just position long ago laid down by Varro," and which he states thus: "First, there was the time from the beginning of mankind down to the first deluge—a time wholly unknown. Secondly, the period from the first deluge down to the first Olympiad, which is called *the mythical period*, because many fabulous things are recounted in it. Thirdly, the time from the first Olympiad down to ourselves, which is called the *historical period*, because the things done in it are comprised in true histories."

According to this "position," mankind did nothing important, and appear not to have risen much above barbarism previous to the first Greek Olympiad. It assumes that actual history begins with the Hellenes; and Grote appears to take for granted that civilization, culture, and even language were in their infancy when Hellas rose. He finds in the mythical traditions nothing to indicate previous civilization or previous nationalities; he fails to recognise the influence of the Phœnicians and Egyptians; and his eyes are blind to the fact that the civilization of Ionia was older and greater than that of Hellas. He finds "prodigious improbability" in the legendary account Herodotus gives of the oracle of Dodona, not seeming able to comprehend that no "prodigious improbabilities" can exceed those put forth in support of this scheme of confident skepticism, which sees nothing but "fictions" in the traditions and mythological legends of antiquity, and attributes them wholly to the "creative imagination" of the Greeks.

He states very justly that, in Hellas, or Greece proper, "physical astronomy was both new and accounted impious in the time of the Peloponnesian war," and that even Plato "permitted physical astronomy only under great restrictions and to a limited extent." And yet he fails to notice, in such a manner as faithful exposition of Greek history demanded, that Thales, Pythagoras, and many other Ionians had a science of astronomy which included correct knowledge of the solar system. It seems impossible to inquire carefully without perceiving that Hellenic culture was preceded by a great development of civilization, science, and art, which it inherited, but could not wholly make its own, and which, in Ionia, was superior to anything known afterward at Athens, excepting, perhaps, in elegant literature, sculpture, and certain forms of philosophical speculation.

What is usually talked of as Greek culture had its origin in Asia Minor, and was richly developed there long before its light appeared at Athens. The earliest intellectual movement that found expression in the Greek language was wholly Asiatic. It appeared in Ionia, the country of Homer, Thales, Pythagoras, and Herodotus, where, during many ages before the Ionians and their language became predominant, another people had richly brightened the land with their culture. The literature, language, and sway of that older people were superseded or absorbed by the Ionic family of the Greek race, just as in Italy, some centuries later, the speech, culture, and dominion of Etruria were superseded by the Romans. The cities of Ionia, and of the whole coast of Asia Minor, were built and occupied originally by the race represented by the Phœnicians, followed by the Pelasgians; and in that beautiful region, whatever culture was known to Arabia, Egypt, Chaldea, and the East, received its most elegant development. The scholars of Ionia itself studied in the schools of Phœnicia and Egypt. They reached a degree of intellectual independence and of progress in science never equaled by any community on the other side of the Ægean.

Only a small portion of the literature of Ionia has been preserved; but the earliest Greek writers known or mentioned were all natives of Asia Minor, or representatives of its culture. Homer was born and educated there; Hesiod's parentage and literary training were both Ionian; Archilochus, "the first Greek who composed iambic verses according to fixed rules," was born on that coast in the eighth century before Christ, and had a fame "second only to that of Homer." There appeared the first development of what has been called the "Greek philosophy," and Herodotus tells us that Thales, "the father of Greek philosophy," was "of Phœnician extraction;" he was born at Miletus in the seventh century before Christ. Pythagoras was a native of Samos, one of the most important Ionian cities. All the early historians who wrote in Greek were born and educated in Asia Minor; Herodotus was a native of Halicarnassus; Hecateus was a native of Miletus. Tyrtæus, born at Miletus nearly 700 years before the Christian Era, was one of those who carried Ionian culture to Athens; and in the same century appeared, on the Asiatic side of the Ægean, Terpander, Aleman, Alcæus, Sappho, and other brilliant Grecian lyrists. In Asia Minor rose the most elegant and beautiful order of Greek architecture—the Ionic. At the beginning of the sixth century before Christ the Greek world had two matchless temples that moved all beholders with admiration and wonder; they were both in Asia Minor, one being the temple of Hera, at Samos, the other the temple of Diana, at Ephesus. Artistic architecture had not then made its appearance in Hellas.

The intimate relations of Athens with Ionia contributed more than anything else to make that city superior in culture to any other community on the Hellenic peninsula.

In this region, the people generally, like the Spartans, never reached a very high degree of cultivation; but the Hellenic writers left no histories of literature to show what the Greek race inherited from the enlightened civilization of other and older peoples, or to point out distinctly their own relation to Ionia. Herodotus showed that religion, letters, and civilization came to the Greeks from the Phœnicians and Egyptians; but in Hellas his statements were severely attacked, Plutarch describing them as "the malignity of Herodotus;" and, until recently, modern scholars, swayed by Hellenic influence, took a similar tone, and treated him as an untrustworthy fabler. It is now understood that no Greek historian was more truthful or more intelligent.

We should study the Greek myths and traditions, not as indications of a "legendary and heroic age of *Greece*," nor with that stultifying skepticism which represents them as nothing more than "interesting fictions," but as imperfect, confused, and idealized recollections of civilizations, peoples, events, and persons that had become ancient before the time of the first Olympiad. Without the aid of regular history, we can see that ancient Thrace and Phrygia were enlightened and important nationalities, that flourished and declined several ages before the period to which the Trojan War is usually assigned. To their time belongs the later period of the oracle of Dodona; and contemporary with them, probably, were Mycenæ and "sacred Tiryns." It is quite as absurd to call Olen, Orpheus, Musæus, Eumolpus, and Minos, Greeks; as to call Livy, Virgil, Cicero, Pliny, Hannibal, and Scipio, Frenchmen. They did not belong to the nation or age of Plato, Euripides, Xenophon, and Socrates. Some of them were Thracians; and the Thrace of Orpheus must have been nearly as distant in time from Hellas, as the Rome of the Cæsars was from the France of Philip Augustus. Between them were " middle ages" to which belonged Troy, Argos, the origin of the oracle of Delphi, with the earlier periods of the kingdom of Lydia and of the Ionian confederacy. The language of Thrace and Dodona must have been a dead language before the time of Homer; and the hymns of Olen, Orpheus, and Musæus, preserved by use in celebrating the Eleusinian Mysteries, must have needed translation in the time of Onomacritus, even if the language in which they were written had been neither Pelasgic nor "Ammonian," but, instead, some ancient dialect of the Greek family.

It is not a fortunate circumstance that our studies of antiquity have been so much influenced by Hellenic narrowness and egotism; nor is it creditable to the scholars of Hellas that they said so little, and appeared to know so little of the ancient history of that beautiful region around the Ægean, where civilization was as old as the commercial enterprise that created Sidon. Their influence has given us histories of Greece in which nearly everything in that region is made subordinate to Hellas, which is set forth as the beginning, middle, and end of all the enlightened culture it ever knew. It should be sufficient to appeal to the Greek language itself against this method of writing histories of the Greeks. The extraordinary development of this language appears in its oldest literary monuments that have been preserved, making us feel that they cannot be the oldest in its history. Its substantial identity in all the dialects shows that it was the speech of a civilized and cultivated people before dialects began to appear. Whence came this development? It shows a history in which Helhas occupies only the last ages. We know something of Ionia and the other Greek communities on the coast of Asia Minor, and we are sure that the beginning of that history cannot be made a "fiction" by the obscurity in which it is hidden.

Three thousand years hence, when all the living languages of the present time have been long dead, and all the literature connected with them lost, some writer belonging to a nation and using a language that will first appear in the world two thousand years after our time may undertake to write the history of America. To do it as some have written the history of Greece, he will begin with some great epoch in our history yet to come, perhaps, previous to which authentic history will be found impossible; but mythical and traditional recollections of Europe and of the first ages of American history will remain, and these will be grouped together and referred to as a "legendary and heroic age" of America. Alfred the Great, William the Conqueror, Shakspeare, Napoleon Bonaparte, Luther, Dante, and possibly Julius Cæsar, Alexander the Great, and Mahomet, will all become mythical Americans. Another historian of that future age may protest, with the air of excessive wisdom, that the mythical and legendary recollections are merely "interesting fictions," and signify nothing. They will agree, however, that actual history begins with the given epoch.

The Hellenes are not the only people whose audacious egotism has assumed and believed them to be the selectest people on earth—the matchless blossom and glory of humanity, while all others were outside barbarians; but it may well be doubted whether this weakness in any other people ever had such a powerful and far-reaching influence.

I do not believe the history of America can be written, three thousand years hence, as ignorantly and meanly as I have supposed. The culture of the present time, with all its defects, is so much larger and nobler, so much more observant of what is true and just, in its treatment of the past and the present, than was ever realized in Hellas, that it cannot transmit to future ages the same misleading influence.

Bryant, in his "Analysis of Ancient Mythology," discusses the narrowness and self-conceit of the Hellenic spirit with much intelligence and force. He points out gross mistakes in Hellenic writers on Mythology, and shows that they were too ignorant of their predecessors, and too bigoted and egotistic, to treat this subject in a proper manner. He maintains that the most useful Greek writers on subjects relating to antiquity are those who did not reside in Hellas, and names Lycophron, Callimachus, Apollonius Rhodius, Homer, Nonnus, who wrote "Dionysiaca," Porphyry, Proclus, Iamblicus, Diodorus Siculus, Pausanias, and the Christian fathers Theophilus, Tatianus, Athenagoras, Clemens, Origen, Eusebius, Theodoret, Syncellus, and others. In such writers he finds a more unprejudiced reference to antiquity, and a more candid record of what was known of the older nations. It would, however, be too much to expect, anywhere in Greek literature, a just and cordial appreciation of the great civilization that prevailed around the Ægean and the Mediterranean for ages before the Greek race came into history. It is not there. The lost literature of Thrace, Phrygia, Ionia, Etruria, and Phœnicia would tell us more; but its beginnings were in very remote times, and successive changes of race and language so wasted the early records and monuments, that a complete history had become difficult, if not impossible, to the later generations.

Some of the most important Grecian works on archæological topics are lost, or known only in preserved fragments of them. Who that is drawn to these studies would not like to have a complete copy of the *Ethnica* of Stephanus of Byzantium? or of the more ancient mythological history of Pherecydes, who is said to have obtained his knowledge from the secret books of the Phœnicians? or of the genealogical, chronological, and historical works of Hellanicus of Mytilene? or of that very ancient work of Thymœtes, of "Asia Minor," written in a language older than the Greek, to which Diodorus Siculus and others refer in their accounts of Dionysus or Bacchus? A vast library of such lost works would fail to satisfy half our questions, but it would add much to our knowledge of the past; and how greatly would this knowledge be extended could we add to it the lost mythological and historical literature of Phœnicia, Arabia, Egypt, and Chaldea, with those "ancient histories of Iran" mentioned in the Dabistan and other Eastern writings!

PRE-HISTORIC TIMES.

Those "ancient histories of Iran," long since lost, would tell us much that we desire to know, not only of the early history of the Aryan people, whose great antiquity it is now impossible to deny, but also of the great people of ancient Arabia, whose civilization was much older and more enterprising, and who were known to the Hebrews as Cushites, and to the early Greeks as Ethiopians. It seems to me impossible to inquire carefully without being led to the conclusion that Arabia, in very remote antiquity, was the

C

seat of a brilliant civilization, which extended itself throughout Southwestern Asia, and spread its influence from the extreme east to the extreme west of the known world. The wonderful people of ancient Arabia—the revered and mysterious Ethiopians of ancient tradition—seem to have filled the world, as they knew it, with their commercial activity, their maritime enterprise, their colonies, and the light of civilized life. Their traces are still found everywhere. Their civilization may have originated in Southern Arabia; it may have been due to the influence of some older people. This problem cannot be solved; but those who are using the disentombed records of Assyrian and Chaldean culture to reconstruct linguistic, ethnic, and political history, may see in them that "third race, neither Indo-European nor Semitic," which "laid the foundation of the culture which was adopted and developed there by the other races, as they later, one after another, succeeded to the supremacy."

By pre-historic times I mean the ages between the creation of man and the beginning of authentic history. If we accept the usual method, and begin regular history with the Greeks and Romans, we must exclude from it the history of China, and pretty much the whole of Rawlinson's history of the "Five Great Monarchies of the Ancient Eastern World;" we must place in pre-historic times all that relates to the old Egyptians, since Menes as well as before his time, not to speak of the older Aryans and Cushites, or Ethiopians, who belong there; and we must find nothing historical in any part of Western Europe beyond the accounts given by the Romans. This method is open to very effective criticism. The limit of history should be moved farther back into the past, and more importance should be allowed to some existing documents which it disregards; but it is unnecessary to engage in controversy with those who begin history with the first Greek Olympiad, provided they do not deny all previous civilization, and maintain that everything in human affairs previous to that date is either unknown or fabulous.

We know much of the history of times more ancient. Egypt has been unveiled. We know much of the Assyrian empire from its beginning to its close; and when the inscriptions discovered in the Assyrian and Mesopotamian ruins, amounting now to "whole libraries of annals, and works of science and literature," shall be fully explored and deciphered, the veil may be partly withdrawn from the history of that great race which created Egypt and Chaldea, and whose characteristic traces still show the extent of its influence. The Cushite element is already clear to the best interpreters; and, apart from linguistic inquiry, what was known already, rightly studied, was sufficient to warrant a prediction that it would be found there.

The great period of the Cushite or Ethiopian race had closed many ages previous to the time of Homer, although separate communities of that race remained, not only in Egypt, but also in Southern Arabia, in Phœnicia, in Africa, and elsewhere east and west. The distance in time from our age to that of Homer is much less than that from his age to the very remote period when the Cushites of Arabia colonized Chaldea. When we consider the exclusiveness of the Hellenes, and their lack of disposition to study and comprehend the past, it is not surprising that they knew so little of the history of more ancient nations; on the contrary, we can see more reason for surprise that their literature and traditions furnish so much to indicate the ancient civilization and greatness of the people whom they called Ethiopians.

We cannot write an authentic history of the ancient people of Arabia, nor of any other pre-historic people; but we can study what is known of them, inquire at every new source of information, and draw such conclusions as the facts may warrant. Inquiry concerning the condition of the human race in pre-historic times cannot now be avoided. It is forced upon us by the constant and increasing influence of progress in linguistic and physical science. That the antiquity of man is much greater than our chronologies have allowed is coming to be an established fact. Should the later reports of geology on this subject be fully confirmed by future discoveries, this inquiry will become more active, and assume higher importance.

Advocates of what is called the "development theory," as well as champions of the narrow chronologies, find it convenient to assign the first appearance of civilization to a very modern date in the great pre-historic past. Their hypothesis, suggested by speculation on the origin of species, and unsupported by any facts, sets forth that the "human race was evolved out of the most highly organized and endowed of the inferior mammalia;" and that "the farther back we trace man into the past, the more shall we find him approach, in bodily conformation, to those species of the anthropoid quadrumana which are most akin to him in structure." Brutes became men by virtue of the assumed "tendency of varieties to depart indefinitely from the original type," brute instinct, meanwhile, by a like wondrous change, being transformed into all the great attributes of the human soul. According to this theory, the first appearance of man on earth was followed by a vast period of human savagery, which lasted until the ever-progressing development had made the race capable of civilization.

It is mere hypothesis, accepted by its advocates as true, but, as they admit, not proved. Geology says nothing in its favor, for the oldest human remains discovered by geologists are those of men already capable of improvement, and most of them consist of arms, implements, and utensils of human manufacture. Sir John Lubbock and others mention only two human skulls that can be referred to the most ancient period of the Age of Stone, and the antiquity of one of these is doubtful. Of the other, known as the Engis skull, Mr. Huxley says, in his "Man's Place in Nature," "There is no mark of degradation about any part of its structure. It is, in fact, a fair average human skull, which might have belonged to a philosopher, or might have contained the thoughtless brains of a savage." Sir J. Lubbock says "it might have been that of a modern European, so far, at least, as form is concerned." This seems to be an explicit contradiction of the "development theory."

Moreover, it cannot be shown that communities more or less civilized did not exist on some portions of the globe at the oldest period to which these remains can be assigned. Northwestern Europe is but a small portion of the globe we inhabit. To suppose the existence of such communities at that time is inconsistent with nothing but this unproved hypothesis; and to say they did not exist, because we have no record of their existence, is mere assumption, with no more claim to the consideration due to ascertained fact than the supposition itself.

Archæological investigation has brought to view civilized peoples much farther back in the past than history has ever supposed possible. Linguistic science enables us to trace others much older. Who can show that many civilized communities and family groups of language did not successively appear, run their course, and perish in the veiled ages of pre-historic time? Who can make it certain that the first appearance of civilization in those ages was at a comparatively modern date? If we must have a hypothesis concerning the condition of mankind in the most obscure pre-historic ages, let it not be inspired entirely by the generalizings of physical speculation, but rather let it come from the higher dictates of reason, and be honorable to human nature. There is much to suggest such a hypothesis as I have indicated, not only in the nature of man, but also in the widespread traces of pre-historic civilization. For instance, we are not the first civilized inhabitants of North America, as the almost obliterated but still unmistakable evidence of an ancient civilization throughout the Ohio and Mississippi Valleys clearly shows.

These reflections, however, are somewhat beyond the scope of our present inquiry, which relates chiefly to the antiquity and character of the ancient people of Arabia, and their influence in promoting the civilization of the Semitic and Aryan races; therefore I close them with the following from Humboldt's Cosmos: "We will not attempt to decide the question whether the races at present termed savage are all in a condition of original wildness, or whether, as the structure of their languages often allows us to conjecture, many among them may not be tribes that have degenerated into a wild state, remaining as scattered fragments from the wreck of a civilization that was early lost."

III.

PRE-HISTORIC GREATNESS OF ARABIA.

In our researches into the beginnings of culture in the oldest nations mentioned in history, we perceive that they did not originate civilization. It preceded their existence, and came from an older people. They gave it new forms, each developing an individuality of its own; but it came originally from abroad. On this point tradition is uniform and explicit. In Eastern Africa, the civilizers proceeded from the south toward the Mediterranean, creating the countries in the valley of the Nile. The traditions of inner Asia bring civilization from the south, and connect its origin with the shores of the Erythræan Sea, meaning the Arabian shores of the Indian Ocean and the Persian Gulf; and these traditions are confirmed by inscriptions found in the old ruins of Chaldea. These inscriptions reveal also the fact that the first civilizers were neither Semites nor Aryans, but a "third race," which ethnic and linguistic investigators have been slow to recognise.

Meanwhile, it is distinctly apparent in the religions, mythologies, institutions, and customs of these ancient nations that they all had the beginnings of their civilization from the same source. The foundations of their culture were all laid by the same hand, whose traces are still visible in its ruins—in the remains of its most ancient religious forms, its most primitive architecture, and its most archaic styles of writing. This is so plain that some writers, not able to see the vast extent of pre-historic times, or to comprehend the possibility of human development in ages too remote for their chronology, have sought to show that some one of these nations gave civilization to all the others. Some have suggested that it came from Egypt, a hypothesis which neither facts nor probability can allow. Some have said it went from India to all the other nations, which is still more improbable. Other clever theorists have found the primeval source of ancient civilization in Chaldea, where, as both tradition and the ruins testify, it was not original, but came in from an enlightened people belonging to more ancient times.

AN EARLY CIVILIZATION IN ARABIA.

In studying the influence of this more ancient culture, and seeking to discover the source from which it proceeded, we are led to Arabia, and to a people known in remote antiquity as Ethiopians and Cushites. It is evident that, in ages older than Egypt or Chaldea—ages away in the Past, far beyond the limit of Usher's chronology—Arabia was the seat of an enlightened and enterprising civilization, which went forth into the neighboring countries, and spread its influence "from the extremity of the east to the extremity of the west." At that time Arabia was the exalted and wonderful Ethiopia of old tradition—the centre and light of what, in Western Asia, was known as the civilized world. There are traditions of the ancient eastern world, which, rightly interpreted, can have no other meaning; and modern research presents linguistic and ethnological problems that can have no other satisfactory solution.

The geographical position of Arabia, as well as the characteristics of the great race by which it was occupied, must have given it this early pre-eminence. A peninsula of great extent, lying between the Red Sea and the Persian Gulf, having at command the shores of the Indian Ocean and the Mediterranean Sea, within easy reach of the valleys of the Indus and the Euphrates, the eastern coast of Africa, the Nile Valley, and the regions on the Eastern Mediterranean, and with an atmosphere and other physical relations that gave it cosmical importance, it had all those conditions by which commercial and intellectual development are most powerfully stimulated. It is not surprising to hear what the oldest traditions say of the wonderful Ethiopians, nor to find indications that they were the civilizers of Egypt and Southwestern Asia. If, as Heeren says, "the first seats of commerce were also the first seats of civilization," the civilization of Western Asia must have begun with the people who, previous to the time of Alexander the Great, had, from time immemorial, monopolized commercial and maritime enterprise.

ARABIA WAS THE ANCIENT ETHIOPIA.

In the early traditions and literary records of the Greeks, Arabia is described as Ethiopia; and this name was applied to other regions occupied or controlled by the Arabian Cushites. In modern times, it has commonly been assumed, without proper inquiry, that the Ethiopians were of course Africans. This grave mistake has been the source of much misunderstanding and confusion. Another fruitful source of misapprehension is that notable exercise in etymology which derives the word Ethiopia from the Greek words αἴθω and ὤψ, and makes it a designation for all the dark-colored races of Africa. Careful students of antiquity now point out that "the people of Ethiopia seem to have been of the Caucasian race," meaning white men, and that the word was, to the Greeks, "perhaps really a foreign word corrupted."* The Greeks themselves used the appellation as a sacred term in the religious vocabulary they had received from the Phœnicians and Egyptians. It is supposed to have been originated by what is called the "serpent worship" of the Cushites. To derive it from the Greek would be as little reasonable as to derive some Greek name, such as Hellas, from modern Hungarian. Eustathius (Schol. in Homerum) says: "Æthiops is a title of Zeus;" Διός ιπίθιτον Αιθίοψ. Lycophron describes Prometheus as Δαίμων Προμαθεύς Αιθίοψ; Prometheus Æthiops, the dæmon or tutelary deity. The appellation had a religious significance, but no reference whatever to complexion.

Arabia was the original Ethiopia, or Land of Cush. The countries on the Upper Nile were called Ethiopia because they were at first colonies or dependent provinces of ancient Arabia. At a later period, when the ancient and long-continued sway of the Ethiopians of Arabia declined, and gave way to the rise of great monarchies in Western Asia and India, the Cushite regions of Asia received new masters and took new names. Arabia itself was reconstructed by new forms of political organization; and, finally, the later Greeks and the Romans introduced the custom of confining the name Ethiopia to certain African countries on the Nile, above Egypt.

In the Hebrew Scriptures Arabia is uniformly described as Cush, or the Land of Cush. In our English Bible, as in the translation of the Seventy, this term is usually rendered Ethiopia. In the eighth chapter of Esther, where the hundred and twenty-seven provinces of the Persian Empire

* See Smith's Classical Dictionary.

are described as extending "from India unto Ethiopia," this word means Arabia; and the Ethiopian wife of Moses was an Arabian woman, being the daughter of a priest of the Midianites. In Ezekiel, that part of Northwestern Arabia which approaches Egypt is called "the border of Ethiopia," or Cush. The Arabian king, Tirhakah, who marched against Sennacherib, is called an Ethiopian, or Cushite; and the same ethnic name is applied to the Arabian Zerah, who waged war against Asa. That the Hebrew Scriptures constantly designate Arabia as Cush or Ethiopia will not be questioned by any Hebrew scholar. Rev. Charles Forster, in his work on the "Historical Geography of Arabia," and Rev. Dr. Wells, in his work, "The Historical Geography of the Old and New Testament," have placed this fact in the clearest light by collecting and examining many texts in which the name appears. Dr. Wells thinks it incontestable "that the nation of Cush did first settle in Arabia;" and Mr. Forster says: "It is a matter of fact, familiar to the learned reader, that the names 'Ethiopia' and 'Ethiopians' are frequently substituted in our English version of the Old Testament where the Hebrew preserves the proper name 'Cush.' And the name 'Cush,' when so applied in Scripture, belongs uniformly, not to the African, but to the Asiatic Ethiopia, or Arabia" (vol. i., p. 12).

The testimony of the older Greek literature is no less conclusive. The fact is incontestable that, in the early traditions and writings of the Greeks, this name, Ethiopia, seldom refers to any region in Africa. Strabo (bk. i., ch. ii.) says: "I assert that the ancient Greeks, in the same way as they classed all the Northern nations with which they were familiar as Scythians, etc., so, I affirm, they designated as Ethiopia the whole of the Southern countries toward the ocean." This includes with Arabia all the adjacent regions between the Mediterranean and the Indian Ocean, and all the coasts in that direction. Again, in the same book and chapter, he says: "And if the moderns have confined the appellation Ethiopians to those only who dwell near Egypt, this must not be allowed to interfere with the meaning of the ancients." The following is from the treatise of Ephorus on Europe: "If the whole celestial and terrestrial world were divided into four parts, the Indians would possess that towards the east, the Ethiopians that towards the south, the Kelts that towards the west, and the Scythians that towards the north." Of course, this classification refers to a period long subsequent to that when the Ethiopians controlled not only India, but also the regions occupied by the Kelts, and a portion of the countries assigned to the Scythians. Ephorus says also: "This family of Ethiopians seems to me to have extended themselves from the winter tropic in the east to the extremity of the west."

Homer describes the Ethiopians as "divided," and "dwelling at the ends of the earth, towards the setting and the rising sun." Strabo favors the following explanation of Ephorus: "The Ethiopians were considered as occupying all the south coasts of both Asia and Africa, and as 'divided' by the Red Sea (anciently called the Arabian Gulf) into Eastern and Western Asiatic and African." It is added that "this is an ancient opinion of the Greeks." This is undoubtedly true, as far as it goes. Arabia was the original Ethiopia, and its name was applied to all its colonies and affiliated communities, whether established at the west by the people called Phœnicians, or at the east from the southern and eastern shores of the peninsula.

They appear to have had colonies in Northwestern Africa at a very remote period. Strabo himself (bk. ii., ch. v.) mentions "Western Ethiopians, who are the most southern of the nations below Carthage;" and his description locates them on the Atlantic coast of Africa.

At one time, as the early Greeks say, the term Ethiopia was used to describe not only Arabia, but also Syria, Armenia, and the whole region between the Mediterranean and the Erythræan Sea, which means the Indian Ocean and the Persian Gulf. Tradition celebrates Kephous as one of the great sovereigns of this ancient Ethiopia. The following can be found in the fortieth "Narrative" of Conon: "The kingdom of Kephous was in the country afterwards called Phœnicia, but then Iopia, from Joppa; and it extended originally from the Mediterranean to the Arabians who dwell on the Erythræan Sea." Quotations showing how the appellation Ethiopia was used by the older Greeks can be multiplied. Prof. Rawlinson has abundant warrant for his statement that "the uniform voice of primitive antiquity spoke of the Ethiopians as a single race dwelling on the shores of the Southern Ocean," and "from India to the Pillars of Hercules."

It appears to have been understood, also, that the earliest civilization appeared in Arabia. This was manifestly the belief of the most ancient Hebrew writers, who described its first inhabitants that had cities and civilized life as Cushites. They recognised no country as older than Cush or Ethiopia, which was intimately associated with the oldest traditions and recollections recorded in their Scriptures. A belief of the ancient Greeks was expressed by Stephanus of Byzantium as follows: "Ethiopia was the first established country on earth; and the Ethiopians were the first who introduced the worship of the gods, and who established laws." This was probably a recollection of what, in earlier times, had been historical. The same belief appears in those glowing passages of the older Greek literature where the Ethiopians, and especially those dwelling on the Erythræan Sea, are described as the greatest and most admirable people ever known. Heeren was strongly impressed by this fact, and in his "Researches" spoke of it thus:

"From the remotest times to the present, the Ethiopians have been one of the most celebrated, and yet the most mysterious of nations. In the earliest traditions of nearly all the more civilized nations of antiquity, the name of this distant people is found. The annals of the Egyptian priests were full of them; the nations of Inner Asia, on the Euphrates and Tigris, have interwoven the fictions of the Ethiopians with their own traditions of the wars and conquests of their heroes; and, at a period equally remote, they glimmer in Greek mythology. When the Greeks scarcely knew Italy and Sicily by name, the Ethiopians were celebrated in the verses of their poets; and when the faint gleam of tradition and fable gives way to the clear light of history, the lustre of the Ethiopians is not diminished. They still continue to be objects of curiosity and admiration, and the pen of cautious, clear-sighted historians often places them in the highest rank of knowledge and civilization."

To Heeren the ancient Ethiopians were "mysterious" as well as "celebrated," because, not having made a clear discovery of the Cushite race, he was preoccupied by the assumption that Ethiopia was entirely an African country. If he could have released his mind from this assumption, and inquired, with his usual sagacity, what the old tradi-

tions and records mean by the term Ethiopia, he would
have seen the mystery dissipated in a clear light of intelligence, and the record of his "Researches" would present a
knowledge of the old Cushite race, and of their native country, which it does not now contain. As it was, no investigator of his time showed more penetration, or approached
the truth so nearly. He saw that a single race (which he
calls Semitic), speaking one language divided into various
dialects, "at an epoch beyond the reach of history, occupied the extensive plains between the Mediterranean Sea and
the Tigris, the most southern point of Arabia, and the Caucasian Mountains." He thinks the Phœnicians belonged
to this race, and says "it appears likely that they came
originally from Arabia." He also finds it probable that
the Arabians gained extensive control in India in pre-historic times, and that "distinct Arabian colonies may have
been settled on the coasts of Hindustan." Inquiring at
the present time, he would comprehend the Ethiopians, and
discover the historic importance of Arabia.

The ancient Ethiopia, or Land of Cush, of Greek and
Hebrew antiquity, is clearly described in the oldest geographical writings of the Sanskrit people of India. This
testimony, no less remarkable than conclusive, shows the
existence, in very ancient times, of a great Cushite empire
or people, occupying Arabia and other regions in Western
Asia; and it is noteworthy that the old Sanskrit books, like
the Hebrew Scriptures, describe the country occupied by
this people as Cusha-dwipa, the Land or Country of Cush.[*]
The old Sanskrit scheme of geography, as found in the Pu-

[*] For some account of this old Sanskrit geography, see Wilford's papers
in "Asiatic Researches," vols. iii. and viii.; and also Maurice's "Ancient
History of Hindustan," vol. ii.

ranas and other ancient writings, divides the world into seven parts, or *dwipas*, to wit: 1. Jambu-dwipa, the centre of the world and ancient home of the whole Aryan race; 2. Anga-dwipa, in Northeastern Asia, the seat of a great Manchu or Mongol people, probably, who, in later times, successfully invaded China; 3. Yama-dwipa, or the ancient Chinese empire; 4. Yamala-dwipa, which included the peninsula of Malacca, with the many important islands of Southeastern Asia, anciently occupied by that great and enterprising Malayan empire, which still existed, in a state of weakness and decline, when the Portuguese first went to the Indian Ocean; 5. Sancha-dwipa, which meant Africa in general; 6. Cusha-dwipa, the Land of Cush, which comprised Arabia and other regions extending from the borders of India to the Mediterranean; 7. Varaha-dwipa, or Europé.

In this geography Cusha-dwipa appears as one of the great divisions of the world, not on account of its position, which alone could not have given it such importance, but evidently on account of the importance and power of the civilized people by whom it was inhabited. A later division of the world added six new dwipas, or, rather, sub-dwipas, contained within the seven great dwipas. Among these we find a second Cusha-dwipa, situated in Africa beyond the straits of Bab-el-Mandeb, and called Cusha-dwipa *without*, or the exterior Cusha-dwipa, because it had been created by emigration and colonization from the original Cusha-dwipa, now called Cusha-dwipa *within*, or the interior Cusha-dwipa. The great or primal Cusha-dwipa is described as extending "from the shores of the Mediterranean and the mouths of the Nile to Sirhind on the borders of India."

The old Sanskrit geographers applied the term Cusha-dwipa to very nearly the same regions which the ancient Greeks described as Ethiopia. It included Arabia, Asia Minor, Syria from the mouths of the Nile, Armenia, the countries on the Euphrates and Tigris, a large part of the region north of the Persian Gulf, and, finally, an extended region in Africa. In remote pre-historic times it was the richest, most populous, and most enlightened portion of the world. Cusha-dwipa was in two parts; so, according to Homer and the Greeks, was Ethiopia " divided" into two parts, one being Asiatic and the other African. All accounts agree in stating that this African Cusha-dwipa was created by emigration from Arabia and from countries connected with it, and it seems to have extended not only northward, but also down the southeastern coast of Africa, and so far into the interior as to include the *Soma-Giri*, or Mountains of the Moon, and the lake regions around the sources of the Nile.

The geography found in the old Sanskrit books is manifestly that of the Aryans before they entered India, and not that of the more enterprising and traveled Cushite race. It describes the world as a circular plain, with a slightly convex surface, sloping gently on all sides to a surrounding ocean. Beyond this ocean, which inclosed the world in a vast river-like circle of waters, was a circular range of mountains supporting the ocean, called the Loca-loca Mountains, beyond which none but the most powerful gods could pass. In the centre of the world, at the highest point of its surface, stood Mount Meru, with Jamba-dwipa, the primeval home of the Aryan race, spread out around it, bordered with the other six dwipas or grand divisions of the earth. At a later period the Hindu scholars obtained more correct notions of the world. Ages before Copernicus, Aryabhatta taught in his writings that "the earth is a sphere, and revolves on its own axis." He learned this, probably, from the Cushites.

That the other scheme was the ancient geography of the Aryan race is shown by the fact that it was carried to the Mediterranean by those families of the race who migrated westward before the Sanskrit people occupied Northern India. We find it in Homer and Hesiod, and it is mentioned and ridiculed by Herodotus, who says (bk. iv., ch. xxxvi., Rawlinson's translation): "I cannot but laugh when I see numbers of persons drawing maps of the world without having any reason to guide them, making, as they do, the ocean stream to run all round the earth, and the earth itself to be an exact circle, as if described by a pair of compasses." This is said to have been the geographical scheme of the Greeks in their early times; Herodotus seems to say it was prevalent among "the Greeks who dwell about Pontus." Its existence in both India and Greece shows that it must be older than the period when these branches of the Aryan family separated.

It would be unreasonable, in my view, to deny or doubt that, in ages further back in the past than the beginnings of any old nation mentioned in our ancient histories, Arabia was the seat of a great and influential civilization. This fact, so clearly indicated in the remains of antiquity, seems indispensable to a satisfactory solution of many problems that arise in the course of linguistic and archæological inquiry. It is now admitted that a people of the Cushite or Ethiopian race, sometimes called Hamites, were the first civilizers and builders throughout Western Asia, and they are traced, by remains of their language, their architecture, and the influence of their civilization, on both shores of the Mediterranean, in Eastern Africa and the Nile valley, in Hindustan, and in the islands of the Indian Seas. These people had a country which was the home of their civilization. These civilizers, this "third race," now so distinctly reported by scientific investigators, but not yet well explained, must have been very different from a swarm of nomads, or a flood of disunited tribes moving from region to region, without a fixed country of their own. Those wonderful builders, whose traces reveal so plainly the habit of fixed life and the spirit of developed nationality, were not a horde of homeless wanderers. They had a country of their own, from which their enterprise and culture went forth to other lands, and this country must have been Arabia.

It is apparent that no other race did so much to develop and spread civilization; that no other people had such an extended and successful system of colonization; that they seem to have monopolized the agencies and activities of commerce by sea and land; and that they were the lordly and ruling race of their time. The Arabians were the great maritime people of the world in ages beyond the reach of tradition; as Phœnicians and Southern Arabians they controlled the seas in later times, and they were still the chief navigators and traders on the Indian Ocean when Vasquez di Gama went to India around the Cape of Good Hope.

IGNORANCE AND MISAPPREHENSION CONCERNING ARABIA.

It can be objected that the common estimate of the Arabian peninsula does not accord with such views of its ancient history as I have indicated. The reply is, that no part of the globe has been so little known or so greatly misapprehended in modern times as Arabia. It is commonly assumed that the whole interior of the country is a dreary waste of deserts, and that the only portions of it where civilized communities can exist are certain districts on the coast, the rest of this great peninsula being given up to nomads, or "wandering Arabs." This assumption, though very old and very confident, is wholly incorrect; its picture of Arabia is a fancy sketch to which the reality has no resemblance. That lack of knowledge which makes such pictures possible is due partly to the extreme isolation of the Arabian peninsula, since the rise of Western Europe changed the route to India, and took away its commanding importance as the central country between India and the West, and partly to Mahometanism and the decline of civilization in Western Asia. But its isolation from the Western countries began earlier. The later Greeks knew but little of Arabia, the Romans knew less, and in modern times intelligent travelers have journeyed along the coast in some districts of the Hedjaz, Yemen, Hadramaut, and Oman without making an actual discovery of the country.

Lieut. Wellsted surveyed nearly the whole coast-line of Arabia, and traveled extensively in Oman, and yet so little did he know of Central Arabia that the printed record of his travels begins as follows: "Arabia has been aptly compared to a coat of frieze bordered with gold, since the only cultivated or fertile spots are found on its confines, the intermediate space being filled with arid and sandy wastes." Even Humboldt, relying on the old assumption and the reports of travelers, supposed "the greater part of the interior of Arabia was a barren, treeless, and sandy waste." Ptolemy, living at Alexandria, gained some knowledge of the country, which appears in his geography, where cities and towns are located in the interior; but in Mr. Forster's work it is pointed out as a very grave mistake that "the Ptolemaic map prepared by Mercator" represents the "uninhabitable desert as clothed throughout with towns and covered with inhabitants." In the same way modern ignorance has criticised and discredited the Arabian geography of El Edrisi, because, as it alleges, through "invincible dislike to large blanks in a map," he filled up "the uninhabited country" of the interior with towns and villages. Mr. Forster's notion of the extent of this "uninhabited country" may be seen in his account of one of its deserts, which, according to his description, fills two thirds of the whole peninsula. Meanwhile it remains true that Ptolemy and El Edrisi had a much better knowledge of Central Arabia than is possible to the invincible assurance of such imaginative constructors of its geography.

In 1862-3, Mr. William Gifford Palgrave, whose long residence at the East, intimate knowledge of the Mahometan world, and perfect knowledge of the Arabic language gave him admirable qualifications for such a tour of observation, spent six months in Central Arabia, traveling through it from west to east. He tells us that he began this journey "supposing, like most people, that Arabia was almost exclusively the territory of nomads." His preparations for "traffic and intercourse with the natives" were made in accordance with this supposition, which, he adds, was "a grievous mistake, of which we soon became aware." Instead of nomads and "uninhabitable wastes," he found a rich and beautiful country, a settled and civilized population, and, throughout nearly the whole of his journey, cities, towns, tillage, and regular government, "where Bedouins stand for little or nothing." The nomads, found chiefly at the north, constitute scarcely one seventh of the population; and he seeks to impress upon his readers that the wandering Bedouins must not be taken as representatives of the Arabian race, for "they are only a degenerate branch of that great tree, not its root or main stock." In a word, they are a debased and roving population, "grown out of and around the fixed nation," and nowise like the fancy-formed "sages and noblemen of the desert" shown us in the portrayals of romance.

Mr. Palgrave discovered that Central Arabia is an extensive and fertile table-land, diversified by hills and valleys, and surrounded by a circle of waste and desert soil. He estimates that this great plateau comprises nearly half of the whole peninsula, or about 500,000 square miles, which is twice the extent of France. He found it occupied by two kingdoms, Shomer and Nejed; the former containing five provinces, Djebel Shomer, Djowf, Kheybar, Upper Kasseem, and Teyma; and the latter eleven provinces, 'Aared, Yemamah, Harock, Aflaj, Wadi Dowâsir, Seley'yel, Woshom, Sedeyr, Lower Kasseem, Hasa, and Kateef. In reality, there seemed to be but one nation there; and, in times not very distant, when Kasseem and Sedeyr were metropolitan provinces, there was, probably, but one supreme government. The industry, culture, and general condition of the people seemed to be above what is found in the neighboring countries of Asia. "The soil belongs in full right to its cultivators, not to the government, as in Turkey; nor is it often in the hands of large proprietors, like the zemindars of India or the wealthier farmers of England." He noticed that the show of civilization increased as he proceeded eastward. In the province of Sedeyr, where Mr. Palgrave seems to have had very cordial communication with the people, he found "elegant and copious hospitality," with much dignity and politeness in the manners of the people. He says, "The dominant tone of society, especially in Sedeyr, is that of dignified and even refined politeness."

He touched the kingdom of Shomer first at Wadi Serban, and came soon to the Djowf, an oasis or valley belonging to that kingdom, described as the western vestibule to the central country. It is fertile and very beautiful, and has, besides many smaller towns and villages, two cities containing over 30,000 inhabitants. Hāyel, the capital of Shomer, "surrounded by fortifications twenty feet high, with bastion towers, some round, some square, and large folding gates at intervals," had from 20,000 to 22,000 inhabitants; but "its area would easily hold 300,000 or more, were its streets and houses close packed like those of Brussels or Paris." It has spacious gardens and pleasure-grounds within the walls, while the plain "all around the town is studded with isolated houses and gardens, the property of wealthy citizens." All along the route he traveled were towns and villages, "clean and pleasant, and not unlike those of Jafnapatam and Ceylon."

Coming to the plain of Lower Kasseem, he saw it as follows: "Before us, to the utmost horizon, stretched an immense plain, studded with towns and villages, towers and groves, all steeped in the dazzling noon, and announcing everywhere opulence and activity." Kasseem is an ancient seat of Arabian civilization. Two of its cities which he saw contained, one over thirty thousand inhabitants, and the other over twenty-five thousand. Riad, the capital of Nejed, is "large and square, with high towers and strong walls of defense, a mass of roofs and terraces," with "edifices of remarkable appearance here and there breaking through the maze of gray roof-tops; and "for full three miles over the surrounding plain waved a sea of palm-trees above green fields and well-watered gardens, while southward the valley opened into the great and even more fertile plains of Yemamah, filled with groves and villages, among which Manfoohah, hardly inferior to Riad itself, was clearly distinguished."

Such, in reality, is that "uninhabited country," that "vast and dreary world" of "arid and sandy wastes," that imagined land of "treeless and waterless deserts"—Central Arabia. The extent of the fertile countries along the coast had already become known. The whole peninsula contains over a million square miles, and probably three fourths of it are now excellent for cultivation. In the great days of Ethiopian supremacy a still larger portion of Arabia was used for agricultural purposes, and for the various wants of a settled population. Even now a sufficient supply of water for irrigation would transform most of the desert districts into luxuriant fields and gardens. The ancient Arabians provided for this want by means of immense tanks similar to those still existing in Ceylon. Mr. Palgrave speaks thus of the Syrian desert: "These very lands, now so utterly waste, were, in old times, and under a better rule, widely cultivated, and full of populous life, as the numerous ruins strewn over their surface still attest." The same may be said of other desert districts in and near Arabia. There is no reason to doubt that very considerable portions of the desert region between Nejed and Hadramaut, usually called "the Dahna," were formerly cultivated, and occupied by towns, villages, and plantations.*

This remarkable country had no lack of fitness to be the home of a great people, and in the days when Balbec and Petra were flourishing cities, and Arabia was the busy commercial centre of the civilized world, it could have supported a hundred million people as easily as France now sustains forty million. It had no lack of resources for the great part played by its people in human affairs. If England and Spain could colonize and fill the whole American continent in the space of two or three centuries, what might not be done by the ancient Arabians in the course of twenty centuries? The great power and far-reaching activity of this people had declined many ages before the time of Ptolemy, and yet he enumerated 170 cities, ports, and large towns existing in his time within the region described by him as Arabia Felix.

THE TWO RACES IN ARABIA.

At the present time Arabia is inhabited by two distinct races, namely, descendants of the old Adite, Cushite, or Ethiopian race, known under various appellations, and dwelling chiefly at the south, the east, and in the central parts of the country, but formerly supreme throughout the whole peninsula; and the Semitic Arabians — Mahomet's race — found chiefly in the Hedjaz and at the north. In some districts of the country these races are more or less

* According to Arabian tradition, Ad, the primeval father of the pure Arabians, settled in the region occupied by this desert, where he built a city that became great and powerful. The Mahometans say the city and people were destroyed on account of the unbelieving wickedness of the Adites.

mixed, and since the rise of Mahometanism the language of the Semites, known to us as Arabic, has almost wholly superseded the old Ethiopian or Cushite tongue; but the two races are very unlike in many respects, and the distinction has always been recognised by writers on Arabian ethnology. To the Cushite race belongs the oldest and purest Arabian blood, and also that great and very ancient civilization whose ruins abound in almost every district of the country. To the Semites belong the originators and first preachers of Mahometanism, and also the nomads.

The Semites claim to be descendants of Ishmael, and they first appeared in Arabia at a period comparatively modern, probably not much older than the time of the Hebrew settlements in Canaan; the Cushites are connected with the oldest traditions of the country. For this reason, the Semitic Arabs, who settled at the north and in the Hedjaz, have always given precedence to the Arabians of the central and southern districts, and conceded their superior antiquity. In Arabic speech the Arabians of the old race are called *Aribah*, that is to say, Arabians of pure blood, Arabians *par excellence*, while those of Mahomet's race are described as *Moustarribes*, people of foreign origin, who were grafted on the pure stock by the marriage of Ishmael with a princess of the Cushite race.

Heretofore both tradition and the Oriental historians have agreed in saying that in ancient times a language was spoken in Arabia wholly different from the Arabic of Mahomet. Modern research has confirmed this statement. That old language has been discovered. We have it in what are called the Himyaric inscriptions; and modern dialects of it are still spoken in two or three districts of the peninsula, and to a considerable extent in Eastern and

Northern Africa, where it is written as well as spoken. It is found, also, in the ruins of Chaldea; and, in remote antiquity, it seems to have been spoken throughout most of Western Asia, and also in Hindustan, where it is probably represented at the present time, in a corrupted form, by the group of languages called Dravidian. It cannot properly be classed in the same family with the Arabic, but is closely related to the old Egyptian. It has been called "a new form of speech," because it was new to those who first discovered it; but it is very ancient, existing now only in disentombed inscriptions, in sentences preserved, without history, on the stones and rocks of old ruins, and in fragmentary and obscure communities representing the great pre-historic people by whom it was used. In the terminology of linguistic science, this language is called Ethiopic, Cushite, and sometimes Hamitic.

Mahometan fanaticism applied the term "Djohal," or "Ignorants" (or anti-Christ, as Christians might say), to all who dwelt in Arabia previous to the advent of its prophet; and the fierce blaze of this fanaticism consumed the old Cushite or Ethiopian literature, in which it saw nothing represented but accursed thoughts and feelings of the previous ages of "heathenish wickedness." The strange tongue of the "godless Djohal," which gradually fell into disuse, made this destruction easy; but, as we can see in Mahometan literature, there remained a prevailing consciousness of the great eminence, influence, and antiquity of the old race; and the wealth of the old culture in Arabia, Phœnicia, and Syria is seen in the superior development of the Arabic language, in the civilization that gave such lustre to the empire of the caliphs, and in the knowledge of science and philosophy brought to Western Europe by the

Saracens. This ineradicable consciousness of a great ancient history of the Arabian Cushites appears in the studied attempts of Mahometan historians and traditionists to connect with them the origin of Mahomet's race. Mahomet, they say, inherited the purest of the "blue blood" through the marriage of an ancestor with a princess of Yemen; and one tradition, which has been issued in many editions, represents that Joktan, son of Heber, recognised for this purpose as the most ancient father of the Semitic Arabians, was identical with Kahtan of Cushite history, described as the first king of Yemen.

These Mahometan inventions have confused and falsified the traditions of Arabian antiquity. William Muir, in the introduction to his learned and elaborate life of Mahomet, says: The identification of Joktan with Kahtan "is one of those extravagant fictions which the followers of Islam, in their zeal to accommodate Arabic legends to the Jewish Scriptures, have made in defiance of the most violent improbability and the grossest anachronisms." He adds: "It is no better than that of the Medina party, who tried to prove that Kahtan was a descendant of Ishmael, and therefore had no connection with Joktan." The Joktan invention is treated in the same way by Caussin de Perceval. These fictions are not as old as Mahometanism; and their chief purpose was to connect the founders of this religion with the prestige of the more ancient race, which still lived in the popular mind throughout the peninsula.

The connection of the Arabian Semites with the Hebrews, to whom they had claimed relationship through Ishmael, was older than Mahomet, and had made them acquainted with the Hebrew Scriptures. When, under the lead of Mahomet, they first emerged from obscurity, and aspired to lordly supremacy in the whole country, they began to appropriate to themselves the antiquity and the great names of the old Ethiopians, or Cushites, whose grand career had long since closed. Then arose the legends that sought to ennoble Mahomet's race by giving it the oldest Arabian blood, and even attempted to Semitize the Cushites by transforming the ancient Kahtan of that race into their imagined or traditional ancestor, Joktan.

In reality, neither history nor tradition has knowledge of more than two races in Arabia—the very ancient Cushites, who were a great and enterprising people in remote pre-historic times, and the Arabian Semites, who were not there during the grand periods of Arabian ancient history, and did not appear there until many centuries after the extended empire of the Cushites, or Ethiopians, had declined and become disunited. These Arabic Semites, who have chiefly occupied attention, and whose history has been allowed to obscure the ancient and true Arabians, were an unimportant, and probably a nomadic people, when they first appeared in the country, and they remained very obscure until the beginning of the seventh century after the Christian Era. They are generally called *Moustarribes* by their own writers, while those of the ancient race are called *Aribah*, or Arabians of the oldest and selectest blood. Ibn-Dihhyah, an Arabic historian, keeping up the fiction about Joktan, in a modified form, describes three distinct classes of Arabians—the *Aribah*, the most ancient tribes of Arabian tradition; the *Moutarribes*, created, though not clearly defined, by the Joktan fable; and the *Moustarribes*, or descendants of Ishmael. His *Moutarribes* may be dismissed from consideration. Mahometan writers cannot be safely trusted when they touch this question of Arabian ethnology, discourse about Joktan, and seek to connect the race of their prophet with everything ancient or great in Arabian history.

CONCERNING THE OLD RACE.

According to Arabian tradition, the old race, or the Cushites, consisted originally of twelve tribes, with the following designations—Ad, Thamoud, Tasm, Djadis, Amlik, Oumayim, Abil, Djourhoum, Wabar, Jasm, Antem, and Hashen. Some writers mention only nine ancient tribes of pure, unmixed Arabians; others mention more than twelve. As these traditions were not created by Mahometan assumption, they may preserve recollections of ancient names of tribal communities, or of cities and districts organized as separate municipalities, and governed by hereditary chiefs subordinate to the supreme authority. I shall endeavor to show that this method of political organization was a marked peculiarity of the Cushites. One of the names, Amlik, is biblical, being the same as Amalek. The saying, "old as Ad," is used in Arabia to designate the remotest period in the past; but we have no means to determine either the antiquity or the historical facts that may be indicated by these traditional names. In the traditions, the ancient people to whom they are applied are described as wonderful builders, who were rich in gold, silver, and precious stones. They have glowing descriptions of the magnificent cities and sumptuous palaces of the Adites and the Thamoudites.

But, as I have shown, we have more conclusive testimony than Arabic tradition to indicate that Arabia was the land of Cush, or Ethiopia; and the great and extended influence of the Cushite race in distant pre-historic times is now admitted by all careful investigators. The Arabic Semites were a foreign people, very modern in Arabian history, and had nothing to do with the country in the ancient times concerning which we inquire. That old Cushite race, so great and influential in its time, and so intimately connected with the most ancient civilization of which we have any knowledge, has almost wholly disappeared from the earth by mingling with other races in the widely-separated regions where it established colonies and civilization; with the Aryans, and perhaps with an aboriginal population, in Southern and Western Europe; with Semites and Aryans in Western Asia; with Semites in Arabia, and with a dark brown race found by the ancient Cushites in India and Africa. But few communities of pure Cushite blood can now be found even in Arabia. Its great mission was fulfilled in the grandest way centuries before the beginning of what is called authentic history, and now we have only scanty remains of either the race or its language. The great natural superiority of this race is still manifest wherever it is found with a tolerable approach to purity of blood.

Some communities of the old race found in Arabia claim to have unmixed blood. They strongly impressed Mr. Palgrave, who invites attention to them. At the northwest, where the Semites settled, there has been a greater decline of civilization than elsewhere. Mr. Palgrave points out that the show of civilization increased as he proceeded through the peninsula from Ma'an towards the east; and, after much communication with the inhabitants of cities and towns along his route, he recorded and published his opinion of the people as follows: "After having traveled much, and made pretty intimate acquaintance with many races, African, Asiatic, and European, I should hardly be inclined to give the preference to any other over the genuine unmixed clans of Central and Eastern Arabia." He says they represent "one of the noblest races earth affords," but does not appear to comprehend the real significance of these fragments of the old Cushite race, once so grand and powerful, now almost hidden from observation among living races. He says again, in another part of his book, "I am inclined to regard the Arabians, taken in themselves and individually, as endowed with remarkable aptitude for practical and material science, and hardly less adapted to the railroad, to the steam-ship, or to any other nineteenth century invention or natural research, than the natives of Sheffield or Birmingham themselves; but lack of communication with other countries has kept them back in the intellectual race." It would not be reasonable to doubt the natural capacity of a race whose people were anciently represented by the marvelous manufacturing skill and commercial power of Sidon and Tyre. Arabia, once foremost, has been made the obscurest of countries by great changes in the seats and routes of commerce. The Cushite race has not been "kept back" from a great part in human affairs; it has declined from a great position, and was made obscure by that influence of time which brought the world's great changes and made another race imperial.

ANCIENT ARABIAN RUINS AND INSCRIPTIONS.

Ruins representing ancient civilization exist in every part of Arabia, from Balbec and Petra to Mareb and Zhafar. They have not been carefully explored, and only a few of them have been visited. No excavations have been made, but a considerable number of Cushite or Himyaric inscriptions have been secured that furnish important information concerning the language and race of the ancient inhabitants of the country. None of the ruins already visited belong to the earlier periods of Arabian ancient history, and it is nowise likely that ruins representing times so very remote still exist for examination; nevertheless, some of those to which attention has been drawn are very old.

The discovery of these antiquities, especially the inscriptions, seems to have been connected incidentally with measures taken by the English to facilitate communication with India through Egypt and the Red Sea. About thirty-five years ago, nearly the whole coast-line of Arabia was surveyed or carefully explored by naval expeditions fitted out by the British East India Company. Some of the accomplished officers engaged in these surveys traveled in Oman and Hadramaut, and visited ruins in Yemen and along the shores of the Red Sea. Among those who made important discoveries were Lieutenants Wellsted and Cruttenden, Dr. Hulton, and, later, Captain Haines. Carsten Niebuhr had previously reported the existence of inscriptions, and two or three had been very imperfectly copied by Dr. Seetzen.

Wellsted and Cruttenden made the first discovery of Himyaric inscriptions that were carefully copied. Wellsted visited important ruins at Nakab-el-Hadjar, between Hadramaut and Yemen. He found there the remains of an immense wall, originally from thirty to forty feet high, and ten feet thick at the foundation. It was built around a hill of considerable extent, on a line above the base, and was flanked by square towers standing at equal distances from each other. The blocks of grayish marble, of which it was built, were hewn and fitted by the builders with surprising nicety, indicating science and skill in construction of a high order. Within the inclosure were the remains of edifices by which the slopes of the hill had been covered. Wellsted says of the wall: "The magnitude of the stones used, and the perfect knowledge of the builder's art exhibited in the style and mode of placing them together, with its towers and great extent, would give this structure importance in any part of the world." Describing one of the ruined buildings, he says: "That it owes its origin to very remote antiquity is evident by its appearance alone, which bears strong resemblance to similar edifices found amidst Egyptian ruins. We have the same inclination of the walls as in them, the same form of entrance, and the same flat roof of stones." Important inscriptions in the old language and character, found on the smooth face of the great blocks of stone at this place, were copied.

M. Fulgence Fresnel, in the *Journal Asiatique*, discussing Wellsted's discoveries at Nakab-el-Hadjar, is sure, and with good reason, that these ruins mark the site of the ancient city of Meyfah, which, he thinks, is the same as the "Mempha" of Ptolemy. It is undoubtedly the same as the old city of "Mepha," not "Mempha," which Ptolemy places in the valley of Meyfah, where these ruins are found.

Among the ruins visited by Wellsted are those at His'n Ghorab, on the coast in the same region. His'n or Hassan Ghorab is a hill about five hundred feet high. It is now connected with the main land by a low, sandy isthmus, but was formerly an island. All around it, and scattered over its slopes to the summit, are ruins of houses, walls, and towers. It is a remarkable field of ruins, some parts of which are almost inaccessible. Everything indicates that a commercial emporium formerly stood here—a city which in ancient times must have been of the first importance.

It is doubtless, as Fresnel and others suppose, the site of that celebrated commercial emporium anciently known as the city of Kana. Here, too, Himyaric inscriptions, engraved on the smooth face of the rock, were discovered and copied by the English visitors.

On the coast, in the northern part of Hadramaut, are the ruins of a great commercial city called Zhafar, the Sapphar of Ptolemy, and supposed to be the Saphar of the Hebrew Scriptures. The name Zhafar is now applied to a series of villages situated on and near the coast. It is supposed that the ancient Zhafar, or Saphar, stood at some distance from the sea, and was connected with it by a port or second city at the place called El Belid in Arabic, and Kharekhâm in the Ehkkili or Himyaric tongue; but these ruins, said to be very remarkable—"splendid ruins" Fresnel calls them—have not been explored as carefully as their importance demands. Perhaps what have been mentioned as sites of the city and its port are in reality sites of an old and a new town, a Pælus-Zhafar and a New Zhafar. Both are now desolate. The "splendid ruins" are found at the place called El Belid, where the blocks of stone used by the architects, cut with geometrical precision, show marvelous perfection in the workmanship of the builders. It is evident that the whole district now called Zhafar would yield rich results to careful investigation by competent explorers.

In July, 1843, Thomas Jos. Arnaud, a French gentleman, visited the ruins of the very ancient city in the interior of Yemen known as Saba, and also as Mareb and Mariaba.*

* Abulfada says: "There are some who say that Mareb was the surname of a king who reigned over Yemen; but others say that Mareb was the royal arsenal, and that the city was Saba," which seems most probable.

He is the first European who has visited those ruins in modern times and returned in safety. Arnaud went to Saba from San'a, remained there four days, and returned to the coast by the same road. He was five days on the road from San'a to Saba. Within a day's journey of Saba he found very extensive and noteworthy ruins of a great city, which he could not examine carefully. They occupy "a spacious site" on the great plain of Kharibah. He was told of other ruins in that part of the country, which he did not see, and particular mention was made of ruins of an ancient city situated about a day's journey northeasterly from Kharibah. A village called Mareb, surrounded by extensive ruins, is all that now remains of the ancient and celebrated Saba, once the populous and magnificent capital of Southern Arabia. At one period the whole country was known to the Greeks as Saba (called Sheba in the Hebrew Scriptures), and the people as Sabæans; and language scarcely sufficed to express their conception of its riches and magnificence.

At Mareb Arnaud examined what remains of the "Great Dike," or tank, so famous in Arabic tradition, but he does not describe it satisfactorily. The embankment appears to have been a very long and exceedingly massive structure, and he tells us that the basin of the tank or reservoir was a depression between two mountains called "Balak." This dike is probably one of the oldest structures in Arabia of which we have any knowledge. The history of its origin was lost before the time of Queen Belkis, who is supposed to have lived in the age of Solomon, but may have lived at an earlier period. It was then so very ancient that the solid and vast embankment was going to decay through age.* Queen Belkis repaired it, but her repairs did not restore its original strength, for, a few ages later, it burst with such disaster to the whole district as made the event an epoch in the history of Yemen.

Some writers, whose facility in reading Oriental languages is far superior to their capacity for comprehending archæological facts, and studying antiquity with penetrating intelligence, have allowed themselves to talk in a doubtful, hesitating way in support of the strange and most incomprehensible vagary that this dike was not built earlier than the beginning of the Christian Era. They forget that it was incontestably as old as the ancient city of Saba, if not much older, and that both the city and the dike had decayed long before Christ. Mahometan assumption itself never invented a more unwarranted, a more extravagant, or a more senseless fiction.

Wellsted mentions the ruins of Kilhát, on the southern coast of Oman, which "cover an extensive tract," and he was told of other ruins in the interior which he could not visit. Strabo, Pliny, Ptolemy, and others, as well as the Hebrew writers, speak of great cities in Arabia which no longer exist. We can not well doubt that diligent exploration would bring to light numerous ruins of great importance to archæologists which at present are entirely unknown, and which the present inhabitants of the country cannot explain. The Mahometan natives residing near the

---

* Hamza of Ispahan says: "The Himyarites relate that Belkis, having become queen, built in Saba the dike called *Arim*. The other inhabitants of Yemen dispute this, and maintain that the dike *Arim* was constructed by Lokman, the second son of Ad; and they say that time having brought it to a condition of decay, Belkis, on becoming queen, repaired the damage it had suffered." See *L'Univers*, vol. x., p. 58.

ruins visited by Wellsted said, in reply to his inquiries, that these old cities were built by their "infidel" ancestors. He pointed out to them that their "infidel" ancestors must have been vastly superior to the present generation of Arabians, and capable of much greater works; to which they answered that their ancestors were assisted by "Jins," or "Devils." Wellsted's suggestion has more significance than he himself seems to have appreciated. Whether we study Arabia in its traditions, in its ruins, in the remains of its old language, or in the present characteristics and condition of its people, we cannot easily evade the conclusion that this country was anciently the seat of a great civilization, that declined from its highest condition long before the Christian Era, and of which only traces of its impression on the country, and confused recollections of its greatness, still exist.

The old Arabian or Cushite inscriptions found in El Harrah, a part of the region justly described as "the remarkable country south of Damascus," belong to Arabia. Mr. Cyril C. Graham gave an account of them in the "Asiatic Journal" for 1860. El Harrah is southeast and east of Haurân, where ruined or deserted cities exist with the houses still nearly perfect. In El Harrah Mr. Graham found similar remains of cities, with abundant inscriptions. He tells us that when copies of the inscriptions were laid before the Royal Asiatic Society, "a high authority" declared them to be "the most ancient form of Phœnician writing yet seen." Also, "Barth was immediately struck with their great similitude to the inscriptions of the Touaricks." He mentions reports of similar inscriptions in Jebel Shammar, and adds that "Wallin secured two inscriptions at Belad Sôf, in Central Arabia," like those at

El Harrah, and that "he found these characters constantly recurring." One of the alphabetic characters in these inscriptions is found nowhere else save among the Runic letters, and another only in the Etruscan alphabet. Such antiquities abound in the mysterious land of Cush, but they have not been explored, and in many respects Arabia is still an undiscovered country.

Mr. Palgrave's lack of opportunities to study Arabian antiquities, and perhaps a not very active interest in this department of study, did not enable him to add much to our knowledge of the ruins and other remains of the ancient condition of the country. But, in his account of the old castle at Monûmah, on the largest of the Bahreyn islands, we can see how strongly that venerable structure invites attention. He points out the ruins in the Syrian Desert, and he notices in the construction of the old castle at the Djowf evidence of its very great antiquity. This castle has been several times rebuilt in part, or repaired, so that only the south wall now preserves its first line of construction. In this wall, "the huge size and exact squaring of the stones in the lower tiers indicate the early date of the fabric, while several small windows, at a height of ten or twelve feet from the ground, are topped by what is called the Cyclopean arch, a specimen of which may yet be seen in the so-called palace of Atreus at Mycenæ." In Kasseem he found the remains of an ancient structure similar to Stonehenge in England, and he learned from his Arabian companions that two others like it could be found in districts not far away from his route, which they named.*
He says, "There is little difference between the stone wonder of Kasseem and that of Wiltshire, except that one is

---

* See Palgrave's Travels in Central Arabia, vol. I., p. 251.

in Arabia, and the other, more perfect, in England." The huge stones, standing on end, about fifteen feet high, were arranged in a circle like those of Stonehenge. These structures evidently had the same purpose, and the builders in each case were directed by the same thought.

THE ANCIENT ARABIAN LANGUAGE.

In some respects, the most important discovery made in Arabia is that which brings to light the old language of the country, and shows its affinity with that of Egypt and of Western Asia in the earliest times. In these studies nothing is more reliable than the historical revelations of the science of language. They present facts which no romancing of tradition or mythology can obscure. It has been determined by scientific inquiry that the people who first established civilization in Western Asia used a language that has been called Cushite, or Hamitic. Some scholars, like George Rawlinson, attracted by the fanciful linguistic scheme of Bunsen, have suggested a derivation of this language from the "Turanian," a designation that has no very definite meaning in the science of language, and which at first was used loosely to include nearly all languages that could not be classed as either Aryan or Semitic. Hence Mr. Rawlinson sometimes talks of the earliest speech of Western Asia as "Turanian," but points out that it was developed there as the Hamitic, or Cushite tongue, which in the most ancient times prevailed "from the Caucasus to the Indian Ocean, and from the shores of the Mediterranean to the mouths of the Ganges." Among the ancient peoples who spoke this language he classes "the Southern Arabians, the early Canaanites, the early Chaldeans, and the Susianians." He might have added, what is now well known, that dialects of this tongue were spoken in Egypt, and throughout Northern and Eastern Africa. The best linguistic scholars, those whose judgment is least affected by fanciful theorizing, explicitly reject the "Turanian" speculation, and incline to the belief that these Hamitic or Cushite dialects must be classed by themselves as a distinct family.

It is now beyond question that this Cushite tongue, found in the Chaldean ruins, and traced throughout Western Asia, was the ancient language of Arabia. No other language was spoken in the country until, at a late period, the Ishmaelitish Semites went there. The Himyaric inscriptions show conclusively that tradition and the Eastern historians are correct in saying that the old language of Arabia was entirely different from what is known as Arabic. We learn from Arabic writers that dialects of the Himyaric or Cushite tongue were spoken in Hadramaut, Mahrah, and some other parts of Eastern and Southern Arabia, as late as the fourteenth century. They are still spoken in Mahrah, an extensive region in Eastern Arabia, including the district where Mirbat and Zhafar are situated, and in the mountainous districts of Cape Mesandum; and the Arabic used in many of the other eastern and southern communities is so filled with the vocabulary and forms of the old tongue that Semitic Arabs from the north cannot understand it. Dr. H. J. Carter, in the Bombay Journal of July, 1847, said: "The Mahrah dialect, as spoken by the Mahrahs themselves, is the softest and sweetest language I have ever heard." El Edrisi called this language "the language of the people of Ad, which is ancient and unknown to the Arabians of our day."

It was formerly a saying of the Semitic Arabs that " whoever enters Zhafar Himyarizes," which indicates that the old language maintained itself there long after it had been superseded in most of the other districts. In the *Journal Asiatique* for June, 1838, Fresnel stated that the Himyaric language then spoken at Zhafar and Mirbat was somewhat different from the dialect spoken in Mahrah, adding that, according to the best information he could obtain, the only difference was that "the Mahri contained a larger proportion of Arabic words." Fresnel (not aware, probably, that Wellsted and his companions had found Himyaric inscriptions somewhat earlier) claimed to be the discoverer of the Himyaric language. But his first perception of its importance was not very clear, for he announced this discovery to his scientific friends at Paris as follows: "I have discovered the language spoken at the court of the Queen of Sheba, which is still spoken by the savages of Mahrah!" He did not comprehend Arabia, and perhaps his chronology would not allow him to go much farther back into the past. Dr. Forster, in the appendix to his work on Arabian geography, glowed over the Himyaric inscriptions in a somewhat different way, finding in them "the oldest language in the world," and "the first alphabet of mankind."

Neither the dialect nor the alphabet of the Himyaric inscriptions already discovered can be regarded as extremely ancient in the history of Cushite development, certainly not as ancient as the cities which the ruins represent. We have older forms of both. The alphabet carried to Greece, Italy, and Western Europe by the Phœnicians belongs to a much older period, as we can see in the number and form of the letters; and the characters of some inscriptions and writings found in Western Asia evidently belong to an earlier age. The dialect of the Himyaric inscriptions, however, is ancient and difficult to decipher, and the contents of many of them show that they are much older than Christianity, if not older than those found at Sidon. In publishing the Himyaric inscriptions preserved in the British Museum, Mr. Birch notices the suggestion of M. Caussin de Perceval that they may belong to a period of Arabian history beginning not earlier than 100 years before Christ, and adds this criticism: "As the later kings were greatly inclined to Judaism, it is possible that monuments such as these, full of invocations to idols, may belong to earlier times of the empire." The Himyaric alphabet, described as the Musued, had been preserved by several Arabic writers, and was easily understood. The difficulty in translating arises chiefly from the antiquity of the dialect, which, nevertheless, is much later than that of the Chaldean inscriptions.

CONCERNING THE ORIGIN OF ALPHABETICAL WRITING.

It is found necessary to admit that the various styles of alphabetic writing used by the nations of antiquity were all derived, directly or remotely, from a common source,—from a single form of writing, originated by some older people in the course of their own development. They all belong to the same family, just as genetically related dialects and forms of speech constitute one family group, and furnish demonstration that they all proceeded from a single primeval language. According to the Phœnicians, the art was invented by Tanutus, or Taut, "whom the Egyptians call Thouth;" and the Egyptians said it was invented by Thouth, or Thoth, otherwise called "the first Hermes;" in which we see clearly that both Phœnicians and Egyptians referred the invention to a period older than their own separate political existence, and to an older nation from which both peoples had received it.

Sir William Drummond, in his "Origines," said on this point: "There seems to be no way of accounting either for the early use of letters among so many different nations, or for the resemblance which existed between some of the graphic symbols employed by those nations, than by supposing hieroglyphic writing, if I may be allowed the term, to have been in use among the Tsabaists in the first ages after the flood, when Tsabaism (planet worship) was the religion of almost every country that was yet inhabited." Sir Henry Rawlinson, directed by the influence of scientific inquiry, and with the facts before him in a clearer light, says: "So great is the analogy between the first principles of the science (of writing), as it appears to have been pursued in Chaldea, and as we can actually trace its progress in Egypt, that we can hardly hesitate to assign the original invention to a period before the Hamite race had broken up and divided. A system of picture-writing, which aimed at the communication of ideas through the rude representation of natural objects, belonged, as it would seem, not only to the tribes who descended the Nile from Ethiopia, but to those also who, perhaps, diverging from the same focus, passed eastward to the valley of the Euphrates." (See Rawlinson's Herodotus, vol. i., p. 443.)

It seems reasonable, therefore, to infer that Taut or Thoth represents the origin of the art of writing among the Hamitic or Cushite people in the earlier ages of their existence, when they still dwelt together as a single united people, before the time of Egypt and Chaldea; but the home of their civilization, from which their colonies went forth east and west, was not an African country, as Sir Henry Rawlinson appears to assume; it must have been Arabia, as I have shown.

Alphabetic writing would naturally have its earliest development in the country where the hieroglyphic or picture style originated; and, this country being Arabia, the development of the simpler and more practical alphabetic style must have been hastened by the commercial habits and wants of the people. The nation that became mistress of the seas, established communication with every shore, and monopolized the commerce of the known world, must have substituted a simple phonetic alphabet for the hieroglyphics as it gradually grew to this eminence; while isolated Egypt, less affected by the practical wants and tendencies of commercial enterprise, retained the hieroglyphic system, and carried it to a marvelous height of perfection, deriving from it, however, two simpler forms of writing—first the *hieratic*, and at length the *demotic*.

The ruins of Egypt are covered with hieroglyphics, the perfected Egyptian style appearing on the oldest monuments. That this form of writing was laid aside very early by other branches of the Cushite or Hamitic race is evinced by the fact that the only fragments of it found in remains of other peoples of this race appear on a broken tablet from the Mesopotamian ruins, now in the British Museum. Sir Henry Rawlinson finds in the writing on this tablet "several of the primitive forms of natural objects from which the cuneiform characters were subsequently elaborated." There are not less than six different styles of the cuneiform writing, that found in the Chaldean ruins seeming to be the oldest. There is nothing to show how many forms of hieroglyphical writing came into use before this style was perfected in Upper Egypt, and superseded elsewhere by alphabets.

The oldest Cushite alphabet known to us is that which the Phœnicians carried to Southern and Western Europe, which, however, was not preserved without modification. The names of its letters, and some of their forms, show that it was derived originally from hieroglyphics. Aleph means an ox; Bit, Bith, or Beth, a house or temple; and Gamel or Gimel, a camel, an animal very naturally represented in ancient Arabian hieroglyphics, but not likely to appear in a hieroglyphical system originating in any country where the camel is not found.

The invention of this alphabet, from which all the alphabets of modern Europe have been derived, was attributed to the Phœnicians. Pliny (lib. v., ch. xii.) ascribes to the Phœnicians "the great glory of inventing letters"—"*ipsa gens Phœnicum in gloria magna literarum inventionis.*" This appears to have been commonly said among Greeks and Romans. They could have said, more correctly, that letters originated in the country of which anciently Phœnicia was one of the more important districts. And so, when Pliny described the Phœnicians as "the first discoverers of the sciences of astronomy and navigation," he would have been more accurate if, instead of "the Phœnicians," he had said the 'ancient Ethiopians or Cushites of Arabia. The original country of the Cushite race, to which the Phœnicians belonged—the original home where this culture had birth, and from which the Cushite colonies and influence went forth in every direction to spread civilization, and create such nations as Egypt and Chaldea, was not merely the little district of Phœnicia—it was the whole Arabian peninsula.

ANCIENT HISTORY OF ARABIA.

I can imagine nothing that would shed so great a light on the pre-historic ages as an accurate history of Arabia from the beginning of its civilization. Histories of that country were undoubtedly written before and after the time when Menes united Upper and Lower Egypt under one government, for in that old time, so far away from us in the deepest antiquity, Arabia was the foremost country of the world. The people that originated the art of writing did not fail to have writers of their own annals. Nevertheless, their ancient history cannot now be produced, for not only their own literature perished, but also that of the next succeeding nations, and, for more than twenty-five hundred years, no other country with which our civilization is connected has been so completely withdrawn from the observation of what we call history. It has been a mystery, an unreal country, and failure to see its historic importance has left many important problems of Ancient History without proper solution.

And yet a weird influence of its great past is felt whenever inquiry turns to its ancient history; and now and then a writer wonders that " a nation whose history ascends without interruption to so remote an origin, and whose name has been so celebrated, should have its political infancy shrouded in so thick a mist of doubt and oblivion." Even from this writer its grandest ages are hidden under that phrase " its political infancy." These ages are shrouded in doubt and oblivion, partly because they are remote. We consider Egypt and Chaldea very old, culture and political organization of the Arabian were much older; they belong to what both F and Chaldeans regarded as antiquity. Time, that wastes all things human, and buries nations out of sight, has not spared the primeval history of this oldest of civilized peoples. Add to this that the distance from us in time of the beginnings of the Cushite civilization is so vast as to frighten the current chronologies into absolute lunacy, and we shall cease to wonder that the early history of Arabia has been so buried in oblivion, and so discredited by the chronologists that it has failed to command much attention, or even to be thought of as a reality.

This antiquity of civilization in Arabia is necessary to explain the facts that, in the oldest recorded traditions, Arabia is the land of Cush, the celebrated Ethiopia of very remote times, and that, according to the testimony of linguistic and archæological science, the first civilizers in Western and Southwestern Asia and in the Nile Valley were a people described as Cushites or Hamites. These facts are incontestable; but, while it is necessary to accept what they signify, we have no chronology for the scheme of Arabian history which they suggest. Guided, however, by what we know of the antiquity of civilization in Egypt and Chaldea, we may suppose as probable that the history of the ancient Cushite civilization was somewhat as follows:

1. There was the primeval period of first development and growth. Did the original culture of the Cushite civilizers come to them from a still older civilization? or was it originated entirely by themselves, without assistance or stimulus from abroad? We cannot answer these questions. Man was created capable of improvement, and no very long period could have elapsed before the use of reason and the almost spontaneous activity of the aptitude for in-

vention in providing for the wants of life began to create civilization. This development would necessarily be greatest and swiftest in the most highly gifted families and under the most favorable circumstances. If the first appearance of the human race on earth be as far back in the past as it seems necessary to believe, the Cushite civilization could not have been the oldest development of civilized life in human history. It is, however, the oldest of which we have any trace. It may have been original; and therefore the period of its beginning, and its growth to the condition out of which grew its eminence in commercial and colonizing enterprise, may have been very long.

2. The period of colonizing enterprise, commercial greatness, and extensive empire. Early in this period Cushite colonies were established in the valleys of the Nile and of the Euphrates, which in subsequent ages became Barbara, Egypt, and Chaldea. Its beginning could not have been later than 7000 or 8000 years before Christ, and it may have begun much earlier. The Cushites occupied India, Western Asia to the Mediterranean, and extensive regions in Africa. In this period they brought to full development that knowledge of astronomy and of other sciences, fragments of which have come down to us through the nations they created and by which they were succeeded. The vast commercial system by which they brought together "the ends of the earth" was created, and that unrivaled eminence in maritime and manufacturing skill was developed, which the Phœnicians retained down to the time of the Hellenes and the Romans. In this period were the grandest ages of the great empire of Ethiopia, or Cusha-dwipa.

3. The period of disintegration, when Egypt and Chaldea became separate countries, and the Sanskrit branch of

the Aryan race invaded and occupied Northern India.
This period may have begun about 5000 years before the
Christian Era. But the Arabian Cushites, having control
of Arabia, Southern India, many colonies on the Mediterranean, and extensive districts in Africa, were still unrivaled
in power and commercial dominion. At length came a
time, for which there is nothing to suggest a probable date,
when, under control of the people called Phœnicians, Northern Arabia, Syria, and the connected communities on the
Mediterranean became a separate dominion. There is
some reason for supposing (as I shall presently show) that
the rest of the peninsula was divided into two kingdoms,
not later than from about 3000 to 3500 B.C.—one including Yemen, Hadramaut, the Hedjaz, and other western districts; and the other consisting of Oman, the districts towards the Persian Gulf, and the whole region known as
Irak Arabi to the Euphrates, of which Zohak, celebrated in
Iranian history, was a famous ruler.

4. The period of continued decline, which finally brought
the Arabian peninsula to its present condition. Much of
what is usually written as "the History of Arabia before
Islamism" belongs to this period. The country was divided into five or six separate kingdoms, of which that described by the Greeks as Saba was the most important.
The Phœnicians, finally restricted in Asia to the little district immediately connected with their great cities, and
the rich and still enterprising people of Southern Arabia,
called Sabeans and Himyarites, continued to represent what
remained of the old Cushite civilization down to a period
comparatively quite modern. But the ancient glory of the
country departed previous to the rise of the Assyrian empire, in the thirteenth century before Christ; and, not long

before the beginning of the Assyrian period, the whole northern portion of the peninsula was invaded and overrun by Semites, chiefly nomadic, who occupied the Hedjaz, became permanent inhabitants, and finally originated Mahometanism. The Land of Cush was transformed.

In the absence of regular historic annals, any scheme of Arabian history that takes in all its periods must be chiefly hypothetical. Beyond a few important facts that may be used to guide supposition, there is nothing to enlighten us. We learn something from the traditions of antiquity; the Hebrew Scriptures tell us something; the old ruins of the East furnish some light; and in Mahometan histories of Arabia there are passages that seem to present a few confused recollections of what was written in the lost annals of the country; but a regular and accurate historical account of ancient Arabia is no longer possible. If the Greeks had studied the country carefully, and written its history with such intelligence as the libraries of Egypt and Phœnicia then made possible, it would have had a prominent place in our studies of ancient history. But to them Arabia was already very obscure, and their knowledge of the peninsula was nearly as vague and visionary as that which has prevailed in modern times.

GREEK NOTICES OF ARABIA.

Herodotus, writing more than twenty-three centuries ago, had no perception of the historic importance of Arabia. To him it was a land of rare and marvelous productions, but he seems to have had no knowledge whatever of the great commerce with India and other countries at the East, still monopolized by the Southern Arabians. He says: "Arabia is the farthest of the inhabited countries towards the South; and this is the only region in which grow myrrh, frankincense, cinnamon, and ledanum. All these, except myrrh, the Arabians gather with difficulty." Then follows a rehearsal of certain cunning stories, worthy of the "Thousand and One Nights," put in circulation by the Arabians to hide their commerce from the Western nations. It was understood that all spices and perfumes, and most other rich and royal products, came from that country; and Herodotus, like others of his time, supposed they were all produced there. His knowledge and appreciation of the country seem to have been fully expressed in his exclamation, "There breathes from Arabia a divine odor!"

He knew no more, and nowhere else in the Greek literature of that age, or of any subsequent age, do we find a more intelligent account of Arabian history, geography, or commerce. Enough was known of the country to create a feeling of something rich and strange, something uncomprehended and mysterious, and Greek writers who gained some general knowledge of Southern Arabia were moved to exhaust the power of language in attempts to describe its riches. There may have been something more in the lost geographical work of Artemidorus of Ephesus, although the extract in Strabo indicates little more than visionary ignorance; but nothing beyond this has been preserved. Diodorus Siculus, after an extravagant description of "the perfumes of Arabia, which ravished the senses," and "were conveyed by the winds to those who sailed near the coast," proceeded (bk. iii., ch. iii.) as follows:

"Having never been conquered, by reason of the largeness of their country, they flow in streams of gold and silver; and likewise their beds, chairs, and stools have their feet of silver; and all their household stuff is so sumptuous and magnificent that it is incredible. The porticoes of their houses and temples, in some cases, are overlaid with gold. The like wonderful cost they are at throughout their whole buildings, adorning them, in some parts, with silver and gold, and in others with ivory, precious stones, and other things of great value, for they have enjoyed a constant and uninterrupted peace for many ages and generations."

Agatharchides is quoted thus:

"The Sabeans surpass in wealth and magnificence not only the neighboring barbarians, but all other nations whatsoever. As their distant situation protects them from all foreign plunders, immense stores of precious metals have been accumulated among them, especially in the capital. Curiously-wrought gold and silver drinking vessels in great variety; couches and tripods with silver feet; an incredible profusion of costly furniture in general; porticoes, with large columns partly gilt and capitals ornamented with wrought silver figures; roofs and doors ornamented with gold fretwork set with precious stones; besides an extraordinary magnificence reigning in the decorations of their houses, where they use silver, gold, ivory, and the most precious stones, and all other things that men deem most valuable. These people have enjoyed their good fortune from the earliest times undisturbed."

These descriptions bring out one important fact. The Greeks believed Arabia had been a seat of enlightened civilization and of a great commerce "from the earliest times;" and yet, so far as we know, it never occurred to any Greek scholar to study the history of this land of marvelous wealth, and trace "from the earliest times" the development of its civilization and commercial enterprise. The Greeks of the Hellenic period knew less of distant countries than was known in the time of Homer. Their geographical knowledge was confined chiefly to the regions around the Ægean and the Eastern Mediterranean. The prevalent ignorance of more distant regions is shown by a statement of that insatiate reader and collector of information, the Elder Pliny, who says (lib. vi., ch. xxiv.): "Taprobane (Ceylon), under the name of the 'land of the Autochthones,' was long looked upon as another world; the age and arms of Alexander the Great were the first to give satisfactory proof that it is an island." Telling what he had learned concerning the Arabians, he says, "Arabia is inferior to no country throughout the whole world." Speaking of the "Omani," or people of Oman, he refers to "their once famous cities," which "at the present time are wildernesses." He mentions "Homna and Attana, which, our merchants say, are at the present time the most famous towns on the Persian Sea." His estimate of the Arabians is summed up as follows: "Take them all in all, they are the richest nation in the world."

ARABIAN RECOLLECTIONS OF THE PAST.

Mahometan writers on the history of Arabia give us a few vague recollections of the ancient condition of the country; but the old Cushite literature, locked up in a strange tongue, and fiercely cursed by their religion, had all disappeared long before they began to study the subject. Moreover, their first writings on the history of Arabia were several centuries later than the time of Mahomet. The Arabian Semites were probably the rudest and least civilized inhabitants of the peninsula. Most of them were nomads, although they had some settled communities, and some knowledge of reading and writing. The first Mahometans were not a literary people, and no attempt was made to write even the life of their prophet until more than a century after his death, towards the close of the Ommiade dynasty of caliphs. The culture for which the caliphate was celebrated did not come from Koreish Arabs, nor did it greatly affect them, but it affected the Arabic language; and the literary activity it created produced not only poetry, philosophy, and science, but also biographies of Mahomet and histories of Arabia. Among those who wrote on Arabian history and geography with most care and ability were Al Tabiri of Tabreez, who wrote in the 10th century of the Christian Era; El Mas'udi, who died about 957 A.D.; Nuwayri, surnamed Al Kendi, who died about 1340 A.D.; Abulfeda, prince of Hamah, in Syria, who died in 1345 A.D.; Hamza of Ispahan, who died about 908 A.D.; and El Edrisi, who was born about 1000 A.D.

The time of Mahomet was becoming ancient when these men wrote. They had no materials for a regular and intelligent history of even the later periods of the country, and, if they had been supplied with such materials in abundance, the overwhelming influence of Mahometan prejudice and assumption would have made a proper use of them impossible. Mahometanism, treating everything Arabian but itself as antichrist if it could not be made tributary to the Prophet and his race, was incapable of being a faithful historian of the old Cushite civilization. Nevertheless, Mahometan writers give us traditions and facts, in which successive periods of the ancient history of Arabia are clearly indicated. They all agree that Kahtan, celebrated in the most authentic traditions, represents a great epoch, which was preceded by the misty ages of Ad and other representative persons or names, and followed by historical periods beginning with great political changes, represented by Saba and Ilimyar. The Mahometans, by substituting the Semitic Joktan for Kahtan, and by attempting to reconstruct all Arabian history around the Himyarite kings, have entangled the subject in great confusion. This was quite sufficient; but the rabbinical spirit and chronological dogmatism of modern times have gone farther, and made this confusion a hopeless jungle of absurdities. To see anything clearly, we must put aside these perverting interpretations, and consider the traditions and facts for ourselves without regard to what has been said of them by Mahometan egotism, rabbinical ignorance, or false chronology.

1. The traditions quoted as authentic by all Mahometan writers on Arabia describe a period of civilization before the time of Kahtan. To this period are assigned Ad, Thamoud, and the representative names of persons and peoples associated with them. Arabian tradition knows nothing older than Ad. It associates with him and with his time the beginnings of civilized life. It represents the Adites, Thamoudites, and their contemporaries as enterprising, rich, and powerful, says they had great cities and wonderful magnificence, and declares that they finally disappeared from the earth under the curse of heaven on their pride and arrogant idolatry. Mahometan ardor tells romantic stories of their marvelous cities, and of the miraculous judgments by which they were blasted. This traditional lore evidently preserves faint and confused recollections of a great period of civilization that had decaying monuments, ruined cities, and mysterious antiquities before the

time of Kahtan. Its wondrous creations and grand political supremacy disappeared, not in fiery storms of wrath from heaven, but under the influence of time and change.

2. In Arabian tradition Kahtan occupies a position similar in some respects to that of Kaiamors in Iranian history. It is pointed out that there were ages of civilization before his time, and yet he is described as the ancestor of nearly the whole Arabian people. According to the traditions as reconstructed by Mahometanism, his descendants repeopled the country with the race known as the *Aribah*, or Arabians of pure blood, and he is celebrated as the primal personage of the Arabian world. Laying aside the Mahometan fables, we may suppose, not unreasonably, that Kahtan represents the time when the old Cushite communities in Southern, Eastern, and Central Arabia were politically separated from those at the north. That must have been a very important epoch in Arabian history. Egypt and Chaldea had already become separate empires; the Aryans had entered Northern India; other important changes had occurred; and now what remained of the old Cushite empire was divided, by a line running through Arabia itself, into two separate dominions—one at the north, under Phœnician supremacy, the other at the south and east, reorganized, we suppose, by Kahtan. Whether Kahtan actually represents the beginning of this new era must, however, be left to conjecture; an accurate history of that time might give the historical significance of this personage a different explanation. He belongs to a remote age, and could not have been later than the time when Martu or Marathus, mentioned in the earlier Chaldean inscriptions, was the ruling city at the north.*

* Among the notes which El Mas'udi added to his "Meadows of Gold

3. In the traditions, Saba, described as a descendant of Kahtan, is the next personage who represents an important historical epoch. The legends connect him with the southwestern quarter of the peninsula, and with a kingdom that seems to have included Yemen, Hadramaut, the Hedjaz, and other districts. That very ancient Cushite temple—the oldest temple in existence—known as the Caaba was situated in the Hedjaz, and for this reason, it may be, the traditions say much more of this kingdom than of any other part of Arabia. Saba may represent the time when the provinces included in the kingdom of Saba and the Himyarites were separated from those in the opposite quarter, including Oman and the districts on the Persian Gulf. It is known that such a division existed long before the Christian Era, and that the southwestern kingdom, less affected by the great changes in Western Asia, and more largely devoted to commerce and maritime enterprise, preserved its existence much longer than the other. Saba was probably the first sovereign of this monarchy after the separation. Nuwayri makes him its founder and first ruler; and Djennabi, who wrote in the sixteenth century of the Christian Era, gives it a duration of three thousand years.

4. Himyar, a descendant of Saba, is another royal personage to whom special but unexplained historical importance is attached. He begins the line of Himyarite kings,

and Mines of Gems" is the following: "There are two famous places on earth, the Iwán (of the Kosrous at Ctesiphon), and the Ghomdán (of the kings of Yemen) at Sana; and there are only two great royal families, the Sassanians and the Khatanites." We have not been accustomed to see in Arabia one of the greatest and most ancient royal families. It was different in El Mas'udi's time.

and his name has been given to both the people and language of the country. Nuwayri places the beginning of his reign in the year 1400 B.C., and says there were sixteen sovereigns between him and Queen Belkis, whose reign began in the year 991 B.C. This makes Belkis contemporary with Solomon. According to Hamza of Ispahan, the Himyarite monarchy was divided "during fifteen generations," at a very indefinitely dated period after the time of Himyar. This division was the result of a feud between the descendants of Himyar and those of his brother Kahlan. During the time of this division, one family reigned at Saba, while the other reigned at Zhafar. Other writers mention this fact. The kingdom was finally reunited under Harith-el-Raiseh. He was called *Tobba*, as the Egyptian kings were called Pharaohs, "because," it is said, "the united people followed (*tabbahou*) his laws;" and all his successors bore this title. This explanation of the title, however, may not be correct; it is not shown that it was not in use before the separation. The rule of the Himyarite kings was terminated nearly a century and a half before the time of Mahomet by an invasion from Abyssinia.

The varying and contradictory dynastic lists of kings after the time of Saba, constructed by Mahometan writers, would be masterpieces of confusion and absurdity if they were not outdone by the insane chronology, and worse than Mahometan assumption, of those learned Orientalists who place Himyar only 381 years before Christ, and bring Belkis into the first century after Christ. It seems necessary to remind these astonishing chronologists that the Hebrew Scriptures make it certain that a "queen of Sheba" ruled this kingdom in the time of Solomon. This must be accepted as an established fact; but, while the dates of the Mahometan historians are more credible and respectable than those of some modern scholars, who have applied a false chronology to the history of Arabia, it is necessary to admit that neither their dates nor their dynastic lists can be trusted. Their dates lack the evidence that would make them authentic, and their lists of Sabean and Himyarite kings include sovereigns who evidently belong to ages more ancient, while in other respects they are confused, arbitrary, and unwarranted. Nevertheless, among the materials collected by these writers there are royal names and brief historical fragments that engage attention.

FRAGMENTS OF OLD ARABIAN HISTORY.

An ancient Arabian sovereign, usually called Zohak, is mentioned in the traditions as an enterprising and powerful conqueror. He is sometimes connected with the most ancient people of the country, but there is nothing in Arabic literature to make certain the time of his reign. It is stated in the chronicle of Tabiri that "Zohak was in possession of the whole of Irak Arabi, with Tabristan, Khezlan, Gûrgan or Jurgan, and, in short, of all the territory in this direction to the very borders of Hindustan, which he (and his successors) governed with paramount sway during a period of 260 years." The Iranian historians give a more particular account of Zohak. According to some of them, he was the son of an Arabian king named Mirtas. Others add that his mother was a sister of Jemshid. All agree that he was an Arabian. It is stated that he dethroned Jemshid, and made himself master of the kingdom of Iran or Hiras; that "he slew and partook of all animals indifferently, whether destructive or harmless" (which was in violation of the religious code of Iran), "so that the detestable practice became general;" and that, long afterwards, "when Feridun had purged the land of Zohak's tyranny," the "detestable practice" could not be entirely overcome.

In the Iranian books Zohak is described as Deh-ak and Dizakh, "the Tasi," usually translated "the Arabian." A note in the Desatir says, "Taz is the supposed father of the Tasis (or Arabians)." The word Taz reminds us of the original Arabian tribe of Tasm. Zohak probably claimed descent from Tasm. The commentary on the Desatir tells us that "Zohak was of the race of Taz," and that "he paid assiduous worship to Yezdam (the Supreme Being) and to the stars, on which account Yezdam granted him his wishes; but, during his reign, he annoyed harmless animals." He is also charged with grave crimes. Much of the accusing execration bestowed upon Zohak is probably due to the fact that his religion was that of the Arabians, and not that of the Iranians or Hirasis.

According to Berosus, a foreign dynasty of kings, called "Median," ruled Chaldea during 224 years. This dynasty was probably the result of a conquest of the country by Zohak. The term "Median" has occasioned much doubtful speculation; some supposing it to mean Turanians or Magians, and others, in despair, suggesting a corruption of the word actually used by Berosus. But Madian or Midian was the name of an important branch of the Arabian people; and in Irak Arabi there was a district and a great city called Madain. Sadik Isfahani said in his geography, "Madain was a celebrated city of Irak Arabi. It was called Madain because it was the largest of the seven Madain, or cities of Irak." Wherein is it unreasonable to suppose that Zohak, having conquered Chaldea, selected from his immediate followers a Madian prince to be its ruler? Or that he annexed it to the Madain territory of the prince or king who ruled under him in Irak Arabi, with which Chaldea was immediately connected? I shall show, in another place, that the "Median" dynasty of Berosus could not have begun in Chaldea much later than about 3000 years before Christ; and an average of the varying statements of Iranian writers gives this as very nearly the date of Jemshid and Zohak.

An Arabian sovereign called Schamar-Iarasch, and also Schamar-Iarasch-Abou-Karib, is described by Hamza, Nuwayri, and others, as a powerful ruler and conqueror, who carried his arms successfully far into Central Asia. It is said that he became master of all the countries in that direction, occupied Samarcand for a long time, and even invaded China. In proof of the conquests of this sovereign, Hamza states that an edifice formerly existed at Samarcand bearing this inscription in the Himyarite or Cushite language and characters: "In the name of God, Schamar-Iarasch has erected this edifice to the sun, his Lord." And Abulfeda says in his Geography, "Ibn-Hankal states that he saw on one of the gates of Samarcand, called *Kesch*, an iron plate bearing an inscription said by the inhabitants to be Himyaric; and they told him that the gate was built by the king or *Tobba* of Arabia." Ibn-Hankal added that this gate was destroyed during a sedition that arose while he was there. Langles states in a note on Norden's "Travels" that such inscriptions still existed at Samarcand in the fourteenth century; and Humboldt, referring to these facts, is sure that "some connection existed between ancient Ethiopia and the elevated plain of Central Asia."

At what time in the past did these extensive Arabian

conquests take place? Not during the time of either the Assyrian empire, or of the Persian empire established by Cyrus the Great, and, certainly, not at any later period. It was previous to the period of the Assyrian empire, which, according to the best estimates, began in the year 1273 before Christ. The History of Berosus informs us that, during the 245 years previous to the rise of Assyria to imperial power, Chaldea was governed by an Arabian dynasty of nine kings. The time of these Arabian kings extended from 1518 to 1273 B.C., and this is the latest period to which the conquests of Schamar-Iarasch can be assigned. He, or some other Arabian monarch, conquered Chaldea at the beginning of this period. We may, therefore, reasonably suppose that the occupation of Central Asia, and the invasion of China by Arabians, was connected with this conquest.

There is mention of Arabian monarchs who marched far into Africa and waged war with "Maghrib;" and one of them, called Afrikis or Afrikin, is said to have marched his army to the Atlantic Ocean. Maghrib is an ancient name of Mauritania, which is sometimes called *Maghrib-ul-Aksa.* The old Arabian Cushites, in the great days of their empire, occupied or controlled the larger part of Africa, as I shall endeavor to show in another place. Doubtless their establishments in Central Africa were retained down to the first period of the Himyaric kings. Under these circumstances, wars with Maghrib were not unlikely; and a march through Africa by a monarch occupying its central countries could not have been a very difficult affair. Harith-el-Raisch, by whom, it is said, the divided kingdom of Hadramaut and Yemen was reunited, is celebrated as a sovereign of remarkable genius and character. He made the reunion complete and permanent, greatly enlarged the power of the kingdom, and extended his conquests to India.

None of these historical fragments and traditions, however, refer to the earlier periods of Arabian civilization and greatness; none of them reach back to the ages previous to the epoch when the northern provinces and colonial possessions of Arabia were politically separated from the rest of the peninsula; but they show distinctly that the country was very great and very powerful, even in its periods of disintegration and decline. The Greek and Sanskrit traditions and mythological narratives relate to more ancient times, and give us the names of some of the earlier rulers of the Land of Cush, such as Dionysos, Kepheus, and others. It is unreasonable not to see what is signified by the traditions concerning Dionysos. He was one of the greatest and most influential sovereigns the world has ever known, if we may judge by that ineffaceable impression of his greatness left behind him in Egypt, India, and throughout Western Asia. In Egypt he was deified as Osiris, and I shall speak of him more at length in what I have to say of the Cushite origin and civilization of that country.

THE CUSHITE SYSTEM OF POLITICAL ORGANIZATION.

The ancient Arabians had a peculiar system of political organization, which went with them to every land they colonized. The traces, remains, and, sometimes, nearly perfect forms of it still remaining in countries where their influence was most powerful and permanent, should be classed with the characteristic and suggestive antiquities of that legendary race. We see the Phœnicians come into history with a political system radically different from that of any other people of antiquity, excepting those peoples on the Mediterranean who were originally formed by their influence. Their cities, with connected districts, were separate municipalities, completely organized, and controlled more or less by popular influence. They established the same system in Greece, and along the coast of Asia Minor, long before either Greeks or Pelasgians were mentioned in those regions. They carried it to Italy and Northern Africa. It prevailed anciently in Arabia from Phœnicia to the Indian Ocean, and it exists there still. We see it in Mr. Palgrave's account of the political organization of the kingdom of Oman. He says:

"Oman is less a kingdom than an aggregation of municipalities; each town, each village, has its separate existence and corporation; while towns and villages, in their turn, are subjected to one or another of the ancestral chiefs, who rule the provinces with an authority limited, on one side, by the traditional immunities of their vassals, and, on the other, by the prerogatives of the crown. These prerogatives [of the crown] consist of the right to nominate, and (on complaint) to depose local governors, although the office remains always in the same family; to fix and levy port and custom-house dues; to have exclusive management of the navy; to keep a small standing army of six or seven hundred men; and to transact all foreign affairs, for alliance or treaty, peace or war. The administration of justice and the decision of criminal cases are reserved to the kadis and the local royal judges. In short, the whole course of law is considered to be entirely independent of the sovereign, except in very extraordinary circumstances. Again, the taxes levied on land or goods (sea-port commerce excepted) are fixed and immutable save by local or municipal authority; the sultan enjoys, but can not change them."

Here we have the remains of that ancient political system

of the Arabian Cushites which regulated the organization of the Phœnician communities, created similar communities in Asia Minor and around the Ægean Sea, and thus determined the conditions that, in later times, brought into existence the Ionian confederacy, and the "fierce democracies" of the Grecian peninsula. Some of the best preserved forms of this system are found among the African Berbers, such as the McZabs and the Touaricks; but remains or traces of it appear, with other antiquities of that old race, in India, as well as in Africa, and even in Western Europe. The local municipalities, or "village republics," as they have been called, still existing in India, were noticed by Arrian, and they are described in English accounts of the country; but I shall speak of them more particularly in another place. The "free cities" of the Middle Ages of Europe, which were recognised but not created by the governments of the newly-organized nations, must have had their origin in this old system, especially those of France and Spain.* They were organized municipalities long before Spain and France existed, as we know them. The same system has been universal among the Basques from time immemorial; and their right to live under their own laws, and manage their own affairs without dictation, was not interfered with until, under the late sovereign of Spain, Queen Isabella, their municipal prerogatives were suppressed because they took the side of Don Carlos in the civil war.

Could we have a complete and authentic history of the

* The maritime towns of the south of France entered into separate alliances with foreign states, as Narbonne with Genoa in 1166, and Montpellier in the next century. At the death of Raymon VII., Avignon, Arles, and Marseilles affected to set up republican governments, but were soon brought into subjection.—*Hallam's Middle Ages*, vol. I., p. 206.

various municipalities of Phœnicia from the time of Martu to the beginning of the Carthaginian period, the actual character of this old Cushite system might be seen more clearly. Probably it was not very democratic. Very likely there were "principal classes" who controlled the commonwealths. There may have been a more or less exclusive system of citizenship. At the head of each municipality there appears to have been a hereditary local prince or chief. Among the Phœnicians, as we see them in history, the general organization seems to have been a loose fraternal confederacy, much looser probably than circumstances made possible under the great kings of ancient Arabia, much farther removed from consolidation than the present governments of the Arabian peninsula. But a people so active and enterprising, and so largely devoted to manufactures, commerce, and maritime undertakings, would naturally demand and secure a political system based on municipal organizations that would allow them to manage their own affairs.

The traditions of the Cushite race in Arabia indicate that they had this system from the beginning. Their traditionary myths and legends, unlike those of most ancient peoples, do not describe a national beginning—when they were formed and organized by a great sovereign who taught them civilization, overwhelmed their enemies, and gave them national existence. On the contrary, they tell us that this Cushite nation first appeared in Arabia in nine or more tribes or communities, separately organized, and governed by chiefs whose names are given. At the head of these chiefs or princes was Ad, who appears to be recognised as the first ruler of the nation. The significance of these traditions is unequivocal. They show us that, in the earliest times, the Cushite system made the nation consist of an "aggregation of municipalities." There is no recollection of any other system, and we find no other that can be traced to this race in any part of the world where their colonies and their influence were established.

CUSHITE SCIENCE, ASTRONOMICAL AND NAUTICAL.

There is a passage in Aristotle's *De Cœlo*, lib. ii., cap. xii., frequently cited or mentioned, which reads as follows: τὴν δὲ σελήνην ἑωράκαμεν διχότομον μὲν οὖσαν· ὑπεισελθοῦσαν δὲ τῶν ἀστέρων τὸν τοῦ Ἄρεος, καὶ ἀποκρυφέντα μὲν τὸ μέλαν αὐτῆς, ἐξελθόντα δὲ κατὰ τὸ φανὸν καὶ λαμπρόν· ὁμοίως δὲ καὶ περὶ τοῖς ἄλλοις ἀστέρας λέγουσιν οἱ πάλαι τετηρηκότες ἐκ πλείστων ἐτῶν Αἰγύπτιοι καὶ Βαβυλώνιοι, παρ' ὧν πολλὰς πίστεις ἔχομεν περὶ ἑκάστου τῶν ἄστρων· which may be translated, *We have seen the moon, one half bright and the other dark, pass between us and the planet Mars, which disappeared under the dark side and came out from behind the shining part. Similar observations of other stars are described by the Egyptians and Babylonians, who anciently, and for many ages, made astronomical observations, and from whom many things worthy of credit have come to us concerning the several constellations.*

Aristotle might have given, from the records sent him by Callisthenes, a more extended account of the great attainments of the Chaldeans in astronomy, unless we are to suppose he lacked a competent knowledge of the language in which those records were written. The priests of ancient Egypt were skilled in astronomy. During many ages they were accustomed to make and record observations. According to a statement of Diogenes Laertius, he had ascertained that they had preserved records of 373 solar and 832 lunar eclipses. Bunsen assumed, too readily, that the eclipses observed were all total, or nearly so, and therefore "must have extended over 10,000 years." The assumption being unwarranted, the inference fails; in Egypt, however, the study of astronomy was very ancient; there, as well as in Chaldea, in the more ancient times, we must suppose it reached higher results than were attained in later times. In Egypt, and "other countries at the East," Pythagoras and other Greeks found the heliocentric system, which we call Copernican—a system which they accepted without fully comprehending the science that produced it, and which the Greek world, more remarkable for literature and art than for mathematical and astronomical science, could not retain.

It is folly—the folly of prejudice and preconceived criticism—to deny, against the testimony of all antiquity, that the Chaldeans and Egyptians, especially the former, had great knowledge of astronomy. I need not cite the familiar passages in Greek and Roman literature which show this; but it may be said with confidence that, if there had been at Athens a great observatory similar to that in the temple of Belus at Babylon, associated in the same way with reports of eminent attainments in astronomy, our inquiries concerning it would not be regulated by doubt and incredulity. On the contrary, if we now obscure the wiser peoples of antiquity with clouds of incense offered blindly to the Greeks, we should, in that case, believe extravagantly, and might lose our wits beyond recovery in the vehemence of our adoration.

We must give attention to one fact that has peculiar significance. The zodiac, representing the apparent path of the sun in the heavens, with the names and symbolical figures of its signs substantially the same, was common to Chaldea, India, Egypt, and Arabia. Sometimes eleven signs were counted, the claws of the scorpion representing the sign known as Libra. Sextus Empiricus and others stated that the zodiac, as we have it, came directly from the Chaldeans. The great similarity of the zodiacs used in Egypt, India, and the countries of Western Asia shows that they must have had a common origin, and to find their origin we must go to the older people who gave all these countries civilization, and prepared them to become great nations.

The science of astronomy prevalent in Chaldea, Egypt, and other old nations, so generally, although imperfectly noticed by Greeks and Romans, and of which so many fragments have come down to us, must have been originated by the ancient Arabians in the earlier periods of their civilization. The starry heavens naturally engage attention even among barbarians, and a systematic study of the stars has so many practical uses that astronomy must have been one of the earliest sciences. Add to this the peculiar genius of the old Arabian race and their favorable atmosphere, with the fact that they were pre-eminently planet-worshippers, who, from the earliest times, had been largely devoted to maritime enterprise, and we cannot reasonably fail to see that they must have originated the science of astronomy, and carried it into all the communities that grew up under their influence. The zodiacs so closely resembling each other, found in different countries, whose origin must be traced to Arabian or Cushite influence, must have come originally from Arabia.

The Egyptians regarded Taut, or Thoth, as the originator of astronomy; the Phœnicians and other Cushite peoples traced letters and science to Taut. In the work on Astrology attributed to Lucian, the author says: "It is commonly understood that the Ethiopians were the first who invented astronomy, being led to this science by their cloudless sky and favorable climate, and by their surpassing intellectual sagacity, subtilty, and force." I have shown what country the ancient Greeks described as Ethiopia. The Greeks indicated not only the great antiquity of the sphere, but also the people by whom it was invented, by connecting its origin with Atlas and Hercules.

There was astronomy in Arabia when the book of Job was written, but the great ages of Cushite civilization closed at a period which at that time was very ancient. The Arabians were eminent for their knowledge of astronomy and mathematics while any influence of the old culture remained; but in the later times, the old books had perished not only in Arabia, but also in Egypt and Chaldea. The astronomy of the Arabians, after the time of Mahomet, was not the system learned by Pythagoras and his followers of the Chaldeans and Egyptians. It was that of Ptolemy. They brought it to Europe, and they brought with it something better, namely, mathematical science, giving Europe even the nine digits, or "Arabic figures," with algebra, of which the old Greeks knew nothing. The word Al-manac, like the word Al-gebra, is Arabic.

It is easy to deny an ancient civilization when its records have perished and its remains have become scanty, and demand something as conclusive as mathematical demonstration, but it is not reasonable to do so. The astronomical science of the Chinese is generally admitted; but, if China were now as far back in the past as Chaldea, with no more record or remains of its civilization left to enlighten us, stupid skepticism, feeling very wise, would deny everything. Its denials, however, could neither destroy the fact nor lessen the significance of such traces of it as might remain for study. Inquiry tends more and more to show that we must give up the vain assumption that not much was known previous to the rise of Greece, and not much at any time out of Greece, until Western Europe became enlightened. There was much more in the past than we have been accustomed to admit; but this is seen only when the aim of our inquiry is to discover, and not merely to deny.

The nautical science of the old Arabians must have been equal to the wants of their great commercial enterprise; for the faculty to invent what was necessary did not wait until our time to make its first appearance in the human mind. It is seen that the Phœnicians, when they came out of the obscure pre-historic ages into history, were immeasurably superior to every other people in maritime skill. No other people had such naval constructions; no other people were so much at sea, or made such long voyages, or had such skill in navigation. Some ages later, the Athenians had ships; but they had nothing like the great Phœnician ships that came regularly to Athens in the service of commerce, and were always regarded there as marvels of naval architecture. What the Phœnicians were on the Mediterranean, the Southern Arabians were on the Indian Ocean, although history, necessarily, has much less to say of them; and these peoples representing in the later ages of its decline the great race that had been, for not less than six millenniums probably, foremost in human affairs, give us some notion of what must have been the attainments of that race in the ages of its highest development and power. The marvelous skill of the Phœnicians in manufactures would have been impossible without unusual intellectual activity, aided by great attainments in science. Is it reasonable to believe that the nautical science of such a people, with whom maritime enterprise was a chief business, could have been poor and mean? Such a belief is possible only to the prodigious incredulity of egotistical skepticism.

It has been usual to assume that nautical science never existed anywhere much previous to the beginning of the fourteenth century, and that such things as the mariner's compass, the astrolabe, and other scientific instruments to aid navigation, were not heard of previous to that age. The mariner's compass, it has been said, was invented by Flavio Gioja, at Pasitava, near Amalfi, in Italy, in the year 1302. Unfortunately for the prestige of orthodox wisdom, it has been shown that the mariner's compass was in use long previous to this date. Raymond Lully, in his "Fenix de las Maravillas del Orbe," published in 1286, states that the seamen of his time used "instruments of measurement, sea-charts, and the magnetic needle—*Tenian los marcantes instrumento, carta, compas y aguja.*" A Latin letter or essay of Peter Adsiger, dated in 1269, and cited in Rees's Cyclopædia, speaks of the mariner's compass as if it had been in use for a long time, gives a very particular description of it, and says: "Take notice that the magnet, as well as the needle that has been touched by it, does not point exactly to the poles; the south point declines a little to the west, and the north point to the east." In the year 1180, the mariner's compass was very fully described in a poem of one of the Provençal Troubadours, named Guyot de Provins. He described the magnet, the method of preparing the needle, and the certainty with which it points to the polar star, *l'estoile qui ne se muet.* He stated that the needle, fixed to

F

bits of straw, was made to swim on water in a dish. Then it turned steadily to the pole and could not lie, but was a sure guide to the mariner in the darkest night.

> "Puis se tourne la pointe toute
> Contre l'estoile, si sans doute
> Que j'a nus hom n'en doutera
> Ne ja por rien ne faussera."

Guyot de Provins was at the court of Frederick Barbarossa, at Mentz, in the year 1181. The date and authenticity of his poem are both undoubted. To him the mariner's compass was one of the common things which had been in use for a long time, and might have existed from time immemorial. Some have supposed that Marco Polo brought the magnetic needle from China in 1295, and taught Flavio Gioja how to produce the mariner's compass; but Guyot de Provins wrote that poem long before Marco Polo was born. It is known that the early Venetians used the compass, making the needle swim on water by fixing it to a piece of cork. Plautus, in his *Mercatore*, act v., scene 2, has the following: *Huc secundus ventus est, cape modo vorsoriam.* The word *vorsoriam* has been interpreted to mean the mariner's compass, although some critics have tried to see in it a rope, or the helm of a ship. Pineda and Father Kircher argued earnestly to show that the compass was used by the Phœnicians and Hebrews in the time of Solomon, which was much more reasonable than the claim that it was first invented in Europe.

It is found necessary to admit, and therefore Humboldt (Cosmos, chapter on the Period of Oceanic Discoveries) states as a fact, that the mariner's compass was brought to Europe by the Arabians. He says: "The Arabic designations *Zophron* and *Aphron* (south and north), given by

Vincenzius of Beauvais, in his 'Mirror of Nature,' to the two points of the magnetic needle, indicate, like many Arabic names of stars which we still use, the channel and the people from whom the Western countries received their knowledge." Humboldt suggests that the Arabians may have received the compass from the Chinese, who appear to have used the magnetic needle in the time of Hoang-ti, more than 2700 years previous to the Christian Era. Could we have a complete history of Arabia previous to that date, it might appear that the Chinese themselves received it from the Arabian Cushites. Be this as it may, we cannot reasonably suppose that such a people as the ancient Arabians, endowed with remarkable aptitude for making science practical, constantly engaged in navigation, and perpetually incited to contrive nautical instruments and improve nautical science, were less likely to invent the mariner's compass than the Chinese. To believe this requires greater credulity than reason can tolerate.

Flavio Gioja represents the age when nautical instruments first came into general use among the present peoples of Western Europe, but he does not represent the age when they were first invented. The people we call Moors, Saracens, and Arabians inherited the remains of the old Cushite civilization. They had the mariner's compass, but they did not claim to have invented it. They had "always" used the compass, and we must suppose (for no other supposition is probable) that it had come down to them from the Phœnicians. When Vasques di Gama went to India round the Cape of Good Hope, he found the mariner's compass, the astrolabe, and other important nautical instruments in general use among the Southern Arabians, who controlled maritime enterprise on the Indian Seas. Barlow, in his "Navigator's Supply," published in 1597, states that he had ascertained by personal inquiry and observation that "instead of our compass they used a magnetic needle about six inches long, suspended on a pin, in a white China dish filled with water, in the bottom of which were two cross lines marking the cardinal points." This method of using the needle is the same as that employed by the Arabian race on the Mediterranean. It indicates that they all had the compass from the same source.

We have some very plain indications of the existence of the mariner's compass among the Phœnicians. The magnet was described as "the stone of Hercules;" and we have very significant accounts of "the cup of Hercules," which reminds us of the cup in which the later Arabians floated the needle. Hercules, it is said, departed on his great maritime expedition to the West with a cup which he had received from Apollo. The cup is associated with Hercules not only in the myths, but also in sculptured and other representations, which show him with a cup in his hand. Nothing could have been more natural to the Phœnician mariners than to associate the magnetic needle with the gods, and regard it as a divine oracle. When not in use, the place of the compass would be in a temple, apart from familiar approaches. The Bætylia, or "stones having life," which, we are told in Sanchoniathon, were made by Ouranos, are supposed to indicate ancient experiments with the magnet.

Knowledge of the properties of the magnet existed in very remote times. We find traces of it everywhere. It appears in the old Sanskrit myths. Wilford says: In the *Chatur-varga-chintámáni*, it is said that when the *daityas*, being defeated, fled before the gods and found no shelter,

Sucrácháryya created an immense magnet, like a mountain, by which the iron-tipped arrows of the gods were attracted; whereupon Indra struck the mountain-like magnet with his thunder, shivering it into numberless splinters, which fell upon the land and into the sea, existing thereafter as magnetic rocks.

The credulous skepticism that believes the old Arabians, with their practical spirit, their penetrating intellect, and their nautical wants, could have the magnet and understand its properties without producing the magnetic needle, greatly needs the wholesome discipline of reason. It is certain that the mariner's compass was not originated in Europe, nor among the later Arabians from whom we received it. Where did it originate? How shall we reasonably explain its origin if we refuse to believe it was invented by the greatest maritime people of antiquity—the great people who monopolized maritime enterprise for so many centuries, not to say millenniums, and who created the ancient civilizations? Its history, so far as we can trace it, leads us directly to this explanation; no other is so obvious, so probable, or so necessary to a just comprehension of antiquity itself.

But, it is said, "If the Phœnicians and their predecessors had the mariner's compass, why did not the Greeks and Romans make a full record of this fact? and how did it happen that all knowledge of the compass was lost?" Knowledge of the compass was not lost by those who used it. Perhaps the Greeks and Romans knew more of it in a general way than they have told us; and if they did not know enough of the compass to explain it, or if, knowing something of it, they regarded it merely as a thaumaturgical instrument of no practical importance, they would not be likely to make it a topic in their writings. The Greeks must have known much concerning the history, manufactures, enterprises, and nautical science of the Phœnicians which they did not write down in their books. They did say something. Strabo, referring to the opportunities afforded by the cities of Phœnicia for studying geometry, astronomy, and other sciences, says: "The Sidonians are said by historians to excel in various arts, and they cultivate science, and study astronomy, arithmetic, and *night sailing*, each of which concerns the merchant and the seaman." Night sailing! What does that mean? It was a science peculiar to the Phœnicians. We hear of it nowhere else. Strabo himself, probably, could not have explained it.

It should be remembered that, among the enlightened peoples of antiquity, the methods of communication were different from ours. The current knowledge of their time was not published every morning in newspapers. The progress of science was not regularly announced to the public either in monthly bulletins or annual reports; and, what is more, the higher studies in science and philosophy were not conducted openly before the public so much as in secret societies. Pythagoras found it necessary to undergo a very severe ordeal of initiation before he could be allowed to pursue his studies in Egypt. In the matter of learning and its mysteries, exclusiveness and secretiveness were much more common among the ancient peoples than publicity and frank communication. No ancient people hastened to communicate to all others its wisdom in the arts and sciences; on the contrary, the rule was to conceal and hold it as the exclusive possession of those to whom it belonged; and, to a great extent, the highest and boldest developments of science and philosophy were carefully shut up in secret societies.

It is well known that the Phœnicians, as far as possible, drew the curtain of secrecy over the whole business of their commerce; and we see in the statements of Herodotus that the Southern Arabians pursued the same policy. Can it be supposed, or even imagined, that these wonderful navigators and traders, having the mariner's compass, would go into all the public places of the known world, and there announce it, explain it, and, giving it to all other peoples, invite them to become their commercial rivals? No; they would have hidden it from observation with the most jealous care. Nothing else connected with their business would have been kept in profounder secrecy. A means of maritime supremacy so sure, and to other peoples so mysterious, would have been withdrawn from the scrutiny of Greek and Roman curiosity as carefully as the most sacred things of their religion were secured against the blaspheming impertinence of its enemies. The people who braved shipwreck to hide the Cassiterides from the Romans were not likely to make it possible for Greeks and Romans to understand and describe their greatest treasure, the mariner's compass. Therefore, when the mariner's compass has been fairly traced to the Phœnicians, it is preposterous to object, seriously, that the Greeks and Romans have given us no account of it.

A good old lady living in one of the most secluded valleys of the Green Mountains was visited one day by a little company of romantic pleasure-seekers. She asked them where they lived when at home; and on being told that their homes were in Boston, she exclaimed with raised hands, "How can anybody be willing to live so far off!" It is to be feared that some persons contemplate antiquity with intelligence very similar to that of this most excellent old lady. They find it difficult, if not impossible, to believe there could have been anything worthy of attention in ages "so far off." They are sure that nothing of much importance could have existed previous to our time. This style of intelligence is always preposterous; but it reaches the superlative degree when allowed to guide the judgment of scholarly gentlemen whose chief aim is to establish a reputation for "critical discrimination."

IV.

THE PHŒNICIANS.

HEEREN, pursuing his inquiries concerning the nations of antiquity, was constrained to say, "The severest loss Ancient History has to mourn—a loss irreparable—is the destruction of those records that would inform us of the affairs, the government, and the enterprises of the Phœnicians." Heeren's "Researches" have great value. His ethnic assumptions are not always correct, and his conception of antiquity was not sufficiently extensive to take in the whole career of the old Cushite race, to which the Phœnicians belonged; but he wrote more than fifty years ago, without aid from the later discoveries. The lost records of this whole race would indeed shed a great light on the past; nevertheless, it will be readily admitted that a complete history of the people known as Phœnicians, or even a complete record of Sidon or Tyre, giving a history of its maritime operations from the beginning, its manufactures, its commerce, its colonies, and its commercial and political relations with the rest of the world, would be an invaluable acquisition.

The term Phœnicia is of Greek origin. The Greeks applied it to a small district on the Mediterranean, which appears to have been the only Asiatic territory controlled by the people called Phœnicians after the date of the first Olympiad. This was only a fragment of their more ancient dominion, and they themselves were only a fragment of the still more ancient empire of the Arabian Cushites. The term Phœnicia did not come into use until long after the Phœnician dominion—in Asia Minor, on the Black Sea, and on the islands and coasts of the Ægean and Eastern Mediterranean—was broken. We call certain people Moors who never knew themselves by the name we give them. So did the Greeks and Romans describe a certain people of antiquity as Phœnicians. We can not have a regular history of this people; but we know that the early Greeks called them Ethiopians. Notices of them are found in Greek literature; tradition gives some account of them; traces of their character and civilization are found in the many regions where they had colonies or commercial establishments; and there is something for study in the unexplained yet unavoidable impression of their greatness felt by every student of ancient history.

ORIGIN OF THE PHŒNICIANS.

Herodotus, beginning his record of historical events among the "Greeks and barbarians," states, on the authority of "the learned among the Persians," that "the Phœnicians migrated from the shores of the Erythræan Sea to the Mediterranean." The Greek writers frequently mention ancient historical works, relating to Western Asia, that would tell much we desire to know. Strabo mentions "ancient histories of Persia, Media, and Syria;" and we know from statements in Oriental books that there were "ancient histories of Iran." It is probable that Herodotus had some knowledge of such works. He states that the Phœnicians themselves had the same tradition concerning their origin. In book vii., ch. lxxxix., he repeats his first statement thus: "The Phœnicians, as they themselves say, anciently dwelt on the Erythræan Sea; and, having crossed over from thence, they settled on the sea-coast of Syria." Eratosthenes found the same tradition in certain islands of the Persian Gulf, named Aradus and Tyrus or Tylus, supposed to be the same as the Bahreyn Islands of modern times, one of which is still called Arad. These islands are on the coast of Arabia, in a bay that extends from the Persian Gulf.

It will appear that the people called Phœnicians were a branch of the great Cushite race, and that the country they occupied was originally a part of that empire of Cusha-dwipa which extended from the Erythræan Sea to the Mediterranean. At that very remote period, when the first Cushite settlements were established on the Mediterranean, there was undoubtedly a great movement of the Arabian Cushites in that direction from all parts of the peninsula, and especially from the commercial districts on the southern and eastern coasts; and probably there were other migrations, at subsequent periods, whenever a new city was founded, or some new commercial opportunity stimulated enterprise to seek that coast. The tradition reported by Eratosthenes appears to signify, at least, that, when Tyre was founded, its builders from Sidon were joined by immigrants from the Bahreyn Islands and the Arabian coast with which they are so closely connected. Political considerations may have done something to incite this migration, for the unity of the ancient Cushite dominion must have disappeared before Tyre was built, and the independent nationality of the Phœnicians must then have reached that great condition of prosperity which it maintained for centuries afterwards.

Linguistic and archæological research have made two points very clear: first, that the oldest traces of a civilized people found in Asia Minor, especially in the coast regions, are those of the Cushites, or Ethiopians; and, second, that there was a very close relationship between the Phœnicians and the ancient people of Southern Arabia, or, to translate the words of a distinguished French explorer and philologist [Ernest Renan]: "It must be admitted that singular relations exist between the ethnographic, historic, and linguistic position of Yemen and that of Phœnicia." These points are now so generally admitted by those familiar with the evidence on which they rest, that an elaborate discussion of this evidence is not required.

Mr. Rawlinson, in his essay "On the Ethnic Affinities of the Nations of Western Asia," states the admitted result of investigation to be that Hamites or Cushites preceded Semitic and Aryan civilization throughout that whole region; and he names "Arabia, Babylonia, Susiana, Philistia, Sidon, Tyre, and the country of the Hittites" as points where their traces are especially noticeable. His essay is by no means all that can be desired on this subject, while his Turanizing speculation cannot be very satisfactory to himself. Any theory that classes the languages of the Egyptians, Himyarite Arabians, early Chaldeans, and early Canaanites as "Turanian languages," should not expect much success. Nevertheless, he says: "The primeval Canaanites, indeed, were of the race of Ham (*i. e.*, they were Cushites), and no doubt originally spoke a dialect closely akin to the Egyptian." In another place he points out that Hamites, or Ethiopians, "were the original founders of most of the towns" occupied by the Phœnicians, including even Sidon itself, and starts these questions: "Are we to identify the Phœnicians with the Canaanites, and understand a Hamitic migration from Chaldea or Susiana in times long anterior to Abraham? or are we to distinguish between the two races, and to regard Herodotus as describing a long' subsequent immigration of Semites into these parts—a settlement of Phœnicians, as we know them in history, among the Canaanites, a people of quite a different character?"

This is creating difficulty where none exists, and where none can be felt save by those who are predetermined to class the Phœnicians as Semites, and whose untenable chronology forbids a just comprehension of the past. The Phœnicians, "as we know them in history" written under these influences, are very poorly understood. Should Mr. Rawlinson study the case with entire freedom of mind, he could not allow himself to doubt that Herodotus meant a Cushite immigration "in times long anterior to Abraham"—not "from Chaldea or Susiana," which is pure invention, but "from the shores of the Erythræan Sea, from Southern Arabia." It may also be suggested that the Phœnicians meant by Herodotus, according to his own statement, founded Tyre about 2760 years before the Christian Era, and carried letters and civilization to Hellas (or to the country that afterwards became Hellas) long previous to the date fixed for this imagined "immigration of Semites into those parts," to become the Phœnicians.

We have seen, in another place, that the whole Asiatic region on the Mediterranean was anciently a part of Ethiopia, or the Land of Cush, and that Joppa (Iopia), one of the most ancient Phœnician cities, was the royal city of "Kepheus the Ethiopian." Among the notes to Hamilton and Falconer's version of Strabo are the following: "We have before remarked that the Ethiopia visited by Menelaus was not the country above Egypt, but an Ethiopia lying around Jaffa, the ancient Joppa." Again: "The name of Ethiopians, given by Ephorus to fugitive Canaanites, confirms what we have before stated, that the environs of Jaffa, and possibly the entire of Palestine, anciently bore the name of Ethiopia." The most ancient Greeks, in their writings and traditions, knew nothing of that name, Phœnicians, but they did know and use such names as Ethiopians, Sidonians, and Aradians. Ethiopia was the term most commonly applied to the country afterwards called Phœnicia; and this term, as an appellation to describe some of the communities and districts that were under Phœnician control, did not pass out of use until after the beginning of the Christian Era.

Jerome, in his catalogue of ecclesiastical writers, mentions that St. Andrew preached the Gospel in towns on the two Colchic rivers, Asparus and Phasis, and calls the people Ethiopians: "Ubi est irruptio Aspari et Phasis—illic incolunt Æthiopes interiores." He says the same of Matthias: "In alterâ Æthiopiâ, ubi est irruptio Apsari et Hyssi portus, prædicavit." This ancient name, lingering still in later times, is sufficient to determine the ethnic character of the Phœnicians. They were Arabian Cushites—the Ethiopians of Greek antiquity—who came to the Mediterranean and established that "multitude of flourishing commercial cities," which, as Heeren says, "adorned the countries of Phœnicia and Asia Minor, and formed an almost unbroken line from the Straits of Byzantium to the confines of Egypt." In most of their communities there seems to have been a remarkable mixture of races, but there is no reason to doubt that their dominion over this whole region was maintained for a long time after the decline of the great Cushite empire in Western Asia, the "great Sidon" being, at an early time, their metropolitan city, preceded, however, in ages still earlier, by Martu or Marathus. It finally gave way, and their Asiatic territory gradually shrunk to the small district in which authentic history found them.

THE IMMIGRATION DOUBTED.

Some writers, in discussing what Herodotus says of the Phœnicians, have discredited such an immigration as improbable in the highest degree, if not impossible. They have said, "The great difficulties of such a migration from the Erythræan Sea to the Mediterranean, at that remote period, made it utterly impracticable." Those who have used, in this connection, the phrase "at that remote period," have deemed it very powerful and conclusive. They have assumed, and supposed everybody else would admit as a matter of course, that all men were ignorant barbarians "at that remote period," destitute of the arts of civilized life. "That remote period," they are quite sure, was not far from the dreary "Stone Age" in the unwritten history of Western Asia, when the noblest naval structure was a loose raft of logs, and hunting and fishing with the rudest stone and bone implements the most serious undertakings of the people.

The confident critics who raised this objection have seemed deliciously unconscious of its absurdity. They are not as numerous now as formerly; but those who believe there never was any civilization worth taking much account of previous to the time of the Greeks are liable to such magnificent flights in the dark. That brilliant skeptic, Voltaire, writing on this subject with more wit than wisdom, supposed the migration must necessarily have been impossible without a sea voyage around Africa; and he ridiculed this supposed sea voyage with immense satisfaction to himself, therein making plain that brilliant wit is not sure to save a man from stupidity.

Movers, in his elaborate work on the Phœnicians, urges two arguments against the migration described by Herodotus. In the first place, he is sure it cannot have taken place because it is not mentioned in the Bible—a style of argument not well considered. The Bible does not describe the building of Petra; it does not relate the history of Balbec; it does not tell us when Sidon was founded; it fails to explain either the origin or the ethnic character of the Philistines. Moreover, the first settlements of the Ethiopians on the Mediterranean were made many centuries before the time of Abraham, and were no more likely to be discussed by Moses or his successors than any other event of general history far away in the past. In the second place, Movers urges that, according to Sanchoniathon, the Phœnicians were the original people of the region where they dwelt, and the human race itself appeared first in their country. But the authorities tell us that "it is now generally agreed among scholars that the work attributed to Sanchoniathon was a forgery of Philo Byblius." It is very true that what "is generally agreed among scholars" in such cases—like some of the judgments in which churchmen, or medical scientists, or representative men of other professions are, from time to time, both agreed and disagreed—are not infallible. The work may be a forgery; but is it not quite as probable that an ancient Phœnician should have written such a work, as that an eminent scholar of Philo's time should have forged it? The general judgment of scholars, however, should have due weight;

therefore Sanchoniathon cannot be safely used to prove anything, although many scholars, entitled to great respect, have believed the work authentic.

At the same time, should the work in question be generally accepted and used in these investigations as a genuine production of an old Phœnician writer, it would not sustain the argument of Movers. The immigrants who built the old Phœnician cities did not go out of their own country; they did nothing more than extend its borders and its population to the Mediterranean Sea. Their country was Ethiopia or Cusha-dwipa, and the new settlements were as essentially a part of it as the older communities on the Erythræan Sea. The Cushites who settled on the Mediterranean might justly claim that their ancestors were part of the original people of the ancient Ethiopia, without meaning that they were the original occupants of that particular portion of it. The argument of Movers had some force in his own mind, because he assumed that the little district called Phœnicia was all the country ever known or claimed in any age by the ancient people known in history as Phœnicians.

RENAN'S THEORY.

Ernest Renan, in his work on the Semitic Languages (bk. ii., ch. ii.), after showing that, in the time of the Hebrews, the Phœnicians called the district then occupied by them *Chna* or *Cna*,* and that the Hebrews designated the whole Phœnician people as Canaanites, making them a different race from the Semites, speculates on the subject as follows:

* Stephanus of Byzantium, and also Hecateus, states that the country was called *Chna*.

"As the Phœnicians spoke a Semitic language, the philologist is invincibly borne to the conclusion that they were themselves Semites. The historian, however, sees grave difficulties in the way of this conclusion, and is in suspense in regard to the real origin of this people, who played a part so important in the history of civilization. From the first the Hebrews obstinately spurned all fraternity with Canaan, and connected him with the family of Ham. For a moment criticism is tempted to be of their opinion. We said at the beginning, the peculiar characteristic of the Semites is to have neither industrial enterprise, political spirit, nor municipal organization; navigation and colonization seem repugnant to them; their action has remained purely Oriental, and has entered the current of European affairs indirectly only, and by repercussion. Here (among the Phœnicians), on the contrary, we find an industrial civilization, political revolutions, the most active commerce known to antiquity, and a nation incessantly spreading abroad its influence, and mixing itself with the whole life of the Mediterranean world."

Communities have sometimes changed their language; but for one race to borrow, at will, the essential peculiarities of another race, is impossible. With his belief in profound and ineradicable distinctions between races—a belief which in him is emphatic and sometimes extreme—he might have seen that the civilization of the Phœnicians made it impossible to class them with the Semitic family; and also that if, at any comparatively modern period of their history, they were found using a Semitic dialect, it was because unexplained influences had enabled that dialect to supercede their original tongue. No hypothesis should have been permitted to set aside a fact so plain as the manifest distinction of race. But with him, as with some others, it was a foregone conclusion that the Phœnicians were Semites, and he saw nothing to do but to remove the difficulties as cleverly as possible. The emphatic testimony of the Hebrew Scriptures that the Phœnicians or Canaanites did not belong to the Semitic race he treats as follows:

"The affinity established by the Hebrews between Ham and Canaan seems at least to signify that, in their view, the Canaanites came from the south. Perhaps the part taken by the Hebrews to make Canaan an accursed race influenced their ethnography, and led them, notwithstanding the evident similarity of language, to withdraw the Phœnicians from the elect race of Shem, and place them in the infidel family of Ham."

To solve the problem without yielding his assumption, he resorts to the mountains of Kurdistan, where he finds Ur of the Chaldees (as will be shown in the chapter on the Chaldeans) and his Aryan Chaldeans (les Kasdes ou Chaldéens primitifs, que tout porte à rattacher à la race arienne). These mountains now become "the common cradle of the Semitic race," from which the Phœnicians went forth first into the great world and traveled to Babylonia, where they remained an indefinite number of ages, long enough to become civilized and undergo a profound change of character. These Semites from Kurdistan were transformed into a kind of "Semitico-Cushites," and "became to their unchanged pastoral brethren objects of execration." They left Babylonia and settled in Canaan about 2000 years B.C., he thinks long before his chronology finds Abraham there, and five centuries before the Israelites entered the land from Egypt; and yet, during all this time, and through all these changes, these two closely related Semitic families preserved, unchanged and inviolate, the language, common to both, which they brought from the Kurdish mountains. The similarity of language remained, for the Hebrews were still Hebrews of the old style in this respect, and, "more faithful to their language than to their faith and their manners, the Phœnicians were still Semites in speech." It is due to Renan to say he did not originate this hypothesis; he borrowed it from M. Guigniaut, who gave it to the world in his "Religions de l'Antiquité." Its improbability, from beginning to end, is so great and so palpable, that a formal attempt to refute it would be as absurd as the hypothesis itself.

It is nowise likely that Abraham ever spoke Hebrew, a language that seems to have been developed after his time, probably by some Semitic community in Syria that may have become, for a time, sufficiently powerful to control the whole region known as Canaan and Palestine. His family belonged to the nomadic Semites of Mesopotamia; and it is not improbable to suppose he spoke a Semitic dialect that was exchanged for Hebrew, in Palestine, by his descendants—perhaps by the family of Jacob, perhaps at a later period. It may be affirmed with confidence that Hebrew was not the original language of the people called Phœnicians; they were Cushites in race, language, and civilization; and if, in the later ages of their existence as a people, they did actually speak Hebrew (which is not quite so clear as some have assumed), the Kurdish mountains can furnish nothing to explain the fact. Such linguistic changes are possible; history shows us how to understand them; and the ethnologist who does not take proper account of them is liable to go astray.

THEIR CUSHITE RELIGION AND ARCHITECTURE.

If the Cushite or Ethiopian origin of the Phœnicians were not so distinctly apparent in the records of antiquity, in their civilization, and in the other evidence of the Cushite character of the first civilizers of the region they occupied, it would still be convincingly manifest in their religion, and in the architectural remains of their ancient cities. The Hebrew Scriptures show us their religion, and enable us to see its identity with that of all other peoples of the same race. They worshipped "the host of heaven," the planets, as representatives of the Supreme Being; and among these, Baal and Astarte, or Ashteroth, represented the generative and productive powers of nature. It was the Cushite system found not only in Phœnicia and Arabia, but also in Egypt, Chaldea, India, and wherever the influence of this race was established in ancient times. It is brought to light in the old Phœnician ruins. Ernest Renan, who directed an exploration of the ruins of that very ancient Phœnician city which the Greeks called Marathos, and described the results in his "Mission de Phœnicie," says on this point: "The Egyptian aspect of these monuments should not surprise us. More and more, in the course of this work, we shall see Phœnicia, in a religious point of view, become a province of Egypt." He might have said, more correctly, that, in a religious point of view, Egypt and Phœnicia were both provinces of their mother country, the ancient Ethiopia or Cusha-dwipa.

The Cushite origin of the Phœnicians is shown no less distinctly by the architectural remains of their oldest cities. In every country and on every shore, where the old Cushite settlements are traced, are found the remains of vast constructions that astonish and perplex beholders. They are found in Egypt, Nubia, Arabia, India, Greece, Italy, Great Britain, and Phœnicia. In Chaldea, where there was no stone, there were immense structures of brick. The stone-work shown by some of these constructions is amazing, and nowhere more so than in Syria and Phœnicia. Since Maundrell published the record of his travels and observations, we have been familiar with this peculiarity in the ruins of Balbec. One particular in the description of these ruins is that, at one place in a remaining wall, twenty feet above the ground, three vast blocks of stone, twelve feet deep and twelve feet wide, and each more than sixty feet long, are seen lying end to end. The hand of old Cushite architects is seen in the wondrous rock constructions of Petra, and it is visible in the ruins of ancient Phœnician cities that have been explored.

For instance, at Ruad, the Arvad of Genesis, known in remote Cushite times as Arad, the French explorers found the ancient wall that encircled the island city. It was constructed of immense blocks of stone, nearly eleven feet square and fifteen or sixteen long. The beautiful antique reservoirs, hewn out of the rock, are still used by the people of Ruad. The report in the "Mission de Phœnicie" says: "The wall is a work of the old city, without doubt, and a work truly Phœnician. Nowhere more than at Ruad is one impressed by those gigantic rock-works which constitute a dominant trait of Phœnica and Palestine." Ruad is an island very near the Syrian coast. On the main land opposite, and intimately connected with it, were five other cities — Paltus, Balanea, Carné, Enhydra, and Marathos, the "daughters of Arvad"—whose ruins exist. Probably there were others. The French explorers say: "The grand totality of what may be called the Arvadite civilization is represented in our day by a vast mass of ruins, which cover the coast on a continuous line of three or four leagues. Carné, Antaradus, Enhydra, and Marathos must have nearly touched each other, it being now very difficult to say where one began or another ended. Marathos alone, among these centres of population, had an individuality distinct from the insular city." Antaradus, built on the ruins of an older city, was comparatively modern, not being older than the Roman period. It was not mentioned by Strabo, and appears first in the geography of Ptolemy.

Marathos was more ancient than Arvad, and seems to have had a great history of its own before Arvad and "the daughters of Arvad" appeared, or, at least, before the insular city became important. In the more ancient Chaldean inscriptions there is frequent mention of a region on the eastern shore of the Mediterranean called *Martu.* It is usually understood to mean Phœnicia.* Was *Martu* an ancient Cushite name of the Phœnician city called Marathos by the Greeks, and now, in its ruins, known as Mrith or Amrit? and was this city, older in importance certainly than Sidon, sufficiently great and powerful, at some period of its history, to give its name to that region? These questions must be answered in the affirmative.

* A note to George Rawlinson's Essay on the Phœnicians says: "Martu was probably the original form of Marathos, and is the ordinary term in the early Cushite or Hamitic Babylonian for 'the West,' and is especially used of Phœnicia and the Mediterranean." Sir Henry Rawlinson finds the name in the oldest inscriptions at Ur, in connection with one of the most primitive kings, and says: "It was applied by the primitive Hamitic Chaldeans to Phœnicia." This makes Phœnicia as old as Chaldea, and effectually disposes of the theory that the Phœnicians were Semites, and first appeared as a people in the thirteenth century before Christ.

Mrith or Marathos "is the central point of a field of ruins nearly a league square." In the thirteenth century these ruins were visited by the Dominican Brocard, who used the strongest terms of admiration in speaking of "those pyramids of surprising grandeur, constructed of blocks of stone from twenty-six to twenty-eight feet long, whose thickness exceeded the stature of a tall man." Six hundred years can work great changes even in ruins, but these are still very remarkable. The city was built partly on a plain and partly on a chain of rocky hills. Some of the most important monuments of its ancient greatness are the remains of structures hewn out of these rocks.

In Renan's report on the ruins of Marathos there is some account of an edifice called "el Maabed," the Temple, which shows "a vast court, 156 feet wide and about 180 feet long, scooped out of the rock in such a manner as to be level with the soil of the valley." Wonderful traces of skill in rock-sculpture appear in the finish and appurtenances of this temple. "The aspect is Egyptian, with something original." Another structure, named "Burdj-el-Bezzák," now a retreat for brigands, he describes as a mausoleum of enormous dimensions, and says: "This is the most considerable and best-preserved building of ancient Phœnicia still existing. It was constructed of immense blocks of stone, and was formerly crowned with a pyramid, of which we found nearly all the materials." Another structure, hewn out of the rock, he describes as "an immense stadium, about 738 feet long by about 100 feet wide. Ten rows of seats surrounded the arena, and the stadium terminated in a circular amphitheatre, from which two parallel passages communicated with the outside, probably to let in the chariots and horses."

Other remains of rock-sculpture and Cyclopean building were noted at Marathos; and so it is throughout Phœnicia. The Cushite origin of these cities is so plain, that those most influenced by the strange monomania which transforms the Phœnicians into Semites now admit that the Cushites were the first civilizers and builders in Phœnicia. Those old builders, whose sculpture produced such astonishing effects in coarse rock, resorted to wood and metal for the finish and ornamentation of their work. The stone they used was not Parian marble, therefore they covered it with ornaments of another material; and "what remains of their monuments is not the monument itself, but the gross support that served to bear the whole system of decoration under which the stone was concealed."

ANTIQUITY OF THE PHŒNICIANS.

The doubts and perplexities that have troubled inquiry concerning the Phœnicians are due chiefly to the influence of chronological dogmatism. Investigators have created most of them by assuming that the commonly accepted scheme of Ancient History must not be disturbed. To explain the facts presented for consideration, we must disregard this influence, and be entirely free to admit any conclusion that shall seem necessary. The great antiquity of the people called Phœnicians was acknowledged by the ancients. Herodotus, evidently, did not suppose it could be denied. Josephus, while pointing out that "almost all which concerns the Greeks happened not long ago," mentions as a fact generally understood that the antiquity of the Phœnicians was as great as that of the Chaldeans and Egyptians. He says, writing against Apion: The Greeks acknowledge "that they were the Egyptians, the Chal-

G

deans, and the Phœnicians, who preserved the memorials of the most ancient and most lasting traditions of mankind."

In the tenth chapter of Genesis, the Hebrew belief in the antiquity of the Canaanites (called Phœnicians) is shown by the statement that Canaan, Cush, Mizraim, and Phut were brothers. These names are made to represent the beginnings of the several branches of the Hamitic race. This important chapter, which preserves the earliest ethnological traditions of the Hebrews, is, in a geographical and ethnical point of view, of great value. George Rawlinson, while assigning his imagined Semitic Phœnicians to a comparatively modern period, can not deny that civilized Phœnicia itself was very ancient. He says, in his Herodotus, vol. iv., p. 245: "Hamitic races seem to have been the first to people Western Asia, whether starting from Egypt or from Babylonia it is impossible to determine. These Hamites were the original founders of most of the towns, which sometimes retained their primitive names, sometimes exchanged them for Semitic appellations." This admission, however, really yields the whole question, and overthrows the chronology he desires to save.

The arrival of the Israelites in the land of Canaan, from Egypt, is usually placed in the fifteenth century before the Christian Era. At that time the Phœnician cities were very old. Some of them had declined. Arad or Arvad had superseded Martu or Marathus. Many ages had gone by since Joppa or Iopia was a royal city. The great days of Phœnician dominion in that part of Asia had departed. It does not appear that any great city was built in Phœnicia after this date; some of the old cities may have had new extensions, but no new city was founded. From that time onward the history of Phœnicia was the history, not of young vigor and rising greatness, but of development already mature and of progress towards decline. And yet Mr. Rawlinson makes his Semitic Phœnicians begin their residence there in the thirteenth century before Christ—two centuries later than the Israelites! To speak very moderately, and as respectfully as possible, this astonishing hypothesis is unreasonable.

THE PERIODS OF PHŒNICIAN HISTORY.

There are some dates and facts which constrain us to believe that the Phœnician settlements and cities, on the eastern shore of the Mediterranean, were quite as old as Egypt. Herodotus gives us the age of Tyre, one of the latest of those cities; and it is clear that cities much more ancient than Sidon were the earlier seats of the commerce and power of that people, such as Joppa or Iopia, Berytus or Berut, Byblius or Gebal, and Marathos or Martu. The history of the people called Phœnicians can be divided into four great periods;* and the first of these periods, as described in the "Allgemeine Encyklopädie," may be subdivided into three or more. The elaborate and learned article on the Phœnicians, published in that great work, arranges Phœnician history as follows: 1. The ante-Sidonian period, or the time previous to the rise of Sidon to supremacy; 2. The period of Sidon; 3. The period during which Tyre was the ruling city; 4. The period of the Assyrian, Babylonian, Egyptian, and Persian invasions, to the final decline of Phœnicia. The first, second, and third of these periods are greatly crowded and confused by the writer's deference

* See the "Allgemeine Encyklopädie," article "Phœnizien," p. 333–840.

to the popular chronology; and, in other respects, the article is more valuable for the learning it shows than for clear views and just conclusions; but the division adopted is obvious and useful. In using this natural arrangement of the history, I shall divide the first period into three, and the fourth I shall describe as the Carthaginian period.

1. The ante-Sidonian period. This period begins with the first commercial settlements of the Hamitic or Cushite people on that part of the Mediterranean coast—with the time when the Arabian Cushites began to occupy that coast for maritime purposes. That this time was in very remote antiquity is made manifest by the uniform testimony of linguistic and archæological investigation, which shows that the Cushites preceded the other races in that part of Asia, and were the first to establish civilization there. According to an old tradition, the first cities built were Gebal or Gebeil, which the Greeks called Byblus, and Berut, or Berytus as the Greeks made it, now called Beyrut; but others may have been older.

The time previous to the supremacy of Sidon must have been divided by events into several distinct historical periods. 1. There was a time when Kepheus, king of Ethiopia, reigned at Joppa, and his kingdom is described as extending from the Mediterranean to the Indian Ocean. Phœnicia or Canaan was then an integral part of the great kingdom of the Arabian Cushites; but we cannot suppose the time of Kepheus to have been during the first ages of the maritime settlements in that district. 2. There was a time when Berut or Borytus, with its Poseidon and Cabiri worship, was the great city, and the principal starting-point for commercial and colonial enterprise. The earliest colonists may have gone forth from this city. Poseidon-worship seems to have been a peculiarity of all the colonies previous to the time of Sidon. 3. There was a time when Martu or Marathos was the metropolitan city, and gave its name to the whole region.

The ruins of Marathos show it to have been a city of great importance. Diodorus Siculus describes it as a city celebrated for the religious objects guarded in its sanctuaries. It is mentioned in the older Chaldean inscriptions, which shows its great antiquity. Like Byblus and Berytus, it had ceased to be a chief city long before the time of Joshua.[*] It was then secondary to the later island city known as Arad or Arvad, which, however, may have been as old as Sidon. Arad, which inherited the political and commercial importance of Marathos, may have been older than Sidon, to which it finally became secondary. The Arvadites are prominently mentioned in the tenth chapter of Genesis, and Arvad had evidently been a chief city for a long time when that chapter was written or compiled.

2. The period of Sidon. There is no record to tell us when this period began. It belongs to the time when the Phœnician cities, with their many colonies on the islands and shores of the Mediterranean, had become a separate

---

[*] There are indications that Marathos was one of the most primeval cities of Phœnicia, and that the Marathos whose ruins now exist was a new city, built near the site of an older Marathos. This new city was already a mass of ruins in Strabo's time. The French explorers say its structures were much older than the Greek epoch, and yet they found in them materials taken from remains of older structures that had become ruins before they were built. Throughout the vast walls of the building called Burj-el-Bezzāk, blocks of stone were found, evidently taken from the ruins of more ancient structures. Dr. Gaillardot, of the French exploring party, in the "Mission de Phœnicie," discusses the evidence of this fact at length, and shows it to be conclusive.

and independent dominion. This separation, which was probably more political than commercial, may have commenced when Martu or Marathos was the great city, and when the ancient Chaldean inscriptions described that whole region as Martu. In Homer, Tyre is not named, but Sidon and the Sidonians are mentioned in such a way as to make two facts apparent—first, that, in ages previous to his time, "the great Sidon" had been the ruling city; and, second, that the cities in Asia Minor and around the Ægean Sea had recognised its controlling influence. Kenrick says very justly: "This exclusive mention of Sidon cannot represent the actual state of things when the poet wrote, for in that age Tyre had already assumed the ascendency; but it indicates his traditional knowledge of the time when the power of Phœnicia centred in Sidon, and Tyre was insignificant."*

Movers, shackled by submissive reverence for the popular chronology, suggests that the supremacy of Sidon may have begun about the year 1500 B.C. At that date it was already in a state of decline. It must have begun more than a thousand years earlier. We know from the Hebrew Scriptures that, in the fifteenth century before the Christian Era, "the great Sidon" was already a very ancient city. Its greatness was mature and old; its origin was hidden from the Israelites in the mist of remote ages; and they spoke of it as one of the earliest cities of the land. The Hebrew writers could not have spoken of Sidon in this way if at that time its days of great power and influence had just begun.

It is possible that the cities of Asia Minor were separated from Phœnician control during the period of Sidonian

* See Kenrick's "Phœnicia," page 341.

sway, but there is nothing to suggest the date of this separation beyond the fact that, after this period, Phœnician enterprise and influence went chiefly in other directions, while throughout that region, and on both sides of the Ægean, grew up an independent political organization of the Pelasgians, old acquaintances of the Phœnicians. This was followed by subsequent organizations of other peoples, of the same race doubtless, until, in the eleventh century before Christ, we may suppose the famed Ionian confederacy came into existence.* Sidon, whose importance had depended largely on its power and commercial sway in this part of the Mediterranean world, very naturally began to decline under the influence of these changes several centuries previous to the year 1500 B.C.

3. The period of Tyrian supremacy. Herodotus informs us that Tyre was founded about 2700 years before the Christian Era. He learned at Tyre that the city was founded 2300 years previous to the time of his visit there. This date, taken from the annals of the city, is just as authentic

---

* Ernst Curtius, in his "Die Ionier vor der Ionischen Wanderung," shows that the Ionians and other Greeks previous to this time dwelt chiefly in Asia Minor. When Ionia was created, many of those who had passed over into Greece returned to Asia. This is all there is to excuse the absurd representation of Hellenic egotism that the cities of Asia Minor were colonies established by emigration from Hellas, which was politically a much younger country. In concluding his essay, Curtius says:

"In Asien sahen wir die Griechen von der phrygischen Nation sich ablösen als ein besonderes Volk; in Asien sesshaft, bilden sie uns, was an Sprache und Sitte als der gemeinsame Typus des Hellenischen anerkannt werden muss. Sie gliedern sich in zwei Hauptstämme; aus dieser Gliederung wird eine Spaltung; der eine der Stämme bleibt in Asien und besetzt die ganze Westküste, der andere wandert aus durch Thracien und Macedonien."

as any other historical date. It excited in Herodotus neither doubt nor surprise. It implies more past time than the chronologies of modern times can afford; therefore some attempts have been made to bring it into discredit, but without any show of good reason, and without success. When we fairly consider what is known of the history of Tyre, the date given by Herodotus appears not only reasonable, but even moderate. As known to us in history, it consisted of an ancient town on the main land, called Palæ-Tyrus, or Old Tyre, and a later city, or extension of the city, built on an island very near the shore, called New Tyre. Herodotus, after careful inquiry, recorded the age of the old city. Those who would discredit the date he gives put entirely out of view the building of the ancient city on the main land, and begin the existence of Tyre with the building of the new city. According to Josephus, the insular city, or New Tyre (for it was to this he referred), was 240 years older than Solomon's Temple; that is to say, it was built in the thirteenth century before Christ. Two hundred years earlier, when the Ismelites settled in Canaan, the old city, described by them as "the strong city, Tyre," had evidently existed for ages. There is nothing extravagant, nothing improbable, nothing that should be doubted, in the explicit statement of Herodotus that its first foundations were laid about 2700 B.C.

Tyre was built by a colony from Sidon. When it grew to be important, its enterprise seems to have been directed chiefly towards the west, and to countries that could be reached by sailing down the Red Sea. It established close relations with Spain, and with the northern and western coasts of Africa, where the Arabian Cushites established colonies and civilization in the earlier periods of their history on the Mediterranean, probably as early as the time when Byblus and Berut were the chief cities. Those early communities, which in Northwestern Africa and Spain may have been as old as Egypt, grew to be important nations, as appears in the myths, became independent, and assumed control of their own commerce. After a long history, indicated by the myths, they must have declined greatly, for Tyre was able to resume, in those regions, the occupation and influence which the Cushite cities on the Mediterranean had lost many ages earlier. The Tyrians secured complete possession of all those countries, and went beyond them—to Britain for tin, and to regions near the Baltic for amber.

Without being able to determine precisely when Tyre became the ruling city, we can see that it had reached this condition previous to the Hebrew times. Its greatest eminence is apparent in the biblical history of David and Solomon. With an admirable degree of enlightened civilization, with marvelous skill in manufactures, mining, and commerce, and with a range of traffic that included most of the known world, the Tyrians became a mighty, renowned, and magnificent people, such as history found them—such as we can see so distinctly through the lurid storm of prophetic denunciation poured forth in the 27th chapter of Ezekiel.

The Tyrians built Carthage on the site of an older town which had more than once been renewed. A statement of Philistus the Sicilian, preserved by Eusebius, says it was founded "by the Tyrians, Zorus and Carchedon, fifty years before the Trojan war." This makes it as old as New Tyre. It is usual to assign a later date, but not with much certainty. It is probable that the sites of both Carthage and

Utica were occupied by the people called Phœnicians at a very early period, and that the reports of their having been built at various dates, in later times, refer only to subsequent enlargements of the old towns by which they became important cities.

4. The Period of Carthage. The decline of Tyrian supremacy began with those rapacious invasions of the Assyrians, Egyptians, Babylonians, and, finally, the Persians, which troubled its Asiatic commerce, and at last destroyed its independence. On the commencement of these troubles, many of its wealthiest and most enterprising citizens removed to Carthage; and this important migration may have given rise to the common representation that Carthage was built about 813 B.C.

After this time the old security and importance of Phœnicia disappeared. The country was repeatedly ravaged and subjugated by invading armies of the great powers of inner Asia. The ancient condition of Phœnician greatness, no longer possible on that coast, was henceforth represented by Carthage, which succeeded Tyre in the supremacy over Northern Africa and Spain, and became one of the most celebrated cities of its time. The period of its supremacy lasted about 500 years, and was terminated violently by the Romans, who, after a long and malignant warfare, overthrew its power and destroyed the city.

Carthage had over 700,000 inhabitants even at the time of its destruction. Its vigor had not declined; for more than a thousand years longer it might have played as grand a part in the Mediterranean world as the greatest of its predecessors, if Rome had not risen to become its rival. But the great career of the Cushite race was finished. Carthage was the last representative of its enterprising civilization. The time had come when peoples of the Aryan race were to stand foremost in civilization and power, possess the world, and make its history. They can be great enough to see clearly, and with becoming admiration, what they have inherited from their Cushite predecessors.

Ernst Curtius suggests that the order in time of the many Phœnician colonies around the Mediterranean may be traced in the particular form of religious worship established by the first settlers. The colonies of Sidon carried with them the worship of Astarte, while those of Tyre were distinguished by the worship of Melcarth or Hercules. This guidance is not sure; but we may add to his suggestion that the ante-Sidonian period can be traced in the colonies by the worship of Poseidon and the Cabiri. Berytus, which, according to all tradition, was the earliest metropolitan city, was the chief seat of this worship; and we find that it was carried to Spain and to Northern Africa, but most abundantly to Italy, to many of the islands, and to the regions around the Ægean Sea. In Thrace, Poseidon, and also the Cabiri, were worshipped in the earliest times.

The mysterious Cabiri, called sons of Sydyk the Just, and also sons of Vulcan, were peculiarly Phœnician, or more probably Arabian; but their worship, as well as that of Poseidon, belonged to the more ancient period of Phœnician or Cushite civilization, the Cabiri being divinities that presided over navigation, metallurgy, and mining. Traces of the worship of Hercules, nowhere wanting, are most abundant in the western regions on the Mediterranean and beyond the Straits of Gibraltar, where it was established in times far more ancient than either the Tyrian or the Sidonian period.

THE BUILDING OF GADES.

The city of Gades seems to have been founded by the Tyrians about 1100 years before the Christian Era, in pursuance of measures they had taken to occupy the country which had long been politically separated from the Phœnician cities, although commercially connected with them. We are told that their aim was to establish themselves in the most western region occupied by Hercules. That is to say, they sought to regain a country which, in the most ancient times, had belonged to the ancestors of their countrymen. This reference to Hercules distinctly recognises that early occupation of Spain and Northwestern Africa by the Arabian Cushites, which to the Tyrians themselves must have seemed very ancient.

Gades was built near the old city of Erythia, famed in the myths in connection with Hercules and Geryon; and north of it, on an island at the mouth of the Tartessus, now the Guadalquiver, was the equally ancient city of Tartessus, which no longer existed in the time of Strabo, for he says: "They say that on the piece of land inclosed between the two outlets of this river there formerly stood a city named, like the river, Tartessus." When Gades was built Spain had long been an old country, full of old cities, and rich in the monuments of an old civilization, then probably, like the political condition of the country, in a state of decline.

Before the time of Gades, not only the colonizing enterprises and other great events signified by the legends concerning the Cushite Melcarth or Hercules, but also many subsequent ages of the Cushite civilization in Spain, had become mythical. The Temple of Hercules, at Tyre, was then nearly 1700 years old when Gades was built, while in the myths of both Phœnicia and Egypt he was much older. One of the first edifices built at Gades by the Tyrians was the Temple of Hercules. Before going to the island on which Gades was founded, they sought a location for their city on another island, nearer the straits, which, from time immemorial, had been consecrated to Hercules. The whole region was filled with memorials of the ancient Cushite influence that gave it civilization. We can see all this in the old records and myths of the Greeks; and yet some writers have blindly assumed that the first colonizing settlements of the people called Phœnicians, in that part of Europe, were made by the Tyrians. This denial of the past is due mainly to that besotted influence of dogmatic chronology which has done so much to obscure antiquity. The more ancient times must be covered with darkness and left unseen, because its scheme of human history cannot afford to recognise them. This chronological infatuation is not respectable; no deferential forbearance or compliance of eminent scholars can make it so.

Strabo said of Gades, "Its inhabitants equip the greatest number of ships, and the largest in size, both for our sea and the exterior ocean." The best materials for ship-building appear to have been very abundant in that part of Spain. Gades, and Tartessus at the mouth of Guadalquiver, were probably noted for their naval constructions, and especially for the construction of large ships suitable for use on the great "exterior ocean." If we suppose Tartessus to have been the Tarshish of the Hebrew Scriptures, may we not find in the great ships for which that locality was famous an explanation of what was meant by the celebrated "ships of Tarshish?" Some of the ancients placed the

"Pillars of Hercules" near Gades, identifying them with the "Gates of Gades;" by others they were placed as far north as the entrance to the Baltic. These mythical pillars were supposed to be columns set up by Hercules to mark the most western point reached by his expedition; and the Tyrians, it is said, went forth to find them when they sought a location for their new city in the west. El Mas'udi speaks of these columns as "the idols of copper."

EXTENT OF PHŒNICIAN INFLUENCE.

In presence of the manifold traces of their influence, and of the uniform testimony of tradition, it could not be denied, with any show of reason, that the Arabian Cushites, called Phœnicians, were the first civilizers not only in Western Asia, but in Thrace, in Thessaly and Epirus, in the Grecian Peninsula, in the Mediterranean Islands, throughout Southern Europe, and in Northern Africa. In all these regions the Phœnicians are apparent in the oldest architectural remains, the earliest culture and modes of writing, and the methods of political organization. Such antiquities as the Cyclopean structures at Mycenæ and Tiryns, and those in Calabria and Sicily, show at once their origin. Scarcely an alphabet has been known, during the historical period, that did not arise from that of the Phœnicians. But, if there were no other evidence, a controlling Phœnician influence, at the beginning of civilization around the Mediterranean, could be inferred from the Phœnician or Arabian method of political organization everywhere prevalent—an organization in which everything else was subordinate to separate municipalities, completely organized, and more or less controlled by popular influence. What could be more indubitably Phœnician than the political methods of the Ionian confederacy, of Italy in early times, and of peninsular Greece as known in history?

The Phœnician establishments in Scandinavia, where so many traces of their influence are found, could not have been later than the early part of the Tyrian period; and the earliest Cushite-Arabian establishments there must have been much older. The letters and literary culture of the ancient Scandinavians were incontestably Phœnician. It is freely admitted that the Runic letters of the Norsemen, sixteen in number, found in the old inscriptions on the rocks and stone monuments of Denmark, Norway, Sweden, and the neighboring districts of Germany, and used in Norse literature, could have no other origin. A circular of the "Royal Society of Northern Antiquaries," published in the Journal of the Bombay branch of the Royal Asiatic Society for January 1842, says: "From a remote antiquity commercial relations existed between Asia and the north of Europe. Abundance of *Cufic coins*, and other matters, are frequently discovered in excavations, which lead to the inference that such commercial intercourse had no unimportant influence on the north, and also on the countries by which it was originated." The great article of commerce in Northwestern Europe was amber.

The Phœnicians can be traced far down the western coast of Africa, where it is well known they had cities and trading stations. They occupied the Canary Islands, and left there a dialect of the Cushite tongue closely related to the language of the Berbers, which may indicate that their settlements in these islands were older than the period when the language of Phœnicia is said to have been Semitized. Traces of their traffic are found on the coast of Guinea. Some suppose that "sika," as the name of gold, was carried to that coast by the Phœnicians. Be this as it may, the remarkable "Popoe beads," found there in the soil, are evidently remains of their wares. Travelers in Western Africa have frequently called attention to these "beads," which are mysterious to the natives, who prize them beyond gold, and which no manufacturing skill in Europe can imitate. They are described as "semi-mineral beads of many kinds." John Duncan, in his "Travels in Western Africa," vol. i, p. 100, speaks of them thus, in a description of Popoe, and of "the famous market-town of Gregapojoe," three and a half miles distant from Popoe: "The Popoe beads are found sometimes in digging the earth in and around the town. They are generally from half an inch to an inch in length, and of a tubular form, much resembling a stout pipe-handle broken into small pieces. They are of a light red coral color. I believe they have been minutely examined by scientific men in Europe, but the result has not proved satisfactory."

The only reasonable explanation is, that those wonderful manufacturers, the Phœnicians, had a trading station at Popoe in remote times, where they trafficked with the natives for gold and ivory. Urquhart, in his "Pillars of Hercules," describes articles found among Phœnician relics in Morocco, which, he says, are similar to those dug from the earth at Popoe. It was estimated that the Phœnicians had three hundred towns and cities on the Atlantic coast of Africa; and Strabo mentions an account of a ship from Gadeira, or Gadès, that was wrecked on the eastern coast in older times. When Necho, king of Egypt, as Herodotus relates, ordered a vessel to sail round Africa and return to Egypt through the Straits of Gibraltar, he knew such a voyage was possible. Nothing can be more probable than the existence of a Phœnician trading station on the coast of Guinea.

Heeren shows that there was a great overland commerce between the Black Sea and "Great Mongolia" in early times; and he mentions that a "Temple of the Sun" and a great caravansary in the desert of Gobi seem to have been connected with this commercial intercourse. It is not improbable to suppose this caravan commerce began very early, and that it did something towards creating the northern portion of that unbroken line of Phœnician cities "from the Straits of Byzantium to the confines of Egypt." Probably the civilized life and activity it infused into "the tribes of the north" gave political and historical existence to that people of many races, known to the ancients as Scythians.

Arminius Vambéry, in his "Travels in Central Asia," describes very important ruins near the eastern shore of the Caspian Sea, at a place called Gömüshtepe. Connected with them are the remains of a great wall, which he followed "ten geographical miles." He thinks the bricks in these ruins are like those at Balkh.* Between Gömüshtepe and the Little Balkan he found other important ruins, where, according to the Turkoman story, the Caaba was placed before it went to Mecca. In connection with the ruins at Meshedi-Misriyan, he mentions the remains of a

* The Moslem Arabs have traditions of a prodigious wall, or "rampart of Yajûj and Majûj," built by an Arabian king surnamed "*Dzu-l-Carnain*," and situated in that region. They applied the same surname to Alexander, it is said, and the wall has been improperly connected with him. The bricks, which resemble those at Balkh, indicate much greater antiquity. Vambéry reports abundant ruins in that part of Central Asia, extending to China.

vast aqueduct, extending 150 miles to the Persian Mountains. These are not works of Tartars or Mongols, as we know them in history. Would a thorough exploration tell us what they signify?

THE PELASGIANS.

There is evidence to show that at one period—very remote certainly, more than 2000 years before Christ, we may suppose—a people known as Pelasgi, or Pelasgians, began an organized dominion which included Asia Minor, the Grecian Peninsula, and the whole of Northern Greece. The historical traditions of the Greeks relating to this people refer chiefly to the time when the Pelasgians were broken into many separate tribes or communities under various names. But there are references to the older time, previous to the breaking up of their extended dominion known as Pelasgia. Strabo says (bk. xiii., ch. iii., sect. 3) "that the Pelasgi were a great nation; history, it is said, furnishes other evidence, for Menecrates of Elea, in his work on the foundation of cities, says the whole of the present Ionian coast, beginning from Mycale and the neighboring islands, was formerly inhabited by the Pelasgi." Again (bk. v., ch. ii., sect. 4), "Almost every one is agreed that the Pelasgi were an ancient race, spread throughout the whole of Greece;" and "many have asserted that the nations of the Epirus are Pelasgic because the dominions of the Pelasgi extended so far." In bk. vii., ch. vii., sect. 10, he says: "The oracle of Dodona, according to Ephorus, was established by Pelasgi, who are said to be the most ancient people that were sovereigns in Greece." Herodotus says (bk. viii., ch. xliv.), "The Athenians, when the Pelasgians possessed that which is now called Hellas, were Pelasgians."

A knowledge of this Pelasgian nation seems to be recorded in Sanskrit literature, which shows considerable information relative to Europe and Western Asia, and a better acquaintance with Western Europe in ancient times than we find in Greek literature. Wilford, in the 8th volume of "Asiatic Researches," describing what old Sanskrit books say of certain sub-dwipas, quotes and comments as follows: "The third [sub] dwipa is Placsha, or the country abounding in fig-trees. It is called Palangshu by the mythologists of Bootan, and included the Lesser Asia, Armenia, and other countries. The name still remains in *Placia*, a town of Mysia, whose inhabitants, with those of Scylace, had a peculiar language (according to Herodotus), which was the same as that spoken by the Pelasgi at Crestone or Crotone in Italy, and by the Pelasgi who lived on the shores of the Hellespont. Thus the appellation Placsha, or Palangshu, appears to be the same with Placia and Pelasgia." We have no means to determine whether the Greek or the Sanskrit word most resembles the old name used by the Pelasgians themselves, but this Sanskrit sub-dwipa, or country of Placsha or Palangshu, formed in the northwestern part of the more ancient Cusha-dwipa, can mean nothing different from that ancient nation of the Pelasgians, which, according to the Greeks, occupied the same territory.

Research has shown very conclusively that the Pelasgians belonged to the Aryan race. Their language seemed "barbarous" to Herodotus, because it differed so much from the dialect he used that he could not understand it. The Greeks, who, it is said, were "insignificant in the earlier times," were undoubtedly a family group of this people, with which many other Pelasgian tribes or communi-tics were finally incorporated. The Pelasgians doubtless represented a mixture of several branches of the Aryan family, and, to some extent, a mixture of races, for in later times there were, in the cities of Asia Minor, Ionians like Thales, who claimed to be "of Phœnician extraction." There was probably a mixture of races in the Phœnician cities of Asia Minor in the earlier periods of their existence. The national organization known as Pelasgia or Placsha could not have lasted many ages. What Hesiod said of the Leleges, an important branch of the Pelasgian people, was doubtless true of the whole; they were "a people gathered from among the nations of the earth." Strabo says: "The Pelasgians were a nation disposed to wander, ready to remove from settlement to settlement, and they experienced both great increase and sudden diminution of their number." It is nowise surprising that these Pelasgians went in such large numbers to Italy and Southwestern Europe, leaving the Greek family predominant in Ionia and Hellas.

Clinton (Fasti Hellenici, vol. i., p. 5–10) says: "A dynasty of Pelasgic chiefs existed in Greece before any other dynasty is heard of in Greek traditions. Excepting in this line, none of the genealogies ascend higher than the ninth, or eighth, or seventh generation before the Trojan War. Danaüs is in the ninth, Deucalion in the eighth, Cadmus in the seventh generation before that epoch. But in the Pelasgic branch of the nation, Phoroneus is in the eighteenth before the Trojan War; the founder of Sicyon is his contemporary; and the Pelasgic chief who planted the Pelasgians in Thessaly is five generations earlier than Deucalion. Inachus, the father of Phoroneus, was the highest term in Grecian history." The lists name nine Pelasgian kings who reigned previous to the time of Danaüs, beginning with Inachus. But none of these lists can be received as accurate in all respects, nor can it be reasonably assumed that Phoroneus, like some of the later kings named in them, reigned at Argos.

The extensive Pelasgian kingdom established by Inachus and Phoroneus must have begun to break up before the time of the expulsion of the Hyksos from Egypt, which appears to have sent several Cushite leaders and colonies into Greece. Clinton seems to favor the chronological estimates which give the year 1875 B.C. as the first year of the reign of Inachus, and places that of Phoroneus twenty-five years later. It is probable that the realm of the king of Argos who was displaced by Danaüs was a fragment only of what had been the kingdom of Phoroneus. According to Eratosthenes, the probable date for Danaüs at Argos is 1400 B.C.; and he gives 1753 B.C. as the date of Phoroneus.

MINOS AND HIS CONQUESTS.

There is neither a record nor a tradition relative to the date of Minos that has sufficient probability to deserve attention. His time may have been older than any date that has been assigned for it. To claim him as a Dorian Greek is improbable and absurd. He and his people were Phœnicians or Arabian Cushites, for Crete was an important part of the territorial possessions of that people. He may have lived at the close of the Sidonian period, when, as a successful revolutionist, he may have driven the Sidonians from the islands and other regions around the Ægean; or he may have been the successful conqueror who broke up the kingdom of the Pelasgians. Tradition connects Minos with the Phœnician race. He was, perhaps, the first ruler who gave Crete a separate and independent government. This appears to be signified by the statement that "the Cretans traced their legal and political institutions to Minos." The oldest traditions celebrate him as a just lawgiver; and one, of later date, makes him a brother of Rhadamanthus; but Ephorus, quoted by Strabo, says: "Minos was an imitator of Rhadamanthus, an ancient personage, and a just and wise man." There is an old tradition that Rhadamanthus was a king of Arabia. Herodotus says: "Minos was a great conqueror, and prospered in all his wars."

According to the uniform testimony of antiquity, Crete, in the time of Minos, was a powerful maritime state; and it is said that he not only suppressed piracy, but also made himself master of the Ægean Islands. Many traditions connect Cretan supremacy with the cities of Asia Minor. For instance, the building of Miletus is assigned to Cretans, while the more correct representation, according to Pausanias, seems to be that a body of Cretans, led by Miletus, took possession of the city and changed its name. "Before their arrival the place was named Anactoria, and more anciently Lelegis." It appears most probable that Minos waged war against the Pelasgians, and that he gained control of all the maritime regions around the Ægean. Like that of the Pelasgians, the empire he established seems to have been of short duration. It must have terminated several centuries previous to the beginning of the Ionian confederacy. An authentic history of Minos and Pelasgia would show us something of the lost history of Phœnicia, and make clearer the "Legendary and Heroic Age of Greece."

THE PHŒNICIAN LANGUAGE AND LITERATURE.

According to the uniform and explicit testimony of Greek and Roman antiquity, the art of alphabetical writing was brought into existence, or first diffused, by the Phœnicians. This art was evidently originated by the Arabian Cushites in ages older than Egypt or Chaldea. It is said, also, that the Phœnicians had an extensive literature. It could not be otherwise with the most enlightened people of antiquity —a people celebrated in all the nations of their time for intellectual activity, and skill in the art of writing; but their literature has perished. Not one book, or fragment of a book, in the Phœnician language, has been preserved.

We have a Greek translation of Hanno's record of his voyage down the west coast of Africa, and translated fragments of a "History," imputed to an ancient Phœnician author named Sanchoniathon, but supposed by some to be a work of the later times, and perhaps a forgery. We have also extracts, preserved in Greek by Josephus and others, from Phœnician histories by writers whose names are given as Dius and Menander. In quoting them, Josephus stated as a fact well known that "there were (in his time) records among the Tyrians that took in the history of many years, and that these were public writings kept with great exactness." Phœnician writers were eminent for works on science, philosophy, and theology. Strabo states that, in his time, they were eminent for culture in astronomy, mathematics, and "night sailing"—that astronomy and arithmetic came from Phœnicia—and adds: "At the present time, these cities afford the best opportunities for acquiring a knowledge of these and of all other branches of philosophy."

It is generally assumed that the Phœnicians spoke Hebrew, or a dialect almost identical with the Hebrew. The correctness of this assumption, however, has not been clearly demonstrated, while modern researches have shown that the earliest language of the country was Hamitic or Cushite. If we suppose, what seems necessary, that the first settlements in Phœnicia were quite as old as Egypt or Chaldea, we must suppose, also, that the ancient Cushite tongue first used there underwent important changes with the progress of time, and was more than once developed in new forms during the thirty centuries previous to the rise of Assyria. We have no specimen—not even an epigraph—to show any form of the language during that period, excepting the words that have been preserved by geography and mythology, which are not Hebrew.

Various epigraphs and a few inscriptions, none of them older than the sixth century before Christ, and most of them several centuries later, furnish the most important linguistic remains of Phœnicia. A great number of medals, coins, and epigraphs have been recovered, chiefly in Cyprus, Crete, Cilicia, Sicily, Malta, Southern Spain, and Northern Africa. These, with an inscription discovered at Marseilles, all belong to the Carthaginian period, when Phœnicia had declined, and when the Cushite speech of the Phœnicians, if not already superseded by a Semitic dialect, must have become so corrupted in its vocabulary, and in some of its forms, by Semitic influence, as no longer to resemble itself.*

* Sir Henry Rawlinson mentions Phœnician inscriptions, found in Assyrian ruins, that are as old as the reign of Tiglath Pileser, 744-726 B.C. He says, "They are among the most ancient specimens we possess of Phœnician writing." See the Journal of the Royal Asiatic Society, New

The first attempt to explore the ruins of Phœnicia was made in 1854, at Sidon (or Saida), by the French. Gold coin of the age of Alexander the Great was found, and, also, an important sepulchral inscription on a royal sarcophagus. This inscription, now in the Museum of the Louvre, tells us that the sarcophagus contained the mortal remains of Ashmunazer, a king of the Sidonians. Ernest Renan, who has had charge of the explorations, thinks it belongs to the sixth century before the Christian Era. In 1860, excavation in the ruins of Phœnicia was renewed by direction of the French government. Several fields of operation were selected; and excavations were made at Ruad or Aradus, Tortosa or Antaradus, Marta or Marathos, Gebal or Byblus, Sidon, Tyre, and a place now called Oum-el-Awamid. Several other inscriptions have been found, and some important remains of ancient Phœnicia have been brought to light.

In the fourth edition of his work on the Semitic languages, Renan gives some account of the linguistic discoveries made at Sidon in 1854–5. He assumes, like others, that the Phœnicians spoke a Semitic language closely allied to the Hebrew, but finds that "a great number of passages in the Phœnician texts cannot be explained by such Hebrew as we are acquainted with," and presumes that, "in the separate development of the two peoples so opposed in character and manners, the two languages, although identical at the beginning, became different." He finally takes this view of the linguistic question:

"There is but little doubt that the Phœnician, independently of its similarity to the Hebrew, had its own forms,

Series, vol. i., p. 243–4. He points out only that the characters are Phœnician.

which gave it an individuality of its own in the bosom of the Semitic family; but Phœnician studies are not yet sufficiently advanced, or, if you will, the Phœnician texts are not yet sufficiently numerous to allow us to determine those forms with precision. The epigraphists, who, by means of readings more or less conjectural, create grammatical forms on their own authority, or combine arbitrarily those which they find in neighboring dialects, use a method that is much too convenient."

It is possible that, in the latest period of their history, when the great ages of their intelligence and enterprise had gone by, the people of the little district called Phœnicia used a Semitic dialect. The language of Chaldea was changed in this way during the Assyrian period. A thick veil of obscurity covers the history of Northern Arabia, Syria, and the neighboring countries of Asia Minor for more than a thousand years previous to the invasions by which all those countries were subjected to the sway of Assyria. Important political and linguistic changes may be supposed of which we have no record. If we allow that the Phœnicians, during the ten centuries previous to the fall of Carthage, used a Semitic dialect, it by no means follows that this was their original tongue. The change did not extend to Northern Africa, where Cushite dialects representing the ancient Phœnician language of that region are still used by the people called Berbers.

There are some facts which appear to show that the language of Phœnicia, at the time of the Assyrian invasions, near the close of the ninth century, had become notably different from that of the Phœnician communities in Africa and Spain. The great emigration from Tyre to Carthage, about the year 813 B.C., seems to have carried to the latter city a language quite different from that of the native Carthaginians. It is very significant that Gesenius and others have found it necessary to recognise two classes of inscriptions in Africa: (1.) Those found at Carthage, which resemble all others that represent the direct influence of Phœnicia in its later ages; and, (2.) The inscriptions found in Africa at a distance from Carthage, with which those discovered in Southern Spain must be classed. The differences in the writing are marked, and the fact suggests that the Tyrians who migrated to Carthage took with them a style of writing, and probably a dialect, different from those carried to Northern Africa and Spain by the Phœnicians in earlier times. It may be added that Sallust (Jugurtha, cap. lxxviii.), mentioning Leptis, a city between the Syrtes founded in later times by the Sidonians, observes that, although its laws and worship remained the same, the language of its inhabitants had been recently changed by their intermarrying with the Numidians (*Ejus civitatis lingua modo conversa connubis Numidarum*).

It is not certain, however, that there was an actual change of language in Phœnicia, previous to the Christian Era, from Cushite to Semitic. There may have been great corruption of the Cushite tongue used there, which filled it with Semitic words and affected many of its forms, and this may explain that Hebrew physiognomy of the Phœnician epigraphs and inscriptions which has engaged so much attention. If we had no knowledge of modern Persian beyond a few brief sentences that could be selected from its literature, it might be suspected of Arabic affinities; and modern Turkish, tested in the same way, might raise a dispute between Persian and Arabic claims that would obscure its actual relation to the Turanian or Scythic family. We cannot reasonably be very positive in regard to the linguistic significance of the few Phœnician words and sentences that have been recovered. As Renan says, "Phœnician studies are not yet sufficiently advanced" to bring the question to a satisfactory settlement.

V.

ARABIAN ORIGIN OF CHALDEA.

HISTORICAL skepticism, standing rigidly by the first Greek Olympiad, and refusing to see beyond that anything but a dark realm of unmeaning fiction, must at times find it difficult to maintain self-respect. It cannot be entirely blind. It must now and then turn to the great past, which is not so completely shut up in darkness as it pretends and tries to believe, with a feeling that its bold denials have nothing in common with the excellency of wisdom. The historical skeptic must at times feel stirring in his mind the painful emotions of doubt when his philosophy stands looking, with the helpless stare of foolishness, at the undeniable facts that confound its reasonings and shame its credulity. For instance, how is it possible for this skepticism to consider honestly what is known of Egypt, India, and Chaldea, and still maintain that nothing can be seen in remote antiquity but fables floating in darkness?

The fact that Chaldea, in very ancient times, was a seat of enlightened civilization, has been admitted and discussed from the beginning of what is usually called the historic period. We see it also in writings older than this period —the Hebrew Scriptures. The discoveries made in that country by the Greeks, after the conquest of Babylon by Alexander, gave the Western world some knowledge of the science and general culture of the Chaldeans. Their civilization became an ascertained fact, which subsequent ages have been constrained to recognise and respect. Chaldean science has furnished one of the most important and generally respected dates of ancient history, while, at the same time, Ancient History, as heretofore written, has talked of Babylon, and described the wonderful Babylon of the comparatively modern time of Nebuchadnezzar, without noticing the much more ancient kingdom of Chaldea, and even without admitting the existence in that part of Asia of any monarchy older than that of the Assyrians.

But Chaldea, so distinctly seen through the ages, and so constantly misunderstood, is at length brought more fully to our observation by recent discoveries in the ruins of some of its older cities. We can see now that the Assyrian empire was preceded by a much older kingdom of Chaldea, which existed during a much longer period of time, and, in the matters of race and language, had little or nothing in common with the Assyrians. This should have been discovered by the Greeks of Alexander's time, when there were books as well as monuments to aid inquiry; but the Greeks failed to make a clear report of this fact, because neither their culture nor their spirit qualified them for such investigations; but they saw and admitted the great extent of Chaldean civilization, and the history of Berosus, written nearly a century later, was never discredited in Greece.

CHALDEAN CIVILIZATION AND LEARNING.

At the present time, some writers, enlightened by the results of recent investigation, and not taking due account of the older Cushites and Aryans, have a tendency to exaggerate or overstate both the originality and the influence of ancient Chaldean civilization. George Rawlinsion, in his valuable work — "The Five Great Monarchies of the Ancient Eastern World" — speaks of it thus: "Chaldea stands as the great parent and inventress of Asiatic civilization, without any rival that can reasonably dispute her claims." This awards to Chaldea what belongs to the Cushites and Aryans. The much more ancient Cushite civilization created Chaldea, and that country was originally, for centuries, merely a province of the great empire of Cusha-dwipa. It appears to have become, at a very early period, one of the most important representatives of the civilization of that pre-historic empire. Beyond this there is nothing to warrant the exaggerated representation of Mr. Rawlinson. Millenniums must be counted between the origin of Chaldea and the beginning of human development in Asia. Nevertheless, the beginning of Chaldea was in very remote times.

Among the discoveries made at Babylon by the Greeks there was one of great importance, which in better hands would have been of far more service to the world; but in their hands it has served as a light to show the extent of Chaldean science. Mr. Rawlinson speaks of it as follows:

"We are informed by Simplicius that Callisthenes, who accompanied Alexander to Babylon, sent to Aristotle from that capital a series of astronomical observations which he had found preserved there, extending back to a period of 1903 years from Alexander's conquest of the city. Epigenes related that these observations were recorded in tablets of baked clay, which is quite in accordance with what we know of the literary habits of the people. They must have extended, according to Simplicius, as far back as 2234 B.C., and would seem to have been commenced and carried on for many centuries by the primitive Chaldean people. We have no means of determining their exact nature or value, as none of them have been preserved to us, but we have every reason to conclude that they were of a real and substantial character. There is nothing fanciful or (so to speak) astrological in the early astronomy of the Babylonians."

The Rev. Dr. Roger Long, a learned and enthusiastic astronomer, who wrote on this subject about the middle of the last century, remarked on the astronomical tablets sent from Babylon as follows: "How much it is to be lamented that the observations of 1903 years, transmitted to Aristotle by Callisthenes from Babylon—a treasure in practical astronomy which was probably inestimable, and of which Aristotle was not acquainted with either the use or the value—did not happen to fall into the hands of his contemporary, Eudoxus!"

The regret he expressed was very natural. Others have felt it, and given it similar expression. It is certainly lamentable that those important records, after being examined, talked of, reported to the world for the entertainment of curiosity and wonder, should be laid away to become rubbish, and perish without farther use. Perhaps unacknowledged uses of those records brought some benefit to the science of astronomy in Greece, where all that was known of this science came from Egypt and the East; but they should have been transcribed and studied; Chaldean books and records should have been explored for additional information; and a complete account of the investigation should have been preserved in the works of Aristotle. Evidence of great proficiency in the science of astronomy is found in the oldest Chaldean ruins, and doubtless similar records of more ancient date could have been found in the older cities and temples of the country. Aristotle, in his *De Cœlo*, lib. ii., cap. xii., describing his observation of an occultation of Mars by the moon, refers to the records sent to him by Callisthenes, in a general way, as follows: "Similar observations have been made for many years on the other planets by the Egyptians and the Babylonians, many of which have come to our knowledge."

Ideler, quoted and indorsed by Humboldt, says: "The Chaldeans knew the mean motions of the moon with an exactness which induced the Greek astronomers to use their calculations for the foundation of a lunar theory." Ptolemy, as may be learned from his Almagest, made use of that portion of the Chaldean observations which extended back to the year 721 B.C., obtained, doubtless, from an independent source. In Alexander's time, Chaldean culture was fast declining; its great era was in the past; the great observatory of the Temple of Belus was in ruins; but there were eminent mathematicians at Babylon, the report of whose names is recorded by Strabo, and there were schools of astronomy. That the Chaldeans had great knowledge of astronomy was admitted by the Greeks and Romans. The Greeks, and through them the Romans, had means of being well informed on this subject. The Greeks evidently had knowledge of Chaldean books and records in which the astronomical attainments of that people were abundantly shown. The campaign of Alexander formed a great epoch in the history of Hellenic culture by opening to it a wider view of the world, and bringing it into closer relations with the civilization and science of the East. The gain was great, and it was to some extent acknowledged.

Diodorus Siculus says the Chaldeans attributed comets to natural causes, and could foretell their reappearance.

He states that their recorded observations of the planets were very ancient and very exact. According to Seneca, their theory of comets was quite as intelligent and correct as that of the moderns. He says they classed them with the planets, or moving stars that had fixed orbits (*cometas in numero stellarum errantium poni à Chaldæis, tenerique cursos eorum.—Natur. Quest.*, lib. vii., 2). Their methods for the use of cycles and other astronomical appliances, in arranging and measuring time, showed a correct and profound knowledge of this science. Astronomy implies mathematics; and the Chaldeans, like every other people of Cushite origin, had great knowledge of mathematics. Much progress in astronomy requires the telescope, or something equivalent; and it seems necessary to believe that the ancients had such aids to eyesight. Layard and others report the discovery of "a lens of considerable power" in the ruins of Babylon.* It certainly would be surprising if necessity, "the mother of invention," had not brought such aids to the astronomers of ancient Arabia, Chaldea, Egypt, and India. I have already shown that the genius which made such attainments in astronomy must have been able to contrive whatever instruments were necessary to progress in the science. Thought and invention did not begin with the moderns. It was then quite as possible as now to see and devise what was necessary.

Even the Greeks and Romans, with lower attainments

---

* Layard says this lens was found, with two glass bowls, in a chamber of the ruin called Nimroud. It is plano-convex, an inch and a half in diameter and nine tenths of an inch thick. It gives a focus at 4½ inches from the plane side. Sir David Brewster says, "It was intended to be used as a lens, either for magnifying, or condensing the rays of the sun." See Layard's "Nineveh and Babylon," p. 16, 17, chap. viii.

in astronomy, had aids to eyesight. They are mentioned in *De Placitis Phil.*, lib. iii, c. v., attributed to Plutarch; also in his *Vita Marcelli;* and by Pliny, *Hist. Natur.*, lib. xxxvii, c. v., where he says that, in his time, artificers used emeralds to assist the eye, and that they were made concave the better to collect the visual rays (*smaragdi eidem plerumque et concavi ut visum colligant*). He adds that Nero used such glasses when he watched the fights of the gladiators. There is frequent mention of concave and convex glasses used for optical purposes, and they evidently came from Egypt and the East. Iamblichus tells us, in his life of Pythagoras, that Pythagoras sought to contrive instruments that should aid hearing as effectually as "optic glasses"* and other contrivances aided sight. Plutarch speaks of mathematical instruments used by Archimedes "to manifest to the eye the largeness of the sun." Pythagoras and Archimedes both studied in Egypt and Phœnicia, and probably in Chaldea; for Pythagoras, who lived in the sixth century before Christ, is said to have visited "Egypt and many countries of the East" in pursuit of knowledge; and Archimedes, who lived after the time of Alexander, spent much time in Egypt, and visited "many other countries." It appears that, in the time of Pythagoras, "optic glasses," contrived to increase the power of vision, were so common as not to be regarded as objects of curiosity, and there can be no reasonable doubt that they were first invented and used by the great men who created that profound science of astronomy for which people of Cushite origin were everywhere so pre-eminently distinguished, and which was so intimately connected with their religion.

* νὴ Δία—διὰ διόπτρας.

HISTORY OF CHALDEA BY BEROSUS.

The Greeks failed to give the world such an account of Chaldea as its importance required. Much, however, may have been written on this subject which has not come down to us. Callisthenes wrote a history of Alexander's great campaign against the Persians, which has perished entirely; and there were narratives by Megasthenes, Nearchus, and Aristobulus. Others undoubtedly wrote something on the countries he occupied, but nothing in the literature of the ancients, as we have it, indicates that any Greek undertook to write a history of Babylon and of the country to which it belonged, although much is found in some portions of that literature relating to the Babylonians.

Nevertheless, nearly 300 years before Christ, a regular history of Chaldea, in nine books, was written in Greek by Berosus, a Chaldean priest of Belus. The materials for this work were supplied by archives then existing in the temple of Belus at Babylon. Like many other works of the highest importance, it was allowed to perish. What we know of its contents is found in extracts from it, copied and thus preserved by writers whose works still exist.

Berosus gave the oldest traditions of the Chaldeans concerning the origin of the human race, described Chaldea and its people, related their history, and furnished a list of Chaldean sovereigns down to the beginning of the Assyrian empire, about the year 1273 B.C. Its chief feature was a history of the kingdom of Chaldea previous to the time of that empire—a kingdom that may have counted more millenniums than the Assyrian empire counted centuries. Of course this work could not be properly accepted by any modern system of chronology; therefore it has been set aside as of no account by those schemes of ancient history which modern chronology has indorsed as orthodox; but it was not discredited either by the Greeks for whom it was written, or by the early Christian fathers, who gave it much attention; and modern exploration in the old ruins of Chaldea has confirmed its statements as substantially correct.

Fragments of this work of Berosus have come down to us in the writings of Josephus, Eusebius, Syncellus, and several of the Christian fathers. It does not appear that he gave a particular and complete account of the early ages of the Chaldean kingdom, nor is it certain that his list of the kings goes back to its earliest times. It may be that his enumeration of actual sovereigns begins with that great epoch in the history of the country when the whole was first united under one government. Nevertheless, the list, as it stands, is quite too long to please unreformed chronologists. The extract from his history in which it is found describes the long cyclical antediluvian ages, in which ten fabulous kings reigned 432,000 years. Then, coming to what he considered history, it enumerates 103 kings of Chaldea, who reigned successively from the time when the list begins to the rise of the Assyrian empire. Berosus begins with a dynasty of 86 kings, of whose time he knew nothing. He gave the names of these kings, which are lost. He had no history or chronology of their time, therefore he subjected it to a cyclical calculation, which gives it more a look of myth than of history. In the religious, political, and linguistic changes of the country, the records of the first dynasties had been lost. They had suffered the usual waste of time. The extracts from his work, in passing through the hands of many copyists, have necessarily become more or less imperfect. His list, as we have it, is as follows:

First,	86 Chaldean kings—history and time mythical.		
Second,	8 Median	"	during 224 years.
Third,	11	"	
Fourth,	49 Chaldean	"	
Fifth,	9 Arabian	"	during 245 years.

The rulers of the Assyrian Empire were next added as a sixth dynasty, and the history was brought down to the capture of Babylon by Cyrus the Great. The blank spaces in the list are doubtless the result of careless copying, and of imperfections created in manuscripts by use and time. A great amount of resolute ingenuity has been employed to bring Berosus into harmony with the popular chronology, especially since archæology has begun to remove the obscurity in which ancient Chaldea has been shrouded. Sir Henry Rawlinson, without having himself originated devices for this purpose, has embarrassed his own investigations by using some of the cleverest and boldest of those contrived by others. Admitting freely that " each succeeding discovery has tended to authenticate the chronology of Berosus, and to throw discredit upon the tales of Ctesias and his followers," he has nevertheless looked with too much favor on the efforts of those contrivers of "chronological harmony" who have treated Berosus somewhat as Ctesias treated the facts of Mesopotamian history. He gives prominence to an "emendation" proposed in a pamphlet by Dr. Brandis, entitled "*Rerum Assyriarum Tempora Emendata,*" and describes it as "a most ingenious suggestion of German criticism."

The purpose of this brilliant ingenuity is to make the old kingdom of Chaldea begin with the year 2234 B.C.;

therefore its first step is to declare, in the boldest way, that the first part of the list of Berosus is "fabulous." The first 86 kings are struck out with the best air of historical skepticism, although nothing requires it or justifies it save the "necessities of chronological harmony." It is the same unscrupulous method that was employed against the ancient history of Egypt. Next, the Median dynasty is "left out of consideration," as representing a Magian race who ruled in Babylon before the Cushites went there—a necessary but most unwarranted hypothesis. To these "emendations" two others are added; the next dynasty in order is described as "Chaldean" (which may be correct), and its time is given as 258 years; and a number is devised for the dynasty of 49 Chaldean kings, which makes the whole time of its duration no more than 458 years—a desperate manœuvre, which secures the date required while it insults common sense. The scheme of Chaldean history developed by this operation would amaze Berosus. It is as follows:

First, 11 (Chaldean kings), (258) years, from 2234 to 1976.
Second, 49 " " (458) years, from 1976 to 1518.
Third, 9 Arabian " (245) years, from 1518 to 1273.

The hundred and sixty-three kings of Berosus are reduced to sixty-nine, the popular chronology is rescued temporarily from a great embarrassment, and "ingenuity" wears a crown of laurel. A scheme very similar to this is quoted in George Rawlinson's "Five Monarchies" as "Gutschmidt's revision." In each case it is admitted that astronomical calculations began at Babylon in the year 2234 B.C. It follows, of course, that the great Chaldean culture, the temple of Belus with its observatory, the city of Babylon, and the organized schools of Chaldean science, were all in existence at the very beginning of the Cushite occupation of the country, which is incredible. Such attempts to establish a compromise between Berosus and false chronology must necessarily be failures. They are false and mischievous in all respects.

The hypothesis that the country was occupied by a "Magian" or Aryan race before the Cushites went there is explicitly contradicted not only by Berosus, but also by the testimony of records disentombed from the ruins, which show incontestably that the race which first occupied Lower Mesopotamia and introduced civilization was neither Aryan nor Semitic. Rawlinson himself admits this without qualification. That "Median dynasty" was preceded by long ages of Chaldean supremacy and culture, and, according to Berosus, whose testimony cannot now be invalidated, by a line of 86 Chaldean kings. Those who are not frightened by such amounts of past time as this implies will not be in haste to discredit the testimony by which it is supported. Exploration has found some of the older cities of the country, but the oldest structures and first foundations of those cities were probably long since beyond its reach. We cannot doubt that the discovery of ancient Chaldea will be made still more complete by farther exploration in the ruins and among the records already recovered.

That "ingenious suggestion of German criticism" (not the most intelligent German criticism, however) invents one number which is in itself too unreasonable to win favor. According to its revision, the 40 Chaldean kings reigned only 458 years, which is too improbable for belief. Rawlinson feels this, and objects that it makes the 40 kings reign less than ten years each, an average which he pro-

nounces "quite impossible in a settled monarchy like the
Chaldean." Nevertheless, instead of censuring this reck-
less invention of "ingenuity," he proposes to reduce the
number of the kings! and that, too, without the slightest
warrant for doing so, beyond the desire to reach a given
conclusion. Writers of ancient history have usually paid
great respect to the year 2234 B.C. The astronomical record found at Babylon began with that date; but this
was not the beginning of Chaldean history, and any attempt to make it so is preposterous. Rawlinson himself
mentions a Cushite or Hamitic inscription, found in Susiana, in which there is a date that goes back nearly to the
year 3200 before Christ.

CHALDEAN ANTIQUITIES AND TRADITIONS.

Ancient Chaldea consisted of the lower part of the rich
alluvial region between the Euphrates and the Tigris, although it seems to have included, or to have been very intimately connected with, other territory on the opposite
sides of both rivers, especially the important district
known as Susiana. The name Chaldea comes to us from
Semitic languages—the Aramaic and the Hebrew—through
the Greek. In their inscriptions the people are called Akkadim. Whether described as Cushites or as Hamites in
linguistic reports on the inscriptions, the people represented by the Chaldean ruins were all of the same race. The
uniform statement is that "all the kings whose monuments
are found in ancient Chaldea used the same language and
the same power of writing, professed the same religion, and
followed the same traditions." There are traces of intercourse with other races; Aryan, Semitic, and Turanian elements are noticed; and, in later ages of the kingdom,

there seems to have been a remarkable mixture of races at Babylon. There appears to be some evidence that the Cushite dialect of Susiana was a little different from that of Lower Chaldea, and, probably, other differences of dialect will come clearly to light as the investigation goes forward.*

Berosus stated, as an old tradition of the Chaldean people, that their ancestors and their civilization came originally from a region on the Erythræan Sea, which is confirmed by discoveries in the ruins. By the Erythræan Sea the ancients usually meant the waters of the Indian Ocean and Persian Gulf. He gives, also, an old Chaldean tradition, which seems to preserve a recollection of the first impression made upon the rude aboriginal inhabitants of the country by the beginning of their intercourse with the maritime people of Arabia who gave them civilization. In our day, some of the South Sea Islanders supposed the first ship they saw to be a living creature. This tradition, as stated by Berosus and quoted by Alexander Polyhistor, is as follows:

"In the first year there appeared from that part of the Erythræan Sea which borders on Babylonia an animal destitute of reason, by name Oannes, whose whole body was that of a fish; and under the fish's head he had *another*

---

* The desire to make the Turanian the most ancient ethnic element in Western Asia comes from the wholly untenable theory that Chinese is the oldest language in the world; that Turanian speech was the first development from it; and that the Cushite, Semitic, and Aryan languages were developed from the Turanian. This is romance, not science. Meanwhile, the most ancient ethnic element is so clearly Cushite, that these theorists resort to the device of classing the Hamits or Cushite group of tongues as a branch of the Turanian family.

head, with feet also similar to those of a man. His voice, too, and language, were articulate and human; and a representation of him is preserved even unto this day. This being was accustomed to pass the day among men; and he gave them an insight into letters and sciences, and arts of every kind. He taught them to construct cities, to found temples, to frame laws, and explained to them the principles of geometrical knowledge. He made them distinguish the seeds of the earth, and showed them how to collect the fruits; in short, he instructed them in everything that could tend to soften their manners and humanize their lives. And, when the sun was set, this being, Oannes, retired again to the sea, and passed the night in the deep."

This is plainly a mythical reference to the first remembered appearance in the Euphrates of ships from a civilized country, and of the first introduction into Chaldea of the arts of civilized life. The ship, Oannes, described as a wonderful being and transformed into a sea-god, appeared in that part of the Erythræan Sea which borders on Babylonia; that is to say, it came from the coast of Arabia. The enlightened Cushites or Ethiopians of Arabia, the maritime adventurers, the princely merchants, the enlightened masters in science, the wonderful colonizers of remote antiquity, brought civilization to the barbarous Semites of Mesopotamia. They came in, established colonies, and occupied the whole country, giving it their religion, their science, their manners and customs, and all their arts of civilized life. Even their language was made supreme, excluding the Semitic dialects everywhere, excepting perhaps at the West, and in that part of the country afterwards known as Assyria.

THE CHALDEAN RUINS AND INSCRIPTIONS.

Lower Chaldea, now a desolation thinly inhabited by nomadic tribes, was formerly the most populous region on the globe. William Kennett Loftus, in his record of "Travels and Researches in Chaldea," makes this statement: "In no other part of Babylonia is there such astonishing proof of ancient civilization and denseness of population. Some lofty pile is generally visible to mark the site of a once important city, while numerous little spots, covered with broken pottery, point to the former existence of villages and of a rural population." George Rawlinson names the ruins of twenty-five great cities within that small territory, besides the cities of Ur, Nipur, Larsa, Erech, and Babylon, whose ruins have been explored. He says, in the first volume of his "Ancient Monarchies of the Eastern World," "Farther investigation will probably add largely to this catalogue, for many parts of Babylonia are still, to some extent, unexplored. This is especially true of the tract between the Shat-el-Hie and the Lower Tigris, a district which, according to geographers, abounds with ruins."

The most ancient ruins in Chaldea are those towards the south, such as Ur, Erech, and Senkereh; and here, in the neighborhood of the Persian Gulf (which at that time reached inland nearly 150 miles farther than at present), the explorers place the primitive seat of Chaldean civilization. Mr. Loftus gives the following account of the present condition of the country: "The ruins of Warka (the same as Erech) are in latitude 30° 10' N., and longitude 45° 40' E., and are four miles distant from the nearest point on the eastern bank of the Euphrates. An elevated tract of desert soil, ten miles in breadth, is slightly raised above a series of inundations and marshes caused by the annual overflow of the Euphrates. Upon this are situated not only the ruins of Warka, but also of Senkereh, Tel Ede, and Hammam—all unapproachable except from November to March, when the river assumes its lowest level." How different from what Chaldea was in the great days of her glory, when populous and flourishing cities stood where we now find these almost inaccessible ruins! Neither the soil nor the atmosphere is the same.

The ruins of four of the older Chaldean cities have been explored, to some extent, with very notable results. These four are, 1. Mugheir, the same as Hur, or "Ur of the Chaldees," Mugheir being the modern Semitic name of the ruins; 2. Larsa (now called Senkereh), the same as Ellarsa of the Bible; 3. Warka or Hurruk, the same as Erech or Orech of the Hebrews; 4. Niffer, or Nipur, or Nopher, as the Talmud has it. The Talmudists conjecture, without good reason, that this last-named city was the same as Calneh of the Hebrew Scriptures. We may, with much better reason, suppose it to be the Βαβη of Ptolemy, and the Babel of the tenth chapter of Genesis. Sir Henry Rawlinson says of it, "This city had originally the name of the god Belus, and is, perhaps, the Βαβη of Ptolemy." He thinks "the Greek traditions of the foundation of a great city on the Euphrates by Belus refer to this place rather than to Babylon."

Reports of these investigations have appeared from time to time in the various European journals devoted to Oriental and archæological subjects, and in the publications of English, French, and German scholars engaged in such inquiries, among which none are more important than those of Sir Henry Rawlinson. A good summary of what has been found in the ruins of the Chaldean cities I have named is given in the first volume of George Rawlinson's "Five Great Monarchies of the Ancient Eastern World." Among the important facts discovered are the following:

1. The ruins furnish what appears to be conclusive evidence that civilization was brought to Chaldea from Ethiopia—that is to say, from Arabia. In the inscriptions, the two countries are connected in such a way as makes any other conclusion impossible. Their vernacular name for Ethiopia is Mirukh, and its maritime enterprise is very distinctly recognised.

2. The oldest city and first capital of the country was Ur. It seems to be understood that the settlement of the country began with the building of Ur. At a later period, Erech was for a time the royal city; but the great city of the country, after it became independent and before the rise of Babylon, was the city which, in Semitic speech, is called Nipur and Niffer, and which tradition describes as the city of Belus, or the most ancient Babylon.

3. It is shown, as already mentioned, that the language of ancient Chaldea, found abundantly in these ruins, and that found in the ruins of Southern Arabia, belong to the same family, and that they are radically different from the Semitic tongue of the Assyrian empire. This is the report of all the best investigators who have studied the inscriptions. A Scythian or Turanian theory was started, which made Nimrod a Turanian, and sought support in the Mesopotamian inscriptions. It was never anything more than a very improbable theory.

4. As already stated, the ruins confirm Berosus by showing that Chaldea was a cultivated and flourishing nation, governed by kings, long previous to the time when the city

known to us as Babylon rose to eminence and became the seat of empire. During that long time there were several great political epochs in the history of the country, representing important dynastic changes, and several transfers of the seat of government from one city to another. Such epochs in Chaldean history are indicated by the list of Berosus.

The history of Berosus is confirmed and made authentic beyond reasonable question. There was never anything to discredit his account of Chaldea save the natural tendency of false chronology to discredit literary records, and even the testimony of contemporaneous monuments, which cannot easily submit to its revisions.

The oldest Chaldean cities were in the neighborhood of the Persian Gulf. Ur, or Hur, represented as the first city built by the colonizing Cushites, was situated at the mouth of the Euphrates, with the open sea before it. Its ruins are now at a long distance from both. Sir Henry Rawlinson, in the 27th volume of the Royal Geographical Society's Journal, says: "When Chaldea was first colonized, or, at any rate, when the seat of empire was first established there, the emporium of trade seems to have been at Ur of the Chaldees, which is now 150 miles from the sea, the Persian Gulf having retired nearly that distance before the sediment brought down by the Euphrates and Tigris." A little reflection on the vast period of time required to effect a geological change so great as this will enable us to see to what a remote age in the deeps of antiquity we must go to find the beginning of civilization in the Mesopotamian Valley. No discoveries made in the old ruins of the East are more interesting or more important than those which unveil to us the early history of Chaldea.

THE ORIGIN OF CHALDEA.

The linguistic and archaic obscurities in which some of the questions raised by these discoveries are buried, shut them out from general discussion. Only those scholars whose peculiar acquirements remove this difficulty, and whose profound linguistic studies of the cuneiform records have made them familiar with the intricacies in which these questions are involved, are qualified to speak on the subject with any degree of authority. All the best qualified investigators agree that the evidence already obtained shows conclusively the Cushite or Ethiopian origin of Chaldea. A note which Sir Henry Rawlinson appends to his essay on the "Early History of Babylonia" speaks on this point as follows:

"All the traditions of Babylonia and Assyria point to a connection, in very early times, between Ethiopia, Southern Arabia, and the cities on the Lower Euphrates. In the geographical lists, the names of *Mirukh* (Ethiopia) and Makkan are thus always conjoined with those of Hur and Akkad. The building of Hur, again, is the earliest historical event of which the Babylonians seem to have had any cognizance; but the inscriptions constantly refer to a tradition of the primeval leader by whom the Cushites were first settled on the Euphrates, and one of the names of this leader is connected with Ethiopia in a way that can hardly be accidental."

He finds, also, that the early Chaldeans were largely devoted to maritime pursuits in close connection with the Ethiopians. He says, in the volume of the Royal Geographical Society's Journal already quoted, "The ships of Ur, at any rate, are constantly mentioned (by the inscriptions) in connection with those of Ethiopia; and there is abundant evidence, among the remains of the city (Ur), of the worship of the sea-god, which alone would indicate a maritime people, and which, moreover, is in exact accordance with the early traditions preserved by Berosus."

Is it not absurd to seek at Meroë, or anywhere else on the Upper Nile, for the maritime Ethiopia of these Chaldean inscriptions? If every competent investigator would allow himself to see and comprehend the country which the ancients designated as Ethiopia and the Land of Cush, there would be no failure to recognise Arabia as the mother country of Chaldea; and there would be a more intelligent appreciation of the large amount of ancient tradition which brings the Cushites into that part of Asia, and sometimes describes it as a part of Ethiopia. It was Ethiopian in race, language, and civilization, and constituted a portion of the wide-spread territory occupied by the Cushites, "from the extremity of the east to the extremity of the west."

Mr. Loftus states the common opinion of investigators as follows: "Recent researches made in the interpretation of the cuneiform inscriptions have led to the belief that, in the earliest ages previous to the historic period which began with Nimrod, the region north of the Persian Gulf was inhabited by a Semitic race, which was gradually dispossessed by a powerful stream of invasion or colonization from the south. The Hamitic (or Cushite) element which prevails in the most ancient cuneiform records throughout Babylonia and Susiana points to Ethiopia as the country of these new settlers." The evidence of an immigration from the south seems unequivocal, and the immigrants are everywhere called Akkadim; the terms Akkad and Akkadim are constantly used as ethnic designations, and Hebrew knowledge of them appears in the Akkad or Accad of Genesis. Tradition says these settlers came first in ships, and made their first settlements at Ur and Erech; but Mr. Loftus, having no just comprehension of Arabia, and following the "common opinion," brings the Cushite immigrants from the Upper Nile Valley, across both the Red Sea and the Arabian Peninsula.

THE CUSHITE LANGUAGE IN CHALDEA.

The ruins found in Southern Arabia belong chiefly to the period of the Himyaric and Sabean nationalities, which were long subsequent to the great ages of Cushite supremacy. Some of them are very old, but they have not been so carefully explored as their importance demands. The inscriptions secured by the researches of Wellsted, Arnaud, Fresnel, and others, have furnished important materials for linguistic investigation—important especially in connection with studies of the cuneiform records. Among those who have given them careful examination are Jules Oppert and other French Orientalists, who express in strong terms the result indicated by Sir Henry Rawlinson. They see clearly that the language of the Arabian inscriptions is genetically related to that of ancient Chaldea. Modern dialects of this old Cushite tongue are still spoken in some districts of Arabia and Eastern Africa. Fresnel is sure, on philological grounds alone, that the original Cushites of Chaldea were immigrants from Arabia.

These investigations have interfered with Ernest Renan's theory of the Semitic languages and people, as set forth in the first edition of his "*Histoire Générale des Langues Sémitiques.*" At first he did not appear to recognise the existence of a family of Ethiopian or Cushite languages. In this omission, however, he was not original. This family of languages has not stood so directly in the path of inquiry as to command immediate attention. Renan had not studied carefully the linguistic peculiarities of every branch of the people whom he classed as Semites. Like many others, he had failed to recognise the profound difference between the old Cushite race of Arabia, so celebrated in the olden time, and the modern Semitic Arabs—a difference not likely to be forgotten when once fairly observed.

In the preface to his second edition he had become aware of this mistake; probably Oppert's Chaldean investigations had now effectually engaged his attention; at any rate, he noticed the result of these inquiries, and promised his readers an essay, in which he would "attempt to establish that it is necessary to admit into the history of the civilization of the ancient world a third element, which is neither Semitic nor Aryan, and which may be called Ethiopian or Cushite." It was quite important to notice Hamlet's part in the play; but others before him had failed to discover and describe it. In a revision of the text of his book he referred to the explorations and studies of Arnaud, Fresnel, and Oppert, and said: "If these hypotheses shall be confirmed by a more complete investigation, it will become necessary to establish a group of *Semitico-Cushite* languages, including the Himyaric, the Gheez, the Mahri, and the language of the Babylonian inscriptions."

Semitico-Cushite! something might be said in behalf of *Turano-Cushite;* and even *Aryo-Cushite* might find supporters. Renan and others will probably advance beyond all these prefixes; and when they fully discover the great race that did more than any other to originate and spread the civilization of the ancient world, they will probably drop them all, and include the Egyptian, the Berber, and some of the dialects of Southeastern Africa, with the others named, in a family group of Cushite tongues—a family great in the past, but of which we now have only the perishing remains.

POLITICAL CHANGES IN ANCIENT CHALDEA.

In the very long period that must be allowed for the duration of Chaldea, there were great epochs of political change and reconstruction of which no history can be written. These epochs are indicated in the list of Berosus by the changes of dynasty, made sometimes by successful invasion from abroad and sometimes by internal revolution, and in the cuneiform records by evidence of changes of dynasty and of transfers of the seat of government from one city to another. Should an average of only 20 years each be allowed to the 163 kings who reigned in Chaldea previous to 1273 B.C., excepting the Median and Arabian dynasties, whose time is given, this would carry back the beginning of the Chaldean kingdom of their time to the year 4062 B.C. It would make Chaldea as old as Egypt, which cannot be deemed improbable. Great epochs of political change would necessarily occur during so long a period of time.

The first 86 kings doubtless represent several dynasties; but the past was already hazy around them in the time of Berosus, and had been so, probably, during many ages previous to his time. The succeeding "Median" dynasty represents a successful invasion from abroad, not, however, by the "Medes" of our ancient histories, who belong to a much later period. There have been various conjectures concerning this word "Median," which may be a corrupt form of the designation used by Berosus. Some have supposed these invaders were "Magians" of the Aryan race, from the north; with a greater show of probability, I may suppose they came from the south (led by the celebrated Arabian king Zohak), where "Madian" or "Midian" was the name of an important branch of the Arabian Cushites. Did the prince and people of Susiana take the lead in expelling this "Median" dynasty? and was Susiana represented by the next dynasty of eleven kings, which stands in the list of Berosus, as we have it, without national designation?

The region known as Susiana was politically connected with Chaldea from the earliest times. It was occupied by people of the same race, who, in the course of time, may have developed a Susianian dialect of the common language. This region was probably included in the district first colonized by the Cushites. Its ruins are of great antiquity, and show plainly their Cushite origin. Old inscriptions have been found in the ruins of Susa. Sir Henry Rawlinson mentions some of them, giving the dates according to the chronology he follows. He says: "The inscriptions of Susa, for the most part, belong to the 8th century B.C., the kings named in the legends being contemporary with Sennacherib, Sargon, and their immediate predecessors. There is, however, what appears to be a date in the long inscription of *Sutruk Nakhunta* on the broken obelisk at Susa—two sets of numbers occurring, which may be read as 2445 and 2455. If these numbers are really chronological, the era referred to will be nearly 3200 years B.C."

The political changes that made Erech a royal city, and finally transferred the seat of government to Nipur, must have occurred during the time of the first 80 kings. The inscriptions show that Erech was the capital during two reigns—that of a king whose name is given as *Sin-shada*, and that of his father. There seems to have been a *Sin* dynasty; perhaps all the kings belonging to it reigned at Erech. Probably the kingdom of Chaldea, like most other Cushite nationalities, was a union of separate municipalities, each having a distinct local government and prince of its own, as it is now in the Arabian kingdom of Oman. Occasionally one of these local princes, elevated to commanding importance by his genius, or by some favoring condition of public affairs, may have taken supreme power into his own hands.

One thing is shown clearly by the records explored. Nipur, the great city which had originally the name of Belus, and which Greek tradition frequently confounded with the later city of Babylon, was the capital of the kingdom during the most important period of its existence, and perhaps the longest. Sir Henry Rawlinson thinks the Tower of Babel was at Nipur, where, at the present time, "the remains of a brick tower rise, in a conical form, seventy feet above the plain." He connects Nimrod with this city, and says one of its ancient names was *Tel-Anu*. Did Nimrod cause or direct the political changes that transferred the seat of government to Nipur? The inscriptions have not yet answered the question, and there is no authentic history to give us the desired information. Let me repeat, however, that all this was long ages previous to the time when the later Babylon became the royal city.

Nimrod, under various names, is celebrated in Cushite and Semitic traditions in such a manner as makes it certain that he was one of the greatest personages in early

Chaldean history. All we know of him with certainty is what is told us in the tenth chapter of Genesis. There we learn that he was a personage who rose to great reputation, which became proverbial: "Even as Nimrod, the mighty hunter before the Lord." He is set before us as a great sovereign; and the record says, "The beginning of his kingdom was Babel, and Erech, and Accad, and Calneh." It is not said that he built these cities, but that they were "the beginning of his kingdom." It is usually assumed that Babel here means Babylon. This, however, is conjecture, founded on supposed identity of names. The natural inference from this biblical record, taken in connection with what has been learned from the inscriptions, is that Nimrod caused a political reconstruction of Chaldea; that he began the work by taking control of the cities named; and that he won supreme authority throughout the whole country. Another verse in the same chapter intimates that he showed special favor to the Semitic portion of his subjects, and gathered them together in cities. "Out of that land went forth Asshur," or, as the marginal reading has it, "he went forth into Asshur," and built the Semitic cities—Nineveh, Rehoboth, Calah, and Resen. This was the beginning of Assyria. It may be that Nimrod was the first king who reigned at Nipur. Some identify him with Belus, reasoning thus: "As Bel (Baal), signifying *lord*, may have been the general title of the earliest kings, so Belus and Nimrod can easily have been one person."

THE YEAR 2234 B.C.

I have already called attention to the great respect paid to the year 2234 B.C. by our writers of ancient history. It may be added here that this date has had a singular, if not unaccountable influence on the minds of some learned and eminent archæologists who have sought to comprehend and explain the Chaldean and Assyrian antiquities. Their aim has been to make everything in that part of Asia begin with this year 2234 B.C. That particular record of astronomical observations made in Chaldea, found at Babylon, and sent by Callisthenes to Aristotle, began with this date, therefore Chaldean history must begin with it; no monument of that land must be more ancient; the dynastic list of Berosus must not be allowed to reach farther back into the past; we must reverently accept this date as the chronological limit of human inquiry, beyond which there is nothing but thick darkness haunted by a few shapeless phantoms of fable. No hypothetical scheme of the ancient history of Chaldea, that seeks honestly to comprehend the monuments and the list of Berosus, can be liable to such absurdities as have been occasioned by this infatuation in regard to the year 2234 B.C.

If Callisthenes could have discovered and sent to Greece the records of astronomical observations made at the city of Belus, the more ancient Babylon of Greek tradition (which in its ruins is called Nipur), the royal city of Chaldea in the great ages of Chaldean civilization, our studies of antiquity would not be troubled by this infatuation. The city we know as Babylon was not important until the closing period of the old kingdom of Chaldea. It is assumed as probable, rather than shown clearly, that it was, even in this period, a royal city; therefore to assume that the earliest date we have of the beginning of astronomical observations in that city is the oldest date in the history of the country is preposterous beyond expression. The great city of that old kingdom, the grand metropolis in the ages that saw the highest condition of its civilization, learning, and general culture, must have been the city whose ruins are called Nipur; and the most brilliant age of this city must have been as far beyond the year 2234 B.C. as this date is beyond the first Greek Olympiad; and yet the beginning of astronomical observations at Nipur itself was necessarily later than the beginning of the kingdom, for this was not one of the oldest cities of Chaldea. As a royal city of the country, it seems to have been preceded by at least two others—Ur and Erech.

The Greeks tell us what the later Babylon was in the time of Nebuchadnezzar. They describe its marvelous extent and magnificence when captured by Cyrus the Great. The Hebrew Scriptures describe the city. But Nebuchadnezzar was one monarch of a brief and troubled dynasty of kings, whose whole time was only 87 years, and the first of whom did not appear until the close of the Assyrian period, about 650 years after the old kingdom of Chaldea had ceased to exist. Neither history, nor anything discovered in the ruins, tells us when this city of Babylon was founded. Stephanus of Byzantium, in his work on celebrated cities, indorsed the following statement of an older writer: "Babylon was not built by Semiramis, as Herodotus says, but by Babilon, a wise man, and the son (or descendant) of the all-wise Belus; and this Babilon lived, as Herinnius states, 2000 years before Semiramis." I cite this statement on account of its significance in one respect, which should not escape attention. It assumes, as a matter of course, that the great antiquity of civilization in Chaldea was generally recognised by those to whom it was addressed. For the rest, as Semiramis was supposed to have lived about 1250 years before Christ, this old record, if it should be accepted as authentic, would show that Babylon was founded about 3250 B.C.

Could we have a complete copy of the Chaldean History of Berosus, it would probably make clear many things now involved in obscurity. It might enable us to see when, and under what circumstances, Nipur, the ancient city of Belus, was made the seat of government. It could hardly fail to explain the circumstances that interrupted the Chaldean succession, and brought in the dynasty called "Median." We might or might not learn from that history that the more modern Babylon became the capital at the beginning of the dynasty of 49 kings, not less than 2500 B.C. Meanwhile there is not a trace of evidence to show or suggest that any king of Chaldea began to reign in the year 2234 B.C., or that anything Chaldean began with this date save the records found by Callisthenes.

CONCERNING AN OLD CHALDEAN TEMPLE.

One fact revealed by the cuneiform inscriptions awakens some sense of the great antiquity of Chaldea. The most ancient royal name discovered is given doubtfully, as Urukh, Urkham, or Orchamus. The inscriptions celebrate this king as a worshipper of Beltis and a builder of temples. In the ages previous to his reign, when the great temple of Erech was built, that temple was consecrated to the worship of *Ana*, and *Ana* was the presiding deity of the city. But time works changes. At length the worship of *Ana* in that temple was superseded by that of Beltis, the temple still retaining, as one of its names, the appellation Bit-Ana, house of Ana, and in later inscriptions Beltis being called "the Lady of Bit-Ana," which continued to show its original consecration. There is nothing to give us the date of Urukh's reign; but he was one of the great kings of Ur, it is said, and therefore belonged to an early period of the kingdom. That change in the temple worship at Erech must have taken place in his time, or at some period previous to his reign; but it could not take place during the first day, or year, or century after the temple was built. Many ages of experience, thought, and change were undoubtedly required to make such a religious revolution possible; therefore it shows plainly that a very long period in the history of Chaldea must have passed previous to the beginning of Urukh's reign. In connection with what the ruins say of this king, two lines are quoted from Ovid's Metamorphoses (iv., 212, 213), in which an Orchamus is described as the seventh successor of Belus:

"Rexit Achæmenias urbes pater Orchamus, isque
Septimus a prisci numeratur origine Beli."

Is this a confused reference to the Orchamus, or Urukh, whose name and something of whose history is shown us in the old ruins of Chaldea? Very doubtful. Ovid's Metamorphoses are not history, and it may be added that very queer results must have followed any attempts of that author to write history; but Ovid had some rare learning, and in early life he traveled in Asia. In his time there were Asiatics, and some centuries previous to his time there were Greeks, who could have collected ample materials for a correct outline of the history of Chaldea previous to the rise of Babylon. The annals and archives of the old kingdom were, to a great extent, still preserved in existing temples. In the third century before Christ, the temple of Belus at Babylon, partly in ruins, furnished such materials for that work of Berosus, which the Greeks and Romans allowed to perish.

ASSYRIA AND THE SEMITIC RACE.

The Assyrian empire began with the expulsion of the Arabian dynasty from Babylon in 1273 B.C. A small kingdom of Assyria existed previous to this time. An Assyrian canon, found by Sir Henry Rawlinson, and also the canon of Ptolemy, carries back the history of Assyria to the year 1650 B.C., which is 132 years previous to the Arabian invasion. The obvious explanation is, that "Assyria as an independent kingdom was the natural antecedent of Assyria as an imperial power." In the earlier ages, Assyria was a province of the old Chaldean empire, governed by satraps, four of whose legends, bearing their names and titles, have been found at *Kileh-Shergat*. The "Arabian" dynasty doubtless represented princes of one of the separate kingdoms into which Arabia had become divided. Its territory probably adjoined that of Babylonia. We may suppose that Assyria led the movement by which the Arabians were expelled, and from this beginning went on to become an empire. Babylonia was a province of the Assyrian empire for 650 years, sometimes in rebellion, and never held in very rigid subjection, its vassalage at times being little more than nominal. Sennacherib's inscription at Bavian shows that, in the year 1110 B.C., its princes waged successful war against Assyria, and defeated Tiglath-Pileser in a great battle.

It seems every way probable that Mesopotamia, and perhaps the whole region from Susa and Assyria to Syria, was occupied by uncivilized Semites when the Arabian Cushites first appeared there. They were very likely a nomadic people, divided into tribes, who yielded without a struggle to the enterprising and powerful race that brought them civilization. They were dispossessed, crowded into a few isolated communities, or incorporated with the invaders. Their language disappeared, to a great extent, before the Cushites from the south, and the Aryans from Central Asia who came later, being preserved only in the "Land of Asshur" and in some districts farther west.

The Assyrian empire, which was great in extent and very powerful during nearly seven centuries, wrought another change. It restored the Semitic language, creating the Aramaic form of it. Rawlinson, speaking of the Cushite character and language of the old Chaldeans, says: "It can be proved from the inscriptions of the country that between the date of the first establishment of a Chaldean kingdom and the reign of Nebuchadnezzar, the language of Lower Mesopotamia underwent an entire change." The Cushite tongue disappeared, and the Aramaic took its place. The influence of this Semitizing transformation proceeded westward, encountering effective resistance only where it reached established communities of the Aryans. The marvelous vigor of the Cushite race was passing away; the Aryan race was becoming imperial, and preparing to fill the world with its influence.

A THEORY OF THE CHALDEANS.

I must not leave the Chaldeans without noticing a singular theory touching their origin and character, which has found supporters, and is repeated in Ernest Renan's work on the Semitic languages. This theory locates Ur of the Chaldees in the mountains of Kurdistan, and describes the Chaldeans as a tribe of bold and vigorous mountaineers, who came into Babylonia as mercenary soldiers or favored immigrants used for protection, and speedily rose to be an aristocratic class of "philosophers, naturalists, or soothsayers, whose principal employment was the study of mathematics and astronomy." They were simply a caste in the nation, says this hypothesis, not the nation itself. Renan thinks the Chaldeans belonged to the Aryan race, and describes the Kurds as modern Chaldeans. See his volume published in 1863, book first, chapter second.

Those who begin history in that part of Asia with the Assyrians, placing them at Babylon in the year 2234 B.C., very naturally find the Chaldeans involved in a mystery difficult to explain. Their culture and knowledge were so superior to those of the Semites that they could not cease to furnish the foremost scholars and teachers even when the political supremacy of Chaldea yielded to the Assyrian empire. Therefore, to those who have failed to see the older nation they represented, they have seemed to be a distinct class, a learned and powerful caste in the Babylonian or Assyrian nation of later times. Not aware of the old kingdom of Chaldea, and eager to solve the mystery, they see nothing preposterous in this theory. To undertake a formal refutation of it cannot be necessary. In the light of our present knowledge of Mesopotamian antiquity, it seems more like the production of a fantastic dream than the work of thoughtful inquiry. All antiquity shows us Chaldea and the Chaldeans in Lower Mesopotamia. The Hebrew Scriptures place "Ur of the Chaldees" in that region; and the ruins inform us that this city was situated on the Euphrates, near the Persian Gulf.

CONCERNING CHALDEAN ANCIENT HISTORY.

According to Berosus, there were 103 kings of Chaldea previous to the year 1273 B.C., when the Assyrian empire rose and made that country one of its tributary provinces. Eight of these kings formed a "Median" dynasty, which lasted 224 years; and nine of them formed the Arabian dynasty, which ruled Chaldea 245 years. Now, if we allow each of the remaining 140 kings a reign of twenty years, the whole time of all the dynasties will be 3389 years previous to 1273 B.C.; and the beginning of their time will be placed in the year 4662 B.C., when Upper and Lower Egypt flourished as separate and independent countries, Menes not yet having appeared to unite them. This estimate is moderate; the average is below that of the "Median" and "Arabian" dynasties of kings, whose number and time are both given. It will not be denied that, according to the testimony of Berosus, the 86 kings of the first dynasty represent a great period of very ancient history in Chaldea; the Old Kingdom of the country, the first ages of national existence, of which he could give no history. A complete copy of his Chaldean History might show that he had not only their names, but also a chronology of their time; and perhaps it would explain what was meant by the cyclical additions which, included in their time, extended it to 34,080 years.

Bunsen finds the point of separation between the mythical and the earliest historical periods by deducting from the 34,080 years the nine complete *sari* (astronomical cycles of 3600 years each). The remaining 1680 years he regards as the actual historical time of the 86 kings, to which the nine *sari* were prefixed. These 1680 years, being the fragment of a *sari*, have no cyclical significance, and, therefore, cannot be any part of the cyclical contrivance. They give the 86 kings an average of nearly twenty years each. It must be observed, however, that during the time of these kings the Chaldeans computed by lunar years; after the time of the "Median" dynasty they reckoned by solar years. In dealing with a later period of Chaldean history, Bunsen's methods are less reasonable and his conclusions much less satisfactory. Even Bunsen did not wholly escape the glamour of the year 2234 B.C. He saw clearly, and said strongly, that Chaldean civilization was much older than this date; yet, unlike most other writers on Chaldean chronology, he constrained the "Median" dynasty to begin with it, and thus crowded the subsequent dynasties within still narrower limits. This has no warrant of probability. It is inadmissible. Dismiss all this, strip the year 2234 B.C. of its preposterous pretensions, and give the later Chaldean dynasties such space in time as the number of kings on the list of Berosus so plainly demands, and the beginning of the first dynasty cannot, on any ground, reason, or probability, be placed later than 4500 B.C.

We can see, in what Berosus says of the history of Chaldea, that it was divided into two great periods, very distinct from each other, and as completely separated as the Old Monarchy and the New Monarchy of Egypt. The first is the period of the 86 kings, which began with the royal city at Ur, and was brought to a close after the seat of government had for a long time been at Nipur, by an invasion from abroad, which overthrew the government and established that "Median" dynasty. The next dynasty of eleven kings may have represented the princes of Susiana, elevated to supreme power by their successful leadership in expelling the "Median" power. The second great period of Chaldean history, the "New Monarchy of Chaldea," so to speak, may have begun with the dynasty of 49 kings. It was terminated by a powerful invasion of the "Arabians," who ruled the country until the rise of the empire of the Assyrians.

HYPOTHETICAL SCHEME OF CHALDEAN HISTORY.

A hypothetical scheme of the history of Chaldea, based on the list of Berosus and the results of modern research, may serve to aid the mind in tentative efforts to realize and reconstruct the past. Of course, it will not claim to be authentic history; but it will have more to command respect, and be every way more credible than any scheme that trifles with what is known by beginning the national existence of Chaldea in the year 2234 B.C., with the city we know as Babylon for the seat of government. Every reader will understand that the following scheme is hypothesis, and judge of its probability for himself.

1. At the beginning of Chaldean national existence, and in the first ages of the country, the royal city was Ur, or Hur. This city was then situated at the mouth of the Euphrates, but now, in its ruins, is a hundred and fifty miles above the mouth of that river, the Persian Gulf having been filled up to this extent by accumulations of alluvium. During the previous colony and provincial times Ur had become a great commercial emporium—a grand centre of power. At this early period the more important cities and communities were at the south, between the rivers and in Susiana. Ur very naturally became the political as well as the commercial metropolis, and must have remained so for a long time, until the northern part of the country was filled with inhabitants, and its relations with the interior countries of Asia became important. Ur may have continued to be the royal city during some twenty-five reigns, or

until about 4150 B.C., when some great political change may have transferred the seat of government to Erech.

2. At Erech there may have been ten reigns, from 4150 to 3950 B.C. The names of two kings who reigned at Erech, one after the other, have been found in the ruins of that city. They were father and son. One of their names is given as Sin-shada; the other has not been phonetically rendered. We may reasonably conjecture that, for some reason, to be explained only by circumstances of which we have no knowledge, Erech was made the royal seat of a dynasty to which these kings belonged. The period, after the seat of government left Ur and before it was established at Nipur, may have been unsettled and changeful, so far as relates to the ruling dynasty. There may have been more than one change of dynasty during this period, and more than one royal city; but, whatever may have been the political condition of the country at that time, there came a great epoch of change and reconstruction, which established the seat of government at Nipur. The personage called Nimrod in the Hebrew Scriptures, and the "beginning" of whose kingdom "was Babel, and Erech, and Accad, and Calneh," may have flourished at this time.

3. At Nipur, the city of Belus, we may suppose there were fifty-one kings, in several dynasties, previous to the "Median" invasion; that is to say, from 3950 to about 2950 B.C., a thousand years. In this period must have been the great ages of Chaldean civilization, culture, and power. It was the period of the first eight or nine dynasties of the Old Monarchy of Egypt, when the civilization of that country reached its grandest development. Other civilized countries of great importance must have been contemporary with the Chaldea of that period, not only in Ara-

bia, Africa, and on the Mediterranean, but also in India, and in the neighboring parts of Asia, where a people of the Aryan race, in very remote times, had a great kingdom, of which Balkh was the capital. Many of the Greek traditions concerning Chaldea, inherited probably from the older peoples whom they succeeded, must refer to this period, and to the great city, now called Nipur, still so remarkable in its ruins. About the year 2050 B.C. this old Chaldean monarchy was brought to a close, probably as other monarchies have reached this fortune, after some ages of decline. The country was invaded, the government was broken down, and the nation submitted to the sway of a dynasty of foreign kings described as "Median."

4. These "Median" rulers filled a period between ancient Chaldea and the later kingdom, which is usually called Babylonia, just as the Hyksos in Egypt filled the time between the Old and the New Monarchies. Berosus says their dominion lasted 224 years. It was still in existence long after all those were dead who had seen the time of the last native king. There must have been differences, to some extent, between the later Babylonian Chaldea and that more ancient kingdom. We cannot reasonably suppose that the Chaldean people, under the first king in the next dynasty of native sovereigns, still used precisely the same form of their language in which the latest annals of the old kingdom had been written. If the successful invaders did not destroy the Chaldean books, and seek to obscure all recollections of the great history of the country, time and linguistic change must have so altered the current speech of the people that the old writings had become unreadable to all save adepts at the beginning of that dynasty of 49 kings, which, there is some reason to believe, established

the seat of government at Babylon. There must have been other changes that gave the period of these kings a distinctive individuality; it was the same people, but not the same nation. Some writers, not finding a suggestion for any other hypothesis, have supposed the "Median" kings represented invaders from the north—Turanians, Aryans, or some other northern people. This ethnic term, supposed by some to be a corruption of the word used by Berosus, was probably used by him to describe some branch of the Arabian people, or some princely family of Arabia, who governed Chaldea under the sway of the celebrated Arabian conqueror, Zohak, as I have already explained.

5. The next dynasty of eleven kings, on the hypothesis of 20 years to each king, must have lasted 220 years, or from about 2726 to 2506 B.C. If it represented princes of Susiana, who led a rising of the people that overthrew and expelled the "Median" power, the seat of government during the time of this dynasty must have been at Susa. The supposition that these eleven kings were Susianian princes is the most probable I can suggest. In the list of Berosus, as we have it now, they are without ethnical or national designation; but they stand by themselves, entirely separate from the preceding "Medians" and the following 49 Chaldean sovereigns. We may, therefore, suppose they represent a distinct period of the transition from the downfall of the old Chaldean monarchy to the permanent establishment of the new monarchy under native Chaldean princes, with the seat of government at the city known to us as Babylon.

6. The 49 Chaldean kings on the list of Berosus are associated with the second great period in the history of Chaldea. An average of twenty years to each of these

kings gives 980 years; and the time from 2500 B.C. to 1518 B.C., the year in which the rule of the Arabian dynasty began, is 980 years. Berosus must have given a complete history of this period, for he himself states that the materials for his work were the old archives and historical records deposited in the temple of Belus at Babylon, where annals had been written from age to age, and carefully preserved by the priests. He was one of the priests of that temple, and had unobstructed access to all these documents. How could the Greeks receive his work with so little attention, and allow it to perish! During the time of these 40 kings, Babylon seems to have been the centre of a great commercial intercourse with Upper Asia, India, Arabia, and the countries on the Mediterranean. It became the metropolitan city of Southwestern Asia, and had in it a remarkable mixture of races and tongues—Cushite, Semitic, Aryan, Turanian, and others, perhaps — in which most of their dialects and varying shades of difference were represented. Chaldea was still a grand and famous country, eminent for its culture, wealth, and influence; but finally the sceptre departed, and Chaldean supremacy was broken down by an invasion from Arabia.

7. The Arabian dynasty of nine kings lasted 245 years, from 1518 to 1273 B.C. During this time Assyria and Susiana were probably separate and independent, though not of great importance. An uncertain Greek tradition speaks of an Ethiopian prince, called Memnon, and described as son of a king of Susa, who is said to have led an army to aid his uncle Priam in the Trojan War. Much more trustworthy is the testimony of Sir Henry Rawlinson, that an Assyrian canon found by him carries back the independent existence of Assyria to the year 1050 B.C. I have already

suggested that this second conquest of Chaldea was probably made by an Arabian sovereign known as Schamar-Iarasch, who is said to have extended his conquests far into Central Asia, and whose inscriptions at Samarcand are mentioned by certain Mahometan writers. I find no reason to modify this suggestion, and have no doubt of its correctness.

The most probable explanation of the rise of Assyria, from the condition of a small kingdom to that of an extensive and powerful empire, is, that about 1273 B.C. the Arabian kings were dispossessed and driven out of Chaldea by a revolutionary movement stimulated and supported by the princes of that country. It is certain that the Arabians were expelled at that time, and that there were great political changes which made Assyria an empire, and gave it control of that part of Asia for nearly seven centuries.

Those who may be disposed to accept this scheme for a hypothetical reconstruction of Chaldean history as substantially warranted by probability, will very likely suggest important modifications. The more they reflect on the subject, the more will they see that something like this general outline is required by what has been learned of the antiquity and ancient condition of that country from Berosus, and by means of archæological investigation. Those who may allow themselves to object, criticise, and discredit this scheme, should turn their attention more carefully to the absurdities, incredible theories, audacious "emendations" and "revisions" of facts, and unwarranted assumptions which they must indorse if they reject it. The scheme I have presented is more reasonable, and, I will add, much more truthful, than any arbitrary scheme that emends, reduces, and falsifies the list of Berosus, and modifies or misinterprets facts in favor of dogmatic chronology. Nothing is so liable to absurd exhibitions of credulity and unreason as morbid skepticism directed by invincible prejudice.

VI.
INDIA, SANSKRIT AND ANTE-SANSKRIT.

The Greeks and Romans described as India the whole region beyond the Indus, including in it Hindustan, Burmah, Cochin China, Siam, and Malacca, with the islands of the Indian Archipelago. Their knowledge of that region was very imperfect; but then, as in later times, it had strange power to enchant imagination, seeming to be a marvelous land of riches, magnificence, and everything rare and wondrous. Even in modern times, the influence of this enchantment has led some learned and enthusiastic writers to describe India as the primal source of all knowledge and culture, the radiant morning-land of human civilization.

The name India, however, is most commonly restricted to the great peninsula known in our geographies as Hindustan; and it is this land that has presented so much both to incite the genius of romance and engage the attention of scholars. It is separated into two great divisions by a chain of mountains running east and west, called the Vindhya Mountains. Strictly speaking, the northern division, including the vast and fertile valley of the Ganges, is Hindustan, the land of the Hindus; while the southern division is known as the Dakshin, the south country, a name which the English have transformed into Deccan. The conquests of Alexander the Great gave the Greeks some knowledge of the northern division of the country. At that time its civilization was very old, and presented clear indications of a long and important history.

We are accustomed to associate India with the Sanskrit race and the Brahmanical system of religion; but this gives a very imperfect knowledge of the country. The Sanskrit literature, the superior culture of the Brahmans, and the prominence of their race among the Indian peoples, have naturally drawn attention chiefly to the Hindus or Indo-Aryans; and yet it may be doubted whether the unmixed Indo-Aryans were not always a small minority of the whole population of India. All over the country, at the north as well as in the south, there are communities and dialects that do not belong to the Sanskrit race. The people of this race were a long time in Northern India, and had a long history there, before they attempted to establish themselves in the country south of the Vindhya Mountains; they have never at any time occupied the south country as they occupied the Punjâb and the valley of the Ganges.

The old race constitute the great majority of the population of the Dakshin as well as of many districts of Northern India, and they still use dialects of a language radically different from the Sanskrit. The languages of Southern India, called the Dravidian family, and the aboriginal dialects throughout Central India, cannot be classed in the same family with the Sanskrit. The old books of the Hindus recognise the two distinct races; and they tell us that the original Indo-Aryans were white, while the people they found in India were "dark-skinned." There are now no white Aryans in India save the English and other European residents. The original Sanskrit whiteness was mixed with the darker color of the native inhabitants long before Alexander's time.

K

THE INDO-ARYANS PRECEDED BY THE CUSHITES.

It can be seen distinctly in the antiquities of India, and in the religious ideas, customs, and symbols of the peoples who represent the oldest inhabitants, that when the Indo-Aryans entered that country, it had for a long time been occupied by the Arabian Cushites. There are strong reasons for believing that the Cushites found the country inhabited by a dark-colored race, similar, perhaps, to the Malays, and to the people found on most of the islands of the Indian and Pacific Oceans. It was not the policy of the Cushite race to exterminate peoples found in countries which they colonized and occupied. Their policy was to conciliate, civilize, and absorb them. The present physical characteristics of the people of India indicate that they pursued this policy in that country. Let me state some of the indications that they occupied India long before the Indo-Aryan immigration.

In the first place, it is in the highest degree probable that the Arabian Cushites occupied India. It is unreasonable to suppose otherwise. A great commercial, maritime, and colonizing people, such as the old Arabians were in the remotest antiquity, could not fail to go as colonizers to India, and to many of the islands of the Indian Ocean. It was an ordinance of nature itself that any people controlling the navigation and commerce of that ocean should establish very close relations between India, Ceylon, Southeastern Africa, and Southern Arabia. It has been well observed that there are probably no other extensive and separated regions on the globe where so many causes incite to a mutual commerce. While the older Greeks associated "the sacred wave and coraled bed of the Erythræan Sea" with the wonderful Ethiopians, there was neither trace nor tradition of any other controlling maritime people in that part of the world. They must have occupied all those regions; for it is undeniable that they had uninterrupted supremacy on the Indian Ocean from time immemorial, from ages away back in the deeps of antiquity, until the people of Western Europe found their way to India around the Cape of Good Hope.

Vincent, in his work on the Periplus of the Erythræan Sea, without distinctly recognising ancient Arabia, found himself constrained to speak thus: "The commerce of the Arabians has arrested our attention throughout the whole progress of our inquiry, from the first mention of imports in Scripture to the accounts of the present day. Their connection with the countries in their neighborhood is equally obvious. In the Indian Ocean they are found upon every coast and upon almost every island." There may have been some older civilization than that of the Arabian Cushites, from which they learned their skill in commerce and navigation; but tradition does not go beyond them. It followed, necessarily, that they occupied all desirable regions within their reach. Not only Ceylon, the Spice Islands, and all other important islands in the Indian Ocean, but also the shores, southern districts, and central regions of the continent. Ephorus stated expressly that "the Ethiopians occupied all the southern coasts of both Asia and Africa;" and this accords with the universal testimony of ancient tradition.

In the second place, the ancient occupation of India by the Arabian Cushites is seen in the revelations of linguistic and archæological research; in the religious ideas, customs, and symbols found there; in remains of the oldest architecture; in all the antiquities of the country; and even in remains of ancient municipal organizations that seem to have been peculiar to the Cushite race.

Professor Rawlinson, in his work on Herodotus, book i., Essay ii., says: "Recent linguistic discovery tends to show that a Cushite or Ethiopian race did, in the earliest times, extend itself along the shores of the Southern Ocean from Abyssinia to India. *The whole peninsula of India was peopled by a race of this character before the influx of the Aryans*; it extended along the sea-coast through the modern Beluchistan and Kerman; the cities on the northern shores of the Persian Gulf are shown by the brick inscriptions found in their ruins to have belonged to this race." Archæological exploration and research in the East is unveiling the past, and careful inquirers are gradually getting eyes to see it.

The ancient people of Arabia doubtless went first to India by sea, for they were adventurous navigators and traders, who traveled more by sea than by land. Professor Rawlinson is one of the scholars who misunderstand Arabia. He seeks in Africa that Ethiopia from which proceeded such mighty streams of colonization; but he has learned to see the ancient Cushite occupation of India. Heeren, who failed to discover the original Ethiopia, maintained, nevertheless, that "a very ancient connection existed between India and Arabia, and between India and the opposite coast of Africa, which was dependent on Arabian princes;" and also that "from time immemorial the Arabians had monopolized the carrying trade of the Indian Ocean."

Investigation has brought to light traces of the Cushite religion in every part of India. Their significance was pointed out by Signor Gorresio, who edited and translated

Siva a Cushite divinity.

the Ramayana. He believed the ante-Sanskrit people of Southern India to be of "Hamitic origin;" and, in proof of this, he cited the fact that their religious symbols and devices are serpents, dragons, and the like, all peculiar to the ancient Hamitic or Cushite religion; and that the god they prefer to all others, and whom they especially honor in their sacrifices, is "the terrible Rudra or Siva," certainly a Cushite divinity, called by the Cushites Baal, and by other names. Siva is not a Vedic god. He did not belong to the religious system of the Indo-Aryans; but he was a great divinity of the older people of the country; and the later Brahmanism, seeking to absorb everything that could give it strength and influence, adopted him, and introduced him into its system by means of a conveniently invented avatar.

Siva is not mentioned in the Rig-Veda. The legend of Daksha, in the Vishnu Purana, shows that he did not originally belong to the Brahmanical system, and makes him say, "My priests worship me in the sacrifice of true wisdom where no officiating Brahman is needed." Rev. Dr. Stevenson has published in the Journal of the Royal Asiatic Society, and in the Journal of the Bombay Branch of that society, several papers on the religious peculiarities of the Dekhan. He discusses this point, and urges, on the strongest grounds, that neither Siva nor the Phallus worship, of which traces are so prevalent in India, came into that country with the Aryan race. They existed there long before the Aryan immigration. He says:

"The Lingayats are well known to have a bitter hatred towards the Brahmans, to neglect Brahmanical rules about purification for dead bodies, etc., and to have priests of their own called jangams. On the other hand, the Brah-

mans call them *Pakhandī*, or adherents to a false religion.
And although Achárya, or whoever established that cõm-
promise of sects called the worship of Panchaitana, or the
five principal divinities, has admitted Mahadeva (Siva), under the form of the Linga, into the number, still the person
who attends to dress this image is not, as is the case with
all the rest, a Brahman, but a Sudra of the caste Gurava."

The intense and exclusive fanaticism of the early Indo-
Aryans described the old inhabitants of the country, with
their different religion, as Dasyus, Rakshasas, fiendish creat-
ures, demons, and monsters. Rakshasas was a constant
appellation for the people south of the Vindhya Mountains.
Dr. Stevenson says: "I observe in Turnour's documents
relative to the religion of Çeylon that the whole of that
island was overrun with devil and serpent worship previous to the arrival of Buddha; and I think analogy may
lead us to conclude that the same was the case in India before the arrival of the Brahmans." To the ancient Hindus,
Ceylon was a land of very terrible Rakshasas. The "devils" and "demons" of the Buddhists are easily understood.
The serpent worship is full of significance: this was a great
feature of the old religion of the Cushites; but the word
"serpent" will convey a very poor notion of its meaning
to those who do not understand what it was. The serpent
was regarded as a symbol of intelligence, of immortality,
of protection against the power of evil spirits, and of a re-
newal of life or of the healing powers in nature. It is evident that Brahmanism was never established in Ceylon.
The people of that island retained their old religion until
they were converted by disciples of Buddha. In the same
spirit and to the same effect is the statement of Fa-hian, a
Chinese Buddhist who traveled in India, where he speaks

of Ceylon as "originally inhabited by demons, genii, and dragons, who had, nevertheless, a taste for commerce, and in time became civilized."

Dr. Stevenson describes the festival of Holi, or "the worship of Holika Devata," and says it has a close resemblance to the English festival of the May-pole, which originated in a religious ceremony or festival of the Cushites (called Phœnicians) who anciently occupied Western Europe. As cairns, like those in Western Europe and in other Cushite countries, are abundant in the Dekhan, we may suppose the cairn fires also were formerly known there.

Dr. Stevenson and several other writers have described the "worship of Vetal," which still exists in the Dekhan, in which traces of the old Cushites are very plain. It is remarked that Vetal has no image in the shape of any creature whatever; therefore his worship must have been introduced "previous to the custom of likening the gods to men and animals." Vetal has no temple, but is worshipped in the open air, generally under the shade of a wide-spreading tree. "This circumstance connects his worship with that of the Canaanites, who, in the time of Moses, had no temples." The place where Vetal is worshipped is a kind of lesser Stonehenge. It is a stone circle, or inclosure of stones, generally circular in form, varying from fifteen to forty feet in diameter. This antique worship is not confined to the south of India; it is found in Konkan, Kanara, Gujerat, Cutch, and other districts. The Brahmans call Vetal a demon; he neither belongs to their Pantheon nor requires their services. The old Keltic Druids, probably, would have seen in him something very different from a demon.

The great resemblance of certain customs common to

the Kelts, the Canaanites, and the ante-Sanskrit people of
India, strongly engaged the attention of Lieut. Col. Forbes
Leslie, as will be seen in his work on the "Early Races of
Scotland." It is manifest to those who have studied the
subject closely, that both modern Brahmanism and modern
Buddhism (for Buddhism is much older than the Buddha
of the Ceylonese records) have absorbed many elements
of the old Cushite religion. We may suspect, although we
have no historical records to show, that the most ancient
form of Buddhism began the first development of its distinctive peculiarities under some influence of the Cushite
faith. Mr. James Bird, in his work on "The Buddha and
Jaina Religions," speaks on this subject as follows:

"The more intimately we become acquainted with the
principles of the Buddha religion, the stronger will be our
conviction that such principles have their origin in physical
and metaphysical opinions, made applicable to explain the
phenomena of the world and of human nature; and that
such opinions were closely connected with the worship of
the heavenly bodies and the Sabean idolatry. This Sabaism, too, instead of being ingrafted on the Buddha system,
appears to have preceded it, and to have been the source
from whence it sprung."

The earliest religion of India of which we have any trace
is planet worship, with its usual symbols and ceremonies.
The remains of its influence are found everywhere. In
Ceylon and Southern India, the Bali means planet worship.
The stone circles and Cyclopean fanes mean this. Its symbols are abundant in the rock temples. It used no idols
in its purest form, but inculcated adoration of "the host
of heaven." In Ferishta's Introduction to his "Mahomedan
India," he tells us that before idols were used by the peo-

ple of India in their worship, they, "like the Persians, worshipped the sun and the stars." On this the translator has the following note:

"There appears every day stronger reason to believe that the worship of the Bull, the Linga, and the Yoni is the same as the Phallic worship of Egypt, and as that of the calf and the pillar, emblematic of Baal or the sun, by the nations surrounding the Israelites; that this worship was founded originally on Sabaism; and that the emblems are types of fructification. Abundant proof exists in India of the antiquity of Tauric and Phallic worship over that of idolatry and demi-god heroes. All the temples of the latter are modern compared with those dedicated to Mahadeva," that is, Baal, called Siva by the Brahmans.

I must class with the Cushite antiquities of India the local municipalities still existing in many parts of the country. They remind us of similar organizations left by that race in all the countries they occupied. These remarkable municipalities were noticed by Arrian and other Greek writers who followed Megasthenes. Attention is called to them in Elphinstone's History; and Sir Charles Metcalf described them as follows: "The village communities are little republics, having everything they want within themselves, and almost independent of any foreign relations. They seem to last where nothing else lasts. Dynasty after dynasty tumbles; revolution succeeds to revolution; Hindu, Patan, Mogul, Mahratta, Sikh, English, are all masters in turn, but the village communities remain the same." An article in the Journal of the Royal Asiatic Society for 1865, after citing what was said of them by Diodorus Siculus, Arrian, and Quintus Curtius, says: "There are no data to determine the exact form of these constitutions, though they are seen to have been far beyond any mere intramural municipality. The city clearly dominated over the country around, and constituted, to all intents and purposes, a state." This was the Cushite method in Arabia, in Phœnicia, in Northern Africa, in Spain, in their settlements all around the Mediterranean. These municipal organizations were not originated by Brahmánism; they are foreign to its spirit, by which they have been modified and mutilated, but not entirely extirpated. The Sanskrit race found them in India, and they must be classed with the oldest antiquities of the country.

But there are other antiquities in India which reveal the Cushite occupation. It would now be preposterous for any one familiar with the subject to deny that the remains of a civilized people who preceded the Indo-Aryans exist in every part of the Indian Peninsula. The actual state of the case is presented by Lieut. General Briggs, in a paper on "The Aboriginal Race of India," published in the Journal of the Royal Asiatic Society for 1852, as follows:

"There are incontestable proofs of the aboriginal race having once occupied every part of India; and that, ere the Hindus came among them, they had made sufficient progress in civilization to form large communities, establish kingdoms, and become merchants and extensive cultivators of the soil. There are distinct remains of old castles, extensive excavations, and other monumental ruins. Several of their principalities have continued to the present day; and history has transmitted to us, from the earliest period of which any authentic records exist, occasional proofs of the power this race once possessed."

The writer goes, on the wings of fancy, to the Scyths and Tatars for the origin of this aboriginal race. The character of these antiquities very plainly suggest a much more probable hypothesis. Professor Benfey finds "the whole Dekhan covered with remains of a nation of which, it is highly probable, the several parts were connected by affinity," and says, "we know with certainty" that this nation preceded the Sanskrit-speaking people.

These remains of an ante-Sanskrit race in India consist of ancient temples which Europeans call pagodas, Cyclopean excavations in mountains of rock, Cyclopean fanes, barrows containing human remains, cells formed of large slabs, stone circles, cairns of every kind, cromlechs, dolmens, and many other antiquities of the same class—all similar to those found in Arabia, Syria, Phœnicia, Northern Africa, and the western and southern countries of Europe. In presence of these remains, it is unreasonable to talk of Scyths and Tatars. They show plainly the race to which they belong. Their character and significance cannot be mistaken when carefully studied and fairly understood. Such monuments could not be found in India if the Arabian Cushites had not gone there in very remote times, occupied the country, and filled it with the influence of their religion and their civilization. Lieut. Col. Forbes Leslie describes and discusses such antiquities of the Dekhan as appear to him incontestably the same in character and origin as those of Syria and Western Europe. He points out clearly that these monuments in the Dekhan appear "in all the varied forms in which they are to be found in France and Britain," and in all the countries where the influence of the Arabian Cushites was established—an influence which he does not appear to comprehend. He says: "It will not be disputed that the primitive Cyclopean monuments of the Dekhan were erected prior to the arrival of the present dominant race, the Hindus."

THE ROCK-CUT TEMPLES OF INDIA.

The marvelous and long-deserted temples, formed by excavating mountains of rock, must be considered by themselves. Heeren, admitting that Arabian colonies may have been established on the coasts of Hindustan in very early times, allowed himself to make this very singular observation: "And yet, up to the present time, no traces, I believe, of Arabian architecture have been discovered in India similar to those found in many parts of Spain." What have the old Adite Ethiopians to do with the Saracens of Spain, from whom they were so distant in time, and so different in religion and civilization? Nothing whatever. But Heeren did not know that Arabia itself has ruins which show nothing in common with the Saracenic style of architecture.

The Cushite Arabians left, throughout India, some wonderful specimens of their architecture; not Saracenic in style certainly, but remarkably characteristic of their own spirit and civilization. The rock-cut temples at Elephanta, Salsette or Kanaria, Ellora, Ajunta, and elsewhere in the Indian peninsula, together with many of the old temples called pagodas, show their style, and remind us of similar structures of that race in other regions. Both pen and pencil have described them so often that I need not here attempt another elaborate description.

Niebuhr was the first, in modern times, to call attention to these architectural excavations; but his personal observations were confined to Elephanta, where is found one of these rock-temples a hundred and thirty feet deep by about a hundred and twenty-three feet wide, exclusive of the various rooms attached. The roof is supported by twenty-six pillars and sixteen pilasters. The walls were once covered with a beautiful stucco; if they ever had inscriptions, these have entirely disappeared. In the neighboring island of Salsette, or Kanaria, a mountain of rock is excavated in every direction. Some of the finest of these rock-temples are at Ellora, in Central India, where a semicircular range of rock mountain contains a series of them, more carefully finished and ornamented than those at Elephanta and Salsette. The rock excavated at Elephanta is described as clay porphyry, so hard that no ordinary steel can work it. It must have been worked by means of the celebrated India steel called *wudz*.

These wonderful structures are found in many other localities. The ruins at Mavalipura show the remains of a city that was chiefly hewn out of solid rock. A considerable portion of these ruins has sunk into the sea. There are remains of heavy walls, built of immense blocks of stone piled one above another, after the style called Cyclopean. These excavations must be very ancient. That they belong to a remote antiquity is shown by the fact that there is in India no record or recollection of their origin. They may have been changed and reconstructed in some respects, from age to age, until they were disused; but they are very ancient, and owe their origin to that race whose traces are everywhere unmistakable.

To the same race must be attributed the origin of the pyramidal temples of Cyclopean construction called pagodas, the walls of which were made of immense blocks of stone placed together in the usual style of this method of building. All these old structures remind us of similar remains of remote antiquity found in Arabia, Syria, Phœnicia, Greece, Italy, Sicily, Egypt, and the Upper Nile valley.

Rock excavations are nowhere else so extensive as in India; but similar rock architecture and Cyclopean constructions found in the other countries are in the same style, and show unmistakable traces of the same hand. The most ancient architects of Calabria, Mycenæ, Petra, Ruad, Marathos, Nubia, and India all learned in the same school.

Some writers on these architectural remains have sought to deny their claim to antiquity, not because they have good or even plausible reasons for doing so, but chiefly through the influence of that amazing chronological lunacy which aims so obstinately to obscure the past, and begin the history of civilization with an age comparatively modern. One writer, whose pretensions as an architect are not supported by respectable qualifications for archæological inquiry, affirms, with great confidence in his own opinion, that the structures at Mavalipura were built just previous to the year 1300 A.D. Others have maintained that none of these rock-temples can be older than the ninth century of the Christian Era. We have historical evidence that shows the falseness of these representations.

Near the beginning of the Christian Era, envoys were sent to the Roman emperor Antoninus by a king of one of the Indian countries. In the fragment of a lost work of Porphyry, preserved in the 10th Eclogue of Stobæus, a statement of Bardesanes is quoted as follows: "The Indian messengers report that there is in India a large grotto, under a lofty hill, in which is to be seen an image from ten to twelve ells high, with arms folded across the breast, the right side being man and the left side woman." This appears to be a description of the image of Siva in the rock-temple at Elephanta; and, at that time, evidently it was as completely deserted, unused, and mysterious as it is now.

Bardesanes was born about the middle of the second century, and the rock-temple mentioned must have been described by the Indian messengers, or envoys, previous to the year 200 A.D.

By general consent of geographical writers, Mavalipura, the rock-city on the Coromandel coast, has been identified with the Maliarpha located there by Ptolemy, and by him described as a commercial emporium. Ptolemy was older than Bardesanes. His geography, however, was a revision of an older work by Marinus of Tyre; and there is no good reason to doubt that, in locating the city he calls Maliarpha, he depended entirely on Phœnician geographers, who had given this city the same location at a much earlier date than could be claimed for the geography of Marinus itself. At any rate, here is evidence that the city of Mavalipura existed more than 1100 years previous to the time when certain writers say it was built; and that the rock-temple at Elephanta was forsaken and incomprehensible at least 700 years previous to the earliest date that can be allowed for the oldest of these structures by some writers who speak on the subject with that tone of assurance which belongs only to positive knowledge.

It is surprising that anybody should deny the great antiquity of these works in presence of so many indications of their age, with tradition either standing speechless or muttering nonsense to show its inability to explain them. Their origin could not be so completely forgotten if they did not belong to ages previous to the Aryan immigration. Maurice, in his "Indian Antiquities," says very justly: "One would have supposed that the construction of such astonishing works, which have been called the eighth wonder of the world, would have fixed in any country an era never to be forgotten." He is sure they belong to the remotest antiquity, and that "a species of worship totally different from that now prevailing in India was anciently practiced in these caverns." They are now deserted. The people of the country cannot tell when or why they were deserted. Some of them, if not all, were in the same condition 1700 years ago, when, to the Indian messengers, natives of the country, the rock-temple they described was merely "a grotto," with a big image in it; for if it had then been used for temple worship, their description could not have failed to say so.

It is preposterous to talk of these structures as no older than the ninth or tenth century of the Christian Era. At that period such constructions were no longer possible in India, even if their style of architecture had still been current. The great days of the Sanskrit race had gone by, and new influences were preparing to take possession of the country. In the year 637 A.D., during the califate of Omar, the crusading Mahometans began their invasion of India by sending a fleet from Oman to the Malabar coast. Not much was effected; but in the year 696, a Mahometan army, led by "Muhammed, son of Cassem," occupied the valley of the Indus, overturned a powerful Indian kingdom, and penetrated as far as the country of the Rajpûts. No one familiar with the history of India from this date to the reign of the great Akbar can allow himself to assign these marvelous works to any age within the period in question.

The only semblance of argument against the great antiquity claimed for these structures comes from an assumption that they represent some of the later forms of Hindu worship, especially that of the Buddhists. In nearly all the rock-temples there are sculptured figures, reliefs, and decorations that are assumed to represent their original consecration; but the interpreters of these images and decorations do not agree in their conclusions, nor have they attempted to show that the images and symbolical devices are all as old as the temples. Most of the interpretations have been the work of fanciful conjecture. It has been confidently asserted that the temple at Salsetto was a Buddhist temple; but close and careful examination shows that it was certainly a temple of Siva or Baal, for the Linga and Yoni appear everywhere in its interior recesses. Lieut. Col. Sykes, who has given much attention to the rock-temples, says: "There is not anywhere a rock-temple excavation dedicated to Brahma or Vishnu;" and "Siva is the only god to whom honor is done at Ellora." [See vol. v. of the Journal of the Royal Asiatic Society.]

Some of these temples may have been used by the Buddhists during the time of their supremacy, and for this purpose they may have been changed in some respects. The inscriptions found in them are much later than the beginning of the Buddhist period. Scholars who have studied these antiquities admit that "the larger inscriptions at Ajunta may be long posterior to the excavations." [See Bombay Journal, vol. ii.] Similar constructions in Nubia have bas-reliefs and other decorations in the highest style of old Egyptian art, while the architecture of the original structures is entirely different. Rameses the Great found them existing as mysterious antiquities in his time, and used them to display his devices and record his glories as a conquering hero; but neither there nor in India is the vast antiquity of these structures in any way affected by the later addition of inscriptions, decorations, or images. The supposition that the Buddhists originated these rock-temples is made highly improbable, and therefore inadmissible, by several facts that appear against it.

1. In the first place, these structures appear to have been in existence long before the Buddhism of Sakhya-Muni became the established religion of Magadha. They existed at the time of his death. The Buddhist books give an account of three great convocations of his disciples. The first was convened by his favorite disciple Ananda immediately after his death. The Journal of the Royal Asiatic Society [vol. vi., p. 303] has the following statement concerning it: "The Chinese work, the *Foufa-thsang-yaan-king*, contains the following remarkable notice respecting Ananda: 'After the death of Buddha, he collected 500 pious men in the CAVERN of *Pi-pho-lo* [the tree of Photi], and jointly with them collected the Vinayas.' Of Kassapo, another of Buddha's disciples, the same work says: 'He collected a great assembly in the CAVERN of *Pi-ho-lo* and in other places, and arranged the Abidharmas.' From these passages it appears that cavern-excavations must have been contemporary with, *or even prior* to, Buddha [Sakhya]."

2. In the second place, these excavations are most numerous, in India, away from the region on the Ganges that was the birthplace and immediate home of Buddhism. A note in the volume of the Asiatic Journal just quoted takes notice of this fact as follows: "The remains of Buddhism in the Dekhan are even more magnificent and extensive than in its native seats on the Ganges. The cave-excavations are well known as wonderful monuments of art." Buddhism was never very extensively influential in the Dekhan, and in many districts its influence was scarcely felt. Hinan-Thsang, a Chinese Buddhist who visited India

in the beginning of the seventh century, tells us what he saw in the Dekhan. In Kalinga, he says, "there were few of the orthodox and many heretics;" but there were rock-temples. In the same part of the country he passed through a small state "where a peculiar language was spoken and Buddhism was not practiced." In another district, where the people were "black and savage," he notices "an excavated mountain;" if it had been used as a Buddhist temple he would have said so. It seems apparent that these rock-temples, which were not coincident with the established domination of Buddhism, and do not anywhere measure the extent of its influence, must have existed long previous to the time of Sakhya-Muni, and had their origin in something entirely independent of his religion. The Buddhists may have used them and perhaps remodeled some of them, but they did not originate them.

3. In the third place, the Siva-worship, to which these rock-temples were mainly devoted, had but little in common with Sakhya-Muni's type of Buddhism, which became the state religion of Magadha; therefore this state religion could not have originated these Saivite excavations. Eugene Burnouf was sure that nothing in the teaching of Sakhya could have produced the Saivite Tantras of the Nepaulese collection of Buddhist Scriptures. It is equally certain that nothing in his religion can be held responsible for the Saivite rock-temples; and it was only in behalf of such Buddhism as he and his disciples preached that the power and resources of Magadha were engaged; therefore no other school or sect of Buddhists—and, certainly, no one so different from his as that of the Saivas, which had most in common with the old religion of the country—could have had means to accomplish such stupendous

works. They were originated in times more ancient, by another race, for the uses of that older system of religion of which Hindu Saivism was born. Buddhists of all sects may have used them; but the history of Buddhism has nothing to explain their origin, or to account for their peculiar and very significant style of architecture.

No part of India has more abundant traces of the old Cushite occupation than Ceylon. In addition to rock-temples, traditions of the ancient Bali and serpent-worship, Cyclopean fanes, and other antiquities of the same class, it has immense and very remarkable structures called tanks, which have been well described by Governor Ward in the 27th volume of the Journal of the Royal Geographical Society. After giving some account of the ruins of two great cities, and pointing out that the east side of the island was anciently occupied by a very numerous and intelligent population, he says:

"All we know positively, or can collect from ancient records, is that there must once have been a large population on the west side of the island, in the neighborhood of Manaar and Aripo; that the causes which prompted the selection of this barren coast for a commercial emporium probably determined the choice of Anaradhapura as the seat of government; that other causes, equally obscure to us, forced back this teeming population (leaving everywhere traces of its industry and skill) to the neighborhood of Pollinarus, where its second capital was founded; that this second capital, like the first, is now a wilderness; and that nothing remains to bespeak its ancient magnificence save the long line of tanks that unite it with Tamblegam Bay and Trincomalee."

These tanks are artificial lakes of great size (some of

them over twenty miles in circumference) formed between hills by embankments of wonderful masonry "that seems to defy the hand of time." They were agencies of a vast system of irrigation; but "there is no visible outlet at the point from which the stream issues, yet the stream is perennial. * * * No doubt the run of water is regulated by those ancient sluices, placed in the bed of the lakes, which answered the purpose so admirably, although modern engineers cannot explain their action." The ruins of similar tanks are found in Arabia and Southern India. Wrede found such ruins in the Arabian valley of the Doan; and Arnaud has described the ruins of the celebrated "dike" or tank near the ancient city of Saba. The tanks of Ceylon may not be as old as most of the other Cyclopean antiquities of India; some of them may be comparatively modern, that is to say, not much older than the Christian Era; but they belong to a class of structures that must have been originated by the Arabian Cushites. Maurice, in his "Ancient History of Hindustan," speaks of these antiquities as follows:

"At that period, when the daring Cushite genius was in its full career of glory, it was the peculiar delight of that enterprising race to erect stupendous edifices, excavate long subterranean passages in the living rock, form vast lakes, and extend over the hollow of adjoining mountains magnificent arches for aqueducts and bridges. * * * It was they who built the tower of Belus and raised the pyramids of Egypt; it was they who formed the grottoes near the Nile, and scooped the caverns of Salsette and Elephanta. Their skill in mechanical powers to this day astonishes posterity, who are unable to conceive by what means stones thirty, forty, and even sixty feet in length, and from twelve to twenty feet in breadth [and depth], could ever be raised to that wonderful point of elevation at which they are seen in the ruined temples at Balbec and Thebais. Those composing the pagodas of India are scarcely less wonderful in magnitude and elevation." [Vol. ii., p. 241-2.]

THE DRAVIDIAN RACE AND THEIR LANGUAGE.

The fact that languages exist in India radically different from that of the Indo-Aryans, and that these languages represent the aboriginal speech of the country, was admitted and discussed by the old Sanskrit writers themselves. Mr. Muir has taken some pains to show this in his "Sanskrit Texts." The native writers apply the term *Desi* to this aboriginal tongue, and point out that, to a greater or lesser extent, it enters into all the existing dialects or languages of the peninsula. At the north the influence of Sanskrit has been much greater than at the south, but the old language is largely present in all the northern dialects, "especially among the lower orders of the people, and in the business of common life;" and it is admitted to be the oldest element in these dialects. In the south the old speech is represented by a family of cultivated languages, spoken, says Rev. Dr. Caldwell, in his Comparative Grammar, by thirty-one millions of people, not including the numerous uncultivated "hill tribes" and retired communities of Central India, who use dialects closely related to this family. It is admitted by Lassen, and by all others who have given them any attention, that these languages are fundamentally different from the Sanskrit, and that "their grammatical forms and primary words cannot by any possibility have been drawn from that source."

The five cultivated languages classed as the Dravidian family are used by peoples occupying the most southern part of India. They are the Tamil, spoken by people occupying the extreme southeastern extremity of the peninsula and nearly the whole of Ceylon; the Telugu, or Telinga, used in a larger region north of the Tamil people; the Karnâtika, or Carnarese, spoken in the interior region west of the Tamil and Telugu; the Malayâlam, or Malabar tongue, found in a narrow district on the western coast, extending north from Cape Comorin; and the Tulu, in a smaller territory north of the Malayâlam.

Linguistic scholars have not studied these languages closely. Not much is known of them beyond the information furnished by Dr. Caldwell's excellent Comparative Grammar of the Dravidian Languages, and Mr. A. D. Campbell's Telugu Grammar, with the accompanying note or essay of Mr. Ellis. No very profound study is required to see their radical unlikeness to the Sanskrit. Linguistic investigation has not yet authorized us to go beyond this; and, for the present, we must be content to see that this Dravidian speech, so far as relates to its distinctive character, must, like the Cyclopean remains of the more ancient race, be classed with the ante-Sanskrit Antiquities of India. They belong together, and whatever explains the one will explain the other.

Dr. Stevenson, in the Bombay Journal for April, 1842, describes the Tudas, the chief tribe of the Nilgiri Hills, and says: "The language of the Tudas is a sixth Indian peninsula language. All these languages have but one origin; an intimate relation in grammatical construction and vocables runs through them all." He finds that the language of the other hill tribes has a strong resemblance to that of the Tudas. It is known, also, that a form of speech closely related to the Dravidian family is used by certain peoples in Beluchistan. Dr. Stevenson calls attention to one peculiarity of these languages that has some significance. He says the word "Mag," son, is used in personal appellations as the term "Mac," son, is used in Gaelic, and adds, "Surely, after this, the M'Phersons and M'Gregors of our Highland glens need not hesitate to claim as Scotch cousins the inhabitants of the Indian peninsula." There is more in this than he saw. The African Berbers use this term "Mac" in the same way. Mr. Urquhart takes notice of this fact in his "Pillars of Hercules," and infers from it an ancient relationship between the Berbers and the Scotch Highlanders.

The Sanskrit is not now represented in India by any spoken tongue, as the more ancient speech is represented by these Dravidian languages. Its influence is seen everywhere; its words are found in all the vocabularies; some of the dialects grew up under its direct influence, and are supposed to have proceeded from it, but their formation was so powerfully influenced by the old language that the Desi element appears in them as an essential part of their structure. What scholars represented by the Bombay Journal have said of the Desi element of the Mahratti cannot be said of the Sanskrit element of any existing dialect, namely, that it is more used "among the lower orders of the people, and in the business of common life," than any other element. Between the Mahratti, the Hindi, the Bengali, and the Guzerati there is a close relationship. They come chiefly from the Sanskrit through intervening tongues called Prakrits, or " derived," which, through the continued use of Sanskrit as a literary language, were left almost wholly unwritten. Only one of them, the Pali, or language of Magahda, the birth-place of Buddhism, has been preserved in a distinct literature.

These Prakrits doubtless grew up in mixed communities at the north, composed of the Sanskrit-speaking people and that portion of the aboriginal population that had come under their control. Thus, for the uses of common life, there came into existence, in presence of the literary Sanskrit, new forms of speech, in which the tongues of the two different peoples were assimilated, and, to a greater or lesser degree, amalgamated. This is not the history of the Dravidian languages.

The primeval mother of the Dravidian languages, and of the Desi element throughout India, was much more ancient than the Rig-Veda—quite as old, probably, as the original source of the whole Aryan family. It may have been a composite language, formed by a fusion of the speech of the ante-Sanskrit civilizers with that of the ruder aborigines found in the country. If—as I believe, and as the antiquities of the country so clearly show—these ante-Sanskrit civilizers were Cushites from Arabia, the primal source of the Dravidian or Desi speech must have been a very ancient form of the Cushito tongue, modified by amalgamation with the speech of the aborigines, or by such use as was made of it in the communities created by the civilizing influence of the Cushites. Through how many changes and successive linguistic forms the Dravidian languages came down from that original source cannot be told, nor is it possible to know how many successive dialects and family branches of that old tongue appeared, flourished, and perished during the many ages of that long period.

These languages have been taken in hand by the "Scythian" infatuation, but without success. The old language of Arabia has sometimes been called "Scythian" and "Turanian." It would be pleasant to see those who have been carried away by this infatuation undertake to define clearly what is meant by the "Scythian family," and write comparative grammars of the "Scythian" languages. The truth is, these terms, "Scythian" and "Turanian," represent, in great measure, a mysterious limbo that symbolizes the mythical Babel, and into which are crowded, with a few things that are partially understood, all the vague, uncomprehended, and doubtful peoples and tongues that linguistic science is not yet qualified to explain and classify.

The Dravidian languages are too little known to comparative philologists, and linguistic studies are too little advanced in this direction to allow any scholar to place them in any other family with conclusive reasons for doing so. The first civilizers found in India a dark-colored race. The "Scythians" may claim the original speech of this race if they will. I shall not attempt to discredit their claim, for it will be amusing to see them support the right of that primeval tongue to a place in the "Scythian family." No doubt it belongs there. But the languages of the Dravidian family must for the present be allowed to stand by themselves. Probably the most competent linguistic scholar, if profoundly versed in the Dravidian tongues, and furnished with all possible aid to inquiry, might find it impossible to class them with any other family. With a composite language for their original source, and several millenniums between them and that source, the genetic relations and distinctive peculiarities of the ancient speech from which they came must now be too much obscured for easy recognition.

ARYAN HISTORY AND ANTIQUITY.

All inquiry concerning the origin of the Sanskrit race and their first appearance in India has been greatly embarrassed by the refusal of investigators to accept the meaning of the old Iranian histories. They were histories of the Aryan people in Asia for many years before either Media or Persia became separate kingdoms. But the inquirer, with his imagination occupied and his mind bewildered by historical assumptions and dates, which he does not allow himself to disturb, fails to see this, and puts ridiculous invention in the place of truth. While the ancient history of the Aryan people, reproduced in the old Persian books, is treated as a history of Persia merely, confusion and absurdity will be inevitable. It is no more a history of Persia than a history of the ancient kingdom of Turan or Rûm, of which it says so much, would, if it still existed, be a history of modern Turkey.

According to the old chronicles of Iran or Hirns, the history of the Aryan people began with the reign of the great Abad, who was succeeded by thirteen kings, his descendants. These constitute the Mahabadian dynasty. After the close of this dynasty there came a period of wild disorder, and "everything went to ruin." At length Jai Afrâm, a descendant of Abad, restored order, and began a second dynasty, that was long and prosperous. Shái Gîliv began a third dynasty, called the Sháyián, which was "happy," and lasted many ages. A fourth dynasty, begun by Yásán, and called the Yásánián, had a line of wise and excellent princes; but at its close, "the state of mankind fell into utter ruin," and there was a long period of frightful disorder and bloodshed. Finally, Gilshah, known in Iranian history as Kaiamors, "restored the institutes of justice, gave battle to the vile race," and had an illustrious reign. His successors are called the Gilshayan monarchs, and divided into four dynasties: the Peshdadian, the Kaianian, the Ashkanian, and the Sassanian. The Dabistan says there were long intervals between the several dynasties previous to Kaiamors; and "between Yúsán and Gilshah there must have elapsed multiplied and numerous generations."

Those who can see nothing but Persia in this ancient history coolly dismiss the dynasties previous to Gilshah as fabulous, do nothing, or worse than nothing, with the Peshdadians, and begin the history with the Kaianian dynasty, transferring to it all the more distinguished Peshdadian monarchs. And then, by means of "emendations" in the usual style of the manufacturers of "chronological harmony," they contrive to make it begin about 600 years before the Christian era. By this process it all becomes Persian history, and Zoroaster is made to live in the time of Darius Hystaspes. We are told that Anquetil du Perron treated this matter with remarkable "ingenuity," as follows: "The reigns of the Peshdadian princes, as recorded in the ancient books of of the Persians, are true, or at least probable, when considered in a proper point of view; that is, the reign or dynasty of Jemshid as the Chaldean dynasty of Julius Africanus; that of Zohak as the Arab dynasty of the same author; and that of Feridun as the dynasty of Bélétarán, ending with Sardanapalus." [See the Notes to Shea's translation of Mirkond's History of Persia.] A stroke of genius, no doubt; but excessive brilliancy is not always pleasant.

It was said in the old Iranian books that the Peshdadians governed the kingdom of Hirna, of which Balkh was the capital. The Dabistan (which mentions twenty or thirty such ancient books that are now lost) places the beginning of the reign of Gilshah, or Kaiamors, 5371 years before Christ; Ferdousi's estimate was 3529; and Sir William Ouseley, in his "Epitome," taken from the Jehan Ara, states the mean of various dates referred to in that work to be 3430 B.C. There is no authentic date, but the time was far back in the past. The Greeks, who said Zoroaster appeared 6000 years before the death of Plato and 5000 years before the Trojan War, placed it farther back than either of the dates here named.

We must put away confusion and accept the fact that, in ages long before Persia appeared as a nation, the city of Balkh, or Bactria, was the capital of a great kingdom of the Aryan people called Hiras, Hiran, and Iran. The date given in the Dabistan is more likely to be worth attention than the others named. The territory included within this kingdom, when it was greatest, may be indicated by the Fourteen Aryan Settlements or provinces described in the Vendidad, among which appears Bactria " with the lofty banner," indicating its metropolitan importance. These "Settlements" (following Haug's exposition) are named as follows: 1. Sughdha, or Sogdiana; 2. Móuru, or Margiana, called also Merv; 3. Bakhdi, or Bactria, with Balkh for its chief city; 4. Nisaya, or Northern Parthia, the Nisaia of Ptolemy; 5. Haroyu, or Aria, the Hariva of the cuneiform inscriptions; 6. Vékereta, or Segestan, the home of Rustem, so famous in the old Iranian histories; 7. Urvâ, or Cabul, as Haug has shown; 8. Khnenta, or Kandahar; 9. Haraquaiti, or Arachosia; 10. Hétumat, or the district of Hilmend; 11. Ragha, or Northern Media, where Ptolemy and Strabo place a city of Rhagæ; 12. Kakhra, or Khorassan;

13. Varena, or Ghilan; 14. Haptu-Hindu, or the Punjûb. Haptu-Hindu was in India, being the region between the Indus and the Sutlej, "the land of the seven rivers," called in the Veda, also, the country of the seven rivers, and sometimes the country of the five rivers. It probably included territory west of the Indus.

The Iranian record of kings and dynasties previous to Gilshah, or Kaiamors, doubtless preserves recollections of the history of the Aryan people during their residence in Upper Asia before the family separated. Kaiamors and his successors, with the great kingdom of Hiras, must represent the period when the Zend and Sanskrit branches of the family still lived together as one people and used a common language. In the later ages of this kingdom the Vedic and Zend dialects were developed. There may have been both political and religious division; but we cannot explain the circumstances that led the Vedic branch of the race to invade India beyond the Sutlej, and establish themselves in the valley of the Upper Ganges. Kings must have continued to reign at Balkh, over a lessened kingdom, long after this movement took place; but it is plain that, previous to the movement of the Vedic family to occupy Northern India beyond the Sutlej, they dwelt a long time in Haptu-Hindu, then a province of the kingdom of Hiras.

The refusal to see anything more in the old Iranian records than Persian history is so preposterous, and has created so much confusion and absurdity, that it is not easy to understand how it has been possible. Nearly a hundred years ago, it led an ardent scholar, John Richardson, in his "Dissertation on the Languages, etc., of the Eastern Nations," to deny the truthfulness of Greek history, and speak of it as pure romance. Having dismissed as fabulous all the ages of Aryan history previous to the Kaianian dynasty, and identified the first king of that dynasty with the Median Cyaxares, he read everything in the old chronicles as Persian history after that date; but he was perplexed to find it so totally different from Persian history as written by the Greeks; he declared them to be as much unlike as "the annals of England and Japan." In what he assumed to be Persian history, there was "no mention of Cyrus the Great," nor of any king who could be forced to resemble him; "not a vestige of the famous battles of Marathon, Thermopylæ, Salamis, Platæa, and Mycale," nor a single trace of "the most splendid facts of the Greek historians." Therefore Mr. Richardson, instead of correcting his own falsification of Persian history, accused the Greeks of falsehood and discredited their histories. This is more logical than the "harmonics" attempted by some others who have treated Iranian history in the same way, but it is no less absurd.

THE VEDA AND THE VEDIC AGE.

The Rig-Veda shows us that the earliest seat of the Indo-Aryans was in the upper valley of the Indus, on both sides of that river. This was Haptu-Hindu in Zend, and Saptu-Sindhavas according to the Vedic speech. It was chiefly that country in Northwestern India now called the Punjâb. They must have dwelt there a long time. The earliest songs of the Rig-Veda must have been written in Haptu-Hindu while it was a province of the kingdom of the Hirasis, or not long after the separation. The Veda shows their long residence there, and also the progress of their invading march from the Sutlej to the Sarasvati, in the upper valley of the Ganges, where they were established during the first great period of their purely Indian history.

These invading Aryans were intense and fanatical religious enthusiasts. In the Veda they are described as "the twice-born," "the righteous," "the sacrificers," and the like; while the people they found dwelling in India are impious "Dasyus," demons, devil-worshippers, a vile race, "who observe no sacred rites." Their right to subjugate the country is explained thus: "Indra subjects the impious to the pious, and destroys the irreligious by the religious." They pray to Indra, "Hurl thy shaft against the Dasyu, and increase the might and glory of the Arya;" and Indra, "armed with lightning," moves about, "shattering the cities of the Dasyus," and is described as the destroyer of "the godless cities" of the Dasyus," from which we may infer that the old inhabitants of India, described as Dasyus, had cities, settled life, and civilization. "Ancient cities" of the Dasyus are mentioned; also cities built of stone, and cities which the invading Aryans attacked by blockade or siege.

The Dasyus, or native inhabitants of India, were not like their invaders either in race or religion. Moreover, they were "black-skinned," while the Aryans were white. This is frequently mentioned. The Aryans are "the bright race," while the Dasyus are described as "the dark race," and "the host of black descent;" and Indra is praised because "he destroyed the Dasyus and protected the Aryan color." These expressions are used to mark the difference in color and race between the white Aryans and the aborigines, or native inhabitants, whom they found in possession of the country. They can mean nothing else. Of course, the Veda undertakes no formal description of the aboriginal inhabitants. It has no formal discussions of either their religion, language, or social condition; but their unlikeness to the Aryans is plainly indicated. "Wealthy Dasyus" are mentioned in the Mahabharata, who lived "in a prosperous condition," and tempted Aryan saints to associate with them; but this was at a later period, when the "twice-born" children of the Veda were beginning to humanize that intense and terrible fanaticism which had regulated their treatment of the Dasyus at the beginning.

There are some passages of the Veda that seem to indicate that these intense Aryan invaders saw, in the religion of the Dasyus, either Phallus worship or something akin to it, for they express a feeling like what might naturally be aroused in them by observing the rites and symbols of that worship without comprehending their significance. In the Rig-Veda, vii., 21, 5, the worshipper prays, "Let not the lascivious wretches (or those who make a god of the *sisna*, *i. e.*, of the *membrum virile*) approach our sacred rite;" and in x., 99, 3, we read, "When smiting the [city] with a hundred portals, the irresistible [Indra] overcame the lascivious wretches." Mr. Muir, in his "Sanskrit Texts," calls attention to these expressions, and also to the Vedic word *sisnadevá*. He observes that "Roth thinks the word [*sisnadevá*] is a scornful appellation for priapic or sensual demons." The Phallus-worshipping aborigines were naturally called demons by the "twice-born" Aryans. Mr. Muir expresses some uncertainty; but it cannot be disputed that the Phallic worship connected with Baal or Siva prevailed throughout India in the ante-Vedic ages. The Aryans certainly found it there, and we may reasonably presume that these passages of the Veda express their execration of its rites.

Scholars who have carefully studied the Vedic literature agree in the opinion that the Indo-Aryans paused in the valley of the Upper Ganges a long time—probably several centuries—before proceeding to occupy the country further east, and that "there the Brahmanical institutions must have been developed and matured, and, perhaps, the collection of the Vedic hymns completed, and the canon closed;" or, as Lassen has it, the germs imported from without were first planted, cultivated, and brought to maturity in Hindustan, in the country adjacent to the Sarasvati River. There must have been a long distance in time between the Veda and the Brahmanas. In the matured Brahmanical system Indra is dethroned by Brahma, who does not appear in the Veda as a deity, and the leading Vedic divinities have either disappeared or been transformed. In the literature of that system the Vedic language itself is superseded by Sanskrit.

There is neither history nor chronology of the long period required for these changes, but their character, and what we know of the process by which such changes are effected, indicate its extent. I cannot suppose that the Brahmanical system matured on the Sarasvati was the same as that known to us as modern Brahmanism, which must be a late reconstruction of the old system; but it was so different from the simpler religion of the Veda, both in its divinities and its organization, that many ages must have been required for the gradual growth of the changes by which this difference was produced.

In the next ages, that Aryan country on the Sarasvati was the holy land of the Brahmana. They called it Brahmâvartta. The following is from a frequently quoted passage of Manu: "The tract fashioned by the gods, which

A Mixture of the Races.

lies between the two divine rivers Sarasvati and Drishadvati, is called Brahmāvartta. The usage relating to castes and mixed castes, that has been traditionally received in that country, is called the pure usage." He describes as Aryavartta a region north of the Vindhya Mountains, from the valley of the Indus to the mouth of the Ganges, saying that beyond its limits lay "the country of the Mlechhas," or Dasyus. "Twice-born men" were required to remain within the limits of Aryavartta, "but a Sudra may dwell anywhere." We see, therefore, that Manu appeared later than this first development of the Brahmanical system, and that when he wrote, the Indo-Aryans had left Brahmâvartta to occupy the whole lower valley of the Ganges down to the Bay of Bengal.

Previous to this movement they had occupied but a small part of India, and probably they were at all times much less numerous than the aboriginal population. It may be presumed that fanatical exclusiveness was beginning to relax its severity when they took possession of the country on the Lower Ganges, and that closer relations were established between the Aryas and the Dasyus; for at this period, or at a period not much later, must have begun that mixture of the two races in which the white Aryan color finally disappeared. This mixture is an incontestable fact, but nothing indicates that it could have begun at any time during the Vedic age. It must, however, have begun at a very early period, for it was complete, even in the Punjâb, long before the time of Alexander the Great, who found there but one color, and apparently but one race. We learn from Megasthenes and Arrian that "the natives of India and Ethiopia are not much different in their features or complexion." It was noticed, says Megasthenes, that the people of Southern India were darker in color than those at the north, and also that "the Astaceni and the Assaceni," two Indian peoples dwelling on the west bank of the Indus, were "not altogether so swarthy" as those east of that river.

It may be inferred from passages in the Sanskrit books that after the Indo-Aryans occupied the country on the Lower Ganges known as Maghada and Behar, but more anciently as Kīkata, Brahmanism was affected by some great and successful influence of the aboriginal inhabitants and their religion. Kīkata was probably a civilized and important country of the Dasyus, and most of its people may have become incorporated with the Aryans who conquered and occupied it. At any rate, after the Aryan occupation of that country, the "twice-born" Sanskrit worshippers connected with Brahmâvartta did not regard it as a land of faultless Brahmanism, but rather as a country in which the true religion had lost the holy flavor of orthodoxy. But it was not wholly excluded from the pale of the faithful, as may be seen in the following passage from the Bhagavad Purana, quoted by Mr. Muir in his "Sanskrit Texts," part ii., p. 363: "In every place where those who are devoted to me, who are calm, who regard all things as alike, and who are holy and virtuous, are born, the men [of that country] are purified, even if they be Kīkatas."

Professor Weber, noticing the doubt expressed by some concerning the origin of these Kīkatas, shows, what the Sanskrit books make plain, that they were Aryans who did not faithfully observe the Brahmanical rites. He thinks "they may have been Buddhists, or the forerunners of Buddhism." It is well known that Kīkata, or Maghada, was the birth-place of both Buddhism and the Pali language; and the inspiration of Buddhism came largely from the doctrines of the Cushite system of planet worship, which had prevailed in India previous to the Aryan invasion, and with which the phallic and serpent worship were intimately associated.

At a later period the Sanskrit race went beyond the Vindhya Mountains into Southern India. An invasion of that country, and a war with Ravana, king of Ceylon, furnish the subject of the Ramayana; but they never occupied the Dakshin as they occupied the valley of the Ganges. The Sanskrit did not supersede the aboriginal tongues in the Dekhan, and the invaders found it necessary to absorb, or to reconstruct and modify, the old religion, which they could not exterminate. It may be doubted whether the pure and stainless orthodoxy matured in the holy land of the Brahmana, Brahmavartta, entirely escaped the modifying influence of the old religion in any other part of India. If its modern representative could be submitted to the judgment of the great Brahmans of the Sarasvati, they would unquestionably regard it as a fallen creature, defiled and transformed by unlawful association with Rakshasas.

RELIGIOUS HISTORY OF SANSKRIT INDIA.

Some Oriental scholars have argued with much earnestness and ingenuity to show that Buddhism and the Pali language are older than Brahmanism and the Sanskrit language. They are mistaken in their conclusions, and yet not entirely wrong. They show conclusively that Buddhism must be older than modern Brahmanism, but they do not show that there was not another and much more ancient Brahmanical system, developed and matured while the Sanskrit was in the brightest age of its history as a spoken language, and long before the Pali made its appearance. What we know as the Brahmanism of India cannot be very ancient. It is full of elements foreign to the Sanskrit race; it worships gods whom they did not bring into India, and who were unknown in the Pantheon at Brahmāvartta. Like the modern tongues of the country, it is full of materials borrowed from the "Dasyus" or "Rākshasas," in mixture with whom the Indo-Aryans themselves lost their white color. This cannot be the Brahmanism to which Manu gave laws in the "divine country" on the Sarasvati, nor of any age while Sanskrit was still learned of mothers and nurses, and still used in all the intercourse of common life.

Neither the Sanskrit nor the Pali books give us anything like a regular history of religious development, change, and reconstruction in the various countries of India; but they enable us to see that original and pure Brahmanism—the Brahmanism of the time of Manu—came into existence before the Sanskrit race established their supremacy in the lower valley of the Ganges, and that Buddhism did not appear until the kingdom of Kīkata, afterward called Magadha and Behar, became important and influential. At first, and for a long time, the two systems must have existed as two differing schools in the same religious communion; Buddhism being a visible but undeveloped heresy, with a very distinct and positive individuality in its elements and tendencies, but not yet sufficiently matured and organized to create actual separation.

Buddhism was much older than Gautama, or Sakhya-Muni, the Buddha of the Ceylonese records. He was only one of its prophets. A passage in the Raja Taringini, a religious history of Kashmir, translated by Mr. Turnour, shows (for it plainly has this meaning) that in China, Thibet, and Nepal, "six Arhatas, or mortal predecessors of Gautama" (Buddha), are recognised; and this accords with the fact that the Jainas, whose religious system originated in Buddhism, celebrate Kasyapa, one of these predecessors, as their great prophet, claiming that the Buddhists themselves followed him before Gautama appeared.

Eugene Burnouf found it difficult to comprehend the very intimate relations between Buddhism and Siva worship. Perhaps a clearer perception of the real significance of this worship, with a more careful consideration of the circumstances under which Buddhism came into existence, might have lessened the difficulty. He recognised the antiquity of this system of religion by speaking of Sakhya-Muni as "the last of the seven human Buddhas of whom tradition has preserved recollections." Buddhism was the growth of many ages preceding that in which Sakhya-Muni appeared. Its system of doctrine and practice was completely developed before his time, and this fact explains why the various Buddhist sects have differed and disputed so much concerning the date of his appearance.

Professor H. H. Wilson, finding among these sects not less than twenty different dates for the time of his birth, varying from 2420 B.C. to 453 B.C., made this a reason for doubting whether such a person ever existed. We may reasonably deny that he was the original founder of Buddhism, but he was undoubtedly one of its great teachers. Burnouf thinks his teaching was oral, and doubts whether he left any writings. Fa-hian, a Chinese Buddhist who spent several years in India between 300 and 414 A.D., stated his personal knowledge of Buddhist sects there that specially honored the names of three Buddhas, immediate predecessors of Sakhya-Muni, but refused to honor him as a Buddha.

The successful development and final supremacy of Buddhism in India were due, in great measure, to the power and influence of the kingdom of Magadha. In that kingdom its gradual growth was protected; and when it came to an open warfare with Brahmanism, Magadha was supreme throughout Northern India. Brahmanism was defeated and driven into obscurity, and for ten or eleven centuries Buddhism was the dominant religion of the land. It is probable that both Magadha and the religion it protected had much greater influence with the aboriginal inhabitants than Brahmanism, and were strengthened by their support; for Buddhism opposed the arrogance of caste, and preached equality. It drew much from the religion of the primitive inhabitants, while it won their sympathy and support against the Brahmans. Buddhism appears to have had a somewhat larger influence in Southern India than had been possible to Brahmanism; and it took possession of Ceylon, where Brahmanism never found entrance. It was established in the countries of Farther India; it crossed the Indus; it passed over the Himalaya Mountains into Thibet; it went to China; and, although it was subsequently expelled from India, it is still the religion of nearly one third of the human race.

In the seventh century of the Christian era Magadha no longer existed as an all-powerful kingdom. There were great political changes, and with them came religious changes. Buddhism was declining, and Brahmanism was gaining strength and influence. The reigning princes were no longer all Buddhists; the Brahmans were coming into power. The inscriptions began to mention them, at first with respect, as a class on whom royal favor was bestowed; then as "lords of the earth;" and at last their position is indicated by the terms used in an inscription at Chatapur, dated in the year 1010 A.D., which describes them as those "whose feet earthly kings adored." The downfall of Buddhism seems to have been effected by a combined and persistent attack of the Brahmans, the Saivas, communities representing the ante-Sanskrit religion of the country, and all the Buddhist sectaries who rejected Sakhya-Muni, or made his teachings subordinate to other features of the more ancient Buddhism. The Buddhism of Sakhya was finally expelled from India; but the Brahmanism developed by this successful crusade was no longer that of Manu and the great teachers of the ancient Brahmâvartta.

Sakhya-Muni, instead of being the founder of Buddhism, was merely the representative of one particular and very popular development of that system. The Jainas, who still remain in India, are really Buddhists who profess to follow the teachings of his immediate predecessor. The Saivas, a numerous and powerful sect, probably had their origin in Buddhism, and represented features of that system which did not appear very distinctly in the teachings of Sakhya and his disciples. We must suppose there may have been much in ancient Buddhism that did not appear prominently in that particular development of it which Asoka made the established religion of his empire.

The sect called Saivas may have been anciently a Buddhist school in which the elements drawn from the ante-Sanskrit religion of India were more fully represented than in any other. It had risen to great influence when the Buddhism of Sakhya-Muni was overthrown; and after this event it seems to have been absorbed by the reconstructed Brahmanism that took the place of the fallen system. Like the Buddhists, the Saivas rejected the Vedas; and Burnouf refers to "a considerable number of gods and goddesses, veritable Saivite divinities, such as Mahákála, Yamántaka, Bhúirava, Durgá, Mahákáli, and others that were really borrowed from the popular religion of the Indians."

MODERN BRAHMANISM.

Dr. Stevenson says: "Three different systems of belief have contributed to the formation of modern Hinduism [or Brahmanism], namely, ancient Brahmanism, Buddhism, and the ante-Brahmanical religion of the country." He is sure that the worship of Siva was "an aboriginal superstition of the country," and that the Brahmans adopted it to gain influence with people of the old race. It is plain, however, that they adopted it because the Saivas were a power in the land. As Dr. Stevenson observes, wherever the Brahmans found among the people a god whom they deemed it politic to reverence, they straightway made him an avatár of one of their own gods. He says innumerable local avatárs of gods have thus sprung up throughout the country, and found celebration in manufactured legends or *Máhátmyas* of the Puranas.

The later Brahmans aimed to conciliate and absorb everything; but there are many districts where they have never been able to supersede the old religion; and even the amalgamation of Brahmanism with Siva worship is not perfect. Dr. Stevenson states, from his own extensive observation, that he can vouch for the fact that, in the Maráthi country, where Saivas greatly prevail, no Brahman officiates in a linga temple. The same appears to be true in the Dekhan;

and here it may be stated that the ante-Sanskrit origin of Siva worship is plainly signified by the fact that its chief seats and most sacred places are in those parts of the country where the influence of the Sanskrit race, whether as Brahmans or Buddhists, has always been weakest—in the north-east and at the south, where the worshippers of Siva are far more numerous than those of Vishnu.

The Brahmans could not have been wholly without organization and influence during the Buddhist ages, for they kept the Sanskrit language in use as a literary language, and they carefully preserved the old Vedic and Sanskrit books; but their endeavor to connect the origin of modern Brahmanism with the oldest traditions of their class, and make it appear to be the same system that was developed in the early times at Brahmâvartta, has led them to destroy some of the books, revise and interpolate others, and to do all in their power to hide or obscure the intervening religious history of India. It cannot well be doubted that the Puranas have been reconstructed to a certain extent. While, as Colonel Wilford pointed out, they contain much that bears internal evidence of great antiquity, there are other portions of their contents that cannot be very old. Wilford said: "I am sometimes tempted to believe, from some particular passages in the Puranas which have the true historical style, that the Hindus have destroyed, or at least designedly consigned to oblivion, all genuine records militating against their system." Mr. Wathen believed that, "on the Mussulman conquest of India, the Brahmans destroyed all previous historical documents," and said, "they seem, nevertheless, to have carefully preserved, invented, or adapted such compositions in Sanskrit as attested their own religious supremacy."

While the Puranas undoubtedly contain genuine records of great antiquity, we cannot safely trust those portions of them that relate to the connection of modern Brahmanism with ancient times.

INDIAN HISTORY AND CHRONOLOGY.

There is nothing in the monuments or literature of India that affords materials for a chronological history of the country, or that furnishes a basis for any hypothetical scheme of such a history. There is in the Pali language a history of Ceylon, deemed authentic, that goes back to the year 543 before the Christian Era; and there is a history of Kashmir, the Raja Taringini, of which Professor Wilson spoke as "the only Sanskrit composition yet discovered to which the title of history can with any propriety be applied." It is difficult to believe that written annals of Magadhi, Oude, and other Indian kingdoms never existed. The Jainas accuse the Brahmans of having destroyed "all the historical books in existence wherever they gained the ascendency;" and they assert, also, that the Puranas were originally historical works, and that Parasurama, Ramchandra, Krishna, and others, celebrated as divine heroes, were merely great kings who reigned in Oude and other Brahmanical countries in ancient times. It seems very clear that these charges against the Brahmans are true. The lost history cannot be recovered; but certain facts appear, in the course of these inquiries, that engage attention, and furnish important suggestions.

We see in the Veda itself that the people found in India by the Sanskrit race were a civilized people, who had important cities, and, of course, settled life and political organization. It is preposterous, and utterly unwarranted by any fact whatever, to approach this investigation with the mind and imagination preoccupied by the assumption that the people of India were all savages before the Aryans went there. Nothing to justify this assumption can be found in the Veda, for the terms of religious hatred and execration bestowed upon the native inhabitants by the fanaticism of the invading Aryans cannot have this meaning. When we read in the Veda that the Dasyus, Rakshasas, and demons, as they were called, had important cities, "cities built of stone," "ancient cities," cities that were attacked by siege and blockade, we see clearly that the aboriginal inhabitants of India were civilized.

It is probable that the highest condition of their civilization existed in the kingdoms of the southern country and on the Lower Ganges; but civilization was found in that part of India first visited and occupied by the Sanskrit race. Fa-hian, the Chinese traveler, learned in India that the ancient "Rakshasas" and "demons" of Ceylon were a civilized and commercial people. In the Ramayana, the people of the Dekhan are called not only Rakshasas, but also "monkeys;" but there is mention of their kings, kingdoms, wealth, golden ornaments, and rich gifts to Rama, which very distinctly indicates their civilization. We see it, also, in those antiquities of the country, which must be referred to ages before the Aryan immigration, and which so clearly connect that ante-Sanskrit civilization with the Arabian Cushites. Civilization must have come from Arabia to India at a period that was already in the misty deeps of antiquity when the oldest hymns of the Veda were written.

The history of the Aryan race in India may be divided into four distinct periods. 1. The Vedic age, which began when the Indo-Aryans were dwelling in Haptu-Hindu, and closed at some period after their settlement at Brahmâvartta on the Sarasvati. During this period they occupied but a small part of the country. 2. The ancient Brahmanical period, which began at Brahmâvartta, and terminated when the supremacy of Buddhism was established. This was the period of the Sanskrit language. The Vedic tongue had ceased to exist save in the old books, and there were important changes in the Vedic Pantheon. A very long period of time was required for such changes, to which must be added all the time necessary for the Sanskrit tongue to appear, receive its great development, live its whole life as a spoken language, and finally disappear from common use. 3. The period of Sakhya-Muni's Buddhism, which lasted about twelve centuries, counting from the time of the second convocation in the year 450 B.C. 4. The period of modern Brahmanism, which was beginning to take form and assume importance in the seventh century of the Christian Era, more than eleven hundred years ago.

The kingdom of Magadha was much older than the time of Sakhya-Muni, who is supposed to have been born more than 600 years before Christ. It grew up out of the Aryan occupation of the Lower Ganges, and may have been as old as any attempt to reconstruct its chronology has claimed; but we have no authentic chronology, nor even an authentic list of the kings from the beginning. The Brahmans, who preserved the old Sanskrit and Vedic books, have dealt most villanously with the historical and chronological records of the country. Mr. Turnour, in his Introduction to the Mahâwanso, speaking of the great ingenuity that has been displayed in attempts to unravel and explain the absurdities of Hindu chronology, says: "They all tend to show that the incongruities are the result of

systematic perversions, had recourse to, since the time of
Megasthenes, by the Hindus, to work out their religious
impostures, and that they in no degree originate in barbarous ignorance, or in the imperfect light that has glimmered
on a remote antiquity." And yet these unpardonable falsifiers have not been able to hide the fact that Buddhism,
including all its various schools, has had a far more powerful and permanent influence in India than Brahmanism,
nor to conceal the comparatively modern origin of their
own composite system.

THE ANCIENT MALAYAN EMPIRE.

El-Mas'údí, in his work on history and geography, entitled "Meadows of Gold and Mines of Gems," says: "India is a vast country, having many seas and mountains,
and borders upon the empire of ez-Zanij, which is the kingdom of the Maharáj, the king of the islands, whose dominions form the frontier between India and China, and are
considered as part of India." He represents that "the
splendor and high civilization" of this island empire, called
ez-Zanij, were greatly celebrated. Farther on he adds:
"The Maharáj is lord of the sixth sea," and "king of the
islands from which drugs and spices are exported;" and
says, "the population and the number of the troops of his
kingdom cannot be counted; and the islands under his
sceptre are so numerous that the fastest sailing vessel is
not able to go round them in two years." [See Aloys
Sprenger's translation, p. 176, 187, 355–6, and 397.] The
people of this great island empire, he tells us, were black.

Five hundred and fifty years after the time when El-Mas'údí wrote, the Portuguese made their first appearance
in the Indian Seas, having sailed around the Cape of Good

Hope. At that time this celebrated empire was still in existence, much weakened, and in a state of decline. It included, with the peninsula of Malacca, the great islands of Sumatra, Borneo, Java, and Celebes, and all the other islands between Australia and the China Sea. Renaudot gives the reports of two Mussulman travelers who visited that part of the East in the ninth century, previous to the time of El-Mas'údí. At that time it included Arracan, Chittagong, the Gangetic provinces, and considerable territory on the Coromandel coast. They called it the empire of Zápáge, or Zábája, probably a corruption of the name of the island of Jává, or Jábá, which is also an old name for the island of Sumatra, called Já-bá-din by Ptolemy and Marco Polo. These travelers gave an account of wars between the Mahá-Raja of Zábája and the king of Al-Comr, or Comorin, and other kings in Southern India. Zaba, on the peninsula of Malacca, was a famous emporium in the time of Ptolemy; and Zábája, as a great maritime power, was probably much older than the Christian Era.

This was an empire of the people whom we know as the Malays, who, like the modern inhabitants of Yemen, Mauritania, and Asia Minor, no longer represent the civilization that made their nation great in ancient times. It may reasonably be presumed that in the Malays we see the race found in India by the Arabian Cushites. Mr. Marsden, who has given some attention to their literature and language, is inclined to connect them ethnically with the people of Chinese Tartary. Their color and other physiological peculiarities forbid this classification, and probably their language will do so strongly whenever it shall be thoroughly understood and intelligently described. It has been ascertained that dialects of the Malayan tongue are used by the people inhabiting nearly all the islands from New Zealand to the Sandwich Islands, from Madagascar to Formosa, and from the Indian Archipelago to Easter Island, on the American side of the Pacific Ocean; and that they all have certain rites and customs, which, like their related dialects, indicate a common origin.

These points are discussed in a volume published at London in 1834, which was written by Rev. Dr. Lang, and entitled "The Origin and Migrations of the Polynesian Nation, Demonstrating their Ancient Discovery and Progressive Settlement of the Continent of America." Humboldt and others have stated their belief that America was visited in pre-historic times by people from the Asiatic world, who went there across the Pacific Ocean; the Chinese and Japanese have recorded traditions that say this; and the Abbé Brasseur de Bourbourg points out that the ancient Peruvians had traditions of the arrival in their country of foreigners, who came by sea, and landed on the western coast.

The ancient Malayan civilization, like that of India and so many other ancient peoples, came originally, we may suppose, from the old Arabians. Java and the other large islands have antiquities, including ruins and inscriptions, that have not been explored and studied. The Malays read and write, and have many of the arts of civilized life. They use the Arabic characters, it is said; but formerly, it appears, they used another alphabet. Lieut. Col. Sykes stated, in the Journal of the Royal Asiatic Society, that "there are ancient inscriptions in Java" written in a character like that of "the old inscriptions in the Dekhan." If the antiquities of that old empire of Zábája (which Dr. Lang, in the ardor of his enthusiasm, believed to be as old as the Empire of China) could be intelligently and faithfully explored, something important might be added to our knowledge of the East—something that might give us a better notion of the character and importance of the Malayan people in ancient times, and aid our endeavor to make clear some of the difficult problems of Indian history.

VII.

EGYPT PREVIOUS TO MENES.

ANCIENT Egypt is now a fact that cannot be discredited, but a fact, nevertheless, which the current chronologies cannot accept. It has always been visible, though scarcely ever fully recognised by those who have written history. Greek scholars who visited Egypt toward the close of the New Monarchy, studied in its schools, explored its libraries, observed its monuments, and had access to abundant materials for writing its history, were not incited to write on that country, even as imperfectly as some of them wrote about Persia. They were more disposed to appropriate Egyptian science and philosophy without due acknowledgment; and we find many Greeks censuring Herodotus scornfully because he admitted that Greek thought and culture came largely from the Egyptians and Phœnicians.

Hellenic egotism and exclusiveness could not allow the scholars of Greece proper to write candid histories of "outside barbarians," and show, by clear and formal recognition, that the civilization of any "barbarian" nation, or of any older time, was or could be superior to that of Hellas; and their spirit has been allowed too great influence on the scholarship of modern times. Greek scholars had before them records and monuments of the Old Monarchy of Egypt. Had they investigated carefully, and recorded the result of their investigations in candidly-written histories of the country, our notions of the great past would be regulated by a scheme of chronology more in accordance with truth than that of Usher or of any other rabbinical speculator, and it would be much easier to accept the facts concerning Egypt which modern discoveries have made undeniable.

MANETHO'S HISTORY OF EGYPT.

So far as we know, the only history of Egypt ever written in Greek was that of Manetho of Sebennytus, an Egyptian priest of the highest reputation for learning and wisdom, who wrote about 300 years before the Christian Era. His aim was to give, in the Greek language, a full account of the religious and philosophical wisdom of his country, with a complete record of its history and chronology, basing his work on the ancient annals and sacred books of Egypt. The history was arranged in three parts. In the first part he gave what was known of the history of Egypt previous to the time of Menes, with the first eleven dynasties of the Old Monarchy, which Menes established. The second part closed with the nineteenth dynasty, and the third continued the history down to the overthrow of Nectanebus II., the last native sovereign, by the Persians. According to Manetho, as usually understood, the time from the first year of Menes to this conquest of Egypt by the Persians was 3555 years. During this time there were thirty successive dynasties, and the account of them suggests a division of Egyptian history into three great periods—the Old Monarchy, the Middle Monarchy, or period of the Hyksos, and the New Monarchy, which began with the eighteenth dynasty, and terminated with the reign of Nectanebus II. Manetho states that the rule of the Hyksos lasted 511 years. The reign of Menes began in the year 3893 B.C., reckoning Julian years, or 3803, reckoning Egyptian years.

This important work of Manetho is lost; but fragments of it have come down to us in the works of Julius Africanus, Eusebius, Syncellus, Josephus, and others. Certain passages in Plutarch's treatise *de Iside et Osiri* are supposed to be extracts from that part of it in which he explained the Egyptian doctrines concerning the gods. The most valuable portion of the history thus preserved is the list of Egyptian dynasties. None of the transcribers, however, have preserved it entirely free from error; but in Julius Africanus, copied by Syncellus, and in the Armenian version of Eusebius, we have copies of it so nearly correct that we can see what it was. Our dogmatic chronologists have not been able to receive this list with cordiality; in fact, they have treated it very unworthily; but its correctness has been revealed more and more clearly at every step in the progress of modern discovery in Egypt, which, instead of reducing the time given for the duration of Egypt under all the dynasties, has led some acute investigators to believe it should be considerably increased by additions to the time of the Old Monarchy.

Manetho's eminent character and great reputation made his work an authority in his own time. It was universally accepted as authentic. It does not appear that its accuracy was questioned for 600 years after it was written, or until the beginning of the fourth century of the Christian Era, when certain Jewish Rabbins and Christian writers fell into an obstinate chronological controversy, the Christians aiming to establish certain millennial theories, and the Jews to oppose them. Manetho's chronology found its way into this controversy, but neither Jew nor Christian was in a mood to accept it without revision. Both parties sought to compel his dates to harmonize with the system they profanely called biblical; and the rabbinical dogmatist, who had not scrupled to falsify the genealogies and alter the dates of his own sacred Scriptures, could not be expected to treat Manetho with much reverence. Manetho's earliest chronological date, 3893 B.C., could not be tolerated; therefore it must be denied; and they proceeded to mutilate and falsify his list of the dynasties. This villanous endeavor of falsehood, which was as false to the real chronology of the Hebrew Scriptures as to that of Manetho's history, was conducted in the most systematic and elaborate manner possible to those engaged in it. Manetho's lists and numbers were altered, abbreviated, and transformed in the most unscrupulous way, so as to compress them within such limits as suited the dogmatism of rabbinical theories.

This studied operation of fraud produced two spurious works—the "Old Chronicle" and the "Sothis"—which have, since, more than once deceived and misled honest investigators. To these spurious writings—which almost entirely omitted the Old Monarchy and otherwise falsified the true list—is due most of the confusion introduced into the inquiry concerning Egyptian chronology and ancient history. Their real character is now more generally understood; and yet, since the year 1860, a large and elaborate octavo volume has appeared in England, devoted to a discussion of Egyptian chronology, in which that false "Old Chronicle" is used as the highest authority on this subject.

But it does not belong to my present purpose to engage in this discussion, or to give a history of modern explorations and discoveries in Egypt. My inquiries relate to more ancient times. For all that belongs to the history of Egypt since the time of Menes, I must refer my readers to the works of eminent Egyptologists whose names are familiar to all, and especially to the very thorough and complete essay of Professor Lepsius on "The Chronology of the Egyptians," and to the publications of M. Mariette in France. Lepsius shows how constantly the monuments confirm the history of Manetho; and he observes very justly that "the investigation of Egyptian history will gradually exercise an extensive influence on all branches of archæology—on our whole conception of the past history of man."

ORIGIN AND ANTIQUITY OF EGYPT.

Before the time of Menes, Egypt had a civilization which must have seemed old to those acquainted with it. This is apparent to all who have studied the antiquities of that country. Sir Gardner Wilkinson refers to "the great mathematical skill of the Egyptians in the time of Menes," evinced by the change he made in the course of the Nile, and says: "It may be inferred, from their great advancement in the arts and sciences at this early period, that many ages of civilization had preceded the accession of their first monarch." Upper and Lower Egypt had previously existed as separate countries, each being governed by its own princes. Menes was a prince of Upper Egypt, the oldest of these separate countries. He was born at the city of This or Thinis, which appears to have been the royal seat of a Thinite dynasty of the upper country. That he was a man of remarkable force of mind and character may be inferred from the fact that he was able to unite the

"Two Countries" under one government, and lay the foundations of a great monarchy whose monuments are still studied with admiration and wonder.

There is neither history nor chronology of Egypt previous to the time of Menes. We have only the fact that civilization, letters, science, political organization, and kings existed there long before he appeared, with such knowledge of the early history of the "Two Countries" as may be gleaned from legends, traditions, and mythological narratives. Annals of those early ages were undoubtedly written and preserved in the temples, but they seem to have perished long before the time of Manetho. When we consider that a civilization like that of Egypt in the time of Menes is not the work of a year or of a century, we see distinctly that Egypt had a long existence previous to his reign. Most of the great monuments of civilization now found in Egypt belong to the period of the Old Monarchy, some of the grandest of them being as old as the time of its earlier dynasties.

According to the uniform testimony of tradition, civilization was first established in Egypt by colonies of Cushites, or Ethiopians. The old civilization throughout the whole upper valley of the Nile had the same origin. It came originally from Arabia, and went onward into Egypt, in very early times, before the Cushite race had changed its color by mixture with the dark race of Africa. According to Pliny, King Juba II. stated, in his work on Africa, that the people in the valley of the Nile, from Syene to Meroë, were Arabians. Those who have studied ancient Egypt carefully generally agree in the opinion that the Egyptians must have come originally from some country on the Asiatic side of the Red Sea. Sir Gardner Wilkinson says on this point:

"Every one who considers the features, the language, and other peculiarities of the ancient Egyptians, will feel convinced that they are not of African extraction, but that, like the Abyssinians and many inhabitants of the known valley of the Nile, they bear the evident stamp of an Asiatic origin." And, "In manners, language, and many other respects, Egypt was certainly more Asiatic than African; and though there is no appearance of the Hindu and Egyptian religions having been borrowed from one another, yet it is not improbable that those two nations may have proceeded from the same original stock, and have migrated southwards from their parent country in Central Asia."

How many difficult problems, or problems that seem difficult to many learned investigators, become clear immediately when we recognise the pre-historic greatness of ancient Arabia! Sir Gardner Wilkinson goes to Central Asia to find the origin of the ancient Egyptians, and endeavors to connect them with the Aryan race, which linguistic science forbids. Professor Rawlinson and others go over into Africa, and down the Nile to Meroë, to find the original colonizers and civilizers of Chaldea, which is preposterous. These gropings in the dark will be discontinued when such inquirers have learned to comprehend Arabia, the ancient mother of nations. Sir Henry Rawlinson sees the common origin of the Chaldeans and Egyptians, and finds it even in the character of their writing, which, he thinks, must have been in existence before the two peoples separated; but he does not see Arabia, although he understands very well the impossibility of connecting the origin of either the Chaldeans or Egyptians with any people of the Aryan race. Lepsius draws the same conclusions from the resemblance of Egyptian and other Cushite writing, and thinks the Egyptians may have brought the first elements of theirs "from their original home in Asia."

The ancient Arabians, being what they were, could not fail to occupy the Nile valley, and place colonies in Upper Egypt. It is very easy to see the course taken by their colonizing and civilizing forces. They crossed the Straits of Bab-el-Mandeb, and created a second Land of Cush. They occupied the Upper Nile valley, creating the civilized country long known as Barbara, and afterwards famed as Meroë. At length they went on to the lower valley of the Nile, and planted colonies in Upper Egypt. Sir Gardner Wilkinson says: "That civilization advanced northwards from the Thebaid to Lower Egypt is highly probable." The hieroglyphic legends which give precedence to Upper Egypt, and show that its early cities were the oldest in the country, place this beyond doubt. Civilization certainly came from the south.

Memphis, in Lower Egypt, founded by Menes, has around its ruins the great pyramids, and many other wonderful remains of the Old Monarchy, which astonish beholders; but This, or Thinis, in Upper Egypt, was a royal city, where kings reigned long before the time of Menes. The Egyptian name of Memphis was Misr. When another royal town rose on the east side of the river, this new city was also called Misr, and it still retains this name among the people, for Alkahira, the Conqueress, vulgarly called Cairo, is merely an epithet of the Mahometan Arabs. Hosea calls the city Moph; the Chaldean paraphrase calls it Maphes; Rabbi Kimchi says Moph and Noph were the same town. The Septuagint calls it Memphis, which the Copts and Arabs pronounce Menuf or Menf. Misr was the ancient name of Egypt; and Misraim, the plural or dual, means literally the Two Misrs, Egypt being described on its monuments as the "Two Countries."

It is stated that, when civilized communities were first established in Egypt, the lower part of the country was entirely sea and marsh. Herodotus, who investigated this point and discussed it at length, believed that Egypt was formerly a bay or arm of the sea. In his second book, he speaks thus of its physical condition in the time of Menes: "They say that in the time of Menes all Egypt, except the district of Thebes, was a morass, and that no part of the land now existing below Lake Myris was then above water. To this place from the sea is a seven days' passage up the river." So it was written substantially in the annals of Egypt, and so it was stated by the voice of tradition. Menes drained a part of Lower Egypt by changing the channel of the river. Diodorus Siculus, rehearsing, in his third book, what he had learned from Ethiopian sources, makes this statement: "The Ethiopians say that the Egyptians are a colony drawn out of them by Osiris; and that Egypt was formerly no part of the continent, but a sea at the beginning of the world, but that afterwards it was made land by the River Nile."

Rennell, in his work on the Geographical System of Herodotus, observes that "the configuration and composition of the low lands leave no room for doubt that the sea once washed the base of the rocks on which the pyramids of Memphis stand, the *present* base of which is washed by the inundation of the Nile at an elevation of seventy or eighty feet above the Mediterranean; but when we attempt to carry back our ideas to the remote period when the foundation of the delta was first laid, we are lost in the con-

templation of so vast a period of time." That Egypt is
geologically a "gift of the Nile" cannot reasonably be
doubted, and yet, old as it is, Sir Charles Lyell points out
conclusively that it is much more modern than the "stone
age" of Europe, as revealed by deposits found in the ancient
gravel of the valley of the Somme.

Diodorus Siculus adds to his statement that the laws,
customs, religious observances, and letters of the ancient
Egyptians closely resembled those of the Ethiopians, "the
colony still observing the customs of their ancestors."
Egypt, for several millenniums previous to his time, had
been a "colony" of which the Ethiopians or any other people might feel proud without being unreasonable. It is
true, however, that the origin and close relationship of the
various communities established by the old Cushites were
everywhere shown by the similarity of their mythologies,
religious ceremonies, and social usages. These, quite as
surely as comparative philology, or records found written
on old ruins, still reveal to us the ancient connection of the
Cushite race with Egypt, India, and Asia Minor, and with
many other countries at the East and around the Mediterranean. The very great resemblance between the old
Egyptians and the Cushites, extending to their languages,
which belonged to the same family, makes it undeniable
that one of these two peoples owed its civilization to the
other. But we see clearly, in all the records and traditions
of antiquity, that the civilization of Cusha-dwipa, the Land
of Cush, was much older than that of Egypt—much older
than any other of which there is the slightest trace in the
mythologies, traditions, records, or old ruins of antiquity,
of which we have any knowledge.

The Aryan civilization may have been nearly as old, but

in early times it was not greatly developed; and it was
not so widely prevalent, nor so powerfully controlling in
the ancient world. Certainly it had nothing to do with
the formation and development of Egypt; that was entirely a work of the Cushites, or Ethiopians. This is why
the annals of the Egyptian priests were so full of the Ethiopians, who not only played a foremost and wonderful part
in the affairs of the world, but who had been playing that
part long before Egypt became the abode of a civilized
community.

THE OLD SANSKRIT BOOKS ON EGYPT.

Many references to the pre-historic ages of Egypt are
found in the old Sanskrit books, which contain remarkably
accurate notices not only of Africa, but also of Western
Europe. What the ancient Aryans knew of distant regions came to them probably through the more enterprising Cushites, who preceded them in India, and with whom
they must have maintained a constant intercourse. That
the account of Egypt, given by their Puranas and other
legendary narratives, is based on actual knowledge of a
very early condition of the country, is evident, for it is accompanied by accurate descriptions of the Nile, of the regions through which it flows, and of adjacent regions in
Africa; and it is just as clear that these mythical and legendary narratives of the ancient Aryans of India have a
historical basis. They may have been shaped, more or
less, by the influence of that enchantment which distance
in time and place usually works in the imagination of such
a people. So it was with similar mythical stories of the
Greeks, and so it has been everywhere, from the beginning
of time, in all communities placed in like circumstances.

The facts communicated must flow in the same stream of narration with the feelings, fancies, and prejudices of the narrators; but the facts are not on this account less real, and frequently they stand out with all the clearness of unobscured reality.

Some account of what is told by the Sanskrit Puranas, or mythical stories, can be found in the very elaborate papers of Major Francis Wilford, published in several of the early volumes of "Asiatic Researches." They establish the fact that in very remote times there was a great communication between India and Arabia, and the countries on the Nile, and most of them relate to events that occurred in the ages when the countries of Hindustan were still subject to the sway of the Cushites, who seem to have begun their occupation of India before they went to Egypt. Here is the old Sanskrit description of the Nile:*

"That celebrated and holy river [the Nile] takes its rise from the Lake of the Gods, thence named Amara or Deva Sarovera, the region of Sharma or Sharma-st'han, between the Mountains of Ajagara and Sitanta, which seem part of Sómá-giri, or the Mountains of the Moon, the country round the lake being called Chándri-st'han or Moonland: thence the Cali [Nile] flows into the marshes of Padma-van, and through the Nishadha Mountains into the land of Barbara [Nubia, still known to the natives as Barbara], whence it

---

* Some of Wilford's papers, published in volumes of the "Asiatic Researches" previous to the 8th, cannot be fully trusted, he tells us, because he was deceived by his pundit. But this cannot apply to their account of the Nile, for knowledge of the source and character of this river was prevalent in India and Arabia in very early times. Moreover, Ptolemy, who studied the Phœnician and Arabian geographers carefully, stated that the Nile rose in certain Mountains of the Moon, *from two lakes* lying east and west of each other, near the equator.

passes through the Mountains of Hémacúta into Sancha-
dwipa proper [i. e. Upper Egypt proper]; there, entering
the forests of Tapas [or Thebais], it runs into Cantaca-desa,
or Misra-st'han, and through the woods named Aruúga and
Atavi, into the Sanc'habdhi."

In this description we see an actual knowledge of the
source of the Nile, of the lake region of Africa, and of the
country near the Mountains of the Moon—knowledge
which we have lacked until within a few years; and we
still know much less of those regions than was known in
India when these Puranas were originally written, especially of the Mountains of the Moon, whose very name comes
to us from Arabia and India. We have learned recently
from explorers that the main source of the Nile is a lake
which they call Victoria Nyanza, and that it certainly has
connection with another lake, now called Albert Nyanza.
They tell us, also, that the country around the lakes, at
and near the sources of the Nile, is now called U-nyamúézi
or Moonland; and Speke says: "U-nyamúézi—Country
of the Moon—must have been one of the largest kingdoms
of Africa." The Mountains of the Moon, whose name is as
old, probably, as the first Cushite occupation of that country, have not yet been explored. Traditions of that Cushite invasion and occupation, as well as other traces of it,
remain there to this day.

The country which the Puranas designate as Barbara
was situated between Upper Egypt and Abyssinia, or, according to Wilford, it included "all the country between
Syene and the confluence of the Nile with the Tacazzé,
which is generally called Barbara and Barba at the present time." In this name, perhaps, we see the origin of that
term Barbary, which has been applied to Northern Africa,

and also of the term Berbers, used to designate numerous tribes that occupy the interior of Northern Africa.

According to the Sanskrit books, the first settlers in Egypt were the Sharmicas, who went from Cusha-dwipa. It is said, "they found the country peopled by evil beings, and by a few impure tribes of men who had no fixed habitation." They were followed by other tribes and emigrants, from various parts of Cusha-dwipa within, among whom the most numerous and important were the Pallis, who are shown to have been Cushites, and who, as Wilford points out, were of the same race as the Phœnicians. The term Sancha-dwipa, which became a designation for the whole eastern part of the continent, was originally applied to Upper Egypt. There are legends referring to other emigrants who are said to have gone to that region from Cusha-dwipa and from India, in which we see, woven into beautiful fictions, traditional reports of occurrences there after the first settlements became established communities.

Of course, they give us neither history nor chronology; and there is usually nothing to indicate clearly either the distance or the relation, in time, between the events used for narration in one legend and those used in another. The Puranas describe the reign of "King It" (or "Ait," as he is often called), whose rule seems to have marked a great epoch in the history of Upper Egypt. He belonged to a very remote period. In the Greek traditions he is called Ætus. The Puranas say he came forth from the waters of the Cali, or Nile, and they speak of him as a subordinate incarnation of the god Mrira. He put an end to a period of frightful war and devastation, overwhelmed the *Daityas* or evil beings, protected the *Devatas* or good people, restored order, and ruled those countries with honor and glory. Stephanus of Byzantium says he came from India, which the Puranas do not claim. He may have been a Cushite or Arabian prince who had been employed in India, then largely occupied by the Cushites, and who was afterwards sent to the countries on the Nile to suppress disorder and rebellion, or to defend the settlements against invasion from the interior. He may have remained there a long time as governor of those countries.

The Puranas mention several kings of Arabia, or "the interior Cusha-dwipa," with whom the countries on the Nile had a very intimate connection, and to whom they were subject or tributary. One of these Cushite kings was Divodasa, pronounced Diodas in the popular dialects. It is said that he reigned over the "western districts" of Cusha-dwipa within, which extended from the shores of the Mediterranean to the banks of the Indus and the shores of the Indian Ocean. Wilford remarks that "he seems to have been the Hercules-Diodas mentioned by Eusebius, who flourished in Phœnicia." The story of another king of Cusha-dwipa is told with variations, and with more than the usual activity of imagination, indicating that at some remote period in the past he had a wide-spread fame, and was a favorite theme of popular eulogy. One version of his story is substantially as follows:

On the Mountains of Jwalámuc'ha, in the interior Cusha-dwipa, reigned a virtuous and religious prince, named Charvanayanas, whose son, Capeyanas, had a controlling passion for arms and hunting. At length Capeyanas, being more devoted to his favorite pursuits than to religious observances, was exiled by his father, went to a prince whose territory was in the western part of Arabia, and married his daughter. He distinguished himself as a heroic warrior, rose from the position of a subordinate prince, became the supreme ruler of Cusha-dwipa, governed justly, subdued rebellious tributary princes east and west, made great conquests, and ruled his vast kingdom in glory. He had a daughter named Antarmada, and a son Bhateyanas, who succeeded him on the throne and conquered the King of Meru. Bhateyanas and his sister finally became devotees, and retired to the forest of Tapas, in Upper Egypt. Here Antarmada was sorely persecuted by Mayadeva, who at length chained her to a rock on the sea-shore, from which she was delivered by a young hero named Parasica, whom she married. After death they were seated among the stars, with Capcyanas and his wife Casyapi.

Wilford, having detected his pundit in deceptions and fraudulent copyings from the manuscripts, was for a time in doubt concerning the authenticity of this Sanskrit version of the story of Kepheus, Cassiopeia, Perseus, and Andromeda. But, on careful investigation, the doubt was removed, and different versions of the story were found in the *Yantra-raja* and other books, "with a most ample account of the thirty-six *Deccani* so famous in Egyptian astronomy, and called *Drescan* in Sanskrit." In the Yantra-raja, Perseus is called *Pretasira;* Andromeda, *Vejara;* Cassiopeia, *Lebana;* and Kepheus, *Nripa* or *Nrirupa.* In other Sanskrit books Kepheus is mentioned as a great king, and described "as the father of the Kephenes. Kapesa is Kepheus; and Kápisá is the patronymic of their descendants."

In the Greek legends Kepheus is celebrated as King of Ethiopia, which in the Sanskrit books is called Cusha-dwipa; and Perseus was a prince of Argos, who rescued and married his daughter Andromeda. Here we see again, what is so evident elsewhere, that the Land of Cush furnished both the Greeks and the ancient Aryans of India with materials for their mythological narratives, and therefore had a civilization much more ancient than any other known to them. And a large part of these materials was furnished by personages and events belonging to that period in the history of Cusha-dwipa when Egypt was a colonial dependency or tributary province of that country. It reminds one, as has been observed, of Lord Bacon's remark, that "the mythology of the Greeks, which their oldest writers do not pretend to have invented, was no more than a light air, which had passed from a more ancient people into the flutes of the Grecians" [and of the old Aryans and other peoples also], "which they modulated to such descants as best suited their fancies." All such narratives are "founded on fact," and reveal an ancient history that gave them birth, else they could not exist.

DIONYSOS, CALLED OSIRIS AND BACCHUS.

The narratives relating to Dionysos—known in Egypt as Osiris, and sometimes called the Indian Bacchus—refer to a period more ancient, probably, than that of Kepheus. All the legends of Egypt, India, Asia Minor, and the older Greeks, describe him as a king, very great during his life, and deified after death. The history of Dionysos seems to have been a favorite topic with some of the older Ionian writers; and it was, undoubtedly, still more prominent in the lost literature of Egypt, Arabia, Thrace, and Asia Minor. Diodorus Siculus mentions one old work on this subject that appears to have come down from the ages preceding Ionia, and with which he had some acquaintance. He states that it was composed by Thymœtes of Asia Minor, describes it as a history of Dionysos given in a poem entitled "Phrygia," and says it was written "in a very old language and character." It is added that Thymœtes took pains to secure the most accurate and complete information relative to Dionysos; that he visited Nysa, in Arabia, where he was educated, inquired of records and traditions, and studied the subject carefully. The chief particulars in his account of Dionysos are as follows:

Amon, king of Arabia or Ethiopia, married Rhea, sister of Cronos, who reigned over Italy, Sicily, and certain countries of Northern Africa. Nevertheless, Amon was greatly in love with the beautiful Amalthea, and Dionysos was the child of this love. Rhea, in a violent excitement of anger, separated herself from Amon, returned to Cronos, and became his wife. Dionysos was brought up at Nysa, a city of Arabia, and diligently instructed in the most learned arts and sciences. He was endowed with remarkable genius, and developed wonderful force and brilliancy of mind and character. The relations between Cronos and Amon were constantly hostile, and at length the former became successful in a war against the latter, defeated his armies, and attempted a conquest of his kingdom. With this end in view, he marched against Nysa; but now Dionysos took the field, defeated the army of Cronos in a great battle, drove him out of the country, pursued him to his own capital, dethroned him, and enthroned his son Zeus in his place. It is added that Zeus reigned nobly and won a great fame. The great career of Dionysos followed this beginning. He succeeded his father, and became the greatest of sovereigns. He powerfully extended his sway in all the neighboring countries, and completed the conquest of India, where he spent several years, and built a city called Nysa. He afterwards seems to have given much attention to the Cushite colonies in Egypt, greatly increasing their strength, intelligence, and prosperity.

In classical tradition, Cronos and Saturn are treated as the same personage; but the character of the Roman Saturn is quite different from that of the Greek Chronos. In the mythical legends of Rome, Saturn was celebrated as a very ancient king of Italy, who introduced agricultural industry, social order, and the habits of civilized life. His reign filled the land with plenty, and created the golden age of Italy. He was suddenly removed to the divine abodes and became a god. These legends were ancient, in Italy, long before Rome was built. The Greek, Egyptian, and Ethiopian legends made Dionysos contemporary with Saturn, or Cronos, and his sons. In the legends of Egypt, Osiris, or Dionysos, was a glorious king of that country, who came to a violent death at the hands of his brother Typhon, and whose death was revenged by his wife Isis and his son Orus. He was King of Egypt just as the sovereigns of Great Britain are sovereigns of Canada; Egypt formed a part of his empire. But the Egyptians, in their mythology, appropriated him entirely to themselves, making him the originator of civilization, and especially of the arts of agriculture.

Fresnel, in the *Journal Asiatique*, maintains that the Dhou-Nouwas of Arabian tradition is the same as Dionysos. He quotes Pococke, who has pointed out the resemblances between the Arabian Dhou-Nouwas and the Dionysos of ancient tradition, and says "Pococke was perfectly right in seeking Bacchus in Arabia." Fresnel attempts to locate the city of Nysa "about forty leagues from Zhafar," where there is a mountain which Edrisi calls Lous, although the people of Mahrah call it Nous; but Dionysos and the city of Nysa were many centuries older than Menes, and no such attempt to locate that city can be satisfactory. The very mention of its distance from us, in time, is sufficient to give any dogmatic chronologist a very disagreeable emotion. Fresnel finally comes to the conclusion that the great colonizing and civilizing conquests, which Arabian tradition ascribes to Dhou-Nouwas, must have been the work of several great princes; and he names "Dhou-ons or Dhou-nous, Dhoul Karnayn, Afrikis, Lokman," and others. The fact that traditions of events of such remote antiquity can still be found in Arabia is noteworthy; but the ancient Arabian books that would give us an authentic history of Dionysos had perished long before the Hellenes knew how to read and write.

We naturally expect to find references to Dionysos in the old Sanskrit Puranas. It is not to be supposed, however, that the Sanskrit legends will correspond literally to any of those constructed in Egypt, Asia Minor, or ancient Greece. Saturn and Cronos, undoubtedly the same personage, and by the Greeks and Romans admitted to be so, are differently portrayed in their mythical narratives. We must be prepared to find in all such legends not only the very ancient facts that made them possible, but also the peculiar spirit, genius, and hero-worship of the composers. Some Oriental scholars have sought to identify Dionysos with the Sanskrit Rama, but with no satisfactory result; for Rama was undeniably a native of India, and a prince of the ancient kingdom known to us as Oude. He was much more-modern than Dionysos. The most probable identification is that of Wilford, who finds Dionysos in the great and heroic sovereign celebrated in the Puranas as

Dionysos in India. 287

Nahusha, or Deva-Nahusha, and evidently referred to times more ancient than the Aryan immigration. Wilford points out that Deva-Nahusha is connected with "the oldest history and mythology in the world." He is said to have been a contemporary of Indra, king of Meru, who was also deified, and who appears in the Veda as a principal form or representation of the Supreme Being. The warmest colors of imagination are used in portraying the greatness of Deva-Nahusha. For a time he had sovereign control of affairs in Meru; he conquered the seven dwipas, and led his armies through all the known countries of the world; by means of matchless wisdom and miraculous heroism, he made his empire universal. Wilford says:

"It is declared in the Puranas that, when Deva-Nahusha had conquered the world, he visited the seat of his grand ancestor, Atri, on the Lesser Meru; and, being uneasy to see it neglected, he sent for Vivasa-Carma, the chief engineer of the gods, and ordered him to build on the spot a superb city which he called after his own name, *Deva-Nahusha-Nagara*, which is accurately rendered *Dionysipolis* in Greek. It is called, also, Nahusham, Nahusha, and Nausha, from which the Greeks made Nysa. Nahusha is better known in Hindustan by the emphatic appellation of Deva-Nagara, the divine city. Not a single vestige remains of this ancient Nahusha or Nysa." In the fourteenth volume of the "Asiatic Researches" is the following quotation from Sig. Bayer relative to a passage in a Sanskrit geographical work: "Mention is made of the town called *Nisadaburam* in the Tamul dialect, but in Sanskrit *Nahushapur* or *Naushapur*, from an ancient and famous king of that name, more generally called Deva-Nahusha and Deo-Naush in the spoken dialects. He appears to be the

Dionysos of our ancient mythologists, and reigned near Mount Meru."

Wilson, the English Orientalist, writing on the Dionysiacs of Nonnus, after showing that Rama was not Dionysos, attempts to discredit the view set forth by Wilford, but without producing any substantial reason for doing so. He urges that "the history of Nahusha has nothing in common with that of Bacchus;" and he might have added that the Bacchus of the Greeks, to whom he refers, had nothing in common with Dionysos. A just appreciation of Hellenic mythology should qualify any scholar to make a proper use of this fact. The Greeks distorted the story of Dionysos, and transformed him into their Bacchus, the son of Semele, whom they celebrated as the rollicking and drunken god of wine. It was their custom to reconstruct and misuse the old Cushite mythology whenever they failed to understand it, or sought to appropriate it entirely to themselves. Why should Deva-Nahusha resemble the Greek Bacchus?

Professor Wilson should not have made it necessary to ask this question. He should have seen without effort that such a resemblance would have made it impossible to identify him with Dionysos. Moreover, no one who studies and comprehends the mythical legends of different nations will expect to find exact resemblances in different portrayals of the history and character of the same personage. But in this case there is no such lack of resemblance as will justify Professor Wilson's criticism, while in certain respects the resemblances are very striking. It may be added that Wilford had made the Puranas his chief study, and had gained a more extended and thorough knowledge of the mythical legends of India than any other Oriental scholar of his time. It could not fail to bring important aid to our studies of antiquity if some other competent Sanskrit scholars would emulate his enthusiasm for this kind of investigation.

In Wilford's view, these passages in the Sanskrit books, and many others of similar purport, were important. He saw in them actual recollections of the earliest period of Egyptian history. That they show actual knowledge of the country is very plain, and I can find no good reason to deny that their historical significance is equally incontestable. It would be more satisfactory to have an authentic history of the times to which they refer; but this is impossible. We must be content with such light as can be found in traditions and myths, and may feel safe in believing, with Humboldt, that "myths, when blended with history and geography, cannot be regarded as pertaining wholly to the domain of the ideal world."

We can see in the old Sanskrit books that the Indo-Aryans borrowed extensively from the aboriginal inhabitants of India materials to enlarge their own Pantheon, and enrich the legendary lore that supported and glorified their religious institutions. Thus Siva became one of their chief gods; thus came into their Puranas and Epic Poems old legends, traditions, and mythical personages that did not belong to their history, and had, originally, no connection with their race. This borrowing must have begun very early; not later, certainly, than the beginning of that mixture of the two races in which the "Aryan color" was lost. It appears in the great Epic Poems; we find it everywhere in the Puranas; it is one of the most important and significant facts in the religious history of the Indo-Aryans; and, unless it is fully appreciated, a proper understanding of their mythical lore is impossible. In many cases, this appropriation was carried so far as to include the aboriginal inhabitants themselves. Manu, describing certain aboriginal peoples, maintains that they were originally Khastriyas, or people of the military caste, who had sunk to be Urishalas, or Sudras, "through the extinction of sacred rites, and from having no communication with Brahmans." He specifies the "Paundrakas, Odras, Dravidas, Kâmbojas, Yavanas, Sâkas, Pâradas, Pahlavas, Chinas, Kirâtas, Daradas, and Khasas." The Mahabharata adds to this list the Kalindas, Pulindas, and others, as people who were formerly Khastriyas, but "have become Sudras from seeing no Brahmans." [See Muir's Sanskrit Texts, vol. i., p. 177.] This doctrine was inspired by the policy that aimed to bring the Dasyus, or native inhabitants, especially those who had been admitted into the caste of Khastriyas, to reverence Brahmanism and submit to its authority.

We can see in the legends that Pûrûrâvas, Nahusha, and others, had no connection with Sanskrit history. They are referred to ages very long anterior to the Sanskrit immigration, and must have been great personages celebrated in the traditions of the natives, or Dasyus. It was not to glorify these personages that they were introduced into the Sanskrit legends, but rather to show that, great as they were, terrible punishments fell upon them because they failed to reverence the Brahmans. Brahmans did not exist in their time, but this made no difference. The native legends were reconstructed, and the Brahmans were made to figure in them as supreme lords of the world, to whom the mightiest must submit, whether Aryan or Dasyu. Pûrûrâvas was a king "of great renown, who ruled over thirteen islands of the ocean." Being "altogether surrounded by inhuman (or superhuman) persons," he engaged in a contest with Brahmans and perished. Nahusha, mentioned by Manu, and in many legends, as famous for hostility to the Brahmans, lived at the time when Indra reigned on earth. He was a very great king, "who ruled with justice a mighty empire," and attained the sovereignty of three worlds. Being "intoxicated with pride," he was arrogant to Brahmans, compelled them to bear his palankeen, and even dared to touch one of them with his foot, whereupon he was transformed into a serpent.

According to Herodotus, the Egyptians placed Dionysos, by them called Osiris, near the close of that period of their history which was assigned to the gods. Conversing in a temple with the priests, he was told that 341 kings had reigned in Egypt previous to the time of his visit, and their images or statues were shown in a chamber of the temple. He was told that, at first, "gods had been rulers of Egypt; and that Orus, son of Osiris, whom the Greeks call Apollo, was the last. 'Now Osiris, in the Greek tongue, means Bacchus." It is explained, also, that Osiris, or Bacchus, "was not one of the eight gods called original," nor one of the four subsequently added to these; he was of the third order, being one of those in the early unrecorded ages (certainly without record, and very mythical in the time of Herodotus), "who were sprung from the twelve gods;" that is to say, he was a human sovereign to whom divine honors were awarded after death. In all this we have, at least, the fact that in Egypt the time of Dionysos was placed at a very remote period, at a very early age, in Egyptian history, which agrees with the Indian and other Asiatic legends that made him contemporary with Indra and Zeus.

MYTHOLOGY AND MYTHOLOGICAL PERSONAGES.

Ernest Renan, in his work on the Semitic Languages, assumes that "monotheism sums up and explains all the characteristics" of the genius of the Semitic race, and that this race gave monotheism to the other races. Even "India," he says, "which has thought with so much originality and profoundness, has not yet reached monotheism." This theory, which is encouraged by certain tendencies of our education, may be very convenient for use in eloquent generalizations; but it does not accord with facts. It plainly contradicts what we know of the Aryan race. For instance, Professor Rawlinson, in his account of the ancient religion of the Persians, recognises clearly that it presented a very admirable form of monotheism. He says: "Evidently the Jews and Aryans, when they became known to each other, recognised mutually the fact that they were worshippers of the same Great Being. Hence the favor of the Persians towards the Jews, and the fidelity of the Jews towards the Persians. The Lord God of the Jews being recognised as identical with Ormazd, a sympathetic feeling united the peoples." [See his "Five Monarchies."]

The Desatir, or fragment of the Desatir, found among the Parsees, is certainly very old, whatever may be thought of it in other respects; and its claim to antiquity is supported by internal evidence. The first books inculcate the purest monotheism, with a very simple and inartificial system of religious worship, while the later books show this religion considerably modified by the influence of planet worship. Monotheism was never taught more distinctly, in any age or by any race, than in the first book of the Desatir, called "the Book of the Great Abad."

Mythology implies monotheism, and cannot be intelligently explained without it. How can anything be reverenced or thought of as a manifestation of the Supreme Being where there is no faith in a Supreme Being? It does not follow that peoples of the Aryan race are incapable of seeing the unity of God, because they have brought to religion the highest and most active faculty for poetry and philosophy. Can Renan find anything more distinctly present in the oldest hymns of the Rig-Veda than belief in God and perception of right and wrong? One of these hymns, referring to the Supreme Being, speaks of him as follows: "They call [Him] Indra, Mitra, Varuni, Agni; then he is the well-winged heavenly Garutmat; that which is One the wise call in many ways; they call it Agni, Yama, Mâtarisvan." We read in the Orphic Fragments that all the gods were one alone:

Εἷς Ζευς, εἷς Αἴδης, εἷς Ἥλιος, εἷς Διονυσος,
Εἷς Θεος εν παντεσσι.

Hermesianax is quoted as follows:

Πλουτων, Περσεφονη, Δημητηρ, Κυπρις, Ερωτες,
Τριτωνες, Νηρευς, Τηθυς, και Κυανοχαιτης,
Ἑρμης θ', Ἡφαιστος τε κλυτος, Παν, Ζευς τε, και Ἥρη,
Αρτεμις, ηδ' Ἑκαεργος Απολλων, εἷς Θεος εστιν,

which means that one god are Pluto, Persephone, Demeter, Venus, Cupid, Triton, Nereus, Tethys, Neptune, Hermes, Vulcan, Pan, Zeus, Hera, Artemis, and Apollo. Mythology was brought into existence by recognising the sun, the stars, the forces of nature, and great heroes and sages, as manifestations of some attribute or activity of this one God. No form of religion had a wider or more powerful influence in the great pre-historic past than planet worship, with its phallic and orphic accompaniments; and yet it would have been impossible without monotheism. It was based on the idea of one Supreme Being, who was symbolized or manifested in the sun and the stars, and from whom proceeded the vital forces of nature. It was easy to include among these divine manifestations great heroes and sages, whose influence as deliverers, civilizers, reformers, or rulers, seemed to regulate the destiny and determine the history of peoples where they appeared. A great king or sage, whose life and influence filled and swayed nations, seemed to stand far above ordinary mortals, and thus, after his death, easily became honored as a form or manifestation of the Supreme Being, or of some recognised and greatly venerated form of that Being. He was a man, and, at the same time, more than man; he was an incarnation, an avatar, a special embodiment of divine wisdom and power. Thus were men deified; thus was mythology created.

The Dabistan, citing old Iranian books, gives part of a conversation between a celebrated sage, named Dáwir Háryár, and another person, in which they inquired whether prophets were higher in dignity than the sun. Dáwir maintained that they were not. They were superior to the rest of the human race, but not greater than the sun. "Behold," said he, "what an amount of light is diffused by the solar globe, whereas the bodies of your saints are destitute of splendor; therefore rest assured that his spirit is more resplendent than theirs. Know, besides, that the sun is the heart of the heavens; if he existed not, this world of formation and dissolution could not continue; he brings forth the seasons and the productive energies of nature;" therefore the sun was the highest and brightest manifestation of God known to mortals.

Polytheism can appear only where mythology has become so confused, corrupted, and debased, that the idea in which it originated has disappeared or become obscured. I cannot suppose that polytheism ever was, or ever could be, the first form of religion among any people, for in every case where there are records or monuments to show the earliest religious faith of any people, we find in it the least obscured form of monotheism, with the simplest system of religious worship. Compare the oldest hymns of the Rig-Veda with the later developments of Brahmanism, or the religion of the oldest Iranian books with that of the later age, when Ecbatana stood with its seven differently colored walls, symbolizing the religious system of its inhabitants, or the oldest religion that can be traced in Egypt with that of later times.

But Dionysos, or Osiris, has led me to a discussion of mythology, which requires a volume rather than a few paragraphs. What I have said may serve to explain how he became a personage of mythology. The Egyptians, and all others who speak of him, tell us he was a human sovereign, the greatest known when he lived, and reverently deified after his death. We have no right to take any other view of him. Dionysos was a great monarch of the Cushite Arabians. He seems to represent the epoch when the Cushite race, extending their conquests, gained entire control of the northern and central countries of India. This occurred long ages before the Aryans went there, and many ages lay between that time and the period when Menes began the Old Monarchy of Egypt. When Dionysos reigned in Arabia, both India and Egypt were provinces of his empire. He has been introduced here because his power seems to have been used in the wisest and most beneficent manner to develop the civilization of the Egyptians, for this must be the reason why, as Osiris, he was so intimately associated with the religious thought and feeling of that country.

THE AGES BEFORE MENES.

It is not certain that Menes was the first king of united Egypt. His name heads all the lists, but there is no conclusive reply to those who maintain that this happens merely because he is the earliest king whose name has been preserved on the monuments still existing, and, consequently, the earliest known to the later Egyptian annalists; for we have neither record nor inscription to show that he was actually the sovereign who united Upper and Lower Egypt, or that he was not preceded by other sovereigns of the "Two Countries." We must, however, accept Menes as the first king, for Egyptian chronology begins with him, and, according to Manetho, the regular history of united Egypt began with his reign. From his time onward there is nothing mythical, nothing improbable, nothing that is not supported by inscriptions found in the ruins.

Ernest Renan, reviewing the discoveries of M. Mariette [Revue des Deux Mondes, tome 56], points out that Egypt at the beginning appears mature, old, and entirely without mythical and heroic ages, as if the country had never known youth. Its civilization has no infancy, and its art no archaic epoch. This was true of Egypt in the time of Menes. The civilization of the Old Monarchy did not begin with infancy. It was already mature. But Egypt did not begin with the age of Menes. There was already a very long past in the history of the country when it was united under one government, which consisted, first, of the ages during which the "Two Countries" existed under separate governments; and, second, of the vaguely indicated mythical ages, when, it is said, Egypt was governed by gods and demigods. The first colonists settled in Egypt were undoubtedly civilized; but the country had an infancy, and its art an archaic period, which would be found if there were history to take us back far enough beyond the Old Monarchy and its monuments to reach them.

Megasthenes, reporting Indian traditions, stated that Dionysos founded the first regular monarchy in India, and that he was revered as the sole ruler of the country during the three years he remained there. It is added that, when he left, he established on the throne Spartembas, one of the princes who attended him, and who was most honored with his regard and confidence. Spartembas, having reigned fifty-two years, was succeeded by his son Budyas, who reigned twenty years, and was succeeded by Cradevas; and this dynasty continued to flourish in regular lineal descent for many generations. He reckoned 6042 years between Dionysos and Alexander—an estimate that is more likely to be too small than too large. Could we go back to that age, and visit the countries on the Nile, we should be likely to find Egypt in its infancy. Many investigators, however, are usually more frightened at the mention of such dates than disposed to accept and comprehend the antiquity they indicate. There is always a tendency to reduce dates and contract the past, even when investigators are guided by a free spirit and an honest purpose, because there is always some failure to realize and appreciate the whole extent of remote ages that have become more or less mythical.

Although we have neither history nor chronology of

Egypt previous to Menes, yet we can not avoid the tendency to inquire concerning those earlier ages. They cannot be measured; but the records tell us of a dynasty of ten Thinite kings who reigned in Upper Egypt, and of one or two dynasties that reigned in Lower Egypt, before Menes appeared; and the previous history of the "Two Countries" appears to have been very long. There were still earlier ages, in which demigods and men were rulers; and at the beginning, a vast period created by cyclical invention, in which "the gods reigned." Bunsen believed the history of Egypt previous to Menes was longer than that after his time. Without accepting Bunsen's belief, we can see plainly that the previous history was very long, and understand very well why the civilization of the country was mature, and even old, at the beginning of the Old Monarchy.

Learned and thoughtful Egyptologists generally agree that the empire of Menes in his own time "evidently rested on a basis of previous centuries," during which there had been gradual and great development of civilization and national character; for the people of that country, although previously divided into separate communities, were essentially the same in religion, ideas, character, and enlightenment. Under Menes they were already a numerous, enlightened, and powerful people, and not at all a barbarous nation just emerging from the darkness and disorder of savage life. They had letters, science, and art. Lepsius says, "We learn from the historical accounts relating to the first dynasties, which are still preserved, that even at that time they had '*Annals of the Monarchy.*'" Some of the greatest remains of the Old Monarchy, that show the highest style of Egyptian art, and still engage the wonder of mankind, belong to those first dynasties. Under the fourth dynasty, when the two great pyramids were built, the nation seems to have approached the highest glory of that wonderful development of intelligence and power to which, after the flight of nearly 6000 years, the ruins still bear witness, and to which they will continue to bear witness for ages to come.

The foundations of this greatness were not the work of miracle, therefore they were not laid in a day or a year. They were the result of many ages of preparation in the life, growth, culture, and general condition of the people. It is very true that the Cushite colonists who settled in Upper Egypt brought letters and civilization from their native country, and that their growth to great eminence as a nation was not like that of a people that rises from barbarism by the energy of its own genius, and develops a great civilization. It is not certain, however, that any people, since the first ages of the world, has risen in this way without the aid and incitement of external influences. No people that has become enlightened, since the first ages, was left unvisited by such assistance. But the civilization of Egypt in the time of Menes had assumed a striking individuality of its own. It had become essentially Egyptian. It was already what we find it in the monuments and ruins. This transformation, necessarily gradual and almost imperceptible in its progress, required a long period of time; therefore centuries of Egyptian life and development must have preceded the beginning of the Old Monarchy.

This changed and reconstructed spirit and character of the people, this essentially Egyptian individuality, which had grown silently out of the peculiar forms, conditions, relations, and influences of the physical nature in which they lived, was manifest in everything. Ages of gradual and unconscious development had established harmony between people and country. It appeared even in their admirable system of monumental writing, which, without explanation of its origin, showed already its highest perfection in the oldest ruins. Professor Lepsius says of it:

"From the choice of the pictures in the hieroglyphics, and from other reasons, it appears entirely justifiable to suppose that this wonderful picture-writing of the Egyptians was formed, with reference to its peculiar characteristics, in Egypt itself, without any other influence from abroad, although they may have brought the first beginning of it from their original home in Asia. But that a people should produce anything so perfect as this system of writing, which embraces at once all the stages of human writing, from the most ideographical symbolic writing through syllables, to the equally direct notation of sound by means of vowels and consonants, certainly indicates a long previous development." [Introduction to "Die Chronologie der Ægypter."]

ANTIQUITY OF WRITING IN EGYPT.

In no other old nation of which we have sufficient knowledge to form an opinion on this point was the art of writing so perfect or so largely used as in Egypt, especially for memorial and historical purposes. "Their temples were almost covered with inscriptions; all buildings erected to the gods, to the kings, and to the dead, had representations and inscriptions on all the walls, ceilings, pillars, architraves, friezes, and posts, inside as well as outside." And their book literature seems to have been correspondingly abundant. The library must have been a very early institution. We hear of it even in the fragments of Egyptian history that still remain. Diodorus Siculus, i., 49, describes a great library of Rameses the Great, whom he calls Osymandyas, whose time was in the fourteenth century before the Christian era. The rooms of this library were in the temple of Rameses at Thebes, and they have been found, recognised, and described by Champollion and by Lepsius. The latter says, in his "Letters from Egypt:"

"The description of this splendid building given by Diodorus may still be traced from one chamber to another among its ruins. At the entrance—behind which, according to Diodorus, the library was situated—Champollion perceived, on both sides, the representation of Thoth, the god of wisdom, and of Saf, the goddess of history; then, behind the former, the god of hearing, and behind the latter, the god of seeing. Several hieratical papyri which we still possess are dated from the 'Ramescion,' and it is also frequently mentioned in the so-called historical papyri. I found in Thebes the tombs of two *librarians* of the time of Rameses the Great, and therefore probably belonging to the library described by Diodorus. They were father and son. The father was called Neb-nufre, the son Nufre-hetep, and they both bore the titles of *her scha tu,* 'Superior over the Books,' and *naa en scha tu,* 'Chief over the Books.' We have good reason to believe this library, of which we have incidentally still farther mention, was not the first nor the only one. Thoth and Saf bear among their fixed titles, not only here, but on other monuments of all classes, the former that of *Master,* and the latter that of *Mistress* of the Hall of Books; consequently the idea of gods of libraries had long been familiar to the Egyptians."

Books, and collections of books, in Egypt, were undoubtedly, like the art of writing itself, much older than Menes. Among a people whose monuments show such an eminent degree of the "historical sense," we may suppose that historical productions in the form of Annals, written and preserved in the temples, were the first writings. That old literature has all, or nearly all, perished. Nevertheless, there still exist some Egyptian manuscripts that were written near the beginning of the New Monarchy, and that are from 1500 to 2000 years older than any other original manuscripts now in existence. It was different 2500 years ago, when Solon visited Egypt. Then Egypt had books and libraries in abundance; the old Annals still existed in the temples, and a priest at Sais said to Solon, with entire confidence in the truth of his statement,

"You Greeks are novices in knowledge of antiquity. You are ignorant of what passed, either here or among yourselves, in days of old. The history of 8000 years is deposited in our sacred books; but I can ascend to a much higher antiquity, and tell you what our fathers have done for 9000 years—I mean their institutions, their laws, and their most brilliant achievements."

Neither Solon, who listened to this statement, nor Plato, in whose writings it has been preserved, considered it improbable. They saw no reason why it could not be true. Neither can we. It would have been surprising if the Egyptians, at that time, had not still preserved old records of the early periods of their history; and whatever we, in presence of excited chronological dogmatism, may allow ourselves to think of the "8000 years," we cannot reasonably bring ourselves to deny that the early history of that country extended through many centuries beyond the age of Menes.

ATTEMPTS TO MEASURE EGYPTIAN ANTIQUITY.

In modern times attempts have been made to throw light on the antiquity of Egypt by determining the age of the alluvial deposit that forms the Nile Valley, of which the most important is that of Mr. Leonard Horner, between the years 1851 and 1854. These attempts have proceeded on the hypothesis that the age of the deposit, at any given point, could be discovered by first ascertaining the average depth of the accumulation in a single century, and then measuring the whole depth of the alluvium. Mr. Horner undertook this work at the suggestion of the Royal Society of London, and the necessary funds were furnished by this society and by Abbas Pacha, the viceroy of Egypt. Having secured the most competent assistants, he penetrated and explored the alluvium in different places by means of ninety-five pits or shafts and artesian borings.

Fifty-one of these shafts and borings were on a line crossing the valley from east to west, between the Arabian and Libyan deserts, in the latitude of Heliopolis, and twenty-seven of them on the parallel of Memphis. The character of the deposit was uniform from top to bottom. The bones of quadrupeds were found, such as the ox, hog, dog, dromedary, and ass, all belonging to living species, which shows that the formation of the Nile belongs to what geologists call the Recent Period. Jars, vases, pots, a small human figure in burnt clay, a copper knife, burnt bricks, and other articles of human manufacture, were found, some of them near the bottom of the alluvium. Brick and pottery were found everywhere and at all depths, sometimes sixty feet below the surface, showing that men who used such things must have occupied that valley as soon as any part of it became habitable. It is not improbable, however, that some of the articles brought up from the lowest depths may have found their way into the sediment from boats and other water-craft from the upper country, floating above it, when that part of the valley, or a large portion of it, was still covered with water.

New and interesting facts were brought to light by these explorations, but they failed to settle accurately and conclusively the age of the Lower Nile Valley. The nearest approach to obtaining an accurate chronometric scale for ascertaining the age of the first deposits of sediment at a given point was made near Memphis, at the statue of King Rameses. It is known that this statue was set up about the year 1200 before Christ. In 1854 it had stood there 3114 years, and during that time the alluvium had accumulated around it to the depth of nine feet and four inches above its base, which was at the rate of about three and a half inches in each century. Mr. Horner found that the alluvium *below the base of this statue* was 30 feet deep. His excavations went down 32 feet, but the last two feet were through sand. Assuming the rate of accumulation previous to the erection of the statue to have been the same as afterwards, it follows that the formation of the alluvium began, at that point, about 11,660 years before the Christian Era. Bunsen places entire confidence in this estimate, suggesting only that the period named is too short, because the lower part of the deposit was more pressed together and compact than the upper part. At the statue, pottery was found within four inches of the bottom, and within sixteen inches of the bottom at another point 354 yards distant from it.

One thing is very clear, and does not need entire accuracy in such measurements and estimates to make it more so. These explorations show beyond question that the great structures of the Old Monarchy of Egypt, as well as those of the New Monarchy, were built on a soil which had been previously occupied, for a very long period, by a people who manufactured pottery, used copper, burnt brick, and had other appliances of civilized life; and also that a very large part of the alluvium which forms the valley was accumulated between the beginning of that occupation and the building of those wonderful structures. Whether the first colonists went to Egypt more than 11,000 years before the Christian Era, as Bunsen supposes, which many will regard as romantic theory, or whether they went there at a later period, which appears more probable and more in accordance with other facts, it is nevertheless certain that the communities they established had a very long existence, and, without doubt, an important history before the "Two Countries" they created were united under one government, and began that great career of which we have an authentic chronology, and which can still be studied in its abundant monuments.

VIII.

AFRICA AND THE ARABIAN CUSHITES.

In the popular estimation, Africa is almost wholly a continent of savage negroes. Even intelligent people, who know something of Egypt, Abyssinia, and the Mediterranean coast of Africa, have entertained much the same notion of the whole interior and southern portions of the African continent. Until recently the inner regions were mostly unvisited by Europeans. They were covered with a veil of mystery. Their inhabitants were described by fancy, or were assumed to be the same in race, condition, and character as those found, or, rather, those degraded and brutalized by slave-traders, on the coast of Guinea. In recent times Africa has been extensively explored by travelers, and much has been done to correct this misapprehension. The means of gaining a better knowledge of both the geography and the inhabitants of that great and hitherto uncomprehended division of the globe are now abundant. Nevertheless, the difference between Africa as portrayed by romancing ignorance, and Africa as described by intelligent travelers, is not yet clearly understood by many persons who claim to be enlightened.

The old notion that Africa is chiefly a land of black savages arose from ignorance of the country, which could not be removed, but, on the contrary, was heightened by slave-trading communication with the Western Coast. Slave-traders, whose operations were confined to the coast re-

gions on the Gulf of Guinea, very naturally fostered this
notion. They could not describe truthfully what came under their own observation, but they sought to excuse their
own frightful savagery by describing Africa as a land of
negroes in the darkest and most hopeless condition of debasement. When this had been repeated many times, they
ventured to represent their kidnapping villanies as mis-
sionary agencies, intent on transferring savages to Christian countries for their own good. It was absurd to expect valuable information from this source.

Moreover, but little knowledge of the African continent
can be acquired by communication with that part of the
Western Coast. There has been no exploration of the interior table-land from the coast of Guinea, and only one or
two travelers have penetrated the continent from any other point on the Atlantic. All the great and successful explorations of Central Africa have proceeded from the east
and the north.

THE RACES IN AFRICA.

In point of fact, the great majority of the people inhabiting this grand division of the globe are not negroes. People of the negro race—meaning those described as "typical negroes," with all others who closely approach this
type—occupy but a small part of Africa. They dwell
chiefly on the low coast-lands around the Gulf of Guinea,
but are found in a few other narrow districts in different
parts of the continent. Whether their habitat was more
extensive and their number greater in remote pre-historic
times cannot now be determined, although this seems implied by the extent of an evident mixture of this negro element with the blood of other African races. It is manifest

that Africa at a remote period was the theatre of great movements and mixtures of peoples and races, and that its interior countries had then a closer connection with the great civilizations of the world than at any time during the period called historical.

Africa, away from the coasts, is generally an elevated table-land, mostly well watered, fertile, and healthy. The great body of its people consists of a brown or olive-colored race, occasionally described as the "Red Race," in which some travelers and ethnologists find a resemblance to the Malays; but in Africa this race is seldom found entirely pure; in every part of the country it shows very clearly the signs of intermixture with other races, both white and black. These signs of mixed blood have been noticed by travelers who have described this race, as I shall presently show under another head. Dr. Livingstone calls attention to them while describing the brown race as he found it at the south, and insisting that the "true type" of the African people is not that found on the Western Coast. The Arabian Cushites appear to have found this dark brown or olive-colored race in India and on the islands of the Indian Seas. In its original condition it may have been primitive in both regions, but there is nothing to explain either its origin or its history.

Certain writers have maintained, with great confidence and some ingenuity, that the negroes of Africa are an exceptional people, and not a distinct race. The theory is, that tribes of the brown race, settling in the low districts of the Western Coast, or in other malarious regions, will gradually assume the negro type, being changed by peculiar physical influences permanently operating in such localities; or, to state it in the words of Mr. Reed, one of its advocates, "The true Africans, a red-skinned race, descending from the table-land into the swamps, become degraded in body and mind, and their type is completely changed." He describes a brown tribe, called "Fans," who have lately approached the coast of Guinea, and gives a lively picture of the change that awaits them. In the course of a few generations, he imagines, their fine forms will become ugly, their long, curling black hair will become short, crisp, and woolly, and their fine, olive-colored complexion will turn to a coal black. This is pure hypothesis, very entertaining, it may be, to its inventors, and full of friendship for another unsupported hypothesis that undertakes to explain the origin and early condition of the human race, but with no support save the ingenious devices of fancy. The reply to its advocates is obvious, and sober reason must regard it as unanswerable.

In the first place, it must be said that for a long time there has been quite too much exaggeration and extravagant over-statement relative to the assumed natural inferiority and degradation of the negro race in Africa. The Negroes are chiefly on the Western Coast, where for ages they have felt the savage influence of slave-traders. Debasement could not fail to be the result; and yet, in the portrayals of the most unscrupulous blackguard that has ever written in the interest of slave-traders, we can see that the negroes of the Guinea Coast are nowise inferior to any other coast population of the country, where this brutalizing influence has controlled all intercourse between the natives and Europeans. Nor can it be said that, even as we know them, they are not superior to some of the more degraded families of the brown race, such as the Saabs or Bushmen. When these Bushmen are under consideration, their physical and social degradation is not treated as an essential characteristic of their race; nor is it said by anybody that the great degradation of this family of the brown race has produced a new type of mankind.

In the second place, if the negroes were not a distinct race, the negro type would not be permanent. If they were, in reality, nothing more than tribes of the brown race, transformed by physical influences of the localities where we find them, they could escape from this negro type and recover the lost traits of the race to which they really belong by leaving the low lands and returning to the upper country. Removal from the unfriendly regions of swamp and miasma, where they have become "typical negroes," to the wholesome lands of the interior, or to other countries, would certainly be followed by a return of the physiological peculiarities they have lost. The natural characteristics of the brown race would reappear; the fine form, the long, curling hair, and the olive-colored complexion would come back to reveal and vindicate the race which the bad locality had obscured. But this never happens. No such return from the negro type to the brown type is ever seen, either in Africa or anywhere else; therefore it is certain that the physiological peculiarities of the former are natural and permanent, and that they indicate a positive distinction of race.

In the third place, such a law of transformation as this theory assumes would not confine its operations to the low districts on the Gulf of Guinea. A natural law cannot be capricious. Its operation is uniform. It is steady, sure, changeless, with nothing uncertain or doubtful in its influence. If there were a natural law by virtue of which the brown people of Africa are sure to become negroes if they settle near the coast on the Gaboon River, all similar regions would be inhabited by negroes. The same transforming power would be felt in the great valleys of the Amazon and the Oronoco, and there would have been more negroes in South America than in Africa. The red or brown aborigines of the country could not have escaped that influence. A negro race would have filled those valleys in the earliest times, and they would have been found there in great numbers when the Spaniards discovered and occupied the country. But they were not found there; they have never existed there as an aboriginal race.

A BRIEF ESSAY ON RACES.

Max Müller, in his work on the ancient Sanskrit Literature, speaks as follows: "What authority would have been strong enough to convince the English soldier that the same blood was running in his veins and in the veins of the dark Bengalese? And yet there is not an English jury nowadays which, after examining the hoary documents of language, would reject the claim of a common descent and a legitimate relationship between Hindu, Greek, and Teuton."

This is in a strain that has been common since the discovery of the Sanskrit language; it shows, however, that in Mr. Müller's mind hypothesis had not carefully adjusted its relations with fact. The claim of "a common descent" for Hindu, Greek, and Teuton might have been well founded, or at least not open to serious criticism, had it been urged four or five thousand years ago, while the Sanskrit was still a spoken language, and the Indo-Aryans were not yet changed in race by intermixture with the dark-skinned people of India. It cannot now be admitted without important qualifications. The English soldier who rejects it is more nearly right than the scholar who believes "the hoary documents of language" would constrain an English jury to uphold it. The scholar falls into mistake by attributing to the Hindus of our time what was peculiar to the unmixed, Sanskrit-speaking Aryans of a former age. The native inhabitants of India now present, in their physiological characteristics, a remarkable mixture of races, in which Aryan blood is not the chief element; and this manifest mixture of unlike races extends, in some degree, even to the present dialects of India. In the matters of common blood and intimate ethnic relationship, the people of Hindustan now have more affinity with the Malays of the Indian Archipelago, and the Arabian people of Oman and Yemen, than with the British soldier.

When we consider carefully the various peoples who inhabit the earth and constitute the human family, we cannot easily avoid the conclusion that great primal races must be recognised, whose origin goes back to the first period of human existence. It is no part of my purpose to write a scientific essay on this topic, and undertake an exact classification of the many varieties of mankind; but there are physiological traits presented for consideration, so different and so strongly marked, and families of language so radically unlike, that their origin must have preceded even the first humble beginnings of civilization. This is so plain, and appears to be so incontestable, that some eminent investigators have resorted to the hypothesis that the human race was originally brought into existence by the creation, in different parts of the earth, of several independent and separate family groups, unlike in physical traits and in the conditions that determined the character of their language, but essentially and ineradicably the same in all the distinctive attributes of human nature itself. This simplifies the question, and makes explanation easy; but in scientific inquiries such simplifications should be used with some caution, for they do not invariably furnish the safest way to just conclusions. It is, however, the most reasonable hypothesis yet furnished by science, for it recognises distinctly the "one blood," or natural fraternity of all the different families of mankind, and it does not, like the "development theory," dishonor human nature by denying the independent creation of man, and assigning the origin of the human family to a "progressive development" of lower orders of the animal creation.

When we study, closely and reflectively, typical representatives of the unmixed Chinese, Malay, Negro, and Aryan or Indo-European families, the conclusion seems inevitable that, while they all have the same human nature, they represent very distinct primordial races. If they did not, according to the simplest and readiest hypothesis, proceed from separately created family groups, they must have been completely separated and subjected to very unlike conditions of existence previous to the earliest movements of that development which produced even the lowest forms of civilized life. This is clearly implied not only by the unlikeness of their physical traits, but also by such facts as the profound difference between the Chinese and the Aryan languages. Whether science will at length furnish a clearer explanation, or, without farther explanation, leave the matter to such hypotheses as it has already suggested, I shall not undertake to say. It has rescued the question from the control of myth and fable; it makes us see that certain venerable assumptions have no foundation in truth and no claim to respect; but the origin of the distinct races that constitute the human family is so covered with the darkness of ages beyond the reach of both history and authentic tradition, and presents so much that is now entirely beyond the sphere of human experience, that science may never be able to substitute demonstration for its most reasonable hypothesis.

Moreover, the problem has some other difficulties. For instance, the physiological differences that separate the primitive races are not always coincident with radical differences of language. The families of mankind usually classed as Aryans, Cushites, and Semites, with some of the peoples classed as Turanians or Scyths, in their original, unmixed condition, are physiologically so much alike that the physiologist cannot show why they should not be classed together as one race. And yet they are separated by three or four families of language, so radically different that a common origin seems impossible. Linguistic science suspects, and may yet be able to show, that the Cushite and Semitic tongues are related, and that they may have proceeded from the same original source. But it finds no such relationship between the Semitic and the Aryan families, or between either of these families and the language of the Magyars. Must the linguistic differences in these cases be made to signify original distinction of race? We turn away from this conclusion to find some other solution of the problem; we suggest that some of these peoples may have changed their original speech, or that they separated from a common stock while their speech was yet unformed, and developed language amid associations and controlling influences that had little or nothing in common; but there can be no such demonstration as will satisfy any close inquiry.

Renan and some others have sought to show that the Semites have manifested a striking unlikeness to the Aryan and Cushite families in their development of religious ideas and civilization, but a great deal more is assumed than can be shown; and Renan's hypothesis that the Semites originated monotheism is explicitly contradicted by what is known of the history of other races.

At the present time, the great primitive races of the human family are seldom found entirely pure. In the many countries of Asia and Europe, where the influence of civilization has been felt to any extent, it is not common to find communities where the blood of any of these races is found unmixed with that of one or more of the others. Throughout Southern Europe we find a mixture of two or three of the light-colored races, in which there is a considerable infusion of blood from the dark-skinned people of Africa. Mixture of races is the rule throughout Central and Western Europe. Russia is a country where peoples of one or two other races have been added to the aboriginal Finnic element. The Russian language belongs to the Aryan family, but in the Russian people there is a very large infusion of blood which it does not represent. In Southwestern Asia, from India to the Mediterranean, the Aryan, Cushite, and Semitic races have lost or shaded their white color in mixture with the dark-skinned race that seems to have been aboriginal in India and Eastern Africa. It is now scarcely possible to find anywhere even a small community of unmixed Cushites—the greatest, most influential, and probably the most numerous race of remote antiquity, whose home was Arabia.

But in no great division of the globe is the mixture of races more general or more remarkable than in Africa.

That it exists in the Valley of the Nile, from Abyssinia to Egypt, and throughout Northern Africa, is well understood. The fact that a mixture somewhat different in character, and more or less distinctly manifest, prevails throughout the interior, has not engaged so much attention. I shall speak of it more fully in another place, in connection with the many traces of their influence left in Africa by the old Arabian race.

Humboldt, in his Cosmos, speaks of "the distressing distinction of superior and inferior races." Certain dogmatic writers on this subject, whose doctrines concerning "inferior and superior races" are revolting to reason and unsupported by fact, finding criticism and rebuke in these words of the eminent German whose science they cannot question, have sought to break their force by treating them as an "unfortunate" gush of "sentimentalism." Humboldt's Cosmos, however, is not a sentimental work, and nowhere in it do we find a sincerer expression of his thought, or a more deliberate criticism of an offensive method of treating a great question.

The doctrines relative to superior and inferior races, as usually inculcated, are not the product of serene science, nor of any calm influence of reason. They have sprung either from the arrogant egotism of the race that assumed superiority, or from zeal in behalf of some institution, or of some form of social or political organization, by which undeveloped races or humiliated peoples are maltreated and tyrannously oppressed.

An elaborate and ingenious French work on the "Inequality of Human Races," written in the interest of the reactionary party in Europe, sets forth the doctrine that the downfall of nations is effected, not by luxury and enervation, not by corruption of morals nor by any disastrous influence of misgovernment, but solely by the intrusion of inferior races into the positions of political influence that belong exclusively to the superior governing races. This infallibly brings on degeneracy and ruin, because the blood of the proper governing class no longer flows in the veins of those who govern, or is debased by mixture with inferior blood. The subject classes, in the nations of Europe, are the inferior races, and the old governing classes the superior races. They are useful to each other while each keeps its proper place; but when the lower orders rise and a mixture of races takes place, the dangerous doctrines of human brotherhood and equality in rights immediately appear, and the nation becomes degenerate.

"With the exception of what has passed in our time," says Count de Gobineau, "the idea of a natural, original, and permanent inequality of races has been the basis of nearly all theories of government. The system of hereditary castes, nobilities, and aristocracies has its origin in this idea;" but "when a mixture of the races takes place, this idea is at once disputed, natural superiority is insulted, the right of the superior race to inherit dominion is denied, and this dominion is stigmatized as a tyrannical usurpation of power. The mixture of castes obscures inequality, and gives rise to the political axiom that all men are equal, and, therefore, entitled to the same rights. Indeed, since there are no longer any distinct hereditary classes, none can justly claim superior merit and privileges." And "the political axiom that all men are brothers, and therefore equal, which, like the bag of Æolus, contains so many tempests, is soon followed by the scientific."

Whereupon the gulf opens, and every thing sinks into

the bottomless pit of ruin. He means to say, chiefly, that the governed people of Europe are inferior races, whose claim to equality of rights must be sternly denied, and who must be rigidly excluded from any assumption of political influence. It is evident that, in his view, the ancient order of things, with all that is included in what the monarchies, the aristocracies, and the Church call civilization, is seriously threatened by that progress of republican ideas which aims to make the people supreme in the politics of Europe. It is wholly the result of "ethnical changes," which have been "slower and less considerable" in England than in any other European country, for England has preserved "to this day the basis of the social system of the fourteenth and fifteenth centuries," while "in France the ethnical elements are more numerous, and the mixtures more varied." This degeneracy, he thinks, is fearfully manifest in Paris, "whose population is a motley compound of all the most varied ethnical elements." Having no longer any love or respect for ancient traditions, and being prepared by the influence of inferior races, meaning the people, for "a complete rupture with the past," Paris has "hurried France into a series of political and social experiments, with doctrines the most remote from, and the most repulsive to the ancient customs and traditional tendencies of the realm." It seems expected that this doctrine, imitating the dignity of science and the speech of philosophy, will shame, confound, and paralyze the liberal tendencies of Europe.

The doctrine of superior and inferior races, in a different form, has been used to justify human slavery, and here the question is confined chiefly to the white and the black races. The black race, it is assumed, is wholly incapable of developing civilization in any form, therefore the superior white race, having a natural right to be its master, may enslave it, or subject its existence to any conditions of serfdom which the governing wisdom of the natural master may see fit to impose. It is no part of my purpose to discuss this doctrine at length. I may observe, however, that ethnical speculations which aim to establish a given conclusion are necessarily vitiated by this aim, and therefore cannot be trusted; and that those who seek to give this ethnical hypothesis the authority of science cannot avoid showing that they proceed "with a purpose," and never get beyond the sphere of violent opinions.

Count de Gobineau, whose purpose did not require him to depreciate the black race, takes a very different view of it. He maintains that, in the great civilizations of antiquity, the inspiration of poetry and art came from the black race. The white race organized those civilizations, and established their laws and governments; but "the source from whence their art issued was foreign to the instincts of the organizing civilizers; it lay in the blood of the blacks. That universal power of imagination, which we see enveloping and penetrating the primordial civilizations, came entirely from the ever-increasing infusion of blood from the black race into that of the whites." Again: "The negro possesses, in a high degree, the faculty of emotion from the senses, without which art is not possible." Once more: "It will be said that I am placing a beautiful crown upon the deformed head of the negro, and doing him a very great honor by thus associating him with the harmonious choir of the Muses. But the honor is not so great. I have not associated him with the highest, those in whom reflection is superior to passion." And, finally, "Certainly the black element is indispensable to the development of artistic genius in a race." [See De Gobineau's work, "Sur L'Inégalité des Races Humaines," book ii., chap. vii.]

It will be noticed that this view of the black race is different from that used to authorize enslavement of the blacks; but De Gobineau, who finds the influence of inferior races in European liberalism, did not study the black race to excuse scornful disregard of its rights, nor with any view to the interests of slavery. Those who take a different course are not likely to agree with him, nor to accept any other view save their own.

Should we admit all that is claimed by certain writers concerning superior and inferior races, it would not follow that we must also accept the logic by which they undertake to show that inferiority has deprived the black race of all right to any position in the human family above that of serfdom. Rights cannot properly be made to depend on a discrimination of this kind. In a justly-organized state, the most imperial intellect can have no more rights before the law than the humblest. There is a duty of the strong to the weak which requires something very different from the pretensions of mastership and the parade of superiority, and there is some great deficiency in the civilization of that race or community by which it is not properly recognised. The logic of superiority that sets aside this duty would justify the enslavement of the weak, humble, and unenlightened classes, in every state where they exist, without regard to race, and show that neither slavery, serfdom, nor any condition of abasement under the domination of privileged classes should be abolished anywhere.

But difference in faculty does not necessarily imply inferiority. We are accustomed to assume, without hesitation, that our race is of course superior to all other races that differ from it in faculty or development; in this, however, there may be quite as much egotism as reason. On what grounds can we safely assume that any race, no matter how powerful it may seem to be, comprehends in the highest degree all the possibilities of human nature? Probably we shall find it necessary to revise our conception of what constitutes the superiority of a race. Wonderful force to attack, subdue, and sway other peoples, distinguishes the faculty of our race, and this force is celebrated in song and romance. But is this really the highest and most admirable development of human nature? We cannot reflect seriously without feeling that there is something nobler, something more beautiful, something more richly fraught with blessing that increases the possibilities and heightens the charm of human existence, something that must necessarily revise our ideal of what is superior in peoples and races.

Reason requires us to believe that each race and each distinct family of mankind has some peculiar gift of its own, in which it is superior to others, and that the All-wise Creator may have designed that each race and family shall bring its own peculiar contribution to the final completeness of civilization. A race or family is not necessarily inferior to others because it comes into the history of civilization latest, nor superior because it appears there first. It was not our own proud Aryan race that created the great civilizations of Arabia, Chaldea, and the Old Monarchy of Egypt. Our race was preceded in development by others, and it was in times quite modern that our own family of the race took its place among the foremost. And yet our mission is great—greater than we have been able to comprehend. The marvelous force, energy, and activity of our particular family of the Aryan race are establishing intercourse and the feeling of neighborhood between "the ends of the earth." We are bringing the races and peoples of the human family to that condition of mutual intercourse and appreciation which will teach all races and families to dismiss the old talk of "outside barbarians," allow them to assume harmonious relations, and prepare them to play connected parts in the grand work of realizing the full-orbed, all-comprehending development of the whole united family of man.

THE ARABIAN CUSHITES IN AFRICA.

That the ancient people of Arabia would pass over into Africa nearly at the beginning of their colonizing movements is so probable that we readily accept it as true. They could not fail to do so. They would move across the Straits of Bab-el-Mandeb, and advance not only northward down the Valley of the Nile, but also towards the central and southeastern portions of the continent; for these regions were attractive to enterprise, and would necessarily add greatly to the resources and power of the rising commercial people on the Erythræan Sea.

The ancient Greeks inform us that what was so probable actually took place. They recorded the fact that the eastern countries of Africa became part of Ethiopia, and that they had been so described from time immemorial. This designation is still used, somewhat indefinitely, to indicate regions in Eastern and Central Africa, although it is no longer applied to Arabia. The old Sanskrit books furnish similar information. They tell us that the people of Cusha-dwipa passed over into Africa, took possession of the country, and established there a subordinate country of the Cushites, which they called the exterior Cusha-dwipa; agreeing with the Greeks, who say Ethiopia included both Asiatic and African territory. Add to this that the Cushite race created Egypt, and carried their colonies and civilization into every part of Northern Africa, and we can see that its influence on this continent in pre-historic times must have been very extensive.

We see this, also, in the fact that a majority of the inhabitants of Africa use dialects of the old Cushite or Ethiopian languages. To this family belong the Berber dialects, spoken and written in all the provinces of Northern Africa, as far down as the southern border of the Sahara. The old Egyptian tongue, and the languages used throughout the Valley of the Nile, in Abyssinia, and in Somaulia, have the same origin. It is known, also, that not only the language, but, along with it, the religious ideas of that important people in Eastern Africa known as the Gallas, came originally from the Arabian Cushites. Dr. Krapf states that the Gallas number "six or eight millions." He says the word "Gallas" means "immigrants," and signifies their recent migration towards Abyssinia and the coast. They call themselves "Orma," or "Oroma;" therefore Dr. Krapf designates the country they occupy as "Ormania." It is very probable that dialects, derived from or modified by old forms of the ancient Cushite language, are used by African peoples in the central and southern portions of the continent. Some linguistic scholars claim that the southern dialects belong to this family, and I see no reason to doubt the correctness of their opinion. No form of any other language known to civilization, ancient or modern, has been found in Africa, save the modern Arabic. The prevalence of Cushite dialects is incontestable, and this shows how extensively Africa was occupied by the Cushite race in the great ages of its power.

The people of Arabia have been accustomed to traverse Africa in every direction, from ages of which neither history nor tradition can make any report. They are found everywhere, east, west, north, and south; usually as traders, ready to deal in slaves or in anything else that gives a hope of profit, but frequently as a part of the settled population. Dr. Barth states that not less than 250,000 Arabians were settled in Bornou when he visited that kingdom, and that "this Arab population appears to have come from the east at a very early period." In that part of Africa their policy is to conciliate the favor of the Fulans. To other peoples the interior of Africa has for ages been an unknown region, a land of mystery, of which nothing could be told beyond some Arabian notices of its geography. The only reasonable explanation of this extensive and long-continued intercourse of the Arabians with the interior countries of Africa is that which assumes that it was established by the ancient Cushite occupation, and has never been discontinued.

We do not always realize the whole significance of the fact that some of the most highly civilized nations of remote antiquity were in Northern Africa and in the Valley of the Nile. The Old Monarchy of Egypt, to which belong the grandest ages of that country, was brought to a close about 2100 years before the Christian Era, after a duration of 1800 years. Meroë, very ancient, though not as old as the great Egyptian monarchy founded by Menes, was preceded by a much older and greater kingdom, described as Barbara, a name still preserved in that part of Africa. It is well known that, "from the earliest times, Meroë was the seat of a great commerce carried on by caravans from all parts of Northern Africa." The Cushite Arabians, who created these countries, continued to occupy Africa down to the latest days of their power. Is it reasonable to believe that neither these Arabians, nor the people of the Nile Valley, explored Central Africa? Nothing is more improbable. On the contrary, it is evident that the ancient Arabians occupied the lake regions, and carried their influence into the central countries as far west as Soudan; and that they were accustomed to communicate with the northern coast through the interior. Until lately, all we knew of Central Africa came to us through Arabian geographers. They could describe the sources of the Nile; and they told us of the Mountains of the Moon, which the moderns have not yet explored, nor even located with certainty.

The fact that ancient kings of Arabia marched armies through Africa to the ocean, and carried on wars with Maghrib or Mauretania, is not left entirely to the historical traditions of Arabia for support. Strabo says in his first book, "It was mentioned as a tradition among the people of Tartessus that the Ethiopians once traversed the regions of Africa quite to its western limits, and that some of them came and settled at Tartessus." This must refer to times long before Gades was built. Central Africa, fertile, beautiful, and, in many respects, attractive in itself, abounded in ivory, gold, and other productions adapted to engage the attention of a commercial people. If there were great navigable rivers flowing from Soudan to the Indian Ocean, or if there were great gulfs extending from that ocean far into the central regions, the ancient history of Africa would have been much more important. But the Arabian Cushites, occupying the great lake regions, and controlling the central countries, would naturally communicate with the coasts to any extent required by the interests of their commerce; and it is no more improbable that they were from time to time engaged in wars with "Maghrib," than that, in more recent times, Muley Hamed, emperor of Morocco, should be engaged in wars with the great Songhay Empire, which at one time controlled nearly all Central Africa.

TRACES OF AFRICAN ANCIENT HISTORY.

Modern exploration has shown clearly that the present condition of the great body of the African people is not that of normal barbarism, but rather a state of decline from a better knowledge and use of the arts and appliances of civilized life. The facts reported by modern travelers in that part of the globe require us to believe that, in pre-historic times, some great influence of civilization was felt throughout nearly the whole African continent for many ages, and that a large portion of the primitive African people were raised by this influence to some knowledge of the ways of civilized life. Traces of this influence are visible everywhere; and, if there were nothing to indicate its origin, we could hardly fail to see that it must have come from Arabia.

Arts and methods of civilized life are common throughout Central, Southern, and Eastern Africa, that cannot be accounted for by anything in the present condition of the people. The art of smelting ores and working metals is not an accomplishment of savage life. It did not originate among barbarians. And yet this art is in common use in almost every part of Africa. Dr. Livingstone, giving an account of what he found in the regions near Lake Nyassa, makes this statement: "At every third or fourth village we saw a kiln-looking structure, about six feet high, and two and a half and three feet in diameter. It is a clay, fire-hardened furnace for smelting iron. No flux is used, whether the specular iron, the yellow hæmatite, or magnetic iron ore is fused, and yet capital metal is produced. Native manufactured iron is so good that the natives declare English iron 'rotten' in comparison; and specimens of African hoes were pronounced at Birmingham to be nearly equal to the best Swedish iron." The method here described is almost precisely like that used in Southern India. Dr. Barth makes similar reports of the prevalence of this art in Central Africa. He describes similar smelting furnaces found in Soudan, where they are common; and those travelers who have explored the sources of the Nile tell us that blacksmiths, workers of metals, and remarkable skill in other manufactures, whose origin implies civilization, are common in that region.

Dr. Livingstone, in the account of his "Expedition to the Zambezi" already cited, describes articles manufactured by the African people, and specifies "hammers, tongs, hoes, adzes, fish-hooks, needles, and spear-heads, having what is termed 'dish' on both sides, to give them the rotary motion of rifle-balls." He admires their skill in spinning and weaving, and in manufacturing certain kinds of pottery similar to pottery found in India. He points out that they have admirably-made fish-nets " nearly identical with those now used in Normandy;" a blacksmith's bellows like that used in Central India; "fish-baskets and weirs like those used in the Highlands of Scotland;" and other implements like those found in Egypt and India. He is sure that this striking similarity of manufactured articles in widely-separated countries—articles "from identical patterns widely spread over the globe"—makes it very probable that the arts and usages of these different peoples were derived from the same source. Not seeing any other explanation, he suggests that they may have been given by direct revelation from God. This hypothesis is reverent, but the very interesting fact to which he calls attention can be explained without resort to miracle. The original instructor in these arts was the ancient Cushite civilization, which went into Africa from the east and the north, and was felt for a very long period of time in all its central countries.

No less important are the facts relating to the social and political condition of Central Africa, reported by Dr. Barth and other explorers. Throughout that extensive central region called Soudan there is very effective political organization, an active trade, and, in some districts, a remarkable condition of manufacturing industry. Here, in many places, Dr. Barth found the manufacture of cotton and grass clothes, very fine leather-work, and the working of metals, carried on very skilfully, and to a notable extent. These manufactures find markets not only throughout Central Africa, but also in the cities on the Mediterranean. He gives a particular description of the city of Kano, which, at the time of his visit, was a flourishing manufacturing and commercial emporium, controlled by that branch of the brown African race known as Fulbe, Fulans, and Fellatahs. A remarkable condition of industrial enterprise was noticed not only in the city, but throughout the whole district.

Dr. Barth describes important kingdoms in Central Africa whose history can be traced back nearly to the beginning of the Christian Era, and which are doubtless much older. These kingdoms have had considerable civilization, that is shown to have been greater in ancient times than it is at present. In Ghasr-eggomo, anciently the capital of Bornou, but now a mass of ruins, the principal buildings were made of brick; but "in the present capital not the smallest approach is made to this more solid mode of architecture." Dr. Barth adds:

"It cannot be doubted that the old capital contained a great deal of barbaric magnificence, and even a certain degree of civilization, much more than is at present found in this country. It is certainly a spectacle not devoid of interest to imagine, in this town of Negroland, a splendid court, with a considerable number of learned and intelligent men gathering around their sovereign, and a priest writing down the glorious achievements of his master."

Written chronicles of Bornou, and of some of the other kingdoms, still exist, although the Fulans have sought to destroy them. Dr. Barth says: "Books containing a comprehensive history of the kingdom of Katsena have been destroyed intentionally by the Fulbe or Fulans since their conquest of the country. One tradition connects the origin of the kingdom of Bornou with the Himyarite kings of Arabia. Other traditions say it was founded by white Berbers, which, of course, means that it was created by influences proceeding from the old Cushite or Phœnician communities of Northern Africa. The records state that Selma, the first black or dark-colored monarch of Bornou, began his reign in the year 1194 A.D., many centuries (no record tells certainly how many) after the kingdom was founded.

That the central countries of Africa were occupied or

controlled in ancient times by a civilized white race is shown by the physiological peculiarities of the present inhabitants. The people of those countries present everywhere a remarkable mixture of races. The blood of the original brown race, with its fine forms, long curling hair, and dark olive complexion, predominates in this mixture, and sometimes it is found nearly pure. It is, however, common to find it mixed with that of both the white and the negro races. I am not speaking of the Berbers, the native Egyptians, the Nubians, the Abyssinians, nor even of the Gallas. I refer only to that great body of the native population of Africa represented by the Fulans and the Bechuanas. All these people show traits of a common origin. They are divided into classes or nationalities, and called by different names, although the difference between them is less than is often created among people of the same ethnic family by time and circumstances. The Abyssinians, Egyptians, and Berbers are white men mixed with the brown race of Africa. The Fulans, Bornese, and Bechuanas are this brown race, more or less mixed with the other races.

Traces of white blood in the African people, more or less distinct, are found everywhere, away from the Western Coast. They have been noticed by all travelers, though not always clearly explained. Dr. Barth, being at a village in Adamwa, wrote thus of this mixture of races: "I was struck by the symmetry and beauty of their forms, and the regularity of their features; but I was still more astonished at their complexion, which was different in different individuals, it being in some a glossy black, and in others a light copper." He adds, "The same variety has been observed in many other tribes, as well on this continent as in Asia."

Dr. Livingstone's attention has been drawn to the same physiological peculiarity in the people farther south, where not only mixture with the black race is apparent, but also striking traits that must have been inherited from a white race. He points out carefully that the true type of the African people "is not that found on the West Coast, from which most people have derived their ideas of the African," and, in his descriptions of the brown race, shows us traces of the mixture of races so manifest in other parts of the continent. Speaking of Chinsamba, ruling chief of the Manganjas, he says: "He has a Jewish cast of face, or rather the ancient Assyrian face, as seen in the monuments brought home by Mr. Layard. This face is very common in this country. The majority of the heads here are as well shaped as those depicted in the ancient Assyrian and Egyptian monuments."

The same variety of complexion, with other physical characteristics denoting mixture, is described by those who have visited the lake regions near the sources of the Nile. For instance, Mr. Burton says of the Wagogo: "Many of them are as fair as Abyssinians; some of them are as black as negroes;" and he describes the Watosi as "tall, comely, and comparatively fair." The ruling and aristocratic class in the countries near these lakes, called "the Wahuma," greatly resemble the Abyssinians, although some of them have a darker color; and there is no reason to doubt that the Wahuma, like the Abyssinians and the Gallas, represent the ancient Cushite Arabians, mixed in a greater or lesser degree with the dark-colored people of Africa. The Wahuma have a tradition that Africa formerly belonged to white men, and they claim to represent the blood of these ancient white rulers of the land.

At the present time, the most numerous and powerful people in Central Africa, south of the region occupied by the Berbers, are the Fûlans, a people remarkable there for their intelligence, skill, and restless ambition. Their influence is already established at many of the more important points, from Senegambia to the Nile, near the western border of Abyssinia, and especially in Soudan. They seem likely to become supreme in all the central countries. Every traveler in that part of Africa describes the Fûlans, and speculates vainly concerning their history. They resemble, substantially, the great body of the brown race of the continent, and show the same traces of mixture with other races. Dr. Barth says of them:

"If any African tribe deserves the full attention of the learned European, it is that of the Fûlbe (*sing.* Pullo), or Fula, as they are called by the Mandingoes; Fellani (*sing.* Bafellanchi) by the Hausa people, Fellata by the Kanúri, and Fûlan by the Arabs. No doubt they are the most intelligent of all the [Central] African tribes, although in bodily development they cannot be said to exhibit the most perfect specimens. It is their superior intelligence that gives their chief expression to the Fûlbe. But as to their outward appearance, which presents various contrasts in complexion as well as bodily development, we must first take into account that the Fûlbe, as a conquering tribe, sweeping over a wide expanse of provinces, have absorbed and incorporated with themselves different and quite distinct national elements."

The Fûlans, on account of their prominence and importance, have been a topic of much speculation. One or two writers have assumed that they were not originally an African people. M. Eichwaldt published an essay in the *Journal de la Société Ethnologique* for 1841, in which he sought, by cleverly managed assumption and hypothesis, to connect them with the Malays by way of Meroë. Dr. Barth says: "I myself am of opinion that their origin is to be sought in the direction of the east; but this refers to an age which, for us, is enveloped in impenetrable darkness. * * There may be some remote affinity between the Fûlbe and the South African tribes, but this refers to an age probably not later than the rule of the Pharaohs." The Fulans, nevertheless, are only a branch of the race found everywhere in Central, Eastern, and Southern Africa. Whatever shall explain their origin will explain that of the whole race.

Within the historical period, and since the beginning of the Christian Era, there has been more civilization in Africa than exists at the present time. Dr. Barth shows that Bornou, in Central Africa, has declined from a higher condition of civilization. The ruins of its former capital, its historical literature, and other facts still apparent to those who observe that country carefully, make plain that not many centuries have passed since there was in Bornou a higher knowledge and practice of the builder's art, a more effective political organization, considerable literary culture, and a better condition of manufactures and commerce. That old tradition of the people which connects the origin of this kingdom with the Himyarite sovereigns of Arabia, whether correct or incorrect, is not without significance. There is much in the history of Arabia, as well as in the present condition of Africa, to show that the Cushite Arabians occupied Central Africa in very remote times.

There is a great difference between the present condition of Eastern Africa and that in which it was found by the first Europeans who visited the Indian Ocean. Vasquez di Gama wrote an account of his first voyage, but the manuscript was lost, probably in a dust-hole of some old library. One or two narratives of the voyage, written by other persons, have been printed. We know that the Portuguese found in that part of Africa two important kingdoms, Quiloa and Monomotapa, which excited their admiration and their covetousness; and also that there was constant commercial intercourse between that coast and India. When Di Gama arrived at Mozambique in 1498, he found there cities not inferior to those of Portugal. A narrative of the voyage says of Melinda, one of these cities: "The city was large, with handsome streets, and houses built of stone, several stories high, with terraces on the top." In the ports of all these cities he found "many ships" quite equal to his own; and the officers in charge of these ships used the mariner's compass, the astrolabe, and other nautical and astronomical instruments. Here, as everywhere else in that part of the Indian Seas, the Arabians were foremost in commercial enterprise.

That African civilization has disappeared; those cities and kingdoms no longer exist. The superior military appliances of the Portuguese enabled them to occupy that region, and this Portuguese occupation has brought to the country nothing but debasement and ruin. In place of the flourishing communities and active commerce found there in 1498, we have only barbarism and semi-barbarism, managed in a characteristic way by Portuguese brutality.

NORTHERN AFRICA IN PRE-HISTORIC TIMES.

Enlightened states and cities existed in Northern Africa long previous to the beginning of history. Many considerations make it evident that the origin of these civilized communities must be referred to a very remote period in the past. A very ancient and influential civilization in Northwestern Africa and Spain is plainly signified by the old myths and legends concerning Atlas and the Atlantides. It must have been established there in the first ages of Cushite maritime enterprise on the Mediterranean, if not earlier; and its beginnings must have been very ancient —so ancient as to be mythical at the commencement of the Tyrian period. Its chronological relation to the building of Gades and the rise of Carthaginian supremacy must have been nearly the same as that of the Old Monarchy of Egypt to the building of Alexandria and the Egypt of the Ptolemies.*

The city of Carthage, which, in the days of its highest power and prosperity, controlled most of Northern Africa and Spain, must have contained more than a million inhabitants. It numbered over 700,000 when destroyed by the Romans. The malignant hate of these conquerors and destroyers, seeking to exterminate every vestige of Carthaginian power, civilization, and even history, destroyed all the books and manuscripts of the country, except an elaborate treatise of Mago on Agriculture and Botany,

---

* Sallust (Jugurtha, cap. 18), deriving his information from "Punic sources," tells us that, according to the traditions of the African people, Hercules died in Spain, and that after his death his followers settled in Northern Africa. Hercules, or more properly Melcarth, belongs to very ancient times.

which they translated into Latin and appropriated to themselves. So we are informed by Pliny.

Carthage was the latest development of the Cushite race in Northern Africa, but it was not the greatest. In earlier times, that region, from Egypt to the Atlantic Ocean, had been still more important, and evidently more populous. Previous to the beginning of Tyrian supremacy, Northern Africa and Spain were old in civilization. During the Tyrian period, Northern Africa was full of cities and alive with the busy movements of commerce and agriculture. It continued to be one of the most attractive of civilized countries down to the time of the Mahometan invasion. Tacitus, writing of Germany, its rude people, and ungenial climate, exclaimed "*Quis, Asia aut Africa aut Italia relicta, Germaniam peteret?*"—who would relinquish Asia, Africa, or Italy for Germany! Roman ruins, now found in the interior, show us how attractive that African country was to the Romans, even in its decline.

The old cities and civilization of Northern Africa came from the people known to us as Phœnicians, and some of their settlements in that region must have been much older than the time when Martu, or Marathos, was the ruling city. Those old myths, common to Romans, Greeks, and Phœnicians, are destitute of significance if some of the Cushite communities in that country, and especially in Northwestern Africa, were not many ages older than those on the Black Sea.

The country is still covered with ruins, although every trace of some of the more ancient cities has undoubtedly disappeared. An interesting account of some of these ruins can be found in the work of Mr. N. Davis on "The Ruined Cities of Africa." His explorations, however, were confined to the districts immediately connected with Carthage; but he refers to other ruins not yet described nor even visited. The old city of Moroco, or *Maghrib*, was a ruin in the time of Leo Africanus. He speaks of it as " the great and famous city of Maroco," describes it as " a huge and mighty city," anciently remarkable for its magnificent temples and schools of learning, and says " it had four-and-twenty gates, and a wall of great strength and thickness." Describing one of the great temples, he makes this statement: " Under the porch of this temple, in the olden time, it is said, there were nearly an hundred booksellers' shops, and as many on the other side; but at the present time I think there is not one bookseller in the whole city, and scarcely a third part of the city is now inhabited."

The Romans were succeeded in Africa by the Goths, who were followed by the Mahometan Arabs. The intolerant and fierce Mahometans waged war against the remaining influences of the Phœnician civilization, and, to a large extent, drove the old inhabitants from the coast. Leo Africanus tells us that " they burnt all the African books, for they were of opinion that the Africans, so long as they had any knowledge of natural philosophy, or of any other good arts and sciences, would every day more and more contemn the law of Mahomet." But the old culture was not all destroyed immediately; " the Moors" of Spain are famed for their learning and elegant culture; and some of the African cities, under Mahometan sway, were for a long time equally eminent. All this, however, disappeared finally, and down to our own time Northern Africa was closed against Europe by the inappeasable hostility of Mahometan fanaticism.

THE BERBERS.

All that now remains of the old Phœnician communities in Northern Africa is found in the people called Berbers, who are spread throughout the inland portions of the country from Egypt to the Atlantic. The origin of the Berbers appears in what we know of their history, as well as in their language, which belongs to the Ethiopic or Cushite family, being genetically related to the ancient speech of Arabia, and to the modern dialects used in Abyssinia and Somaulia. Those who assume that the Phœnicians were never anything more than a few communities of manufacturers and merchants, occupying a little district on the eastern shore of the Mediterranean, are necessarily unable to comprehend this fact, and they are no more able to explain the vast extent of the colonial and commercial system of that people.

The assumption has no warrant. In ancient times that system was supported by Arabia, and not merely by the little district known as Phœnicia. The name and traditions of the country show us that the Cushite colonizers of Northern Africa came from the Upper Nile valley as well as from Phœnicia and the Arabian peninsula. It is probable that the earliest civilized communities on the Mediterranean, away from its eastern shores, were in Northern Africa, and that these communities played a great part in human affairs, of which there is no record, although it is dimly visible in the mythologies and cosmogonic legends of the ancient world from Rome to India.

Leo Africanus, in the first book of his work on Africa, states that the people of North Africa, in his time, all used one language, although divided into many tribes and familica. He says the Mahometan Arabs called their speech "barbarous," and adds that, in his view, it was "the true and natural speech of the Africans," although some would infer from its character that the Northern Africans or Berbers "came by lineal descent from the Sabeans, a people of Arabia Felix." The genetic relation of the Berber language to that of the Himyaric or Cushito Arabians seems to have been noticed distinctly by the Mahometan invaders, whose speech was the Arabic of the Hedjaz.

In Leo's time the Berber language was universal in Morocco, and in all the North African countries, excepting that "oyer against Tunis and Tripoli" the Arabic of the invading Mahometans was "spoken very corruptly." He says the Berbers called their language "*Aquel Amariy*, the noble tongue." In his opinion, the Berbers or Africans anciently "had an alphabet peculiar to themselves," which had given place to the Arabic letters used by their invaders; and they had histories, which were destroyed and forgotten. The Cushite origin of the Berbers is shown in his account of their ancient religion. He says: "These Africans had in times past magnificent and stately temples, dedicated to the sun and to fire;" and they worshipped the planets, offering prayers and sacrifices. Leo had no clear comprehension of the origin of "these Africans," but his account of their language and religion shows it very plainly.

Neither ethnology nor linguistic science has yet given such attention to the Berbers as their historical importance deserves, although we have a better knowledge of them than was possible when Leo wrote on Africa. They are found as far south as the southern border of the Sahara, and they seem to have been connected with some of the important political movements of Central Africa. The Berbers, it is said, established the old kingdom of Bornou, and also founded the city of Timbuctu. They undoubtedly controlled the kingdom of Bornou for a long time previous to the beginning of the twelfth century. But the land of the Berbers is Northern Africa, between Egypt and the Atlantic, excepting the districts immediately on the coast-line. They have towns, cities, agricultural districts, political organization, and many of the arts of civilized life. They generally read and write, and have schools and books. Nearly all the tribes now use the Arabic alphabet; but the Touaricks of the Sahara—the purest, proudest, most numerous, and most lordly family of the Berbers—have an alphabet of their own, for which they claim great antiquity, and they have also considerable native literature.

We have some account of the Berbers from travelers who have partially explored Northern Africa; and since the French took possession of Algeria, a few scholarly French officers employed in that country, such as MM. Hanoteau and Boissonnet, have given some attention to this remarkable people. In the *Journal Asiatique* for May, 1847, M. Boissonnet gave an interesting account of the Touarick or "Tifinag" alphabet, with an impression of the characters, showing it to be nearly identical with that used by the Phœnicians in later times. The characters were printed in a comparative table, with the Hebrew letters and those of the Libyan inscriptions. Their identity with the Phœnician alphabet is too manifest to be questioned. That Journal called attention to their close resemblance to the characters of certain ancient Libyan inscriptions, particularly those of the bilingual stone of

Thugga. There is no room to doubt that this alphabet of the Touaricks is substantially the same that was used by the old Phœnician or Cushite communities throughout Northern Africa. Captain Hanoteau promised to furnish for publication a volume of selections from the Touarick literature, with a French translation.

We have some accounts of the Touaricks, and of other Berber communities, in the volumes of modern travelers. In the months between August, 1845, and April, 1846, Mr. James Richardson visited Ghadames, Ghat, Mourzouk, Sockna, and Misratah. He met the Touaricks first at Ghadames, where a large company of them had arrived for traffic. Writing in his journal while in that city, he said: "This afternoon I had a visit from Touarick women, and was astonished to find some of them almost fair. It is evident that the men are dark simply from exposure to the sun." An Arab merchant expressed to him the common estimate of the Touaricks by saying, "The maharee [desert camel] always assumes the mastery over the coast camel, just as the Touarick assumes to be lord over the Arab." In the Sahara, which is much less a desert than fancy has sometimes portrayed, the Touaricks have towns, cities, and an excellent condition of agriculture. They are very skillful in the cultivation of fruit. Their method of political organization is democratic, somewhat after the fashion of the old Cushite municipalities. Mr. Richardson says: "Ghat, like all the Touarick countries, is a republic; all the people govern." And, "The woman of the Touaricks is not the woman of the Moors and Mussulmans generally. She has here great liberty, walks about unveiled, and takes an active part in the affairs and transactions of life."

In a letter published in the *Journal Asiatique* for August, 1845, M. Boissonnet stated that a native traveler told him that "the Touaricks are very white, go always clothed, and wear pantaloons like Europeans." This reminds us of the description given in the 13th century by Ebn-ed-din El Eghwaati, in his "Notes of a Journey:" "The Touaricks are a very powerful people, of very white complexion; they wear pantaloons like Christians."

Captain G. F. Lyon, whose volume was published in 1821, met a company of Touaricks at Mourzouk, and spoke of them as follows: "They are the finest race of men I ever saw; tall, straight, and handsome, with a certain air of independence and pride that is very imposing. They are generally white, that is to say, comparatively so, the dark brown of their complexion being occasioned only by the heat of the climate. Their arms and bodies, where constantly covered, are as white as those of many Europeans." He gives the following account of a community of white Berbers in Fezzan: "The inhabitants of Zuela are nearly all white, and they are particularly careful about intermarriages with Arabs. They are certainly the most respectable, hospitable, and quiet people in Fezzan; and their whole appearance (for they are handsome and very neatly dressed) bespeaks something superior."

Rev. H. B. Tristam, whose book, entitled "Wanderings South of the Atlas Mountains," appeared at London in 1860, describes the Kabyles, the M'Zabs, the Wareglans, and the inhabitants of the Wed R'hir chain of oases, who are all Berbers, and use Berber dialects. The M'Zabs have a republic or confederacy consisting of seven cities and districts. Ghardaïa, the capital, has 13,000 inhabitants. This city is very old, for the ruins of a still more ancient city are connected with it. Beni-Isguen, another of these cities, has 10,000 inhabitants, and not far from it are the ruins of its still more ancient predecessor. At Berryan these M'Zab Berbers told Mr. Tristam that "their nation came hither from Moroco, to which place their ancestors immigrated from Egypt or South of Egypt; but their imauns knew all their story, and it is written in their sacred books, which are preserved in manuscripts at Ghardaïa."

Being at Guerrara, another of these seven cities, Mr. Tristam writes: "The Guerrarans really understand and apply the arch, a proof certainly of more than modern Arab civilization. In many places the resemblance to Egyptian architecture is interesting, especially when combined with the similarity in shape of their vessels, jars, and household utensils to those of ancient Egypt." Speaking of his departure from the city of Beni-Isguen, he says: "When we were about to depart, the djemmûa requested our names and addresses, as they have a register containing all the events of the city, and a record of its visitors for nine hundred years. The book was produced."

The M'Zabs are not the only Berbers who have books and manuscripts. It is probable that all, or nearly all, the tribes have annals and other literary records like those preserved at Ghardaïa, for they all read and write. The Touaricks appear to be the most cultivated branch of the family; their literature has attracted the attention of French officers in Africa. When it can be explored carefully, important historical records may be discovered, although it is nowise likely that much relating to their ancient history has been preserved.

The Berbers, their language, and their books ought to be fully explored and studied. Archæology and linguistic science have lavished enthusiastic and toilsome study on subjects much less worthy of attention, for these Berbers present the remains of a great civilization much older than Rome or Hellas, and of one of the most important peoples of antiquity. Here are "ruins" more promising, and, in certain respects, more important than the buried ruins of Nineveh; but they have failed to get proper attention, partly because a false chronology has made it impossible to see their meaning and comprehend their importance. The Berbers represent ancient communities whose importance was beginning to decline before Rome appeared, and which were probably contemporary with ancient Chaldea and the Old Monarchy of Egypt. Some of them, I repeat it, may have been established by the Arabian Cushites before Menes united Upper and Lower Egypt under one government.

Additional suggestions relative to the earliest civilized communities in Northwestern Africa will become necessary in what I have to say of Western Europe in pre-historic times, for there seems to have been a period in the remote past when these regions were intimately connected. Meanwhile it must, I think, be admitted that the civilized communities, established so extensively in Africa by the Arabian Cushites in the pre-historic ages, occupied, controlled, or influenced to a large extent nearly the whole continent. The Cushite origin of these communities would be conclusively manifest in the dialects they left in Africa, if there were nothing else to show it; and their influence explains what we see in the present condition of the African people, which is so unlike that of normal barbarism, and in which there are so many traces of former acquaintance with civilization.

NAVIGATION AROUND AFRICA.

We have good reasons for believing not only that the Arabian Cushites in the early times, but also the Phœnicians during the Tyrian period, were familiar with every part of the coast of Africa. The old Cushite settlements were extended far down the eastern coast, nearly to the Cape of Good Hope; and, so late as 1408 A.D., when the Portuguese first sailed to India, there were important cities as low down as the Mozambique Channel, in the latitude of Madagascar. We have the testimony of antiquity that the Tyrians had "ancient settlements" on the Atlantic coast of Africa, "which consisted of not less than three hundred cities." It is added that they "were destroyed by the Pharusii and the Nigritæ." Strabo doubted because he could not appreciate either the greatness or the antiquity of the people called Phœnicians. He frequently doubted incontestable facts because his limited view of the world did not enable him to understand them, as in the case of Pytheas and his voyage to the arctic regions. In the present case, his hesitating doubt itself confirms the testimony which he was not quite able to reject.

The Cushites, or Phœnicians, so placed on the Eastern and Western Coasts, could not have failed to sail around Africa, and become familiar with the coast of Guinea, in the days of their greatest enterprise. The contrary supposition is every way improbable. Could we have a complete history of the Phœnicians and Southern Arabians from the twentieth to the middle of the ninth century before the Christian Era, it would probably appear that their navigation was more extensive than any of the moderns have supposed. The knowledge that Africa could be cir-

cumnavigated, so prevalent in countries connected with
the Eastern Mediterranean at the beginning of the sixth
century before the Christian Era, must have come from
recollections and traditions of the navigation of the Phœnicians and Southern Arabians in the earlier ages.

About the year 600 B.C., Necho II., an enterprising king
of Egypt, fitted out an expedition, which he ordered to sail
down the Red Sea, go around Africa, and return to Egypt
through the Straits of Gibraltar. He knew very well that
such a voyage was possible. The same knowledge existed
among the Persians, when Sataspes, one of the Achæmeni-
dæ, guilty of a great crime, was offered escape from capital
punishment if he would sail around Africa in the opposite
direction, but lacked resolution to complete the voyage.
Herodotus, who gives a particular account of the successful expedition sent out by Necho, adds that the Carthaginians knew that Africa was surrounded by the ocean, and
could therefore be circumnavigated. The Carthaginians
sent forth several expeditions, to renew, along the African
coast, the old navigation and commerce of the Phœnicians;
and there seem to have been several Hannos by whom
such expeditions were commanded. We have the "Periplus" of one, who made an extensive voyage along the
coast, sailing from the west. Pliny mentions another Hanno, who sailed from the Straits of Gibraltar to Arabia, and
wrote an account of his voyage in a "Commentary." Po-
sidonius and others give accounts of the voyages of Eudoxus of Cyzicus, "a learned man, much interested in the
peculiarities of different countries." It is stated that he
had great enthusiasm for exploring the coast of Africa on
the exterior ocean, and that he found on the Eastern Coast,
between the Cape of Good Hope and Arabia, remains of

the wreck of a ship from Gades. Strabo doubts what is said of Eudoxus, but it is not, for this reason, to be discredited.

Phœnician commerce at the East was interrupted, and the independence of the great Phœnician cities on the Eastern Mediterranean was destroyed, in the ninth century before Christ, by those Assyrian invasions that reduced to subjection all the countries in that region. In the latter part of that century there was a great migration of Phœnicians from the Eastern Mediterranean, and especially from Tyre, to Carthage. Phœnician navigation around Africa was discontinued. The Carthaginian efforts to renew it were made three or four centuries later. It had been discontinued more than two centuries when the voyage ordered by Necho was undertaken; but it was remembered, as we can see in the general knowledge that such navigation was possible; and the wreck of a ship from Gades on the eastern coast of Africa shows that voyages around Africa had formerly been made from the west as well as from the east.

It is known that the Arabians had an accurate knowledge of the configuration of the southern and southwestern part of the African continent, and that, through knowledge derived from them, this portion of the coast of Africa was accurately drawn on maps before the time of Bartholomew Diaz and Vasquez di Gama, and then what we call the Cape of Good Hope was described as "Cape Diab" [or Dsiab in Arabic].* It seems also to have been

* Long-temps avant Bartholomé Diaz et Vasco de Gama, nous voyons l'extrémité triangulaire de l'Afrique, représentée dans le planisphère de Sanuto, de 1300, annexé au *Secreta fidelium Crucis*, et publié par Bongars; dans le *Portulano della Mediceo Laurenziana*, de 1351, ouvrage

called "Cape Agisymba," if we may believe Ferdinand Columbus, who said the name *Cape of Good Hope* " was substituted for the older name Cape *Agesingua*," which is a corruption of the word Agisymba, as Humboldt shows. Ten years previous to the voyage of Vasquez di Gama, Pedreio de Covilhan, who had visited Calicut, Goa, and Sofala, in Southeastern Africa, wrote from Sofala to John I., king of Portugal, that he had learned from the Arabians that Africa could be circumnavigated; and he described the course by which Portuguese ships could sail round Africa to Sofala and Madagascar.

Rev. Dr. Krapf, and one or two German scholars of reputation, have supposed that the "Ophir" of the Hebrew Scriptures may have been on the eastern coast; but this does not seem probable. Max Müller is sure that it must have been somewhere in India, because he thinks the names of gold, ivory, and the other articles brought from Ophir by the ships of Hiram and Solomon were Sanskrit; but his attempt to show this is not satisfactory. Moreover, if we are to seek Ophir in India, it will be much more natural and reasonable to suppose the names of the articles of commerce mentioned came from the old lan-

génois, que le Comte Baldelli a fait connaître; dans le *Planisferio de la Palatina*, de Florence, de 1417, discuté par le Cardinal Zurla; et surtout dans le fameuse mappemonde de Fra Mauro, tracée dans les années 1457 et 1459. C'est cette dernière carte surtout, anterieure de quarante ans à la circumnavigation de Vasco de Gama, qui offre, avec la plus grande clarté, le promontoire de l'Afrique australe sous le nom de *Capo di Diab*. [Humboldt's *Examen Critique* de l'Histoire *de la Géographie du Nouveau Continent*, etc., vol. i.] Near the close of the same volume he pointed out that the later opinions of antiquity relative to the circumnavigation of Africa were much more incorrect than those of preceding ages: "Chez les anciens les opinions récentes sont souvent moins justes que plusieurs de celles qui les avaient précédées."

guage of the country, and not from the Sanskrit. Could it really be shown beyond question that these words are actually found in the Sanskrit language, it would be necessary to show, also, that their relation to it is not like that of the word "camel" to English, and "camelus" to Latin —words which, as we know, came into Latin and English from the old Arabian name of the animal they are used to designate. Mr. Müller says, very justly, that the names of the articles brought from Ophir are as foreign to Hebrew as *gutta-percha* and *tobacco* are to English; but this does not make them Sanskrit. It is more reasonable to assume that they came either from some native dialect of the country where they were found, or from the language of the navigators and traders who made them articles of commerce.

The word "Ophir," as used in the Hebrew Scriptures, means "the West," and is the same as the words *Aphar*, *Apar*, and *Aupir*. Wilford says very justly, in the 8th volume of the "Asiatic Researches:" "In Scripture, Parvaim and Ophir mean countries at the east and at the west; but these terms are not deducible from the Hebrew. Apar and Aparica are the same as Ophir, Aphar, and Africa." Bishop Lowth pointed out that Ophir, Aupir, and Auphir were all different forms of the same word, from which he derived the name Africa. It is the same word that was used, in ancient times, to describe Mauretania, Spain, and other countries on the Western Mediterranean, as "the West." Therefore, when it is said that the ships of Hiram and Solomon went to Ophir, the meaning is that they went to the countries of "the West;" and, probably, all the countries beyond the Cape of Good Hope were so described. The Ophir visited may have been the region on the coast of Guinea, where gold and ivory were abundant;

and in making these voyages, the ships went not only down the Red Sea, but also through the Straits of Gibraltar, and down the Western Coast. This appears to be the meaning of the following statement: "The king's [Solomon's] ships went to Tarshish with the servants of Huram: every three years once came the ships of Tarshish, bringing gold and silver, ivory, apes, and peacocks," or perhaps "Guinea fowl" [2 Chron. ix., 21]. That is to say, the ships went to Tarshish or Tartessus, on the coast of Spain, and sailed for Ophir from that place, as well as from Eziongeber, on the Red Sea.

This location of Ophir seems to me more probable than any other that has been suggested. To seek it in India, or anywhere else at the East, when its name tells us that it was connected with "the West," is not the most reasonable method of inquiry, and does not take proper account of the fact that, according to the Hebrew Scriptures, it could be reached from Tartessus, in Spain, quite as easily as from Ezion-geber on the Red Sea. If the great extent of Phœnician navigation had always been recognised, there would have been less doubt, and that part of the African coast, near Liberia, to which gold and ivory have given their names, must have been accepted as the Ophir of Solomon and the Tyrians. At any rate, the old Arabian race, that occupied the central countries of Africa so extensively, and established settlements so far down both the Eastern and the Western Coast, must have been familiar with every coast district of the country that produced anything to attract commerce, and must have been accustomed, in the great ages of their power, to make voyages to the Gold Coast from ports at the West, both on the Atlantic and within the Straits of Gibraltar, as well as from the Red Sea and Southern Arabia.

IX.

WESTERN EUROPE IN PRE-HISTORIC TIMES.

Our histories of Western Europe begin with what the Romans tell us of the occupation of Spain by the Carthaginians, and of their own occupation of the Keltic countries. The historians generally can see nothing beyond this. What the Romans have not described or reported is not deemed worthy of serious attention, and minds controlled by Roman and Greek authority have found it easy to slide into a belief that the people of Western Europe generally were never, at any time, much above the condition of barbarians before they were brought under the influence of Roman civilization.

It is a pleasant thing, no doubt, to have reputation for critical discrimination, but it is well to take some account of the fact that ambition to establish such a reputation sometimes paralyzes the faculty of perception. It is more honorable to see wisely what is presented for observation, than to believe there can be anything worthy to be called sound judgment in refusing to see it. Even in the Roman accounts of the Keltic countries of Western Europe, it is manifest that they had an old civilization when the Romans went there. Julius Cæsar tells us that they had the art of writing, and that they used what he called "the Greek letters." Their cities, their arts and manufactures, their knowledge of metallurgy, and their habits of life, indicate their condition. It is to be regretted that the Romans did not describe them more carefully, study their literature, and tell us all that could then have been learned concerning their history. But they were not accustomed to deal justly, in this respect, by the peoples they conquered. Major Wilford, expressing in the "Asiatic Researches" his opinion that the historical records of India had been destroyed by the Brahmans, added: "In this manner the Romans destroyed the books of Numa, consigned to destruction the historical books of the Etruscans, and, I suspect, those also of the Turdetani in Spain." He might have added a reference to their treatment of the Carthaginian books.

AN ANCIENT CIVILIZATION IN WESTERN EUROPE.

It may well be doubted whether the Kelts were much inferior to the Romans in anything save unity and military organization at the time of the Roman invasion. Strabo makes special mention of the culture and intelligence of the Turdetani, in Southern Spain, who had beautiful cities, possessed great wealth, "used silver goblets and casks," were "polished and urbane in their manners," and showed remarkable elegance and refinement in their manner of life. Polybius states that in the time of the second Punic War the Romans discarded the swords they had been accustomed to use for such as were in use among the Iberians, which were superior to the Roman weapon. Ireland, then and afterwards, was held in great repute for its culture and its schools of learning. Mosheim states that in the ninth century its culture was unequaled by any other in Europe. Tacitus tells us that in his time it was widely known through its commerce, which attracted the merchants of other countries.

An important and very ancient civilization in Western Europe is brought to light by the revelations of geology, in what they show us of the "Ages of Bronze and of Polished Stone," whose unquestionable testimony supports that of the old myths and traditions of the Greeks.

In the historical and mythical literature of Greece there is mention of two distinct and widely separated periods of civilization in Spain and Northwestern Africa, or in the regions near the Pillars of Hercules.

1. The oldest of these periods was entirely mythical. It is indicated by the myths concerning Hercules and the Cronidæ, by the representations that Hyperion, Atlas, Saturn, and other great personages of mythology were kings who reigned over countries on the western shores of the Mediterranean, and by the accounts given of the island of Atlantis. The legends that connect Hercules with Northwestern Africa, Spain, and other regions at the West, evidently refer to the most ancient times. They may represent the first occupation of those countries by the Arabian Cushites, in ages older than Egypt, when the first great cities of that race appeared on the Mediterranean. The story of the Atlantic Island which came from Egypt was believed by Solon and Plato. Solon, it is said, knowing that the Egyptians had records of very ancient times, sought to get an account of them from the priests at Sais. They assured him that the Greeks had no knowledge of antiquity, and knew nothing of what had happened anciently in their own country; and then they gave him a history of the ancient times from their own annals. He brought this history to Greece in manuscript notes, intending to make some important use of it, which circumstances, however, prevented. Plato produced some particulars of

it in his "Timœus" and "Critias" by giving the story of the "Atlantic Island." In the remotest age mentioned in the Egyptian annals, there was, in the Atlantic Sea, over against the Pillars of Hercules, "an island larger than Libya and Asia put together." The people of this island, who had great wealth and an admirable condition of civilized life, "extended their empire to all the country as far as Egypt and Tyrrhenia;" and once "a mighty, warlike power, rushing from the Atlantic Sea, spread itself with hostile fury over Europe and Asia." It is added that the Atlantic Island afterwards sunk in the sea, which, in consequence, was no longer navigable. Other legends tell us of kings who reigned in Spain and Northern Africa. There is but one reasonable explanation. These legends preserve the recollection of a great and enterprising people who in very remote times occupied those Western countries, and had communication with America. The Atlantic Island must mean America, and its disappearance in the ocean must mean the discontinuance of communication with it.

2. The second period presented in the Greek records is more historical. It is the period when, after Tyre rose to supremacy, the Phœnicians reoccupied Spain and Northwestern Africa, and established an extensive commerce with Western Europe, going to Britain for tin, and to the Northwestern countries for amber. To this period belongs the building of Gades; and it has been usual to assume that it shows us the first appearance of the Phœnician race in those regions, although this assumption is contrary to both fact and tradition. Strabo seems to have entertained it, for he says in his third book: "I repeat that the Phœnicians were the discoverers [of Mauretania, the Fortunate

Islands, and Spain], for they possessed the better part of Iberia and Libya before the time of Homer." This describes the second period of which I am speaking; but it does not say that civilization in those countries was not older than the time of the Tyrians. In fact, Strabo himself shows that it was older, in what he says of Tartessus in connection with Geryon and Hercules, and in his representation that the Tyrians went forth to find and reoccupy the most western countries reached by Hercules. Nothing tells us how early the Tyrians began to assume possession of Spain; but they were probably established there, and in Mauretania, before the city of Gades was built.

The first settlements of the Arabian Cushites in Spain and Northern Africa cannot have been later than 5000 years before the Christian Era. The Egyptian date connected with the story of the Atlantic Island makes the time much earlier. Menes was about 4000 years older than the birth of Christ, and his time cannot be as old as that indicated by the myths concerning the expedition of Hercules in the West. Spain and Northwestern Africa must have been independent countries before his time, if the myths have any significance whatever. According to the Irish records, the oldest people mentioned in Ireland, the Formorians, came from Africa; and it is said that they had powerful fleets, and were distinguished for maritime enterprise. Probably the Cushite race, religion, and civilization first went to the ancient Finnic people of Britain, Gaul, and the Scandinavian countries from Spain and Africa. The beginning of the Bronze Age in these countries was much older than the period of Tyre. The Tyrian establishments in those Western countries seem to have been later than the Aryan immigration that created the Keltic peoples and languages; and it may be that the Tyrians introduced the "Age of Iron" not long after their arrival, for it was evidently much older than the time of the Romans.

I have alluded to the ancient myths and mythological legends which indicate the existence of civilized and important countries at the West, near the Pillars of Hercules, in the deepest antiquity. They certainly mean this if they mean any thing; and nothing seems to me more preposterous than to assume that they are entirely destitute of significance.

The rationalism of Euhemerus could not be popular in a community where Socrates was put to death on suspicion that he cherished scientific tendencies hostile to the blind assumptions of the prevalent religion; nevertheless, that rationalism proceeded from truth and reason. The wisest persons among the ancients understood that most of the gods in their mythology were deified men. Diodorus Siculus and others point out that the ancients held two opinions concerning the gods; some saying they were always heavenly and incorruptible, and others that they were originally of earthly origin, being deified men who were worshipped as forms or representations of the Supreme Being. It is easy to imagine the mental characteristics of the disputants on each side of this question. A clear intellect, where reason was not overborne by the feeling of wonder or the tendency to illusion, could not very easily see an original, self-existent divinity in a deified hero or sage. Men like Euhemerus could understand why great kings, heroes, and sages had been deified and worshipped after death; but no pious worship of the gods of Olympus, nor any classical consecration of this worship, could hide from them the fact that Saturn and Jupiter were originally kings who reigned over countries on the Western Mediterranean in the oldest times known to tradition. Even the classical dictionaries tell us that "Saturn was a mythical king of Italy."

One account of these personages runs as follows: Hyperion, Atlas, and Saturn or Cronos, were sons of Uranos, who reigned over a great kingdom composed of countries around the western part of the Mediterranean, with certain islands in the Atlantic. Hyperion succeeded his father, but was killed by the Titans. The kingdom was then divided between Atlas and Saturn, Atlas taking Northern Africa, with the Atlantic Islands, and Saturn the countries on the opposite shore to Italy and Sicily. Plato's account of the legend says: The Atlantes (successors of Atlas) reigned over the island of Atlantis, and also, on one side, over all the countries of Northern Africa to Egypt; and, on the other, all the way from the Atlantic to the limits of Tyrrhenia. This version of the story, which came from Egypt, makes Saturn a successor of Atlas. According to some accounts, Saturn was dethroned. Thymœtes said he was dethroned by Dionysos. The common statement is that Jupiter, his successor, became one of the greatest of monarchs. Another version makes Atlas the son of Iapetus, and the nephew of Saturn and Hyperion.

It must be that these ancient myths, however arrayed by fancy, or varied by local prejudice or tradition, rest on a basis of fact. They cannot be pure inventions; this is impossible; there is history in them; and I should feel that I was rejecting light and trifling with reason if I could refuse to see that they preserve recollections of the lost history of very ancient countries in those regions of Africa and Europe to which they refer. The traditions declare explicitly that such countries existed there. There is nothing whatever to make this improbable; and when we consider the great antiquity and enterprise of the Cushite civilization that created Egypt, we feel that the general testimony of these traditions must be true. But, to see it clearly, we must dismiss all narrow views of the past.

THE AGE OF BRONZE IN WESTERN EUROPE.

Let us now turn to a consideration of some of the facts brought to light within a few years by the investigations of geologists. These facts show that the antiquity of the human race in that part of the globe is much greater than even the boldest geologist had allowed himself to suppose. Human remains have been discovered in the geological formation known as "the drift," and in other subsequent formations down to the present time. In the older formations these remains consist chiefly of articles of human manufacture, such as arms and utensils of various kinds. They are all made of stone; at first, and for a long time, of flint, but finally, when greater skill had been developed, various kinds of stone were used, and a higher style of workmanship was displayed.

At length there is a sudden transition from arms and implements made of stone to those made of bronze. The arms, cutting instruments, and other bronze articles, were beautifully manufactured. In form and ornamentation they are very similar all over Western Europe. In his work on the subject, entitled "Pre-Historic Times," Sir J. Lubbock says: "The similarity to each other of the bronze weapons found in very distant parts of Europe implies a more extended intercourse between the different countries than existed in post-Roman times," or in the centuries immediately after the Roman occupation of Gaul. This Bronze Age seems to have been of very long duration. Bronze, however, was superseded by iron long before the Christian Era, for iron was in use in all those countries before the Romans went there. A very long time must have intervened between the beginning of the age of iron and the first invasion of the Romans.

But I do not propose to undertake an elaborate discussion of these discoveries, which have been very carefully described and discussed in many volumes already published in English, French, Danish, and German. They have been made in nearly all the Western countries of Europe, and particularly in France, Switzerland, England, Ireland, Germany, and Denmark. My purpose is to draw attention chiefly to what is described as the Age of Bronze. The preceding age of Stone, according to competent geologists, must have endured for a great length of time; but it was, in part, an age of civilization. Professor Worsäae divides this age into three periods: First, the period of the stone implements found in the drift and in caves, with remains of the mammoth and other extinct animals; second, the period of the stone implements found in the Danish Kjökenmöddings [or shell heaps] and coast-finds; third, the later Stone Age, or the period characterized by arms and implements of stone beautifully worked, and by large tumuli or buried tombs. Sir John Lubbock divides the Stone Age into two periods: that in which the stone implements were rudely manufactured of flint, and that in which they were made with much skill; the former he calls the Palæolithic period, and the latter the Neolithic period.

The Age of Polished Stone manufactures evidently had a considerable degree of civilization. The beautifully worked stone arms and implements, the gold and amber ornaments, and the large tumuli or buried tombs, with massive stone walls carefully constructed, show that age to have been very different from an age of barbarism. The people who manufactured these artistic stone implements, who constructed such sepulchral tumuli as that at West Kennett, England, and those on the Danish island of Moen, and who cultivated wheat, barley, and flax, and wove tissues of linen, were not barbarians. They may have been much farther removed from barbarism than some peoples of our time, who, without merit or effort of their own, have received from civilization all the metals, with many of its useful arts. It appears that they had domestic animals and agriculture; and among the remains of their age, implements have been discovered which are supposed to be stone ploughs. [See "Horæ Ferales," p. 43.]

The Age of Bronze, by which the Age of Polished Stone implements was immediately succeeded, has left a great variety of interesting monuments. It has been studied with special interest in the Danish peat-bogs and in the ruins of lake dwellings in Western Switzerland; but a careful examination of the many tumuli connected with Stonehenge and with the ancient ruins at Abury, in England, shows clearly that these structures belong to the Age of Bronze—Abury to its earliest period, and Stonehenge to a period much later. Abury was the most extensive and imposing of these pre-historic temples. Mr. Lubbock remarks that, according to Aubrey, Abury "did as much exceed Stonehenge as a cathedral does a parish church." When in perfect condition, the temple at Abury contained an area of $28\frac{1}{2}$ acres. If originally used as a temple, as is commonly supposed, it may also have been used for great assemblies of the people for other grave purposes.

The remarkable peat-beds of Denmark have been formed, during a long series of years, in hollows or depressions in the "drift," varying in depth from ten to thirty feet. During the ages that have elapsed since these peat formations began, the trees of many successive forests have fallen into the growing deposits of peat, and been buried out of sight as the accumulations increased. In the lowest strata the buried trees are of the species known as Scotch fir (*Pinus sylvestris*). This tree is now unknown in Denmark, and will not thrive there. In the peat formations next above the Scotch firs the buried trees are oak, described as "the sessile variety;" and these, in turn, are succeeded by oaks of the "pedunculated variety." In the upper strata beech-trees are found. The beech is now the common forest tree of Denmark, and it was so in the time of the Romans.

It will be seen that a very long period of time was required for the growth, decay, and final disappearance, first, of the successive forests of firs, and next of the successive forests of oaks; and yet no record or memory in Denmark knows anything of the time when the Danish forests were not beech. In the lower part of the peat-beds, with the firs and the first layers of oak, human remains are found belonging to the later periods of the Age of Stone. In the strata with the oaks are found swords, shields, and other articles, made of bronze, with the bones of men and domestic animals. The beginning of the Age of Iron coincides very nearly with the first appearance of fallen beech-trees.

Remains of the Bronze Age are abundant in the ruins of the pile-works or lake dwellings of Western and Central Switzerland, where there have been some attempts to estimate the antiquity of these memorials of the distant past, and large collections of bronze articles have been made from mortuary tumuli. It is manifest in these antiquities that the Age of Bronze was an age of civilization. The bronze itself implies this, not to speak of the beautiful form and workmanship of many of the articles. Bronze is a manufactured product, consisting of copper and tin, and implies skill in metallurgy; it must have been introduced into Western Europe by a foreign people.

There have been tentative efforts to estimate the antiquity of some remains of the Age of Bronze, especially of certain pile-works in Switzerland; but these calculations are necessarily imperfect, and cannot produce satisfactory results. One Swiss geologist estimates that certain structures of the Bronze Age in Switzerland are "from 3000 to 4000 years old." They are doubtless much older, and the beginning of the Bronze Age in that country may have been more than 1000 years older than the particular structures used in making this estimate. It is not extravagant to suppose the Age of Bronze began in Britain, Gaul, and perhaps Denmark, where it was older than in Switzerland, more than 3000 years before the Christian Era; nor is it worth while to quarrel with any archæologist who may be inclined to add considerably to these figures, for on this point nothing can be said or assumed with certainty. We are sure only that the beginning of the Age of Bronze must be sought far back in the past. Nevertheless, there are certain facts relating to this age that furnish something like historical intimations.

In the first place, during that age, or a large part of it, the countries of Western Europe, where its remains are found, must have been subject to the influence of a single government or ruling people. Everything indicates remarkable similarity of customs, ideas, and methods of life;

there was a striking uniformity of civilization; the swords, cutting instruments, tools, utensils, and other bronze articles, all seem to have been made after the same patterns, as if these bronze manufactures came originally from the same source; and there was evidently a more intimate and constant communication between these countries than existed when they were first visited by the Romans.

In the second place, it is seen that the use of bronze arms and implements must have begun on the islands and the coast, and been extended to the interior from the West. It seems evident that the Age of Bronze was older in Ireland, Britain, and the islands of Denmark than in Germany and Switzerland. That the use of bronze was spread into the interior from the West is shown very clearly by the discoveries in Switzerland. Remains of the Bronze Age have not been found in the eastern part of that country. It is only in Western and Central Switzerland that these bronze antiquities are discovered. Sir J. Lubbock, stating the result of investigation in that country, says: "Lake habitations of the Bronze Age have as yet been found only on the lakes of Geneva, Luissel, Neufchatel, Morat, Bienne, and Sempach; none in Eastern Switzerland. It has been supposed from this that the Age of Stone lasted longer in the East than in the West, and that flint and serpentine were in use on Lake Constance long after bronze had replaced them on the Western lakes." These facts make it necessary to believe that bronze came to Switzerland from the West, and was introduced into those districts only which became intimately connected with the other countries where the remains of bronze manufactures are found.

It may be added here that no remains of the earliest period of the Stone Age are found in the Scandinavian countries, which leads some geological archæologists to believe that these countries were not inhabited until after the beginning of the Age of Polished Stone. Also, it does not appear that either the Age of Stone or the Age of Bronze can be studied in Spain or Italy, or in any part of the territory occupied by the old Iberians, where, as I suppose, the Cushite civilization was established much earlier than the beginning of the Age of Bronze farther north. I will not undertake to say what discoveries geological archæology can make in these regions, but the distinction between them and the northern countries is manifest, and it must be due to a much earlier civilization in Italy and throughout the Iberian territory.

In the third place, the sudden transition from stone to bronze indicates that the change was produced by the influence of a foreign people, to whom bronze, and the art of manufacturing bronze arms and implements, were already known. A knowledge of copper and tin, and the art of working these metals, must have preceded the appearance of bronze, an article produced by combining them in certain proportions. There must have been necessarily a considerable period of time between the first discovery of both copper and tin, and the development of that knowledge of the peculiarities and uses of these metals which suggested the possibility of producing a more useful material by combining them, and led to the skillful and artistic manufacture of bronze articles, such as now represent the Age of Bronze. If bronze had been an original production of Western Europe, it must have been preceded by an age of copper and tin. Therefore it is necessary to believe, with the most competent archæologists, that bronze is one of those great discoveries which Western Europe owes to the East. Professor Nilsson states that the oldest bronze articles show the most perfect workmanship, seeming to have come from abroad; while inferior workmanship appears in those of later date, indicating that they were manufactured in the countries where they are found. It is certain that bronze had been carried everywhere throughout the East long before the beginning of the historical period by the commercial enterprise of those marvelous manufacturers and traders, the Arabian Cushites, and also by their representatives, the Phœnicians. What we call brass, an article made of copper and zinc, was unknown to the ancients; but they had bronze, which must have been introduced by the Arabian Cushites, who may have discovered and worked the tin mines of Banca at an early period in their history, before they had sailed to the Cassiterides.

In the fourth place, there is much in these antiquities which appears to show in a very conclusive manner that the Bronze Age in Western Europe was introduced by a foreign people of the Cushite race, culture, and religion, and that for a very long period it was controlled and directed by their influence. Professor Nilsson, whose learning, excellent judgment, and thorough study of the subject have made him the highest authority on most questions relating to it, is sure that bronze was brought to that region by the Phœnicians, meaning the race they represent. The Arabian Cushites, or the communities they established in Spain and Africa, are the only people of antiquity who can be supposed to have done this; but he sees their presence and influence throughout the Bronze Age in the peculiar character of the manufactured articles, in the ornaments on the bronze implements, in the engravings found in tumuli of the Bronze Age, in the indications of peculiar methods of reaping and fishing, in the general use of war-chariots, and in the many clear traces of the worship of Baal. He calls attention to two stones from a tumulus near Kivik, on which are representations of human figures that even Sir J. Lubbock admits " may fairly be said to have a Phœnician or Egyptian appearance." An obelisk symbolizing Baal is represented on another of the stones. The festival of Baal, or Balder, celebrated on midsummer night in the upper part of Norway, reveals the Cushite race, for the midnight fire in presence of the midnight sun did not originate in that latitude. This festival of Baal was celebrated in the British Islands until recent times. Baal has given such names as Baltic, Great and Little Belt, Belteburga, Baleshaugen, and the like. Professor Nilsson calls particular attention to two vase carriages, one found in Sweden and the other in Mecklenburg, which are strikingly like the "vases" made for Solomon's Temple, and described in the first book of Kings. But, to appreciate the whole force of his statement of the case, one must read it carefully, without abridgment.

Sir J. Lubbock urges "two strong objections" to these views of Professor Nilsson, which in reality are very weak. He states them as follows: "The first is the character of the ornamentation on the bronze weapons and implements. This almost always consists of geometrical figures, and we rarely, if ever, find upon them representations of animals or plants; while on the ornamented shields, etc., described by Homer, as well as in the decorations of Solomon's Temple, animals and plants were abundantly represented. Secondly, the Phœnicians, so far as we know them, were well acquainted with the use of iron; in Homer we find the warriors already armed with iron weapons, and the tools used in preparing the materials for Solomon's Temple were of this material."

These objections assume too much. It does not accord with either reason or probability to suppose the materials, methods of manufacture, or styles of ornamentation peculiar to the Phœnicians in the time of Homer and Solomon were in all respects precisely the same as those used by another people of the same race more than two thousand years earlier.* The Phœnicians may have had iron in the time of Homer, and they may have introduced the Iron Age of Western Europe, but the older Cushite peoples had bronze long previous to that date. Moreover, these objections do not undertake to deny that people of the Cushite race are directly connected with the Age of Bronze by the religious significance of its remains. What other people could have brought the worship of Baal to Western Europe in pre-historic times? We see them in the stone circles, in the ruins at Abury and Stonehenge, in the festival of Baal that lingered until our own times; and there is something for consideration in the fact that Arabia has still the ruins of ancient structures precisely like Stonehenge. It is probable that the Arabians, or their representatives in Spain and North Africa, went northward and began the Age of Bronze more than 2000 years before Gades was built.

* In his Introduction to Professor Nilsson's "Primitive Inhabitants of Scandinavia," Sir John Lubbock adds this suggestion: "If Professor Nilsson be correct, the bronze weapons must belong to an earlier period in Phœnician history than that with which we are partially familiar." The suggestion is important. He is not likely to deny that the beginning of the Age of Bronze is much older than Gades.

THE ANCIENT RACE OF WESTERN EUROPE.

What race of the human family was found in Western Europe by the people who introduced the Age of Bronze? This question has engaged much attention. The inhabitants of those countries had created the Age of Polished Stone, therefore they had risen from barbarism to a considerable degree of civilization. It is generally agreed among those who have inquired most carefully that the race now represented in Europe by the Finns and the Hungarians was anciently spread throughout nearly all the European countries. It is seen that the Finns have retired or been driven towards the north since the opening of the historical period; and it seems probable that the branch of this race now represented by the Finns and the Esthonians occupied all the countries of Western Europe before the Arabian Cushites went there, and all the countries so far south as to include nearly the whole of France, at the beginning of the Age of Bronze. Doubtless the old Iberians and Ligurians, with the Siculi and Sicani of Italy, belonged originally to this race, but they were formed by the Cushite civilization at a much earlier period. This Finnish race is the oldest in Europe of which we have any clear trace.*

Previous to the beginning of the Keltic age, and proba-

---

* Sir John Lubbock suggests that there may have been "two distinct races" in Western Europe in the Stone Age, because two skulls belonging to that age are differently shaped, one being "long" and the other "round." Craniology is not the surest guide, here or anywhere else. There is not a civilized race in Europe that cannot furnish specimens of skulls of nearly every shape specified by craniologists, while among uncivilized peoples the shape of the skull is by no means so uniform as many assume.

bly before the time of the Bronze Age, Spain, with a narrow district of Southern France extending to Northern Italy, was separate and distinct from the countries farther north, not because it was inhabited by a different race, but evidently because, in the earliest times, some great influence from abroad had modified the character and condition, and perhaps the speech of the people. It appears to show the first occupation of Southwestern Europe by the Cushite Arabians in ages quite as old as Egypt, as signified by the myths relating to Hercules. Before the Finnic race, farther north, had passed from the Age of Stone to the Age of Bronze, Spain and Italy, as well as Northern Africa, came under control of the most enlightened people of what, at that time, was known as the civilized world.

The original inhabitants of Spain (meaning by original the oldest of whom we have any trace) were the Iberians, represented in our time by the Basques who occupy the western slopes and valleys of the Pyrenees in Spain and France. They are the most remarkable, and, in some respects, the most mysterious communities in Europe, for they represent a people who have disappeared, and of whom no other fragmentary group remains on the face of the earth. This people may be, like the Dravidians of India, the only remaining representatives of a very ancient mixture of the Arabian Cushites with the aborigines of the country where they are found. Their language, like that of the Dravidians, seems to have no genetic relationship to any other known language, so far as comparative philology has been able to ascertain. In its structure it has more in common with certain American languages than any others. Some resemblances to languages of the Finnish family have been traced, but nothing that makes it possible to class the Basque tongue with languages of that family. It appears to represent a very ancient group or family of languages, of composite origin probably, that had passed away before the beginning of the historical period, leaving only this fragment of the group in a narrow district on the Bay of Biscay, where it has maintained its existence with wonderful tenacity.

It has been shown, by a careful collection and analysis of local names, that the Basques or Iberians anciently occupied the whole of Spain, and also the southern part of France, where the Acquitani belonged to this race; and they are traced to Italy, Sicily, and Sardinia, where the aboriginal population, or the people found there in the most ancient times, seem to have belonged to the same family, for there are many old names of rivers, places, and tribes that evidently came from the Iberian language.

This philological testimony is not without historical support. Thucydides and several other Greek writers who had carefully explored the old records and traditions of their time tell us that the most ancient inhabitants of Italy and Sicily were the Sicani, and that the Sicani were Iberians. Nevertheless, we cannot suppose Thucydides was able to give an authentic account of the oldest times. The people found in this part of Europe by the ancient civilizers must have been greatly changed by the mixture of races and languages. So it was farther north at a later period, especially in Gaul and the British Islands. In all these countries the aboriginal inhabitants were originally of the Finnish race, we must suppose. It is very certain that they were neither Aryans nor Semites, and that the remote age when they first came under the control of the Cushite influence had become mythical long before the first arrival of the Pelasgians in Italy.

THE ANCIENT HISTORY OF ITALY.

Dionysius of Halicarnassus, justly described as one of the most diligent and accurate antiquaries of his time, states that the first Pelasgian immigrants who settled in Italy went from Arcadia "seventeen generations before the Trojan War." Their leader was Œnotrus; on this account they were called Œnotrians. There is no record or trace of the appearance in Italy of any people of the Aryan race previous to this date, and yet the Pelasgians may have gone there earlier. Dionysius says: "Antiochus, an ancient historian, relates that the Œnotrians were the first [Pelasgic] settlers known to have come into Italy; that one of this race, called Italus, was a king; and that Italus was succeeded by Morges, from whom the Œnotrians were called Morgetes and Italians." The Œnotrians were followed by other Pelasgian colonies from Thessaly, and probably from other districts of the wide region occupied by the Pelasgic race.

Italy was known to the Pelasgians as Tyrrhenia, and its people were called Siculi, Umbrians, and Tyrrhenes. It is said that long and bloody wars ensued between the Pelasgians and the Tyrrhenes; the Pelasgians "pressed the Siculi [or Tyrrhenes] on all sides;" they seized Croton, "a town of the Umbrians, a very ancient people dispersed over many parts of Italy prior to the arrival of the Pelasgians;" and "driving out the Siculi, they took many towns of the Tuscans, the Siculi passing over into Sicily, at that time possessed by the Sicani, an Iberian tribe." But "the Pelasgians, having established themselves in Italy, fell into great calamities." The native inhabitants rose against them, overthrew their dominion, and resumed control of the country. The Pelasgi, it is said, greatly declined; some of them returned to Greece; some may have followed others of the race who had previously gone farther west. Neither Kelts nor the Keltic tongue appeared in Italy through their influence. Those who remained after these troubles were settled chiefly in Latium, and "afterwards founded Rome."

There is no good warrant for believing that any people of the Aryan race appeared in Italy as immigrants except the Pelasgians, who doubtless went there not only from the Hellenic peninsula, but also from Asia Minor. Among the various opinions expressed by scholars and archæologists concerning the original inhabitants and ancient history of Italy, none deserves more respect, or has stronger support from reason and probability, than that of Professor Lepsius, who is sure there was no invasion or occupation of Italy by any foreign people after it was conquered by the Pelasgians. After a duration of several centuries, probably, the Pelasgian power was overthrown by a successful rising of the original inhabitants. This restoration of the Siculi, Umbrians, or original Tyrrhenes to power created what is known to us as Etruria. At a later period, the Pelasgians of Latium rose successfully against the Tyrrhenian race, and established Rome. Niebuhr's theory that the Etrurians were a tribe from the Rhætian Alps is not supported by any record of antiquity, and it overlooks the more obvious and probable explanation of the origin of Etruria. Doubtless there was a close ethnic relationship between the tribes of the Rhætian Alps and the original inhabitants of Italy, but Etruria did not owe its existence to their agency.

We know by their language, preserved in the Eugubine

tablets and in other inscriptions, and by their religious and social customs, that the original inhabitants of Italy did not belong to the Aryan race. This was manifest to Dionysius of Halicarnassus, who says: "That the Tyrrhenes and Pelasgi were different peoples is proved by their languages, which had no resemblance; neither do I think the Tyrrhenes were a colony of Lydians, for there is no resemblance here in language. These two people differed in laws, in manners, and in institutions." The religious ideas and customs, and the institutions of the Tyrrhenes, had a striking resemblance to those of the Eastern nations that had been formed by Cushite influence. This has led many writers into attempts to show that they came to Italy from the East; but, when Cushite antiquity and enterprise are properly recognised, it becomes much more probable that this unmistakable resemblance is due to the fact that the Siculi, or Tyrrhenes, were civilized, and formed, socially and politically, by the Cushite people called Ethiopians. Their civilization appears to have been superior to that of the Pelasgian race. The founders of Rome, in comparison with them, were little better than semi-barbarians; and it may be doubted whether Rome, which far transcended Etruria in political and military power, could justly claim any other superiority to the Etruscan civilization.

I have pointed out that the original inhabitants of Italy, whom Dionysius calls the "Aborigines," were a branch of the Finnic race, anciently spread over nearly the whole of Europe. To the same race probably belonged not only the Iberians and the Ligurians, but also perhaps the most ancient Illyrians, before they were intermixed with tribes of the Aryan race. If the various branches of the Finnic race separated before they were civilized, a very close identity of language and customs, at the period when they first engage the attention of history, would not be possible. The earliest establishments of the Arabian Cushite race in Italy, Spain, and Northwestern Africa may have been more than 3000 years older than the first arrival of the Pelasgians in Italy. Their aims were commercial, their methods of communication with other peoples were peaceful, and we must suppose that the civilization of the Tyrrhenes was originally created by their influence. So far as appears at the present time, the civilization of the Etruscans was much higher than that of the Iberians. But, in this case, appearance is not a safe guide to reality. The Basques do not show us the whole extent of the ancient civilization of their remote ancestors, and it requires no small amount of gratuitous assumption to believe that the pre-historic civilization of Spain was inferior to that of Italy.

The Etruscan language, like that of the Basques, presents a problem which no philologist has been able to solve. It has engaged much attention, and from time to time there have been confident announcements that this and the other ingenious scholar had penetrated the mystery, and found the clew to its genetic relationships, but it remains still without an interpreter. Otfried Müller's learned speculations on the ancient dialects of Italy are worth no more than the curious and very amusing attempt of Sir William Betham to translate the Euguvine tablets; and Betham's translation, which fills them with directions for night-sailing to Ireland, is quite as confident, and perhaps nearly as correct, as that which finds on these tablets " the prayers and ceremonial rules of a fraternity of priests." The Umbrian and Etruscan inscriptions show us what remains of the language of a people who were developed and formed by the Cushite civilization many ages before the Aryans entered Italy, and, it may be, before the Pelasgian tribes came from Inner Asia to the Mediterranean. Of course, this language underwent many changes during the long and eventful history of the ancient people by whom it was used. How much the original tongue of this people was changed or influenced by the Cushite speech of their civilizers, and to what extent it was affected by other influences, can not be known.

WESTERN EUROPE, ANCIENTLY CALLED AFRICA.

Major Wilford's investigations led him to remark, in the 8th volume of the "Asiatic Researches," that "it is well known to the learned that, at a very remote period, Europe and Africa were considered as but one of two grand divisions of the world, and that the appellation Africa was even extended to the western parts of Europe, all along the shores of the Atlantic." His fact will not be questioned; there may, however, be some question relative to its signification. He points out that the word Africa comes from Apar, Aphar, Apara, or Aparica, terms used, in times almost forgotten by tradition, to signify "The West," just as we now, continuing the ancient method of designation, call most of the Asiatic world "The East."

It is only since the time of the Romans that the word Africa has become a name for one of the grand divisions of the globe. In the most ancient times the eastern part of that grand division was called "Sancha," a term that still remains in the words Zengh, Zenghbhar, Zanguebar, Zingis, and the like; while the northern, and especially the northwestern part, was designated as Apar, Aparica, Afarica, and finally Africa. We must suppose that, in early pre-historic times, Northern Africa and Western Europe had strongly engaged the attention of civilized nations in Asia; that in Asia they were described as "The West;" and that this remote Western world had risen to such eminence because it was, to a large extent, occupied by civilized peoples who had made it important. Spain, as Heeren remarks, "was the Peru of antiquity;" but in that Western world there was much besides gold and silver to command attention and attract commercial enterprise.

It seems to me impossible to study the Greek literature carefully without perceiving that the people on the eastern shores of the Mediterranean knew more of Western Europe in the time of Homer than in the time of Strabo, and much more in the ages previous to Homer than when he wrote. I have discussed the fact that many of the oldest myths relate to Spain, Northwestern Africa, and other regions on the Atlantic, such as those concerning Hercules, the Cronidæ, the Hyperboreans, the Hesperides, and the Islands of the Blessed. Strabo, while admitting that Homer described the Atlantic region of Europe in his account of the wanderings of Ulysses, shows, nevertheless, a very remarkable ignorance of that region, which comes out in what he says of Ireland, and especially in his ill-tempered and coarse attack on Pytheas of Massilia, an eminent astronomer and navigator, who, about the time of Alexander the Great, sailed to Thule or Iceland, and to a point in Northern Europe where, from a mountain, he beheld the midnight sun. In the ages previous to the decline of Phœnician influence in Greece and around the Ægean Sea, the people of those regions must have had a much better knowledge of Western Europe than prevailed there during either the Ionian or the Hellenic period, when actual information seems to have given place to imperfect recollections of what had been known in the earlier times. Diodorus Siculus (bk. ii., ch. iii.) records some of these recollections as follows:

"Among those who have written old stories that sound like fables, Hecataeus and some others say there is an island in the ocean, over against Gaul, where the Hyperboreans dwell, so called because they are beyond the north wind. The soil is very rich and fruitful, and the climate temperate. They say Latona was born there, and that Apollo is worshipped in that island above all other gods. In very ancient times the Hyperboreans had a special kindness for the Greeks, especially for the Athenians and the Delians; and in those times some of the Greeks visited the Hyperboreans and left presents, and Abaris, from the Hyperboreans, traveled into Greece, and renewed the ancient league with the Delians." It is said, also, that in this island Apollo "had a stately grove and a renowned temple, of a round form, beautified with many gifts."

The story of Abaris is told by other writers, and there are repeated accounts of sacred embassies and offerings from the Hyperboreans to the temple at Delos. Some of the Irish antiquarians, whose facts are frequently better than their judgment, cite an old Irish poem which describes a journey of *Abhras* and others from Ireland to Greece, and they claim that this Abhras was the Abaris of Hecataeus. Probably the British Islands were all known as Hyperborean Islands; but that supposition seems most probable which identifies the circular temple of Apollo described by Hecataeus with the great temple at Abury, in England. The Arabian Cushites, who created the Age of Bronze on the western shores and islands of Europe, must have had an accurate knowledge of that region many centuries before the Aryan people became important in Asia Minor and Greece, and, through their influence in both regions, sacred embassies from the Hyperboreans to Delos were quite possible. Apollo, according to Herodotus the same as Orus of the Egyptians, was a Cushite deity, borrowed from the Cushites by the Greeks with nearly all the rest of their gods and their mythology, or rather received with many other great gifts of the Cushite civilization. Sun-worship, represented by Apollo under various names, was likely to appear in some form wherever the influence of this people was established.

THE OLD SANSKRIT BOOKS ON WESTERN EUROPE.

This ancient knowledge of Western Europe extended to India. Recollections of it are recorded in the old Sanskrit books, of which Major Wilford gave an account in the eleventh volume of the Asiatic Researches. The Brahmanical mythology, as we have it, combines the gods and mythological legends brought into India by the Aryan race with those of the Cushites which the invading Aryans found there. This may explain why the Sanskrit records tell us so much of Africa and Europe. According to the Puranic traditions, there was, in very remote times, much communication between India and the western part of Europe. The Varaha Purana describes that region with the accuracy of actual knowledge. Wilford, quoting this description, and reproducing an old Puranic map of Western Europe, says: "Here we may trace the Bay of Biscay, the German Sea, and the entrance into the Baltic; but, above all, the greatest resemblance appears in the arrangement of the British Islands and Iceland; this surely cannot be merely accidental."

England is variously designated, but is usually called Sweta or Swetam: "Sweta-Saila, or the White Cliffs, is often used, which is literally the *Leucas-Petra* of Homer, and Al-Fionn in Gaelic." Homer placed his Leucas-Petra at the extremities of the earth, in the ocean, near the setting sun. The Argonautics, ascribed to Orpheus, call England *Leucon-Cherson*, the White Country, and it is placed in the Western Ocean, with Ierne or Ireland. The Sanskrit "Suvarna-dwipa, the land of Suvarna or of gold, is also called Hirnnya, a denomination of the same import. Hiranya and Suvarneya are obviously the same as Ierne, Erin, and Juvernia, ancient names of Ireland. Another name for Ireland is Surya-dwipa, Island of the Sun [or the land of sun-worship]; and it was probably the old garden of Phœbus of the western mythologists." England, "the White Island, is considered as the abode of the mighty; Ravana, in the Ramayana, inquires where the mighty ones dwell, and is told by Narada that they dwell in the White Island. The most ancient inhabitants of Britain, in their romances, called it the White Island, and *Ynys-y-Ceidein*, the Island of the Mighty Ones."

In the Sanskrit books the British Islands are described as "The Sacred Isles of the West." The White Island, or England, was "the land of *Tarpana*," or of "libations to the Pitris;" and it seems to have been the Therapnæ of the Argonautics. It is called the land of *Tapas*, or the most proper country for performing *tapasya* (religious austerity), which Wilford identifies with the blessed Theba or Thebai of the ancient Greeks. "In the *Santiparva*, one of the greater divisions of the Mahabharata, Narada goes to Sweta-dwipa, in the far northwest, to worship the original form of Narayana, which resides in that island." Wilford stated that, in modern times, Hindu pilgrims have attempted to visit the "Sacred Islands of the West," and added: "A Yogi now living is said to have advanced with his train of pilgrims as far as Moscow; but, annoyed by the great and troublesome curiosity of the Russians, he turned back. He would probably have been exposed to similar inconveniences in the Sacred Isles, not excepting *Breta-st'han*, or the place of religious duty."

Before Old Tyre was founded—before Martu or Marathos became the ruling city of the people called Phœnicians, it may be—in the ages when Beirut, Byblos or Gebal, and Joppa or Iopia, were the chief cities of that people on the Eastern Mediterranean, or even previous to the time of their greatness—an important civilization had grown up in Northwestern Africa, in Spain, and in some other places on the Atlantic coast of Europe, under Cushite influence, with which the great civilized peoples of Southwestern Asia were well acquainted. There was constant communication with that region until this intercourse was interrupted by political changes throughout the Mediterranean world, of which history can give no explanation. All this was very much older than Assyria. Traces of it remain in the oldest myths and records of Greece, India, and Egypt, which, however, do not fully reveal their significance to those who cannot see the antiquity and importance of the Cushite civilization of Arabia. Its origin and history were doubtless fully described in the ancient Phœnician records, but the language in which these records were written must have become a dead language before the Assyrian empire appeared.*

THE ANCIENT HISTORY OF IRELAND.

The Keltic countries of Western Europe, when first invaded by the Romans, were all civilized countries. In this respect their condition was much higher than history, directed by Roman influence, is accustomed to admit. It would be unwarranted and improbable assumption to suppose they had, at that time, the highest condition of civilization they had ever known. They must have declined with that decline of Phœnician power and commercial enterprise which interrupted their communication with the East. But they still had intelligence, wealth, and importance. We can see that their skill in many of the arts of civilized life was nowise inferior to that of the Romans themselves. They had a literature which, in some of the countries, was abundant and important, although the Romans give us no account of it. If Roman scholars had carefully studied the Keltic language, literature, and antiquities, and faithfully recorded the result of such studies, we should not now begin our histories of Great Britain with the invasion of Cæsar, nor would the most presuming historical skepticism fail to treat the ancient history of that part of Europe with some respect.

In the time of Julius Cæsar, Turdetania and Ireland appear to have had the most advanced condition of the Keltic civilization. Turdetania, like most of the Keltic countries in Spain and elsewhere on the Continent, became entirely Romanized. The Turdetani forgot their language, lost their literature, changed their manners, and were so entirely transformed by the conquerors that Strabo said of them, "they have, for the most part, become Latins." The Romans did not go to Ireland, although, in their time, its commerce, wealth, and culture made it the most important of the Keltic countries. On this point Tacitus says, in his life of Agricola: "Melius (Hiberniæ quam Britanniæ) aditus portusque per commercia et negociatores cogniti;" that is to say, "the ports of Ireland are better known through commerce, and more frequented by merchants, than those of Britain."

Ireland escaped the destructive influence of a Roman invasion, outlived the Roman empire, and maintained its independence until the time of Henry Second of England—more than 1200 years after the invasion of Britain by Julius Cæsar, and about 750 years after the Romans retired from that country. It retained its Keltic institutions, laws, and literature for more than 1200 years after all the other Keltic countries had been subjugated and transformed. There was but little internal change in Ireland for a long time after the princes of that country, with their king, submitted to the sway of Henry Second. The old Irish language has not yet wholly disappeared from the country, and it is not very long since it was the prevalent speech in all the provinces.

This explains why the Keltic antiquities and ancient writings have appeared to be so much more abundant in Ireland than elsewhere, and why Toland was able to say, with so much truth, "There remain [in Ireland] very many ancient manuscripts undoubtedly genuine," and the Irish "have incomparably more ancient materials of that kind for their history, to which even their mythology is not unserviceable, than either the English or the French, or any other European nation with whose manuscripts I have any acquaintance." In Gaul and Spain the destruction was nearly complete eighteen hundred years ago. In Britain, which was not wholly transformed by the Roman occupation, no remaining literary monuments of any importance escaped the influence of the fierce and successful Anglo-Saxon invasion. Gildas, who wrote in the sixth century, stated that the old Keltic histories of Britain no longer existed in his time, all the ancient books having been destroyed by the ravage of war, or taken to foreign countries and lost by self-exiled or banished natives of the island. The Welsh books are comparatively modern, and of no great account so far as relates to British antiquity; but the Irish books show us, to some extent, the history, institutions, and culture of that country in very ancient times; and we can see in them the truth of Toland's statement, that "the most valuable pieces [of the Irish], both in prose and verse, were written by their heathen ancestors, whereof some, indeed, have been interpolated since the introduction of Christianity, which additions or alterations, nevertheless, are easily detected."

If we had nothing more than that important collection of laws known as the Senchus-Mor or Brehon laws, there would be enough to show the antiquity of the old Irish civilization and literature. This collection is older than the Christian Era, yet it must have been the growth of many previous ages of civilized life. The language in which it was written seems to have become a dead language in the fifth century, when it was revised, "purged of heathenism," and rendered into the current Irish of that age, under the superintendence of Bishop Patricius, usually called St. Patrick, although the true St. Patrick lived more than three centuries earlier.* This expurgating Patricius,

* It is not certain that Patricius had anything to do with this revision of the Brehon Laws, or that he staid long in Ireland. He did not change

or some other fanatic, did more; he collected and committed to the flames a vast number of the ancient books, desiring, with barbarous fanaticism, to wipe out and hide from remembrance everything that related to the Druidical learning and religion. The language of this revision of the Senchus-Mor was itself antiquated and dead in the time of Henry Second, but the work was studied and used long after that time. It has lately been translated into English.

The Irish historical books have preserved a regular list of the kings of Ireland from the earliest times, with brief annals of each reign; 196 kings previous to the arrival of Bishop Patricius in the year 432 A.D. are enumerated, all royally descended except one, who "was a plebeian called Carbry Caithean. Brief annals, kept regularly from year to year, seem to have been very abundant in the olden times, for every local prince, as well as the king, had his Ollamh to write such records. Keating says, in his history of Ireland, "It is evident that in former times there were constantly more than 200 principal annalists and historians in the kingdom, who had handsome revenues. Every nobleman of any quality retained a number of these learned men." The old annals, reproduced and continued from age to age by these men, were used by writers of more extensive histories; but in the year 1030 A.D. they had suffered greatly by the waste of time. In that year a learned Irish nobleman, Ferall O'Gara, took measures to secure a careful compilation of such as then remained. The work was done by four Irish monks. This compilation, known

the Irish Church, which was three centuries older than his time. Some antiquarians doubt his existence; but he was probably the same Patricius who was afterwards bishop of Auvergne.

as "Annals of the Kingdom of Ireland, by the Four Masters," has been printed in seven quarto volumes, with the Irish text on one page and an English translation opposite.

All the histories of Ireland give substantially the same account of the early times, and of the kings who reigned previous to the Christian Era. The greatest event described in Irish ancient history is the conquest of the island by "the sons of Milidh" or Milesius, who came from Spain with a large fleet and a strong army. According to the chronology of the "Four Masters," this took place about the year 1700 B.C.; but more probable accounts fix the date nearly four centuries later. These Milesians had been preceded by other successful invaders. The earliest company of invading immigrants are described as "Parthalon's people," who found in the island a people called Fomhoraice, Fom'oraig Afraic, and Formoragh, rendered into English as Formorians. These Formorians are sometimes described as "natives," and sometimes it is said that they came in ships to fight Parthalon's people and subsequent invaders. The uniform representation is that they came originally from Africa. It may be supposed that they represent the first communities established or civilized in Ireland by immigrants from the Phœnician or Cushite settlements in Africa or Spain. They treated Parthalon's people with invincible hostility. After about thirty years, Parthalon died of a wound received in battle with them, and his colony became extinct.

The next invading immigrants were led by Neimhidh, who captured a stronghold of the Formorians; but after a short time the fortress was retaken by More, the Formorian leader, who had "a fleet of sixty ships, and a strong army." This defeat was so overwhelming to Neimhidh that most of his people fled from the island to Britain. A long period elapsed—about 400 years some of the accounts say—before there was another invasion. Then came the Fir-Bolgs, a strong people divided into three tribes, and called Fir-Bolgs from the name of the principal tribe. They conquered the whole island, and divided it into five provinces; a division, say the Irish writers, that has never been seriously disturbed, excepting that what is now Munster was then divided into two provinces. But the rule of the Fir-Bolgs lasted only 37 years, during which time they had nine kings, who appear in the lists as the first nine kings of Ireland. They were displaced by the Tuatha-de-Dananus, a people evidently more advanced in civilization than any of the previous invaders, who came with a powerful army, and overthrew the Fir-Bolgs in a great battle that is famous in the Irish Annals. Nuadha, king of the Tuatha-de-Dananna, lost his hand in this battle, and "Creidne, the artificer, put a silver hand upon him." All accounts agree in saying the rule of the Tuatha-de-Dananns lasted 197 years, and that they had nine kings, of whom the last three reigned jointly. Their dominion was overthrown by the sons of Milidh.

It can be seen in all these narratives that, in the earliest times to which the records relate, Africa, Spain, and other countries had commercial intercourse with Ireland. The great provocation that led the people of Spain, frequently called Milesians in the Annals, to invade the island, was received during a friendly visit of some of their people to the Tuatha-de-Dananns. They conquered the whole island, and held it until Ireland ceased to be an independent kingdom. Their language and culture were made predominant, being gradually adopted by all the races and peoples in the island. These Milesians were Kelts; but some of the earlier invasions must have taken place previous to that Aryan immigration into Western Europe which, by absorbing the civilized Finnish and Cushite peoples found there, in Spain, Gaul, and the British Islands, created the Keltic race. Perhaps the Milesians were the first Kelts that appeared in Ireland.

It is not creditable to English scholarship that those who represent it have given no more attention to the old language and literature of Ireland, but the explanation is not difficult. We find it in that invincible scorn and disdain of the English for everything Irish by which the relation between the two countries has been made so unprofitable to both, and so injurious to Ireland in all respects. Without friendly and careful investigation, it has been rudely assumed that the Irish language and literature were not worth attention; therefore they have been neglected. It is to be lamented that this important field was not worked carefully two or three centuries ago, when the old manuscripts were more abundant and the language was in general use among the Irish, for much has been lost. Without accepting either the dates, the glosses, or the ethnical speculations of the later Irish writers, we must admit that the general outline and main facts of Irish history furnished by the old records of the country cannot reasonably be discredited nor shown to be improbable. On the contrary, they are in harmony with what we know, or may reasonably presume, concerning Western Europe in pre-historic times. The monuments of the Age of Bronze, as well as what we know of the antiquity and the colonizing enterprise of the Arabian Cushites, make this Irish claim to antiquity probable, and forbid us to treat it

with such contempt as has been so largely bestowed upon
it. This is a case where contemptuous skepticism dishonors those only who indulge it.

We know very well, without reading the Irish Annals, that Ireland was an independent nation, having its own kings, institutions, and civilization more than two thousand years ago, and that it remained so until its princes, moved by papal influence, submitted to the English. It was an independent monarchy in the time of the Romans. Ptolemy described its cities; Tacitus mentioned its importance; and it is prominently mentioned by writers of earlier ages. We cannot reasonably discredit that portion of the Irish Annals which relates to the ages since the Romans began their subjugation of the Keltic countries; nothing but the intolerance of contemptuous prejudice is capable of doing this. It is no more reasonable to reject the Irish claim to antiquity, and treat with disdain the older annals of the country.

The Irish people seem to have reached the highest condition of their civilization and culture in the time of the great sovereign known in their annals as Ollamh Fodhla, who reigned long before the Christian Era; but they were eminent for culture in times as late as the Norman Conquest of England. No one familiar with what is recorded of the history of England between the time of Hengist and that of William the Conqueror has failed to observe that Ireland at that time was the most enlightened country of Western Europe. It had the best scholars and the most advanced condition of learning. Mosheim says in his Ecclesiastical History, "The philosophy and logic taught in the European schools in the ninth century scarcely deserved such honorable titles, and were little better than empty jargon. There were, however, to be found in various places, *particularly among the Irish*, men of acute parts and extensive knowledge, who were well entitled to be called philosophers." Among the learned Irishmen of that age was the celebrated Scotus. Gildas, according to his biographer, went to Ireland for education, and studied in its schools "the highest forms of philosophy and literature;" and Camden tells us that "the Saxons, from all places, flocked to Ireland as the emporium of letters." If the Normans had failed to conquer England, the language and culture of the English race would now be different, and we should have been taught greater respect for the language, antiquities, ancient history, and old literature of the Irish race.

THE KELTIC LANGUAGE.

Philologists arrange the known Keltic tongues in two divisions: the Gadhelic, embracing the Irish, the Gaelic of Scotland, and the dialect of the Isle of Man; and the Cymric, comprising the Welsh, the Cornish, and the Armorican of Brittany. There may have been other branches of this family that became extinct under Roman influence. The language of the Kelts—after much doubt concerning its character, that has been removed by careful investigation—is now classed as a branch of the Aryan family. Its Aryan characteristics were not immediately obvious. Professor Craik, in his "Manual of English Literature," says: "Probably any other two languages of the entire multitude held to be of this general stock [Indo-European or 'Aryan] would unite more readily than two of which only one is Celtic. It would be nearly the same case with that of the intermixture of an Indo-European with a Semitic language. It has been suggested that the Celtic branch must, in all probability, have diverged from the common stem at a much earlier date than any of the others."

An accomplished American scholar, Professor Whitney, speaking of Professor Schleicher's scheme of relationship for all branches of the Aryan family, observes that the position assigned in it to the Keltic languages repels rather than attracts assent. According to Professor Schleicher, their development was later than that of most other branches of the family, and they are more closely related to Latin than to any other Aryan tongue. This close relationship of the Aryan elements of the Keltic speech to that of the Latins cannot be denied; the more carefully and thoroughly the two languages are compared, the more clearly will this fact be presented to the investigator. It suggests that the Aryan people, whose influence in Western Europe created Keltica and the Keltic tongues, were Pelasgians from Italy. These Pelasgians found in those Western countries a people of another race, who, long before their arrival, had been civilized by the Arabian Cushites. What happened in England at a later period, when the Saxons and Norman French were brought together in that country, must have occurred in this case, with results still more remarkable, for here the peoples were not of the same race. There was a fusion of two races, and of two languages that did not belong to the same family. This fusion developed the Keltic tongues. The Pelasgian language, while retaining most of its fundamental characteristics, and thus preserving its relationship to the Aryan family, was, to a great extent, transformed. It became the Keltic tongue. The decay and new growth that obscured its Aryan features may thus be explained, without assuming that the Keltic tongues constitute a branch of the Aryan family, which "separated from the common stem at a much earlier date than any of the others."

Keltica consisted only of Gaul, Spain, and the British Islands. According to the Irish records, the Keltic people and language went to Ireland from Spain, and from Ireland to Scotland. They may have gone to England and Wales from Gaul. In Spain and a portion of Southern France the fusion of races and tongues was never complete. Large communities of the old Iberian people, now represented by the Basques, were entirely unaffected by it. This may have been due not only to the position of the districts they inhabited, but also to some difference in blood and language, caused by important changes in the other Iberian communities, which did not reach the Basques, but left them to represent more accurately the speech and blood of the earlier ages. An authentic record of the ancient times would explain much that is now left to conjecture. Even a history of the Keltic tongues would give us important historical information. But we have no such history, and no trace of any Keltic dialect that does not belong to either the Gadhelic or the Cymric family. It may be that the Gadhelic family represents the language as it was spoken in Spain, and the Cymric the form in which it appeared in Gaul; but our knowledge of the Keltic speech, which is limited to the Irish and Welsh, with a few kindred dialects, does not allow us to speak on this point with any degree of certainty.

There was no such fusion of tongues in any other country of Western Europe. The other branches of the Aryan family kept their language free from corrupting mixtures. In some cases they fiercely expelled the old inhabitants of the countries where they settled. So it was in Scandinavia, where the old Norse immigrants treated the Finns with perpetual hostility, and described them as "jotuns," demons, beings of an accursed race. There is no record or tradition that tells when the first group of the Aryan race appeared in Central or Western Europe. The people represented by the Lithuanians and the Letts appear to have been the earliest immigrants; the old Prussians belonged to this group. Next probably came the Slavonians, who settled in Poland and other countries of Central Europe. The Teutonic family, including several distinct groups, came later to the countries where history found them. It may be that all these immigrations preceded that of the Pelasgians into Spain and Gaul, but it does not seem probable that any group of the Teutonic family appeared in Sweden, Denmark, or even Germany, previous to the beginning of the Keltic age. It is more likely that this family came latest, and that it arrived in Germany and the more Western countries but a few centuries in advance of the Roman invasion, or at a period considerably later than the beginning of the Age of Iron. All these families of the Aryan race, however, may have been in Eastern Europe a long time before any of them appeared at the West.

ANCIENT COMMUNICATION WITH AMERICA.

Was America known to the ancients? I shall not undertake here a full discussion of this question, which requires a careful consideration of the monuments and literary remains of the ancient civilizations found in America when this continent was discovered by Columbus. What I have to say on the subject will be limited to a brief statement of the grounds on which those whose inquiries have been conducted with most care and intelligence believe there was communication between the Old World and America in very remote times. They find the evidence of this communication in the ruins and traditions of the ancient American civilizations, as well as in the traditions and myths of classical antiquity. We will begin with what is found in America.

1. The antiquities of Mexico and Central America reveal religious symbols, devices, and ideas nearly identical with those found in all countries of the Old World where Cushite communities formerly existed. They show us planet worship, with its usual orphic and phallic accompaniments. Humboldt, having traveled in America, and observed remains of these civilizations, was convinced that such communication formerly existed. He found evidence of it in the religious symbols, the architecture, the hieroglyphics, and the social customs made manifest by the ruins, which he was sure came from the other side of the ocean; and, in his view, the date of this communication was older than "the present division of Asia into Chinese, Mongols, Hindus," etc. [See his "Researches concerning the Institutions and Monuments of the Ancient People of America."] Humboldt did not observe symbols of the phallic worship, but the Abbé Brasseur de Bourbourg shows that they were described by Spanish writers at the time of the Conquest. He points out that they were prevalent in the countries of Mexico and Central America, being very abundant at Colhuacan on the Gulf of California, and at Panuco. Colhuacan was a flourishing city, and the capital of an important kingdom; "there," he says, "phallic institutions had existed from time immemorial." At Panuco phallic symbols abounded in the temples and on the public mon-

uments. These, with the serpent devices, the sun worship, and the remarkable knowledge of astronomy that existed in connection with them, show a system of religion of which the Abbé is constrained to say: "Asia appears to have been the cradle of this religion, and of the social institutions which it consecrated." The Abbé Brasseur de Bourbourg has studied American antiquities more profoundly than any other investigator. He has a very important collection of the books of the ancient people of Mexico and Central America, one of which, "The Popol Vuh," he has translated into French; and he has written in the same language, and published in four octavo volumes, a "History of the Civilized Nations of Mexico and Central America during the Ages before Christopher Columbus," the materials for the work being taken from the old books he has collected or examined.

2. The traditions of these countries are still more explicit. Their uniform testimony is, that the ancient American civilization came originally from the East across the ocean. In Sahagun's history, it is stated that, according to the traditions of the people of Yucatan, the original civilizers came in ships from the East. A similar tradition was communicated to the Spaniards by Montezuma. The Abbé Brasseur de Bourbourg, speaking of the earliest civilization of the Mexicans and Central Americans, says: "The native traditions generally attribute it to bearded white men, who came across the ocean from the east." The native histories he has examined describe three classes of ancient inhabitants. First, the Chichimecs, who seem to have been the uncivilized aborigines of the country; second, the Colhuas, who were the first civilizers, and by whom the Chichimecs were taught to cultivate the earth,

cook their food, and adopt the usages of civilized life; and, third, the Nahuas or Toltecs, who came much later as peaceable immigrants, but after a time united with uncivilized Chichimecs, caused a civil war, and secured power. The Colhuas were the bearded white men, who came in the earliest times across the Atlantic. They built Palenque and other cities, originated the oldest and finest monuments of the ancient civilization, and established the great kingdom of Xibalba, which is celebrated in the histories and traditions. It comprised Guatemala, Chiapas, Yucatan, and probably other countries. Désiré Charnay, speaking of the ruins at Mitla, points out that the most ancient architecture, paintings, mosaics, and artistic designs are in the highest style, and show "marvelous workmanship," while the later additions are in a much lower style, and seem to be the work of a people less advanced in culture and skill than the original founders of the city. The finest and most remarkable monuments in these countries seem to be remains of that ancient kingdom of Xibalba. It is said repeatedly that "the Colhuas came from beyond the sea, and directly from the east." The Abbé makes this statement also: "There was a constant tradition among the people who dwelt on the Pacific Ocean that people from distant nations beyond the Pacific formerly came to trade at the ports of Coatulco and Pechugui, which belonged to the kingdom of Tehuantepec." The traditions of Peru told of people who came to that country by sea, and landed on the Pacific coast. The reader will remember that there was anciently a great maritime empire of the Malays, and that dialects of the Malay language are scattered across the Pacific Ocean as far as Easter Island.

Such, very briefly stated, are the chief points in the testimony of the antiquities and traditions found in America. We will now turn to the ancient myths and traditions of the Old World.

In the traditions, legends, and mythical geography of the ancients, there is much that has no meaning if it does not preserve vague recollections of very ancient knowledge of America. The mythical references to a great continent beyond the "Cronian Sea," meaning the Atlantic, Plutarch's mention of a great Cronian or Saturnian continent, the Atlantis of Solon and Plato, and the Merope of Theopompus, all belong to a circle of very ancient traditions, with which many are familiar. There is nothing in the history of the human mind that allows us to treat them as pure fictions. The mythical story of the Atlantic Island which Solon brought from Egypt was not entirely new in Greece. The invasion of the East, to which it refers, seems to have given rise to the Panathenæa, the oldest, greatest, and most splendid festivals in honor of Athena celebrated in Attica. These festivals are said to have been established by Erichthonius in the most ancient times remembered by the historical traditions of Athens. Boeckh says of them in his Commentary on Plato:

"In the greater Panathenæa there was carried in procession a *peplum* of Minerva, representing the war with the giants and the victory of the gods of Olympus. In the lesser Panathenæa they carried another *peplum* [covered with symbolic devices], which showed how the Athenians, supported by Minerva, had the advantage in the war with the Atlantes." A scholia quoted from Proclus by Humboldt and Boeckh says, "The historians who speak of the islands of the exterior sea tell us that in their time there were seven islands consecrated to Proserpine, and three others of immense extent, of which the first was consecrated to Pluto, the second to Ammon, and the third to Neptune. The inhabitants of the latter had preserved a recollection (transmitted to them by their ancestors) of the island of Atlantis, which was extremely large, and for a long time held sway over all the islands of the Atlantic Ocean. Atlantis also was consecrated to Neptune." [See Humboldt's Histoire de la Géographie du Nouveau Continent, vol. i.]

The knowledge of America signified by these myths and traditions must be referred to a very remote antiquity—to a period as much older than the time of the Tyrians as that of the first civilization of Spain and Northwestern Africa was older than the building of Gades. If, as seems probable, this knowledge was a reality, the people who communicated with America must have gone from the great nation created on the Western Mediterranean by the earliest Cushite communities established in that region. If that communication lasted a thousand years, the age in which it was discontinued would have been mythical long before the time when the Tyrians began to establish settlements at the West. What we know of the rise and decline of important nations, and of the great political changes to which such nations are liable, suggests how it may have been interrupted. The Goths and Vandals did not continue the great enterprises of the Romans. There may have been dark as well as bright ages in the history of these great countries at the West.

De Bourbourg, in one of the notes of the Introduction to his translation of the Popol-Vuh, which gives a mythical history of very ancient times in Central America, presents for consideration a remarkable analogy between the kingdom of Xibalba and the mythical account of the island of Atlantis. He says:

"Without seeking to advance any particular opinion on the subject, it seems to me useful to call the reader's attention to the analogies presented between the empire of Xibalba and that of Atlantis as described in Plato's Critias. Both countries are magnificent, exceedingly fertile, and abound in the precious metals; the empire of Atlantis was divided into ten kingdoms, governed by five couples of twin sons of Poseidon, the eldest being supreme over the others; and the ten constituted a tribunal that managed the affairs of the empire. Their descendants governed after them. The ten kings of Xibalba, who reigned [in couples] under Hun-Came and Vukub-Came [and who together constituted a grand council of the kingdom], certainly furnish curious points of comparison. And there is wanting neither a catastrophe [for Xibalba had a terrific inundation] nor the name of Atlas, of which the etymology is found only in the Nahuatl tongue; it comes from *atl*, water, and we know that a city of *Atlan*, Near the Water, still existed on the Atlantic side of the Isthmus of Panama at the time of the Conquest."

In Peru, as in the countries comprised in that ancient kingdom of Xibalba, the oldest civilization was the most advanced, and had the highest style of art and mechanical skill. Here, too, the oldest structures were attributed to bearded white men, who, it is said, worked stone with iron implements brought from their own country. The traditions call them "sons of the sea." It is a remarkable fact, not generally known, that the Incas worked iron mines on the east side of Lake Titicaca. [See Introduction to Popol-Vuh, p. 224.] Planet worship, temples of the sun, and great knowledge of astronomy existed in Peru at a very early period. Montesinos and De Bourbourg say the Peruvians had an accurate measure of the solar year, and a knowledge of the art of writing, together with paper made of banana leaves, "at least 1800 years before our era." De Bourbourg thinks large numbers of Colhuas may have migrated from Central America to Peru.

There is in Diodorus Siculus, book v., chap. ii., an important passage concerning America which is not mythical, and seems to be given as a historical fact rather than as a tradition. He says: "Over against Africa lies a very great island in the vast ocean, many days' sail from Libya westward. The soil is very fruitful. It is diversified with mountains and pleasant vales, and the towns are adorned with stately buildings." After describing the gardens, orchards, and fountains, he tells how this pleasant country was discovered. The Phœnicians, he says, having built Gades, sailed along the Atlantic coast of Africa. A Phœnician ship, voyaging down this coast, was, "on a sudden, driven by a furious storm far into the main ocean; and, after they had lain under this tempest many days, they at length arrived at this island." There have been attempts to believe that the great land of civilized people thus discovered was either the Cassiterides or one of the Canary Islands. Look on the map, and judge whether such a belief is possible to a reasonable mind. The land reached by the Phœnicians of that tempest-driven ship is more likely to have been some part of Central America or Yucatan, where at that time stood the great cities now in ruins.

There is a similar statement in a work attributed to Aristotle (*de Mirab. Auscult.*), in which the discovery is ascribed to the Carthaginians; but the statement of Diodorus is most particular, and evidently most correct. Humboldt [*La Géographie du Nouveau Continent*, p. 191] cites a pas-

sage of Plutarch, in which he thinks, with Ortelius, that
not only the Antilles, but the American continent itself,
is described, for it is the "Great Continent" of which he
speaks beyond the ocean; and one of the speakers in the
dialogue gives an account of what was told of the Saturnian Continent by a stranger who came from it to Carthage.

The extract from Theopompus relating to America is familiar to scholars, but not, perhaps, to general readers. Ælian, in his "Varia Historia" [book iii., chap. xviii.], tells us that Theopompus related the particulars of an interview between Midas, king of Phrygia, and Silenus, in which Silenus reported the existence of a great continent beyond the Atlantic "larger than Asia, Europe, and Libya together." He stated that a race of men, called Meropes, dwelt there, and had extensive cities. The statement of Theopompus went on to say that the Meropes were persuaded that their country alone was a continent. Out of curiosity, some of them crossed the ocean and visited the Hyperboreans. De Bourbourg, referring to those who talk of these distinct references to America as "fictions," says very justly, "If the story of Theopompus is a fiction, it is, like 'The Incas' of Marmontel, founded on fact."

It is now a historical fact that the Northmen, sailing from Iceland, not only discovered America in the tenth century, but also established colonies on the coast of New England, and that they preserved communication with these colonies for two centuries. Most readers are familiar with the story of these discoveries and settlements of the Northmen. It is not so well known, but is, nevertheless, quite true, that they were preceded in Iceland by the Irish, and in voyages to America by the Irish and the Basques.

The Basques, being adventurous fishermen, and extensively engaged in the whale fishery, were accustomed to visit the northeast coast of America long before the time of Columbus, and probably "from time immemorial." [See Michel's "Les Pays Basques," and De Bourbourg's Introduction.] There is no scarcity of reports and traditions of Irish voyages to America, but I will do no more than cite a fact recorded by the Abbé Brasseur de Bourbourg in a note to his translation of the Popol-Vuh. He says:

"There is an abundance of legends and traditions concerning the passage of the Irish into America, and their habitual communication with that continent many centuries before the time of Columbus. We should bear in mind that Ireland was colonized by the Phœnicians [or by people of that race]. An Irish saint, named Vigile, who lived in the eighth century, was accused to Pope Zachary of having taught heresies on the subject of the antipodes. At first he wrote to the pope in reply to the charge, but afterwards he went to Rome in person to justify himself, and there he proved to the pope that the Irish had been accustomed to communicate with a trans-Atlantic world." This fact seems to have been preserved in the records of the Vatican.

It is known that knowledge of the American continent existed in China and Japan long before the time of Columbus. The Abbé de Bourbourg says in his Introduction to the Popol-Vuh, "It has been known to scholars nearly a century that the Chinese were acquainted with the American continent in the fifth century of our era. Their ships visited it. They called it *Fu-Sang*, and said it was situated at the distance of 20,000 *li* from *Ta-Han*." M. Leon de Rosny has ascertained that *Fusang* is the topic of " a curious notice in the *Wa-kan-san-tai-dzon-yê*" (which is the name of the great Japanese Encyclopædia). In that work Fusang is said to be situated east of Japan, beyond the ocean, at the distance of about 20,000 *li* (7000 miles or more) from *Ta-nan-kouēk*. De Bourbourg, who quotes the notice, adds: "Readers who may desire to make comparisons between the Japanese description of *Fusang* and some country in America will find astonishing analogies in the countries described by Castañeda and Fra Marcos de Niza, in the province of Cibola."

The Chinese and Japanese do not give us myths; they tell us what they have actually known for many centuries. The Welsh prince Madog, about the year 1170 A.D., was just as certain of the existence of America when "he sailed away westward, going south of Ireland," to find a land of refuge from the civil war among his countrymen. The Welsh annals tell us that he found the land he sought. Having made preparations for a settlement, he returned to Wales, secured a large company that "filled ten ships," and then sailed away again, and "never returned." In 1660, Rev. Morgan Jones, a Welsh clergyman, seeking to go by land from South Carolina to Roanoke, was captured by the Tuscarora Indians. He declares that his life was spared because he spoke Welsh, which some of the Indians understood; that he was able to converse with them in Welsh, though with some difficulty; and that he remained with them four months, sometimes preaching to them in Welsh. John Williams, LL.D., who reproduced the statement of Mr. Jones in his work on the story of Prince Madog's emigration, published in 1791, explained it by assuming that Prince Madog settled in North Carolina, and that the Welsh colony, after being weakened, was incorporated with these Indians. If we may believe the story of Mr. Jones (and I cannot find that his veracity was questioned at the time), it will seem necessary to accept this explanation. It will be recollected that, in the early colony times, the Tuscaroras were sometimes called "White Indians." The Northmen had settlements in New England long before Prince Madog's colony went to America.

But I must leave this topic, which requires a volume instead of a few pages. The Abbé de Bourbourg thinks ancient America "is still to be discovered." Perhaps he will advance the discovery by finding means to interpret the inscriptions at Palenque. Certainly there is nothing unreasonable or improbable in the supposition that the countries on the Western Mediterranean, associated in the myths with Atlas and the Atlantides, communicated with America in very remote antiquity; nor is it improbable that there was communication across the Pacific. The objections raised against it come chiefly from the gratuitous assumption that such enterprise was impossible in ancient times, and from the influence of thought and imagination preoccupied, perhaps unconsciously, by an invincible determination to deny it.

GENERAL INDEX.

[The figures in this Index refer to pages.]

Abaris the Hyperborean, 377; Irish antiquaries on Abaris, 377.
Abraham and Hebrew, 140.
Abury, its ruins of a vast temple, 15, 360; this temple belonged to the first period of the Age of Bronze, 360; described by Aubrey, 360; by Hecatæus, 377.
Ad and his contemporaries, 78; nothing Arabian older than Ad, 104; he represents the oldest Arabian civilization, 104, 105; political periods between Ad and the Himyarites, 104-106, 115.
Africa not a continent of savage negroes, 306; our knowledge of the interior recent, 306, 825; negroes chiefly on the Guinea coast, 307, 309; races in Africa, 307-311; exploration proceeds from the north and east, 307; the brown races most numerous in Africa, 308; African ancient history, 329; the Africans make and work iron, and have arts of civilization, 328-335; mixture of races in Africa, 330, 331; written histories of Central African kingdoms, 322; the Gallas, 323; the Wahuma, 331; the Fulahs, Barth's statement, 332; Eichwaldt and Barth on their origin, 332, 333; more civilization in Africa formerly than now, 333-337; North Africa in ancient times, 333-331; what the Portuguese found in East Africa, 334; navigation around Africa in ancient times, 345-350; origin of the name Africa, 375.
Age of Bronze in Western Europe, 358-361; it began on the West Coast, 303; a foreign people introduced it, 302, 334; it was of long duration, 359, 361; bronze implies civilization, 302; antiquity of the Bronze Age, 361, 364, 367; was introduced by the ancient Phœnicians or Cushites, 333, 365-367; it reveals Baal worship, Cushite manufactures, etc., 365, 366; it was contemporary with a much higher and older civilization in Spain and Southern France, 369; its oldest remains show the highest manufacturing skill, 363.
Age of Iron traced in the Danish peat, 361; was much older than Roman times,

359; was introduced by the Tyrians, 355, 367.
Age of Stone, it has two or three periods, 359; its latest period shows civilization, 359, 360, 368; it was contemporary in Eastern Switzerland with bronze at the West, 362.
Alphabetical writing, 91-94; the styles used anciently all from one source, 91; the Phœnicians and Egyptians on its origin, 91, 92; Sir William Drummond's theory, 92; Sir Henry Rawlinson's statement, 92, 93; alphabetic writing originated in Arabia, 93; it was preceded by hieroglyphics, 92, 93; the art of writing in Egypt, 93, 94; six styles of cuneiform writing, 93; the oldest known form of the Cushite alphabet, 90, 94; the names and forms of the letters show their origin in hieroglyphics, 94; Pliny on the origin of alphabetic writing, 94.
America discovered by Asiatics in prehistoric times, 395, 396, 401, 402; Atlantis meant America, 334, 397, 399; Mexican and Central American traditions indicate ancient communication between America and countries east of the Atlantic, 392-395, 397; planet worship and phallic symbols in America, 393; tradition in Yucatan, 394; the three ancient races, 394; the Colhuas who came first in ships were bearded white men, 394; they built Palenque and the oldest and finest monuments, 394, 395; the earliest ancient civilization in America the most advanced, 395, 393; legends, traditions, and mythical geography of the ancients, 395-400; the Athenian Panathenæa and Atlantis, 396; Proclus, 396; a Phœnician vessel finds America, 399; Aristotle and Plutarch, 399; statement of Theopompos, from Ælian, 400; the Northmen in America, 400; the Irish and Basques, 400, 401; Virgil on Irish voyages to America, 401; Chinese and Japanese statements, 401; Prince Madog and America, 402; Rev. Morgan Jones and the "Welsh Indians," 402; the Cushite

406 Index.

people on the Western Mediterranean must have gone to America, 391, 403; how the communication was interrupted, 327; antiquity of ancient knowledge of America, 391.

Ancient History, how it is embarrassed, 23; ancient history of Arabia, 96–117; of Iran or Iran, 36, 243–247; ancient historical works that are lost, 130; of Ireland, 352.

Antiquity of civilization and science, 30, 31, 116–125; antiquity of man underrated, 25; antiquity denied because "so far off," 127, 128, 135.

Arabia a very ancient seat of civilization, 21, 42, 54, 56, 57, 64, 67, 76, 66; the ancient Ethiopia, 67–63; origin of the term Ethiopia, 57, 68; Hebrew Scriptures on Arabia, 58, 59; earliest civilization in Arabia, 61, 62; Arabia misunderstood, 67–69; Wellsted, Forster, Ptolemy, and El Edrisi on Arabia, 68, 69; Palgrave on Central Arabia, 69–72; its settled population, kingdoms, cities, and condition, 70–72; the nomads few and unimportant, 70; the desert districts formerly cultivated, 72, 73; its ancient capacity for colonizing enterprise, 78; the two races in Arabia, 73–78; its ancient language, 74, 75; its superior geographical position, 50, 61; its present isolation explained, 63; Arabian ruins and inscriptions, 86–88; Arabian inscriptions in El Harrah, 86, 87; Palgrave's notice of Arabian antiquities, 87; ancient science originated in Arabia, 118; its nautical science, 120–126; the mariner's compass, 121–122, 125; mathematical science and the nine digits came from Arabia, 119; Vincent on Arabian enterprise, 210; the Arabians in Africa.

Arabian Ancient History lost, 96; weird influence of Arabian antiquity, 95, 96; its extent, 97; what linguistic and archaeological science say of it, 96; hypothetical scheme of Arabian ancient history, 96–99; its grand period, 97; its periods of decline, 97–99; the Greeks failed to study Arabia, 99, 100; what they said of it, 100, 101; Arabian tradition on the past, 102–108; Mahometan writers of Arabian history, 102–104; fragments of Arabian ancient history, 108–112; Zohak and the "Median" dynasty of Berosus, 108–110, 212; Schamar-Jarasch and his conquests in Central Asia, 110, 111; political disintegration in Arabia, 105–107; Afrikia, 111; Harith-el-Raireb, 111, 112; Dionysos and Kephens represent earlier periods, 112; the "Arabian" dynasty in Chaldea established by Schamar-Jarasch, 111, 213, 214.

Aristotle, his notice of Chaldean and Egyptian Science, 116, 117; Dr. Long on Aristotle and Eudoxus, 176; Aristotle on ancient knowledge of America, 390.

Arnaud's visit to the ruins of Saba and the dike Arim, 83, 84.

Aryan or Iranian ancient history, 36, 243–247; inquiry embarrassed by refusal to see it, 243; how it is mutilated, 244; a "brilliant" scheme of Anquetil du Perron, 244; the kingdom of Iliras with its "fourteen settlements" and its capital at Balkh, 244–246; dates in Iranian history, 245; the Zend and Sanskrit Aryans dwelt together in the kingdom of Iliras, 246; the whole Aryan family together under the dynasty of Abad, 246; the Vedic race dwelt first in Hapta-Hindu, 246, 247; Michardson's trouble with Aryan history, 246, 247.

Aryans in Europe, order of their coming, 391, 392; the Pelasgians came through Italy and mixed with the old race in Gaul and Spain, 390, 392; this fusion created Keltics and the Keltic tongues, 391; the Lithuanians, Slavonians, and Teutons came through Central Europe, 391; may have stopped long at the East before coming West, 392; the Aryan tongues in Central and Northern Europe unmixed with those of the old race, 391.

Assyria, its origin, 192, 204; its rise to empire, 204, 214; it changed the language of Chaldea, 205.

Astronomy in ancient times, 116–120; its Arabian origin, 118; the later Arabian astronomy, 119; suppose the great Babylonian observatory had been at Athens, 117; astronomy in China, 119, 120; astronomical observations at Babylon, 175, 176; Dr. Long on these discoveries, 176; Greek astronomy came from Egypt and the East, 119; the ancients had aids to eyesight, 178, 179; lens found at Babylon, 179.

Athens learned of Ionia, 44, 45.

Baal in Western Europe, 368.

Babylon, that of the ancient Greeks was at Nifer, 189, 190, 194, 200; the more modern Babylon of Nebuchadnezzar, 201, and of the later kingdom of Chaldea, 213.

Banca tin mines, 363.

Barbara described, 279; this ancient name in North Africa, the Berbers, 279.

Bardesanes quoted, 230.

Barth on iron-making in Africa, 327; on African manufactures, 328; on ruins and written histories in Central Africa, 329; on the mixture of races, 330.

Basques are ancient Iberians unmixed with Pelasgians, 368, 369, 391; their lan-

Index. 407

guage, 369; their navigation, 400; their civilization, 374.

Berbers, their political system, 119; origin of the name, 230; they represent the old Cushite communities in North Africa, 338, 344; Leo's account of them, 339; they read and write, 340; accounts of them by travelers, 340-343; they occupy all North Africa away from the coast, 340; the M'Zabs, their confederacy and their books, 342, 343; their Egyptian style, 343; their history, 343; the Touaricks, 341-342.

Belkis, queen of Saba, 84, 85.

Berosus on the "Arabian" dynasty in Chaldea, 111; his history of Chaldea, 180-185; his dynastic list, 182-184; dogmatic chronology on Berosus, 181-185; he enumerated 122 Chaldean kings previous to Assyria, 181; Berosus on the origin of Chaldean civilization, 185; his history confirmed, 190, 191; he shows two great periods of Chaldean history, 208.

Brahmanism, where first developed, 250; Manu on Brahmavarta, 250, 251; Brahmanism in Kikata, 252; ancient Brahmanism very unlike the Vedic religion, 250; very unlike modern Brahmanism, 253, 254, 257, 258; how Buddhism grew to power, 254; Brahmanism never went to Ceylon, 256; modern Brahmanism explained, 258-260; its eclectic policy, 258, 259, 274; its union with Siva-worship not perfect, 262, 263, 264.

Brasseur de Bourbourg, his study of American antiquities, 393, 394; translated the Popul-Vuh, 394; his comparison of the government of Atlantis with that of Xibalba in Central America, 397, 398; his account of Mexican and Central American traditions, 394; of phallic worship, 393; of Peruvian traditions and antiquities, 393; of Virgil's statement, 401.

British Islands called Hyperborean, 377; described in Sanskrit books, 378, 379; Sanskrit name of Ireland, 379; the Sacred Isles of the West, 379; a Yogi's attempt to visit them, 380.

Buddhism, its probable origin, statement of James Bird, 224; it did not originate the rock-temples, 233-236; the Buddhism of Sakhya-Muni very different from the Siva worship of the rock-temples, 236; Burnouf on Buddhism and the Saivic Tantras, 235; how Buddhism was originated in Kikata, or Naghada, 252, 253; it was later than ancient Brahmanism, but older than modern Brahmanism, 253, 254; older than Sakhya-Muni, 254; many previous Buddhas, 255; Burnouf and Wilson on the Buddhas, 255; Buddhism now the religion of a third of our race, 256; how it was overthrown in India, 256, 257; Sakhya-Muni was merely the oracle of one very popular development of Buddhism, 257; the Saivas were more ancient Buddhists, 257, 258; the Chinese Fa-hian on the more ancient Buddhas, 256, 259.

Bunsen on the date of man's creation, 25, 94; on Chaldean chronology, 207, 209; on Egyptian antiquity, 208, 209.

Burnouf on the Saivite Tantras, 235; perplexed by the intimate relations of Buddhism and Siva-worship, 255; his notice of the "Seven Buddhas," 255; his statement concerning the Saivite divinities, 258.

Chaldea and the Greeks, 173-176, 180; Chaldea discovered in its ruins, 177; Chaldean astronomy, 175-179; Chaldean history by Berosus, 180-185; Chaldea much more ancient than Assyria, 180, 196; the Cushites were first in Chaldea, 184; Chaldean traditions and antiquities, 185-191; tradition of Oannes, 186, 187; the Turanian hobby, 188; Chaldean ruins and inscriptions, 188-191; present condition of the country, 188, 189; the ruins of four cities explored, 189-191; Cushite origin of Chaldea, 192, 193; language of Chaldea, 194-196; discussed by Renan and the French philologists, 194, 195; political and linguistic changes in Chaldea, 196-199, 204, 205; it may have begun 4662 B.C., 196; Tower of Babel, 198; Nipur, the more ancient Babylon, the capital in the great days of Chaldea, 198; Nimrod and this capital, 198, 199; (the year 2234 B.C. discussed, 199-202); a Sin dynasty in Chaldea, 198; history of an old temple, 202, 203; Babylonia became subordinate to Assyria, 204, 209; Chaldea misunderstood because it is not seen, 206; Chaldean history and chronology considered, 206-214; a hypothetical scheme of the history, 209-214; time of the old kingdom, 207, 209-211; the later kingdom, 212, 213.

China, its civilization, 16; its history and historical works, 87, 88; its chronology, 88; the Chinese cycle of 60 years, when established, 88; China invaded by an Arabian king, 110, 111.

Chronology discussed, 24-89; Rollin's chronological difficulty, 24; the past is larger than the current chronologies admit—Bunsen's view, 25, 26; the business of making schemes of chronology, 26; the current chronologies have misused and insulted the Bible, 27-29; "biblical" chronologists disagree, 27; the dicta of Maurice, 24; Christianity wronged by these chronologists, 29;

considerations that should have checked this chronological dogmatism, 30–33; it has been powerful to discredit facts and dates, 33, 34; its absurdities, 34–36; its relations with Chinese history must be adjusted, 37–39; Egyptian chronology, 37–34; chronological stupidity concerning the dike Arim, 65; concerning the time of Zoroaster, 94–97; concerning Arabian history, 104, 105, 106; concerning Gades, 167; chronology emendherosus, 184–187, 171; chronological dogmatism on Manetho, 269, 270.

Civilization, where did it begin? 11; its history, 11–13; its earliest manifestation in Asia, 15, 16; the oldest peoples mentioned in history did not originate their civilization, 59; they had it from a common source, 66; Arabia civilized Chaldea, Egypt, and India, 56; civilization of the Tyrians, 163; civilization, since the first ages, usually aided by external influences, 199; traces of former civilization in Africa, 320–329; an old civilization in Western Europe, 251, 252; a very ancient civilization in Spain and Northwestern Africa, 253, 254; and in America, 324, 325.

Clinton's Fasti Hellenici on Pelasgian dates, 164, 165.

Craniology criticised, 162.

Curtius, Ernst, on the Greek race, 151; his view of the chronological order of Phoenician colonies, 155.

Cusha-dwipa of Sanskrit geography the same as Ethiopia of the ancient Greeks, 63; an African Cusha-dwipa, 64; it includes the Mountains of the Moon, 65.

Cushites the first known civilizers, 17–19, 62; their great periods had closed many ages before Homer's time, 51, 79; the Phoenicians were a portion of the great people of Arabia, 94, 129, 138, 155; did the Cushites originate civilization? 20; Cushite literature, how lost, 109; Arabia the Land of Cush, 18, 63, 64, 65–66, 90; the Cushites the oldest race in Arabia, 74; vastness of their antiquity, 85, 90; the grand period of their history, 87; they were the first civilizers and builders in Southwestern Asia, 60, 61; originally twelve tribal communities, 78; pure Cushites now nearly extinct, 79, 115; Palgrave's opinion of the race, 79, 80; the Cushites originated science, 116; the Cushite religion and architecture, 141–145; Cushite colonies in Northwestern Africa and Spain very ancient, 152, 163; Cushites civilized Chaldea, 172, 173; a Cushite family of tongues, 195; the Cushites preceded the Sanskrit race in India, 218–227; Rawlinson's testimony, 220; testimony of archaeological research, 219–227; Cushite religion traced in India, 220–221; Siva a Cushite god, 221; Cushite political system in India, 222, 223; the Cushites in Africa, 322–336; Cushite dialects in Africa, 323; Cushite traces in America, 324.

Development theory can not admit very ancient civilizations, 52; its assumptions, 52; geology has no favor for it, 53; the Engis skull described, 53; this theory admitted to be unproved hypothesis, 53; if we must have a hypothesis, let it be nobler, 54, 319.

Dionysos, what he represents in the past, 112, 288; how the legends describe him, 282; an old ante-Ionian book on Dionysos, 283, 284; Fresnel on Dionysos and Nysa, 285, 286; Dionysos not Rama, 2–6; he was the Deva Nahusha of Indian tradition, 286–288, 290; contemporary with Indra, 291; his city in India, 291; Professor Wilson on Dionysos and Bacchus, 288; Dionysos belonged to ante-Sanskrit history, 291; Dionysos in Egypt, 291, 295; Megasthenes on his history and date, 287.

Dravidian people and tongues, 238–242; these tongues radically different from Sanskrit, 238, 239; they represent the ante-Sanskrit speech of the country, 239–240; their use of the word Mag or Mac, 140; the speech of the Todas and hill tribes belongs to this family, 238, 239; the Sanskrit writers call this speech Desi, 238; Sanskrit not now represented in India as the old speech is represented by these tongues, 240; how the modern Indian dialects grew up, 241; probable origin of the Dravidian tongues, 241; these tongues and the Basque, 302.

Egypt an incontestable fact, 267; Manetho's history, 268, 269; his dynastic list and dates, 268, 269; how dogmatic chronology has treated them, 269, 270; the "Old Chronicle" and the "Sothic" spurious works, 270; Lepsius and Mariette on Egypt, 271; origin of the Egyptians, 271–274; Sir Gardner Wilkinson on this point, 273; comprehension of Arabia removes difficulty, 273; common origin of Chaldeans and Egyptians shown by their writing, Sir Henry Rawlinson, Lepsius, 273, 274; the ancient Arabians colonized Egypt, 272, 274, 275, 276, 280; Memphis, 274; Menes, a Thinite prince, united the "Two Countries," 271; Egyptian civilization old in the time of Menes, 271, 272, 290, 294, 299, 300; Egypt anciently a bay of the sea, Herodotus, Diodorus, and Rennell, 275; old Sanskrit books on Egypt, 271–283; on the Nile and Moonland, 178, 179; King It, 240; on Divodass and Kepheus, 251, 252; Menes drained part of Lower Egypt, 171, 173; the infancy of Egyptian civilization was long before his time, 290, 328, 292; he may not have been the first king of united Egypt, 296; Egyptian libraries, 301, 302; Egyptian writing, 300; attempts to measure Egyptian antiquity, 303-305; what Mr. Horner found in the alluvium, 303; his estimate and Bunsen's opinion, 304, 305; Egyptian manuscripts the oldest in existence, 302; Solon and the priest at Sais, 307; Diogenes Laertius on Egyptian astronomy, 110, 111.

El Mas'údi, 103; his statements relative to Arabian and Iranian royal families, 103, 100; his description of India and the ancient Malayan empire, 203.

Ethiopia, meaning of the word, 57, 58; was the ancient Greek name for Arabia, 59-61; Joppa one of its ancient capitals, 59; Homer and Strabo on Ethiopia, 59-61; Heeren on the Ethiopians, 62; they were not Africans, 57, 64, 193; why countries in Africa were called Ethiopia, 58.

Etruria, how it originated, 373; its civilization, 373, 374; the Etruscan language, 374; it had a long history, 375; vain attempts to translate the Eugubine tablets, Otfried Müller, Betham, 374; the Etrurians may have been a mixture of Finns and Cushites, 378-379.

Engarine tables, 374.

Euhemerus a Rationalist, 280.

Finns the oldest known people of Europe, 368; their relation to the Iberians, 368, 369; they have been driven northward, 368; they were in Italy and Illyria, 371.

Formorians the oldest known people of Ireland, 883, 885; their resistance to invaders, 885; their probable origin, 883.

Fresnel on the ancient Mepha, 92; on the Himyaric language, 90; on the origin of Chaldea, 194, 195; on Dionysos, 241.

Fusang, a Chinese and Japanese name of America, 401; a Japanese Encyclopedia on Fusang, 401.

Gades, when and why it was built, 156, 354; was preceded in Spain by a very old Cushite civilization, 156, 157; its ship-building, 157.

Geology on the antiquity of man, 10; its estimates of past time, 13, 14; how its testimony has been received, 25; geological changes in Lower Chaldea, 189, 191; borings and excavations in the Nile Valley, 303-305; Geology on the history of Western Europe, 253, 258.

on Gobineau on Races, 316-320.

Greek race, a closely-related group of Aryan tribes, 40; their relation to the Pelasgians, 163, 164; their civilized predecessors, 40-45; what the Greek myths signify, 41, 45; the earliest Greek writers were Asiatics, 44; Greek culture in Ionia preceded that of Hellas, 40-42, 46, 47; Hellas generally less civilized than Ionia, 42-45; the extraordinary development of the Greek language exposes false theories of Greek history, 40; lost Grecian books on archaeological topics, 49, 50.

Grote's historical skepticism, 40; he adopts the position of Varro, 41, 42; his account of the science of astronomy in Hellas, 42.

Heeren on Ethiopia, 62; on the first seats of civilization, 61; his sagacity, 63; what he said of Arabians and Phoenicians, 68; he failed to see the Cushites, 63; on the Phoenicians and their ancient cities, 129, 134; on Indian architecture, 224; on the connection of India with Arabia, 220.

Hellas, its relation to civilization misrepresented, 39-49; Hellenic egotism and ignorance of the past, 39, 40, 44, 48; its treatment of Herodotus, 45, 47; Olen, Orpheus, and others not Greeks or Hellenes, 45, 46; how the history of Hellas has been written, 39, 46; suppose American history so written 3000 years hence, 47; Bryant's opinion of Greek writers on Mythology and Antiquity, 48; limited geographic knowledge of the Hellenic people, 102; their scholars neglected the history of Egypt, 307.

Hercules, Pillars of, 157, 158; Hercules at the West, 162, 179, 194, 325; he died in Spain, 335; his stone and cup, 124; in the myths, 893, 394.

Himyaric inscriptions, when first discovered, 91, 92; they preserve the old language, 89; their probable age, 90, 91, 104; Himyaric inscriptions at Hamarcand, 116; Mr. Birch's criticism, 91.

Himyaric kings in Southern Arabia, 106; date given for the time of Himyar, 107; the Himyarite kingdom divided, and after "fifteen generations," reunited by Harith-el-Raïsch, 107; chronological stupidity relative to the time of Himyar, 107; Mahometan attempts to reconstruct all Arabian history around the Himyarite kings, 104; the Himyarite kingdom destroyed by an invasion from Abyssinia, 107.

Historical skepticism, its hopeless incredulity, 21; illustrated in Grote's history of Greece, 40, 41; must doubt itself at times, 172.

Humboldt on ancient civilizations, 23, 84; on the Ethiopians in Central Asia, 110; on the mariner's compass, 122, 123; on myths, 8–9; on superior and inferior races, 816; on old maps of South Africa, 841, 842; on ancient knowledge of America, 863, 882.
Hyperboreans, 811; their embassies to Delos, 817, 818; where they dwell, 817; visited by the Meropes, 409.

Iberians, probably a mixture of Cushites and Finns, 36–370; the Ligurians and Sicani of this family, 368; the old Iberian territory in Spain and France, 368, 369; the Iberians in Italy and Sicily, 370; antiquity of Cushite influence in Spain, 369, 370, 371.
India, what it includes, 216, 217; the Sanskrit people were a small minority of its inhabitants, 217; its ante-Sanskrit people were dark-skinned, 217, 248; the Cushite Arabians preceded the Sanskrit race, and found a dark-colored race in India, 218; India naturally connected with Arabia and Eastern Africa, 218; Cushite remains in India, 219–227; the rock-cut temples, 225; Goprecko of the ante-Sanskrit religion of India, 220, 221; early Sanskrit or Vedic fanaticism on its predecessors, 220, 248; the Cushite serpent-worship in India and Ceylon, 274; statement of the Chinese Fa-hian, 274, 223; the festival of Holi and our May-day, 223; the worship of Vetal, 223; Col. Leslie on the resemblance of customs of Keltic, Canaanites, and the ante-Sanskrit people of India, 224, 227; planet worship the earliest religion traced in India, Ferishta's Mahommedan India quoted, 224, 228; Indian municipalities, 228, 229; ante-Sanskrit civilization of India, 216, 248, 260, 261; Professor Benfey on the ante-Sanskrit people of the Dekhan, 227; Rev. Dr. Stevenson's statements, 241, 272, 273; ante-Cushite people of India and their language, 242; the Vedic age began in the Punjab and ended on the Sarasvati, 247–250; Vedic notice of the Phallic worship, 249; religious history of Sanskrit India, 253–254; history of India falsified by modern Brahmanism, 259, 262; Wilford, Wathen, Turnoor, and the Jainas on this point, 259, 260, 262, 263; Indian history and chronology, 260–263; the two historical works deemed authentic, 260; the kingdom of Magadha, 262.
Indo-Aryans, they belonged originally to the kingdom of Iliran, 246; their Vedic age, 247–250; their fanaticism, 248; their settlement in the upper valley of the Ganges, 250; they were white,

248; their notice of the Phallic worship of the natives, 240; Manu's description of Aryavarta, 251; the Indo-Aryans on the Lower Ganges, 268; in Southern India, 253; when they began to mix their color with the natives, 251; this mixture in Alexander's time, 251, 252; four periods of Indo-Aryan history, 261, 262; the Indo-Aryans and the old mythology and religion of India, 258, 259, 260.
Ionia had the earliest known Greek civilization, 40–42, 46, 47; its cities originally built by the Phoenicians, 46, 46; Ernst Curtius on the Ionians, 151.
Ireland, its ancient history, 342–351; Formorians the oldest people of Ireland, 346, 349; More the Formorian and Nemidoh, 345; the Fir-Bolgs and the Tuatha-de-Dananns, 345, 346; Nuadha's silver hand, 346; Ireland conquered and held by the Milesians, 240; it is discreditable to neglect Irish ancient history, 351; its probability, 351; we know from other sources that Ireland was an independent nation 2000 years ago, 357, 358; reign of Ollamh Fodhla, 358; Ireland and its learning in the 9th and 9th centuries, 388, 389; Moshelm and Camden on this point, 388, 389; Toland on Irish manuscripts, 257, 373; the Senchus-Mor, 363; Patricius falsely called St. Patrick, 363, 364; Tacitus on Ireland, 354; Ireland outlived the other Keltic countries, and even Rome itself, 322; Annals of the Four Masters, 354; the Irish kings, 8–4; how the old annals were written, 354; date of the Milesian conquest, 848; ancient connection of Ireland with the Cushite people of North Africa, 353, 854, 355; Irish voyages to America, 400, 401.
Italy, its ancient history, 371–375; the first Pelasgians in Italy, 371; how Etruria arose, 371; the ante-Pelasgian people formed by the Cushites, 373, 374; Dionysius of Halicarnassus on the ancient people of Italy, 372; the Cushites were in Italy more than 8000 years earlier than the Pelasgians, 373.

Kahtan represents a great epoch in Arabian ancient history, 103–105; he was a very different personage from the Semitic Joktan, 16; a great Arabian civilization before his time, 104, 105; his position in Arabian history like that of Kaiamors in Iranian history, 104.
Keltic language and countries, 249–392, 341, 362; Keltic civilization, 352, 251; what constituted Keltics, 290; language of the Kelts, two branches of the family remain, 289; Craik's opinion of it, 289; its probable origin, 290; its Aryan elements resemble Latin, 290; no similar

fusion of races and tongues elsewhere in Western Europe, 391; the fusion not complete in Spain, 391; Welsh probably came from Gael, and Irish from Spain, 391; Whitney and Schleicher on Keltic speech, 3*9, 390.

Kepheus, his kingdom described by Conon, 61; he represents an early period in Arabian history, 112; he reigned at Joppa, 133, 143.

Lang on old civilizations, 12; on the Malays, 263.

Language of the Cushite Arabians, 88–91; the Turanian fancy, 88; this old tongue found in the Chaldean ruins, 89; the countries where it was used, 88, 89; it is still used in some districts, 89, 90; Dr. Carter's opinion of its sweetness, 89; it remained long at Zhafar, 90; how Fresnel and Forster spoke of it, 90.

Lepsius on Egyptian history and chronology, 231; on the origin of alphabetic writing, 214; on the ancient history of Italy, 312.

Livingstone on African iron-making and manufactures, 327, 328; on the mixture of races in Africa, 331; on the "true type" of the African people, 331.

Loftus on Chaldea, 189, 191.

Lubbock on implements of the Age of Bronze, 359; on periods of the Age of Stone, 359; on the temple at Abury, 360; on the limit of the Age of Bronze in Switzerland, 363; on Nilsson's views of the origin of the Age of Bronze, 366, 367.

Mahomet's race Semitic, 73, 74; destructive influence of his religion in Arabia, 75; Mahometan literature conscious of the preceding civilization, 75; Mahomet and the old race, 76; Mahometans have confused and falsified the past in Arabia, 76; the Joktan fable, 74; Mahometanism incapable of writing histories of the Cushite civilization, 108; its destructiveness in North Africa, 337.

Malayan empire, 263–266; El Mas'údí's account of it, 263; how the Portuguese found it 550 years later, 263, 264; account of it as it was in the 9th century, 264; Marsden on the Malays, 264; wide diffusion of Malay dialects, 264, 265; Rev. Dr. Lang on this empire, 265; origin of Malayan civilization, 265; Malayan antiquities, inscriptions, etc., 265, 266.

Mariner's compass, erroneously claimed as an invention of Flavio Gioia, 121; it was much older than his time, 121–124; described by Raymond Lully and Peter Adsiger, 121; by Guyot de Provins in 1180 A.D., 122; supposed mention of it by Plautus, 122; it was brought to Europe by Arabians, 122, 123; the old Cushites more likely to invent it than the ancient Chinese, 123; the date of its first use in Western Europe not the date of its origin, 123; Di Gama found it in use on the Indian Seas, 123, 124; it existed among the Phœnicians, 124–126; ancient knowledge of the magnet, 124, 125; the mariner's compass invented by the ancient Arabians, 125; why it was held as a scientific and commercial secret, 125, 126, 127; "night sailing," 126; the stone and cup of Hercules, 124; the old lady and "so far off," 127, 128.

Martu, or Marathus, its antiquity according to the Chaldean inscriptions, 148; its ruins, 144, 145; it was much older than the Hebrew immigration, 146; much older than Sidon, 149; its ruins indicate that the very old city they represent was built of materials taken from ruins of a much older city, 149; Diodorus Siculus on Martu, 144.

"Median" dynasty of Berosus, attempts to explain it, 109, 212; it was probably established by Zohak, the Arabian, 109, 110, 127.

Minos and his time, 163, 164; he was not a Dorian Greek, 163; he may have conquered Pelasgia, 164; he made Crete a powerful maritime state, 164.

Monotheism the earliest form of religious faith, 295; Renan, Rawlinson, and the Desatir on Aryan monotheism, 297; the Veda, the Orphic Fragments, and Hermomanax on this point, 293; its relation to mythology, 294.

Mythology and mythological persons, 292–296; it implies monotheism, 293; how it originated, 294; it precedes polytheism, 295; Euhemerus on mythology, 295.

Myths and traditions, they show facts mixed with fancies and prejudices of the people who transmit them, 277, 283, 2–6; the Greek myths, 41, 45; Wilford and the Indian myths, 238, 239; myths relating to Northern Africa and Western Europe, 335, 336, 348, 353, 354, 356, 357, 378; Atlas and Saturn reigned over countries in the West, 353, 357; the myths contain history, 357, 358; ancient opinions concerning the gods, 358.

Navigation around Africa in pre-historic times, 345; the Cushite settlements on the East and West Coasts made this certain, 345; how this navigation was interrupted, 347; attempts to resume it several centuries later, 348; a ship of Cadiz wrecked on the eastern coast, 347; the Arabians had maps of South Africa long before the Portuguese went there, 347.

348; the old name of the Cape of Good Hope, 347; what the Portuguese had learned of the Arabians, 348; the oldest opinions of antiquity concerning South Africa the most correct, 348; Ophir, 348-350.
Negroes a distinct race, 306-311; the Bushmen not negroes, 309, 310; Gobineau on the black race, 310.
Nilsson on the Age of Bronze, 365; he shows its Cushite origin, 366, 366; Lubbock on his views, 366, 367.
Nimrod discussed, 198, 199.
Northern Africa in pre-historic times, 832 -337; its civilization began in very remote times, 835, 835, 874, 830; Carthage, 325, 836; Tacitus on North Africa, 336; its ruins, 336; Leo Africanus on the city of Morocco, 337; on the destructiveness of Mahometan fanaticism, 1337; the Berbers are remains of the old Cushite communities, 328, 343, 344; Leo on the Berbers, 338, 339; mythical kings and kingdoms of Northwestern Africa and Southwestern Europe, 353, 355, 357; Ireland first colonized from Africa, 356; the term Africa originally meant the West, and became a name of the continent in Roman times, 375; this name anciently applied to Western Europe, 376.

Oman, its political system, 113.
Ophir, where it was situated, 348-350; Dr. Krapf, Max Müller, and others on Ophir, 848; Müller's philological argument has no force, 349; Ophir means "the West," Wilford, Lowth, 849; it was some country west of the Cape of Good Hope, 349, 350; voyages to Ophir were made from Tartessus as well as from Ezion-geber, 350; it was probably on the Gold Coast of Africa, 350.
Origin of separate races and families of language, 16, 812-814; the Cushite, Semitic, and Aryan races seem to have had a common origin, 17; Hebrew traditions, 17, 18; origin of civilization lost in obscurity, 11, 18, 30; origin of Phœnicia, 129-141; of Carthage, 153, 154; of the Egyptians, 271; of Greek and Sanskrit mythology, 283; of Etruria, 372; of Kelkrs, 390.
"Orthodox" learning and progress in knowledge, 10, 20.

Palgrave on Central Arabia, 69-72.
Past, the, schemes for measuring it, 9.
Patricius the bishop not the true St. Patrick, 283, 284; he was three centuries later than St. Patrick, 283, 284.
Pelasgians, their dominion around the Ægean, 161; on their history, 162-165; Greek writers on the Pelasgi, 162; Sanskrit notice of Pelasgis, 163; the Pelasgi were Aryans, their character, 163, 164; Greek account of Pelasgian kings, 164, 165; dates in their history, 165; the Pelasgians in Italy, 871, 374; they created Keltica, 890.
Peru, its antiquities, 396.
Phœnicia, origin of the name, 129, 130; it was anciently called Ethiopia, 129, 184; how it became a small district, 129, 130, 185; its ruins, 143-145; its antiquity according to Sir Henry Rawlinson, 142; Sidon in Hebrew times, 150; Old Tyre in Hebrew times, 163; sarcophagus of a king of Sidon, 169.
Phœnician Language and Literature, 167 -172; no remains of the literature in the Phœnician language, 167; some fragments in Greek, 167; the language assumed to be Semitic, 168; the oldest epigraphs and inscriptions not earlier than the Carthaginian period, 168, 169; Renan on the Phœnician language, 169, 170; writing and dialects of Tyrians and native Carthaginians not alike, Gesenius and Sallust, 170, 171; if a change occurred in Phœnicia, it did not extend to Northern Africa, 170; language of Sidon not like that of Northern Africa, 171; what the change in Phœnicia may actually have been, 171, 172; language of the Canary Islands was Phœnician, 169; of the Berbers, 338.
Phœnician people and history, 122-131; origin of the Phœnicians discussed, 129-140; Hecteu and Herodotus on Phœnician history, 129, 130; the supposed Phœnician immigration, what it means, 130, 131, 187; the Phœnicians a fragment of the old Cushite race, 131; Voltaire and Movers on the immigration, 135-137; when Tyre was built, 133, 151; what the Phœnicians were called by the more ancient Greeks, 134; a Semitic dialect did not make them Semites, 138, 140; their great antiquity, 143, 145, 146; the periods of Phœnician history, 147-155; three or more great periods previous to the rise of Sidon, 148, 149; the period of Sidon older than Homer, 149, 150; date, period, and sway of Tyre, 151-154; Carthage represents the last period of Phœnician history, 154, 155; Berat, Byblus, Joppa, and Marta represent ante-Sidonian periods, 147, 148, 155; Arvad or Raad very old, 149; Movers, false chronology, and Sidon, 150; why the Tyrians emigrated to Carthage, 154; the early Cushite colonies at the West, and the later Tyrian occupation, 152, 153.
Phœnicians, the political system with which they came into history, 112, 113, 115, 153; they attributed letters and sci-

ence to Tant, 91, 118, 119; their nautical science, 120; they had the mariner's compass, 122, 124; it was one of their commercial secrets, 125-127; secrecy of Phœnician and Arabian commerce, 127; Poseidon and the Cabiri, 155; great extent of Phœnician commerce, 158-161; its influence traced around the Mediterranean, 158; in Scandinavia, 159; in Western Africa, 160, 169; in Central Asia, 161.

Pliny on the origin of alphabetic writing, 94; on Ceylon, Arabia, and Oman, 102; on Hanno's voyage to Arabia, 340.

Political system of Ancient Arabia, 112-116; its remains to be classed with Arabian antiquities, 112; where they are found, 112-114; probable character of this system, 112; it is the earliest in Arabian tradition, 115, 116; its remains in India described, 225, 226; in North Africa, 341, 342.

Popoe heads Phœnician, 160.

Pre-historic times defined, 50, 51; in their remote ages, unrecorded civilizations may have existed, 53, 54, 96, 97; inquiry concerning pre-historic times now forced upon us, 52; what they include, as history is written, 51.

Ptolemy's Geography, 291.

Pytheas of Massilia, 376; Strabo's false view of his voyage to the north, 376.

Races in Arabia, 73-78; Wm. Muir and Caussin de Perceval on the Joktan-Kahtan table, 76; races in Africa, 307-311; a theory of the negro race criticised, 308-311; a brief essay on races, 311-322; Max Müller's theory of English and Bengalese brotherhood, 311; origin of races, 16, 312-314; races now seldom found pure, 315; Aryans, Cushites, and Semites physiologically alike, 314; inferior and superior races, Gobineau, 316-320; each race has its peculiar gift, 321, 322; falsely assumed superiority, 316, 320, 321; mixture of races in Europe, 315.

Rawlinson, George, on the ethnic character of the Phœnicians, 132, 133, 146, 147; his Turanian theory, 132; on the earliest race of civilizers and builders in Phœnicia, 143, 146; on Chaldean civilization, 174, 175; on Chaldean ruins, 189; Sir H. Rawlinson on Nipur, 190; on geological changes in Chaldea, 191; on the Cushite origin of Chaldea, 192; G. Rawlinson on linguistic changes in Chaldea, 205; on the Cushites in India, 220; Sir Henry on the origin of the Egyptians, 273; G. Rawlinson on Aryan monotheism, 292.

Renan, his great services in archæological and linguistic science, 91, 92; his view of the relation of Phœnicia to Yemen, 132; his theory of the origin of the Phœnicians, 139, 140; his speculations on their race and language, 137-140; his explorations in Phœnicia, 141-143, 169; what he says of the Phœnician language, 169, 170; of monotheism, 292; of Egyptian civilization, 270; on the Semites, 315.

Rock-cut temples of India, 223-226; Elephanta, Salsette, Ellora, and Mavalipora, 929, 229; these works Cushite in character, 229, 237; denials of their antiquity, 230; early notices of them which confound these denials, 230, 231, 234; what Maurice said of them, 231, 232; they could not have been built as late as the denials say, 231; they were deserted and mysterious more than 1700 years ago, 230, 232; they were made for the worship of Siva or Baal, 233, 235; are older than what we know as Buddhism, 234; they are older than their inscriptions, 233; not coincident with the domination of Buddhism, 234, 235; the Nubian rock-temples older than their inscriptions, 232; the Indian rock-temples not Buddhist works, 234-236.

Ruins, in Arabia, 80-89; how they were discovered, 61; remains of the ancient city of Mepha, at Nakab-el-Hadjar, 81, 82; the ancient Kana, or Hisn Ghorab, 62; the ruins at Zhafar, 63; at Mareb or Saba, 84; ruins of the dike Arim, 84, 85; vagaries of some writers relative to the age of this dike, 85; the Mahometan natives refer the ruins to their infidel ancestors, 66, 86; Strabo, Pliny, Ptolemy, and others describe Arabian cities that no longer exist, 86; ruins in Phœnicia at Arvad, Marathos, etc., 142-145; in Chaldea, 188-191; ruined cities in Ceylon, 236; ruins in North Africa, 336, 337.

Saba the old capital of Yemen, 84; Saba, a king in Arabian history, what his kingdom included, 106.

Saivas, an ancient religious sect in India, 256, 257, 258; they adopted ante-Vedic gods, 258; their influence in developing modern Brahmanism, 257, 258; Siva worship ante-Vedic, 258, 259.

Sancha, an ancient name of Upper Egypt and Eastern Africa, 280; traces of the name still exist, 275.

Sanchoniathon, 155.

Sanskrit or Aryan geography, 63-66; it was that of the early Greeks, as found in Homer and Hesiod, 60; the seven dwipas, 64; Cusha-dwipa important, though not a great division of the earth, 64; the Sanskrit language older than the Pali, 254; Sanskrit books on Egypt, 277; on

Dionysos, 267; on Pelasgia, 163; on Western Europe, 378-390; why Sanskrit books say so much of Africa and Western Europe, 378.

Science in ancient times secret and exclusive, 125; Pythagoras in Egypt, 126; science in ancient Arabia, 118-120; Strabo on Phœnician science and "night-sailing," 126.

Semites in Arabia called Monstarribes, 74, 77; they have chiefly occupied the attention of the moderns, 77, 99; they are comparatively modern in Arabia, 77; they have appropriated the reputation of the old race, 76, 77; the Arabian Semites were not a literary people, 102, 103; the life of their prophet not written until more than a century after his death, 108; Semites found in Chaldea by the civilizing Cushites, 167, 204, 210.

Solon on Atlantis, 353, 354; Atlantis and the Athenian Panathenæa, 396.

Spain and Northwestern Africa anciently closely connected, 375, 376; great antiquity of their first civilization, 355, 364, 374, 380; they were known as "the West," 375, 376; were better known to Greeks before Homer's time than after it, 376; the oldest people in Spain, 359, 370.

Stonehenge a temple of the Bronze Age, 360; Stonehenges in Arabia, 67, 68.

Susiana part of ancient Chaldea, 197; a date in its ruins, 197; it probably led in expelling the "Median" dynasty, 208, 211.

Tartessus and "ships of Tarshish," 154, 157; voyages from Tartessus to Ophir, 350.

Thrace in ancient times, 45, 46.

Touaricks, their Phœnician or Cushite origin, 340, 341; their cities and condition in the Sahara, 341; their language and literature, 340, 341; their inscriptions like those of El Harrah and Central Arabia, 88; Touaricks described by Richardson, Lyon, and others, 341, 342; their political organization and women, 341; their alphabet is Phœnician, 342.

"Turanian" a very indefinite term in linguistic science, 88, 242; improperly applied to the Cushites, 88, 89; the Turanian theory on the Dravidian languages, 242.

Turdetani, a people in Spain, 352; their civilization, 352, 391; their books, 352.

Unity of mankind, 10, 312.

Ur of the Chaldees, where Renan seeks it, 189, 205; its ruins in Lower Chaldea, 189, 190; was the oldest Chaldean city, 191, 192, 209; was the first capital of Chaldea, 189, 209.

Vambéry on ruins in Central Asia, 161.

Welsh books noticed, 383.

Western Europe, its antiquities, 14, 15; how we begin its history, 351; the Kelts not inferior to the Romans in many respects, 352; Cæsar described their civilization, 351; Strabo's account of it, 352; the Romans destroyed the books of other peoples, 325, 352; two periods of Cushite occupation of Western Europe and North Africa, 353-354; the first ancient and mythical in Tyrian times, 353, 355; the Atlantic Island, 353, 367; the ages of Stone, Bronze, and Iron, 355, 358; very ancient Phœnicians created the Age of Bronze, 355, 365-367; its antiquity, 362, 364, 367; the Tyrians created the Age of Iron, 356, 367; the Age of Stone and a Finnic race, 355, 359, 360, 368; in Spain and Northwestern Africa civilization much older than the Age of Bronze, 364, 359, 380; a foreign people began this age, 364; it began on the West Coast, 353, 364; Western Europe described in Sanskrit books, 379; by Homer, 378, 379; its ancient communication with America, 397, 408.

Whitney on Chinese literature, 18; on Prof. Schleicher's theory of the Keltic tongues, 382, 390.

Writings, the oldest, 11.

Xibalba, a pre-historic kingdom in Central America, 396; it was established by men from the East who came in ships, 394, 395; its government resembled that of Atlantis, 397, 398.

Yemen, Khatan its first king, 78; its ruins, 61; its ancient capital and great dike, 84, 85; its relations with Phœnicia, 192.

Zodiac, its antiquity, 117-119; came to us from the Chaldeans, 118; zodiacs used in India, Chaldea, and Egypt similar, 118; they came from the ancient Arabians, 118.

Zohak, famous in Arabian and Iranian history, was an Arabian king, 108; his kingdom, 98, 108; he conquered the kingdom of Iliras or Iran, 108; what the Iranian books say of him, 108, 109; he probably established the "Median" dynasty in Chaldea, 109, 110.

Zoroaster and chronology, 34-37.

THE END.

VALUABLE STANDARD WORKS

FOR PUBLIC AND PRIVATE LIBRARIES,

PUBLISHED BY HARPER & BROTHERS, NEW YORK.

For a full List of Books suitable for Libraries, see HARPER & BROTHERS' TRADE-LIST and CATALOGUE, which may be had gratuitously on application to the Publishers personally, or by letter enclosing Five Cents.

HARPER & BROTHERS will send any of the following works by mail, postage prepaid, to any part of the United States, on receipt of the price.

MOTLEY'S DUTCH REPUBLIC. The Rise of the Dutch Republic. A History. By JOHN LOTHROP MOTLEY, LL.D., D.C.L. With a Portrait of William of Orange. 3 vols., 8vo, Cloth, $10 50.

MOTLEY'S UNITED NETHERLANDS. History of the United Netherlands: from the Death of William the Silent to the Twelve Years' Truce —1609. With a full View of the English-Dutch Struggle against Spain, and of the Origin and Destruction of the Spanish Armada. By JOHN LOTHROP MOTLEY, LL.D., D.C.L., Author of "The Rise of the Dutch Republic." Portraits. 4 vols., 8vo, Cloth, $14 00.

ABBOTT'S LIFE OF CHRIST. Jesus of Nazareth: his Life and Teachings; Founded on the Four Gospels, and Illustrated by Reference to the Manners, Customs, Religious Beliefs, and Political Institutions of his Times. By LYMAN ABBOTT. With Designs by Doré, De Laroche, Fenn, and others. Crown 8vo, Cloth, Beveled Edges, $3 50.

NAPOLEON'S LIFE OF CÆSAR. The History of Julius Cæsar. By His Imperial Majesty NAPOLEON III. Volumes I. and II. now ready. Library Edition, 8vo, Cloth, $3 50 per vol.

Maps to Vols. I. and II. sold separately. Price $1 50 each, NET.

HENRY WARD BEECHER'S SERMONS. Sermons by HENRY WARD BEECHER, Plymouth Church, Brooklyn. Selected from Published and Unpublished Discourses, and Revised by their Author. With Steel Portrait by Halpin. Complete in Two Vols., 8vo, Cloth, $5 00.

LYMAN BEECHER'S AUTOBIOGRAPHY, &c. Autobiography, Correspondence, &c., of Lyman Beecher, D.D. Edited by his Son, CHARLES BEECHER. With Three Steel Portraits, and Engravings on Wood. In Two Vols., 12mo, Cloth, $5 00.

BALDWIN'S PRE-HISTORIC NATIONS. Pre-Historic Nations; or, Inquiries concerning some of the Great Peoples and Civilizations of Antiquity, and their Probable Relation to a still Older Civilization of the Ethiopians or Cushites of Arabia. By JOHN D. BALDWIN, Member of the American Oriental Society. 12mo, Cloth, $1 75.

WHYMPER'S ALASKA. Travel and Adventure in the Territory of Alaska, formerly Russian America—now Ceded to the United States—and in various other parts of the North Pacific. By FREDERICK WHYMPER. With Map and Illustrations. Crown 8vo, Cloth, $2 50.

DILKE'S GREATER BRITAIN. Greater Britain: a Record of Travel in English-speaking Countries during 1866 and 1867. By CHARLES WENTWORTH DILKE. With Maps and Illustrations. 12mo, Cloth, $1 00.

2   *Harper & Brothers' Valuable Standard Works.*

LOSSING'S FIELD-BOOK OF THE WAR OF 1812. Pictorial Field-Book of the War of 1812; or, Illustrations, by Pen and Pencil, of the History, Biography, Scenery, Relics, and Traditions of the Last War for American Independence. By Benson J. Lossing. With several hundred Engravings on Wood, by Lossing and Barritt, chiefly from Original Sketches by the Author. 1088 pages, 8vo, Cloth, $7 00.

LOSSING'S FIELD-BOOK OF THE REVOLUTION. Pictorial Field-Book of the Revolution; or, Illustrations, by Pen and Pencil, of the History, Biography, Scenery, Relics, and Traditions of the War for Independence. By Benson J. Lossing. 2 vols., 8vo, Cloth, $14 00; Sheep, $15 00; Half Calf, $18 00; Full Turkey Morocco, $22 00.

SMILES'S SELF-HELP. Self-Help; with Illustrations of Character and Conduct. By Samuel Smiles. 12mo, Cloth, $1 25.

SMILES'S HISTORY OF THE HUGUENOTS. The Huguenots: their Settlements, Churches, and Industries in England and Ireland. By Samuel Smiles, Author of "Self-Help," &c. With an Appendix relating to the Huguenots in America. Crown 8vo, Cloth, Beveled, $1 75.

WHITE'S MASSACRE OF ST. BARTHOLOMEW. The Massacre of St. Bartholomew: Preceded by a History of the Religious Wars in the Reign of Charles IX. By Henry White, M.A. With Illustrations. 8vo, Cloth, $1 75.

ABBOTT'S HISTORY OF THE FRENCH REVOLUTION. The French Revolution of 1789, as viewed in the Light of Republican Institutions. By John S. C. Abbott. With 100 Engravings. 8vo, Cloth, $5 00.

ABBOTT'S NAPOLEON BONAPARTE. The History of Napoleon Bonaparte. By John S. C. Abbott. With Maps, Woodcuts, and Portraits on Steel. 2 vols., 8vo, Cloth, $10 00.

ABBOTT'S NAPOLEON AT ST. HELENA; or, Interesting Anecdotes and Remarkable Conversations of the Emperor during the Five and a Half Years of his Captivity. Collected from the Memorials of Las Cases, O'Meara, Montholon, Antommarchi, and others. By John S. C. Abbott. With Illustrations. 8vo, Cloth, $5 00.

ADDISON'S COMPLETE WORKS. The Works of Joseph Addison, embracing the whole of the "Spectator." Complete in 3 vols., 8vo, Cloth, $6 00.

ALCOCK'S JAPAN. The Capital of the Tycoon: a Narrative of a Three Years' Residence in Japan. By Sir Rutherford Alcock, K.C.B., Her Majesty's Envoy Extraordinary and Minister Plenipotentiary in Japan. With Maps and Engravings. 2 vols., 12mo, Cloth, $3 50.

ALFORD'S GREEK TESTAMENT. The Greek Testament: with a critically-revised Text; a Digest of Various Readings; Marginal References to Verbal and Idiomatic Usage; Prolegomena; and a Critical and Exegetical Commentary. For the Use of Theological Students and Ministers. By Henry Alford, D.D., Dean of Canterbury. Vol. I., containing the Four Gospels. 944 pages, 8vo, Cloth, $6 00; Sheep, $6 50.

ALISON'S HISTORY OF EUROPE. First Series: From the Commencement of the French Revolution, in 1789, to the Restoration of the Bourbons, in 1815. [In addition to the Notes on Chapter LXXVI., which correct the errors of the original work concerning the United States, a copious Analytical Index has been appended to this American edition.] Second Series: From the Fall of Napoleon, in 1815, to the Accession of Louis Napoleon, in 1852. 8 vols., 8vo, Cloth, $16 00.

BANCROFT'S MISCELLANIES. Literary and Historical Miscellanies. By George Bancroft. 8vo, Cloth, $3 00.

Harper & Brothers' Valuable Standard Works. 3

DRAPER'S CIVIL WAR. History of the American Civil War. By John W. Draper, M.D., LL.D., Professor of Chemistry and Physiology in the University of New York. In Three Vols. *Vol. II. just published.* 8vo, Cloth, $3 50 per vol.

DRAPER'S INTELLECTUAL DEVELOPMENT OF EUROPE. A History of the Intellectual Development of Europe. By John W. Draper, M.D., LL.D., Professor of Chemistry and Physiology in the University of New York. 8vo, Cloth, $5 00.

DRAPER'S AMERICAN CIVIL POLICY. Thoughts on the Future Civil Policy of America. By John W. Draper, M.D., LL.D., Professor of Chemistry and Physiology in the University of New York, Author of a "Treatise on Human Physiology," "A History of the Intellectual Development of Europe," &c. Crown 8vo, Cloth, $2 50.

BARTH'S NORTH AND CENTRAL AFRICA. Travels and Discoveries in North and Central Africa; being a Journal of an Expedition undertaken under the Auspices of H.B.M.'s Government, in the Years 1849-1855. By Henry Barth, Ph.D., D.C.L. Illustrated. Complete in Three Vols., 8vo, Cloth, $12 00.

BELLOWS'S OLD WORLD. The Old World in its New Face: Impressions of Europe in 1867-1868. By Henry W. Bellows. 2 vols., 12mo, Cloth, $3 50.

BOSWELL'S JOHNSON. The Life of Samuel Johnson, LL.D. Including a Journey to the Hebrides. By James Boswell, Esq. A New Edition, with numerous Additions and Notes. By John Wilson Croker, LL.D., F.R.S. Portrait of Boswell. 2 vols., 8vo, Cloth, $4 00.

BRODHEAD'S HISTORY OF NEW YORK. History of the State of New York. By John Romeyn Brodhead. First Period, 1609-1664. 8vo, Cloth, $3 00.

BULWER'S PROSE WORKS. Miscellaneous Prose Works of Edward Bulwer, Lord Lytton. In Two Vols. 12mo, Cloth, $3 50.

BURNS'S LIFE AND WORKS. The Life and Works of Robert Burns. Edited by Robert Chambers. 4 vols., 12mo, Cloth, $6 00.

CARLYLE'S FREDERICK THE GREAT. History of Friedrich II., called Frederick the Great. By Thomas Carlyle. Portraits, Maps, Plans, &c. 6 vols., 12mo, Cloth, $12 00.

CARLYLE'S FRENCH REVOLUTION. History of the French Revolution. Newly Revised by the Author, with Index, &c. 2 vols., 12mo, Cloth, $3 50.

CARLYLE'S OLIVER CROMWELL. Letters and Speeches of Oliver Cromwell. With Elucidations and Connecting Narrative. 2 vols., 12mo, Cloth, $3 50.

CHALMERS'S POSTHUMOUS WORKS. The Posthumous Works of Dr. Chalmers. Edited by his Son-in-Law, Rev. William Hanna, LL.D. Complete in Nine Vols., 12mo, Cloth, $13 50.

CLAYTON'S QUEENS OF SONG. Queens of Song; being Memoirs of some of the most celebrated Female Vocalists who have performed on the Lyric Stage from the Earliest Days of Opera to the Present Time. To which is added a Chronological List of all the Operas that have been performed in Europe. By Ellen Creathorne Clayton. With Portraits. 8vo, Cloth, $3 00.

COLERIDGE'S COMPLETE WORKS. The Complete Works of Samuel Taylor Coleridge. With an Introductory Essay upon his Philosophical and Theological Opinions. Edited by Professor Shedd. Complete in Seven Vols. With a fine Portrait. Small 8vo, Cloth, $10 50.

DU CHAILLU'S AFRICA. Explorations and Adventures in Equatorial Africa; with Accounts of the Manners and Customs of the People, and of the Chase of the Gorilla, the Crocodile, Leopard, Elephant, Hippopotamus, and other Animals. By Paul B. Du Chaillu, Corresponding Member of the American Ethnological Society; of the Geographical and Statistical Society of New York; and of the Boston Society of Natural History. With numerous Illustrations. 8vo, Cloth, $5 00.

DU CHAILLU'S ASHANGO LAND. A Journey to Ashango Land: and Further Penetration into Equatorial Africa. By Paul B. Du Chaillu, Author of "Discoveries in Equatorial Africa," &c. New Edition. Handsomely Illustrated. 8vo, Cloth, $5 00.

CURTIS'S HISTORY OF THE CONSTITUTION. History of the Origin, Formation, and Adoption of the Constitution of the United States. By George Ticknor Curtis. Complete in Two large and handsome Octavo Volumes. Cloth, $6 00.

DAVIS'S CARTHAGE. Carthage and her Remains: being an Account of the Excavations and Researches on the Site of the Phœnician Metropolis in Africa and other adjacent Places. Conducted under the Auspices of Her Majesty's Government. By Dr. Davis, F.R.G.S. Profusely Illustrated with Maps, Woodcuts, Chromo-Lithographs, &c. 8vo, Cloth, $4 00.

DOOLITTLE'S CHINA. Social Life of the Chinese: with some Account of their Religious, Governmental, Educational, and Business Customs and Opinions. With special but not exclusive Reference to Fuhchau. By Rev. Justus Doolittle, Fourteen Years Member of the Fuhchau Mission of the American Board. Illustrated with more than 150 characteristic Engravings on Wood. 2 vols., 12mo, Cloth, $5 00.

EDGEWORTH'S (Miss) NOVELS. With Engravings. 10 vols., 12mo, Cloth, $15 00.

GIBBON'S ROME. History of the Decline and Fall of the Roman Empire. By Edward Gibbon. With Notes by Rev. H. H. Milman and M. Guizot. A new cheap Edition. To which is added a complete Index of the whole Work, and a Portrait of the Author. 6 vols., 12mo (uniform with Hume), Cloth, $9 00.

GROTE'S HISTORY OF GREECE. 12 vols., 12mo, Cloth, $18 00.

HALE'S (Mrs.) WOMAN'S RECORD. Woman's Record; or, Biographical Sketches of all Distinguished Women, from the Creation to the Present Time. Arranged in Four Eras, with Selections from Female Writers of each Era. By Mrs. Sarah Josepha Hale. Illustrated with more than 200 Portraits. 8vo, Cloth, $5 00.

HALL'S ARCTIC RESEARCHES. Arctic Researches and Life among the Esquimaux; being the Narrative of an Expedition in Search of Sir John Franklin, in the Years 1860, 1861, and 1862. By Charles Francis Hall. With Maps and 100 Illustrations. The Illustrations are from Original Drawings by Charles Parsons, Henry L. Stephens, Solomon Eytinge, W. S. L. Jewett, and Granville Perkins, after Sketches by Captain Hall. A New Edition. 8vo, Cloth, Beveled Edges, $5 00.

HALLAM'S CONSTITUTIONAL HISTORY OF ENGLAND, from the Accession of Henry VII. to the Death of George II. 8vo, Cloth, $2 00.

HALLAM'S LITERATURE. Introduction to the Literature of Europe during the Fifteenth, Sixteenth, and Seventeenth Centuries. By Henry Hallam. 2 vols., 8vo, Cloth, $4 00.

HALLAM'S MIDDLE AGES. State of Europe during the Middle Ages. By Henry Hallam. 8vo, Cloth, $2 00.

www.ingramcontent.com/pod-product-compliance
Lightning Source LLC
Chambersburg PA
CBHW030559300426
44111CB00009B/1036